THE WORLD
of the
PHARAOHS

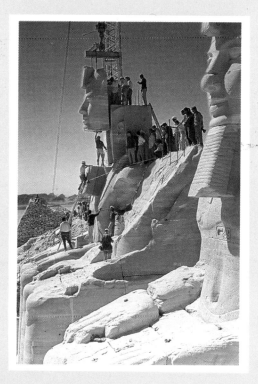

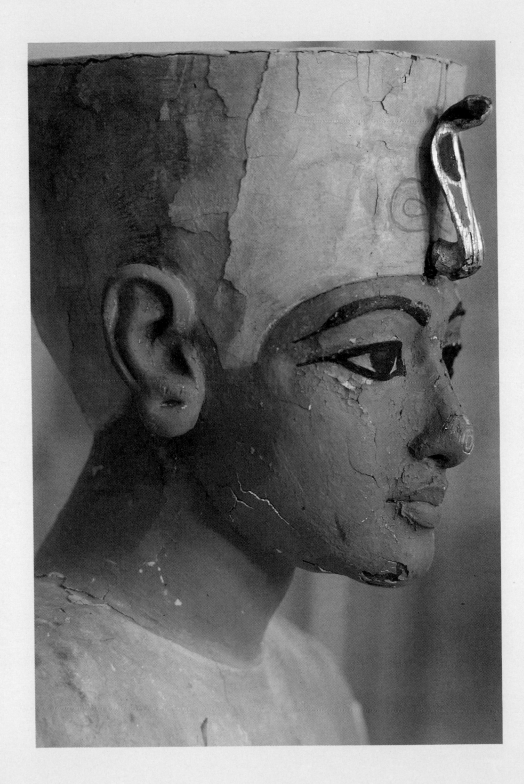

THE WORLD
of the
PHARAOHS

Christine Hobson

FOREWORD BY THOMAS J. LOGAN

Thames and Hudson

First published in the United States in 1987 by
Thames and Hudson Inc., 500 Fifth Avenue,
New York, New York 10110

Library of Congress Catalog Card Number
87-50390

This book was designed and produced by
The Paul Press Limited,
41–42 Berners Street,
London W1P 3AA

Art Editor David Ayres
Project Editor Elizabeth Longley
Picture Research Vickie Walters
Illustrations Ian Bott, Aziz Khan, Chris Moore,
Tracy Wellman
Calligrapher Susanne Haines
Art Assistant Sarah McDonald

Art Director Stephen McCurdy
Editorial Director Jeremy Harwood

Typeset by AKM Associates (UK) Limited
Ajmal House, Hayes Road, Southall, London

Origination and printing by Print Buyer's
Database Limited

Printed in the United Kingdom

TABLE OF CONTENTS

FOREWORD

Christine Hobson has kept abreast of the most recent discoveries in Egyptology. Yet while presenting a comprehensive survey of Egyptian history and culture, she has written it in a non-pedantic style. In so doing she has written a book that fills an important void: one that will be useful to both the general public and the student of Egyptology. It thus provides professors of Egyptology with a good introductory textbook.

The book approaches ancient Egypt through the archaeological discoveries that slowly uncovered and revealed a great civilization that had for so long been 'lost'. It was lost because, as the author so aptly points out, the distance between the modern world and ancient Egypt is enormous. One must keep in mind that fewer years separate us from the Roman emperors than them from the beginning of Egypt. In fact, when Herodotus visited Egypt in 400 BC, Egypt was already almost 3000 years old and, indeed, when the young King Tutankhamun came to the throne the pyramids of Giza were already in decay and over a thousand years old.

As the author indicates, in her discussion on recent discoveries and excavations at such places as Saqqara and Tell el Amarna, much work still must be done in Egypt. She rightly adds that many of the royal tombs of the Twenty-first and Twenty-second Dynasties are still missing. From the earlier period an enormous enclosure to the west of Djoser's Step Pyramid at Saqqara is currently being excavated, and it may turn out to be yet another step pyramid belonging to one of the missing royal tombs of the Third Dynasty. In addition, there are many royal tombs from the Second Dynasty still to be discovered, and very important work is currently being done in the ancient predynastic capital of the north, Buto, by teams of German excavators. Here through modern archaeological technology we are finally able to excavate in the delta, something which was heretofore impossible because of a high water table. Now the importance of the northern predynastic kingdom is finally being uncovered.

The point is simple, much work still needs to be done in Egypt – and is being done. Almost weekly new discoveries are being made. It is to the author's credit that she has kept abreast of modern research. Thus this book will also be useful to those Egyptologists who still rely on the standard but now outdated textbooks.

In sum, Christine Hobson has faced an enormous task: to synthesize and explain a civilization that lasted three-fifths of the recorded history of the Western world using the latest discoveries. This she has done in an enjoyable and exciting way.

THOMAS J. LOGAN

CHRONOLOGY

Principal kings of ancient Egypt

Each king had up to five different names read out at the time of his coronation, but only two were commonly used. The 'Son of Re' name was given to the infant prince at birth, and is the one by which we invariably know the kings, e.g. Ramesses or Tutankhamun. The 'King of Upper and Lower Egypt' name was given to them only when they received the double crown and it was by this name that the Egyptians and other countries knew them.

Egyptologists use the simpler 'Son of Re' name. (The early kings are the only exception because they had no 'Son of Re' name.)

ARCHAIC PERIOD, 3100–2650

First Dynasty
Narmer
Aha
Djer
Djet
Den
Adjib
Semerkhe
Qaa

Second Dynasty
Hotepsekhemwy
Raneb
Ninet jer
Peribsen
Khasekhem

OLD KINGDOM, 2650–2134

Third Dynasty
Sanakht
Netcherikhe-Djoser
Sekhemkhe
Khaba
Huni

Fourth Dynasty
Snofru
Cheops
Radjedef
Chephren
Mycerinus
Shepseskaf

Fifth Dynasty
Userkaf
Sahure
Neferirkare
Shepseskare
Raneferef
Niuserre
Menkauhor
Isesi
Unas

Sixth Dynasty
Teti
Pepi I
Merenre
Pepi II

FIRST INTERMEDIATE PERIOD, 2134–2040

Seventh, Eighth, Ninth and Tenth Dynasties
Ephemeral kings for whom very little evidence has been found.

MIDDLE KINGDOM, 2040–1640

Eleventh Dynasty
Intef I, II and III
Mentuhotep Nebhepetre (*this king is referred to as both I and II*)
Mentuhotep III
Mentuhotep IV

Twelfth Dynasty
Amenemhet I
Sesostris I
Amenemhet II
Sesostris II
Sesostris III
Amenemhet III
Amenemhet IV
Sobeknofru

Thirteenth Dynasty
Wegef I
Amenemhet V
Sobekhotep I
Hor
Amenemhet VI
Sobekhotep II, III, IV, V
This dynasty collapsed after a succession of short-lived and little-known kings.

SECOND INTERMEDIATE PERIOD, 1640–1550

Fourteenth Dynasty
A little-known group of kings contemporary with the end of the Thirteenth Dynasty

Fifteenth and Sixteenth Dynasties
The Hyksos kings, including:
Salitis
Khyan
Apophis

Seventeenth Dynasty
Intef V
Sobekemsaf
Seqenenre
Seqenenre Tao
Kamose

NEW KINGDOM, 1550–1070

Eighteenth Dynasty
Amosis
Amenhotep I
Tuthmosis I
Tuthmosis II
Hatshepsut
Tuthmosis III
Amenhotep II
Tuthmosis IV
Amenhotep III
Amenhotep IV (Akhenaten)
Tutankhamun
Ay
Horemheb

Nineteenth Dynasty
Ramesses I
Seti I
Ramesses II
Merenptah
Seti II
Amenmesses
Siptah
Tawosre

Twentieth Dynasty
Setnakht
Ramesses III–XI

THIRD INTERMEDIATE PERIOD, 1070–712

Twenty-first Dynasty
Smendes
Psusennes I
Amenemope
Osorkon I
Siamun
Psusennes II

Twenty-second Dynasty
Sheshonk I
Osorkon II
Takeloth I
Sheshonk II
Osorkon III
Takeloth II
Sheshonk III, IV, V
Osorkon IV, V

Twenty-third and Twenty-fourth Dynasties
*Ephemeral kings of whom little is known.
The Twenty-fourth Dynasty appears to
comprise two kings, Bakenre (Bocchoris) and
Piankhy (Piye).*

LATE PERIOD, 712–332

Twenty-fifth Dynasty
Shabaka
Shebitku
Taharka
Tantamani

Twenty-sixth Dynasty
Necho I
Psammetichus I
Necho II
Psammetichus II
Apries
Amasis
Psammetichus III

Twenty-seventh Dynasty
Cambyses
Darius I
Xerxes I
Artaxerxes
Darius II

Twenty-eighth Dynasty
*Only one attested king, Amyrtaeus, of whom
little is known*

Twenty-ninth Dynasty
Neferites
Psammutis
Neferites II

Thirtieth Dynasty
Nectanebo I, II

GRAECO-ROMAN PERIOD, 332–AD 395

Thirty-first Dynasty
Alexander the Great
Philip Arrhidaeus
Alexander IV

Thirty-second Dynasty
Ptolemy I–XV, with Queens Cleopatra
I–VII

*After the death of the last Cleopatra, Egypt
came directly under Roman rule, though few
Roman emperors ever went there. When the
Roman Empire divided in AD 395, Egypt
was controlled from Byzantium until the
Arab conquest in AD 641.*

TIME LINE

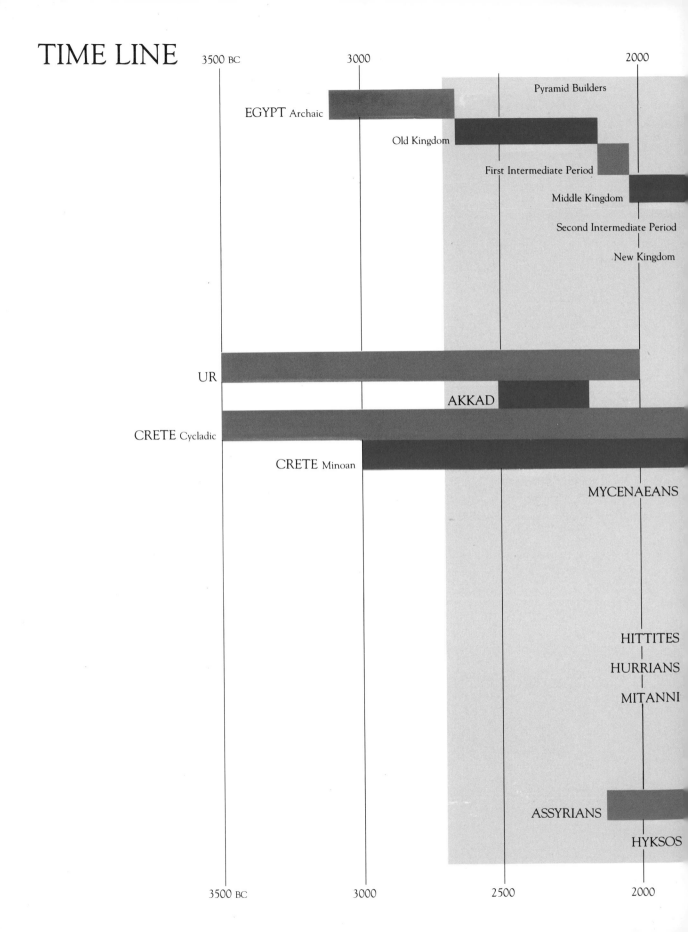

3500 BC   3000   2000

Pyramid Builders

EGYPT Archaic

Old Kingdom

First Intermediate Period

Middle Kingdom

Second Intermediate Period

New Kingdom

UR

AKKAD

CRETE Cycladic

CRETE Minoan

MYCENAEANS

HITTITES

HURRIANS

MITANNI

ASSYRIANS

HYKSOS

3500 BC   3000   2500   2000

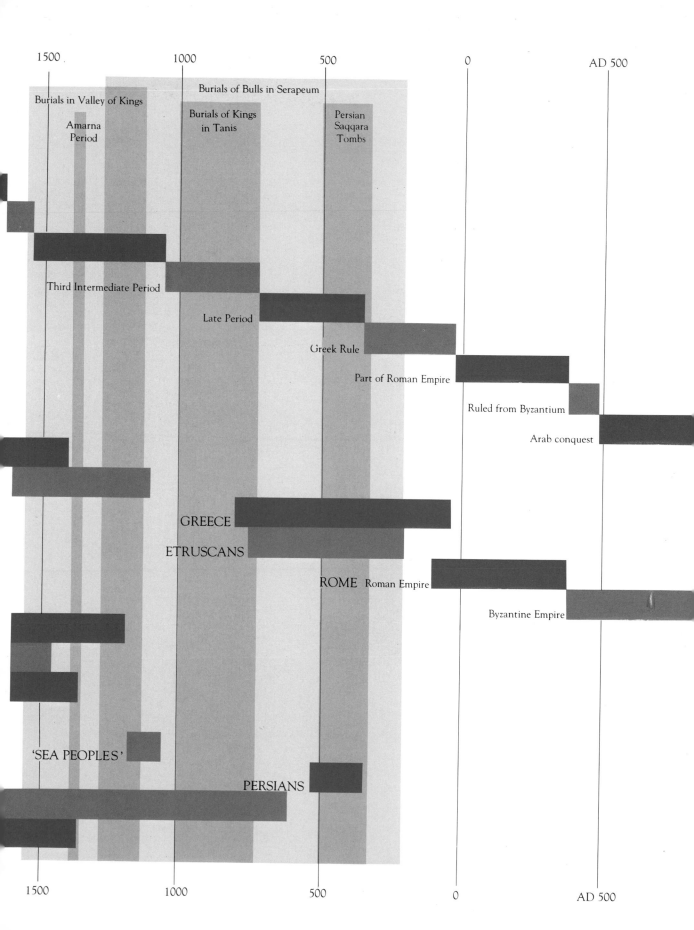

1500   1000   500   0   AD 500

Burials in Valley of Kings

Burials of Bulls in Serapeum

Amarna
Period

Burials of Kings
in Tanis

Persian
Saqqara
Tombs

Third Intermediate Period

Late Period

Greek Rule

Part of Roman Empire

Ruled from Byzantium

Arab conquest

GREECE

ETRUSCANS

ROME   Roman Empire

Byzantine Empire

'SEA PEOPLES'

PERSIANS

1500   1000   500   0   AD 500

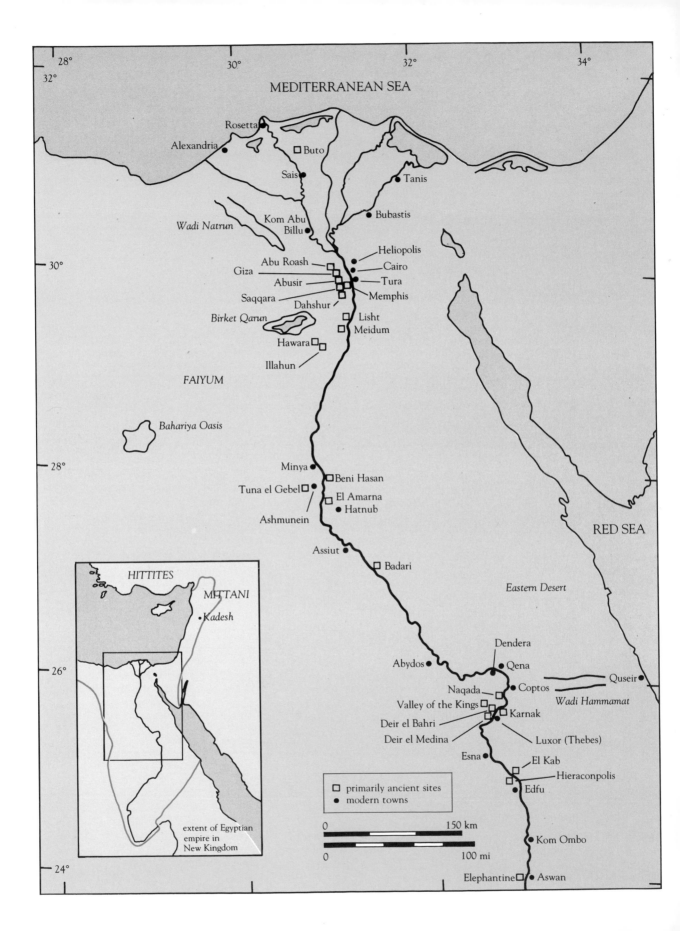

28°　30°　32°　34°

32°

MEDITERRANEAN SEA

Rosetta
Alexandria
☐ Buto
Sais
● Tanis

Wadi Natrun
Kom Abu
Billu
● Bubastis

Heliopolis
Abu Roash ☐
Giza ☐
Abusir ☐
Saqqara ☐
Dahshur
Cairo
Tura
Memphis

30°

Birket Qarun
☐ Lisht
☐ Meidum
Hawara ☐
Illahun

FAIYUM

Bahariya Oasis

28°

Minya
☐ Beni Hasan
Tuna el Gebel
☐ El Amarna
● Hatnub
Ashmunein

Assiut
☐ Badari

Eastern Desert

RED SEA

HITTITES

MITTANI

●Kadesh

26°

Dendera
Abydos ●
● Qena
Quseir ●
Naqada ☐
● Coptos
Wadi Hammamat
Valley of the Kings ☐
☐ Karnak
Deir el Bahri
Deir el Medina
Luxor (Thebes)
Esna ●
El Kab
Hieraconpolis
☐
Edfu

extent of Egyptian
empire in
New Kingdom

☐ primarily ancient sites
● modern towns

0 _____ 150 km
0 _____ 100 mi

● Kom Ombo

24°

Elephantine ☐ ● Aswan

INTRODUCTION

Egypt's history has to a great extent been determined by her geography. The Nile is in a very real sense her life's blood, giving her both water to drink and a unifying route allowing transportation and communication along its length. The great expanses of desert to the east and west of the Nile acted as buffers against foreign invaders and the cataracts in the river itself effectively prevented invasion from the south. Her coast was very narrow and the area of the delta so swampy that invasion from the north would have been impossible. Throughout her long history, ancient Egypt always exerted strong territorial pressure on neighbouring countries. Under the rule of strong kings, both Nubia, to the south, and Sinai, to the east were tightly controlled because of their material assets. The inset map indicates the furthest limit of the Egyptian empire when, under Pharaoh Tuthmosis III of the Eighteenth Dynasty, around 1450 BC, Egyptian armies controlled garrisons from what is now southern Turkey to the Fourth Cataract of the Nile in Sudan. Despite many battles during the Nineteenth Dynasty, Egyptian hold on the area gradually slipped. First the Hittites and then the Persians encroached until Egypt finally fell under foreign domination, about 520 BC.

'The Egyptologist,' wrote Arthur Weigall, a former Chief Inspector of Egyptian Antiquities, in 1923, 'to whom Egypt is not a living reality is handicapped in his labours more unfairly than is realized by him. Avoid Egypt, and though your brains be of vast capacity, though your eyes be never raised from your books, you will yet remain in many ways an ignoramus.'

Weigall's words are as true today as they were 60 years ago. Few civilizations can boast so long a continuity as Egypt and to understand ancient Egypt it is vital to know the Egypt of today. South of the bustling and cosmopolitan city of Cairo, life in the quiet villages remains almost the same as it has been for the 5000 years of its recorded history. The field workers who bend backs to break up the earth with mattocks; those who follow behind ox-dragged ploughs; girls who winnow grain in the light breezes – all can be seen in tomb paintings 4000 years old.

The culture of these ancient Egyptians seems remote and alien to our thinking. The pictures that have survived them show, at first sight, an incomprehensible view of the world. How can one come to terms with a people who seem to have lived solely with the aim of dying, and who spent their short time on earth preparing for, indeed, almost obsessed by it? How can one take seriously people who worshipped gods with the heads of animals, reptiles and even insects?

Never was an impression more wrong. Although archaeology in Egypt has been practised on a scientific basis for barely a hundred years, every week brings new insights into the reality of life in ancient Egypt. It was a past alive with humour, peopled with men and women who had such joy for life that they could never conceive of its ending; it is a history teeming with individuals, with stories of love and hate, of sorrow and pleasure, of endeavour and failure.

THE LAND

Although part of the continent of Africa, Egypt has always remained isolated from its neighbours, absorbing aspects of their cultures yet remaining perfectly distinct. With the Sahara desert to its west, the mountainous deserts and Red Sea to its east, the narrow Mediterranean coast to the north and the rocky, often unnavigable cataracts in the river to the south, the inhabitants of the Nile Valley could live virtually without fear of attack. This splendid geographical isolation was largely responsible for the longevity of the ancient Egyptian culture.

Through what would otherwise be barren wastes of desert runs the Nile, 6741km (4187mi) and the longest river in the world. Only the richness of its river banks brings life to Egypt. For thousands of years, it has been the only constant source of water to supply every need, from irrigation to navigation, from water to wash in to water to drink.

The river of life

The river Nile is fed by three main tributaries: the parent stream, the White Nile, rising in Lake Victoria; the smallest stream, the Atbara, joining the river above the Fifth Cataract near Berber; and the Blue Nile, joining near Khartoum, in Sudan, that gives the river its character. The Blue Nile rises in Lake Tana in Ethiopia. Though narrow and, at its head, unnavigable as it flows through gorges, in the summer months it rises dramatically, swollen with flood waters. So great is its force that at its height, it dams back the White Nile by force of its water alone. As it sweeps northwards it carries alluvial silt with it. Once past the six cataracts it flows into the plains of Egypt, flooding the river banks, leaving only tiny islands of habitation. As it recedes, it leaves behind a rich belt of fertile silt, which the ancient Egyptians called 'Kemet', the black land, soil rich enough to sustain at least two successive crops each year.

As it continues north, the torrent of the river slows and fans out to form the delta. Here the land is always rich and moist. The city of Cairo today stands at the junction of Nile valley and delta, a few miles to the north of the site of ancient Memphis, from where Egypt was ruled for nearly 4000 years. Since 3000 BC the administrators of Egypt have controlled Egypt's wealth from this most geographically strategic spot. The city thus controls two very different areas, what the ancient people called 'the Two Lands': Upper Egypt, the narrow Nile Valley, and Lower Egypt, the delta.

The inundation waters were supplied, according to ancient stories, from the bottomless water jar of the god Hapy, seated in a cavern below the mountains of Aswan and protected by magic serpents. Yet the waters have always been capricious. Should they rise too high, houses built on the edge of the cultivation strip were washed away, making people homeless, while the land became too wet to plant at the right time; if they rose too little, vast areas of ground remained unwatered and unfertilized.

Only in 1971 were the waters of the Nile partially tamed. The building of the High Dam, Sadd el Ali, in Aswan, completely stops up the river and in holding back the annual flood waters, it has created behind it the largest man-made lake in the world, Lake Nasser. It has also changed the face and future of Egypt. Now, water comes to irrigate the land at the turn of a tap; hydroelectric power feeds houses and new industries with energy right to the Mediterranean coast; and in Aswan, for the first time ever, clouds form over the lake and rain occasionally falls. The average monthly temperature in Aswan has dropped by more than 10°C (18°F).

Today the population of Egypt is rapidly expanding. In dynastic times, the land sustained no more than 3,000,000 inhabitants. Today, estimates suggest there are close to 60,000,000, and forecasts indicate that by the end of the century the population may grow by another 50 per cent. Despite the hardships and poverty this brings, Egypt still seems able to withstand all the pressures of climate and changing ecology.

A BRIEF HISTORY

In most ancient times, the two areas of Upper and Lower Egypt were independent of each other, with distinct customs. Earliest pictures carved on slate palettes, used for the grinding of malachite (copper ore), suggest that Lower Egyptian settlements were walled villages, probably built on dry mounds raised well above the marshy plain, while Upper Egyptian settlements were looser gatherings of farming communities.

By around 3000 BC political manoeuvring by powerful leaders in the North, and around the site of Nekheb (ancient Hieraconpolis), and Nekhen (modern El Kab) in the South, resulted in a state of war between the two areas. The king of Upper Egypt triumphed, and the united land of Egypt emerged as a powerful civilization.

This king, whom the Egyptians remembered as Menes, founded a new capital city, Memphis, some 16km (10mi) south of modern Cairo. Here he built a palace and administration buildings which served as the capital of Egypt throughout its history.

The Old Kingdom

The Archaic period rulers of the First and Second Dynasties still faced considerable internal opposition, however, and only by the beginning of the Third Dynasty did a king strong enough to command the country come to the throne.

This king, whom contemporary inscriptions record as Netcheriche, identified by much later sources as Djoser, was able to order the building of his tomb in the form of a Step Pyramid at Saqqara, the first monumental stone building in the world (see pp. 64-7). The organization of labour this entailed, and the power of the government which had to recruit and feed the workers who built it, is an indication of the authority the king had. The reign of Djoser marks the start of the Old Kingdom.

The kings of the Old Kingdom – from the Third to the Sixth Dynasties – were regarded as living gods. Their surviving images are not so much portraits of men as stone embodiments of the power they exuded. Aloof from the people of Egypt, the king alone appeared to have the right to join the gods in the sky after his death with the assistance of the pyramid he had

This large ceremonial mace head, 25cm (10in) high, shows an early king of Upper Egypt known as 'Scorpion' because of the sign near his head. This is, however, probably a title and not a name. The carving on the mace head shows the founding of a building, perhaps a temple, by the king who is breaking the ground with a mattock.

built. The great pyramids of the kings of the Fourth Dynasty, on the plateau of Giza, high above Cairo, mark the zenith of the power of the king and the ability of the economy to sustain such a huge enterprise. The pyramids of the kings of the Fifth and Sixth Dynasties are markedly smaller, reflecting a general impoverishment of Egypt.

The might of the Old Kingdom king was reflected, in his people's eyes, in the well-being of Egypt. But towards the end of the Sixth Dynasty, nature and the Nile combined to bring about the downfall of the old monarchical system. A series of poor inundations resulted in periods of famine. Outside the capital of Memphis, irrigation and drainage ditches filled up.

After the death of Pepi II, who came to the throne as a boy and ruled Egypt for approximately 94 years, the organization of the Old Kingdom failed. Egypt separated again into its distinct parts and, without a king in control, entered a period of general disorder.

This First Intermediate Period lasted for a very short time, certainly less than 100 years. Records are few and often badly written. Various local chiefs vied for power, especially those living in Heracleopolis (modern Ihnasya el Medina, in the Faiyum), each proclaiming himself king and forming his own dynasty, or family succession. During this time, the court at Memphis appears to have been neglected. Instead of being buried near their king, as previously, local governors chose to be buried in their own towns with tomb shafts for family and friends clustered around them.

The Middle Kingdom

The Middle Kingdom (2040 BC onwards) was formed as the result of one strong family from the region of Luxor re-establishing order and claiming the throne for their family. They formed the Eleventh Dynasty. The kings, called Intef and Mentuhotep, reunited Egypt, controlling the administration not from Memphis

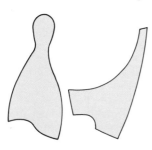

The crown of Upper Egypt (far left), called the white crown, and the crown of Lower Egypt (left), called the red crown, were often combined and worn as a double crown by the king. This is thought to have symbolized his rule over both areas.

The Palermo stone, carved during the Fifth Dynasty, shows the major events of every year of all the preceding kings of Egypt. The vertical bars are hieroglyphic signs for 'years'. The small box at the foot of each group records the height of that year's inundation.

This painted *limestone statue shows Nebhepetre Mentuhotep, first king of the Eleventh Dynasty, who restored calm and order as Egypt moved from the First Intermediate Period into the Middle Kingdom. The king is shown wearing the crown of Upper Egypt and his hands are crossed on his chest in the manner of Osiris. A number of these statues were found lining a processional route that led to his mortuary temple and pyramid on the west bank of Luxor, at Deir el Bahri. The faces of the statues are impersonal and heavy-featured, perhaps indicating the drop in artistic standards which had taken place during the First Intermediate Period.*

but from another town they called 'Itj tawy'. Its actual location is unknown, but scholarly opinion places it probably in the region of the Faiyum. Trading links were rebuilt with other countries and new workshops were established for fine crafts and for the copying of literary texts. The last king of the Eleventh Dynasty, Mentuhotep IV, apparently died childless, for his successor seems to have been his vizier, Amenemhet. This first king of the Twelfth Dynasty also came from the region of Luxor but from a village farther north than that of his predecessors. Despite the new order established by the Middle Kingdom, the local governors still thrived independently and this posed a threat to the monarchy. Amenemhet I was apparently murdered as a result of a conspiracy of his own bodyguard. Succeeding kings of the Twelfth Dynasty, however, were strong enough at home to be able take their armies abroad. A small cache of gold and silver treasure found at Tod in Upper Egypt appears to have been tribute sent from Syria to King Amenemhet II. Only at the succession of Sesostris III were the local governors deprived of their power and made completely dependent again on the monarchy.

The kings of the Thirteenth Dynasty inherited a strong power base. But this dynasty was characterized by a series of short reigns and this no doubt weakened the authority of the throne. At the same time, a great number of foreigners had settled in Egypt, many no doubt brought to Egypt as prisoners of war during the campaigns of the Twelfth Dynasty kings. These foreigners – called Asiatics by the Egyptians – gained power rapidly, establishing their base in the town of Avaris (which they called 'Khut-waret') in the delta. There was a group of minor kings which could be said to have constituted a Fourteenth Dynasty. These kings were probably never really crowned and the Fourteenth Dynasty was most likely to have been contemporary with the Thirteenth and Fifteeenth Dynasties, which consisted of properly crowned monarchs. With the demise of Thirteenth Dynasty kings, Egypt once more fell into chaos, a time known as the Second Intermediate Period.

It seems likely that the foreign kings who claimed Egypt's throne during the Fifteenth and Sixteenth Dynasties were not from any one country, but were a mixture of races of non-Egyptian origin. Egyptian sources called them 'Rulers of the Foreign Lands' (Heka–Khaswt); the Greeks later termed them 'Hyksos'. Archaeological evidence suggests that they adapted well to Egyptian traditions. Certainly their introduction of new technology – the horse and chariot, bronze weapons and the composite bow – ushered in a new era for Egypt.

Once again, it was a warlike family from Luxor who opposed the foreign kings. They rallied the forces of Upper Egypt and sought to evict the Lower Egyptian intruders. A series of fierce battles culminated in the Hyksos kings being driven out of Egypt altogether. The victorious generals from Luxor formed the Seventeenth and Eighteenth Dynasties. With Amosis, who drove the Hyksos out, taking the throne as Pharaoh, the New Kingdom began, in 1550 BC.

The New Kingdom

The warrior kings of the New Kingdom were the superheroes of the ancient world, fearless, tireless, strong, brave and invincible in battle. They were approachable men, keen to advance the positions of worthy supporters, but determined that Egypt should never again fall into the hands of foreigners. In clearing Egypt's borders of foreign threat by establishing per-

manently manned garrisons in towns and cities north of Egypt, they slowly built up an empire dependent on Egypt. Tribute flowed into the Egyptian treasury while the kings continued to extend their hold. Tuthmosis III, mightiest warrior of them all, though only 1.65m (5ft 4in) tall, built ships in Byblos and then had them taken on ox carts over the mountain ridges of Lebanon solely in order to sail across the Euphrates and confront the enemy on the other side.

The accession to the throne of Amenhotep IV (who called himself Akhenaten) proved to be the watershed of Egyptian might. By turning his back on all the old traditions, building an isolated city at what is now Tell el Amarna (*see pp. 106–109*), and accepting the existence of only one god for all mankind, the Aten, he virtually abandoned the Egyptian empire at the very time the Hittite nation was becoming a threat. After his death, although the Ramesside kings of the Nineteenth and Twentieth Dynasties fought valiantly to repel foreign threats, the Egyptian empire was slowly lost.

Even during the lifetime of the last Ramesses – Ramesses XI – Egypt was once more dis-integrating and about to fall into the Third Intermediate Period. In the Temple of Karnak, a priest named Herihor attempted to take control in the south. After the death of Ramesses XI in the delta town of Tanis, a man called Smendes claimed the throne. A story has come down that sheds light on how Egypt was

From the Nineteenth Dynasty onwards, after the end of the traumatic Amarna period, the Egyptians were increasingly concerned about their personal links with the gods. Stelae such as the one shown above were erected to intervene personally with the local god, often to seek justice or offer an explanation for things that had gone wrong in their lives. The deceased is shown kneeling, holding up his hands in prayer. The ears represent those of the god, listening to the plea.

This sphinx (right) bears the face and features of Hatshepsut. In the Eighteenth Dynasty she usurped the throne from her stepson and co-regent Tuthmosis III and ruled Egypt herself as pharaoh for 20 years. At her death, many of her images were smashed or buried, and her name was omitted from the king lists, in an attempt to deny her the immortality that remembrance of her name was guaranteed to bring.

viewed. At this time an unfortunate merchant trader called Wenamun was sent by Herihor to Byblos to fetch wood. At one time, the Prince of Byblos would have complied willingly, but so low had Egypt's prestige fallen that Wenamun was made a laughing stock, being reduced finally to sitting weeping on a beach in sheer frustration.

The Twenty-second Dynasty kings were Libyan chiefs, probably opposed by the contemporary Twenty-third Dynasty monarchs who ruled from Tanis in the delta. Of the Twenty-fourth Dynasty, almost nothing is known.

In 728 BC, a Nubian army under the command of General Piankhy (whom some scholars now call Piye) came northwards and conquered Egypt. Deeply pious, the Nubians restored many ancient Egyptian traditions that had almost died out in Egypt itself. They built huge temples but finally were themselves driven out by Assyrian invaders under the command of Assurbanipal. He appointed a prince of the town of Sais, Necho, to rule Egypt; but order was only restored by his successor, Psammetichus. With a great longing for former glories, these Saite kings revived ancient styles, turning to the Old Kingdom for inspiration. But their desire for the old times was not to be gratified. The Assyrian empire fell to the Persians, and Cambyses appointed deputies, or satraps, to rule Egypt.

Egypt under foreign rule

Persian domination was greatly resented by the Egyptians. When the Macedonian armies, under Alexander the Great, finally conquered Persia and marched into Egypt, in 332 BC, they were welcomed as liberators. The building of the great Hellenic city of Alexandria on the Mediterranean coast signalled a new era. After Alexander's death, Ptolemy, son of Lagos

The towers and stout stone walls of the Citadel (left) still dominate the older part of Cairo. They were built on a hill which is one of a chain at the eastern side of the city, as a fortified palace for Salah ad din (Saladin) between 1176 and 1207. It is rumoured that some of the large limestone blocks used in its building were removed from the pyramids on the west bank of the Nile. Inside the outer walls are many other buildings, chief of which is the mosque of Mohammed Ali, copied from the Blue Mosque of Istanbul, in the 19th century.

(perhaps the half-brother of Alexander), took the crown of Egypt as Pharaoh.

The succeeding generations of Ptolemies and their sister-wives, called Cleopatra, were benevolent though patronizing towards the native Egyptians. While the Greeks absorbed the accumulation of thousands of years of Egyptian knowledge, they tended to regard the Egyptians as little more than ignorant peasants. By exploiting native dependence on the old gods and building temples throughout Egypt, they diverted most of the country's assets into their own coffers.

The dispute between the last queen of the line, Cleopatra VII, and her half-brother, Ptolemy, drew Rome's attention to Egypt. When Julius Caesar intervened with his armies in favour of Cleopatra, Egypt became a satellite of the great Roman Empire and the queen became his mistress. The defeat of the Egyptian fleet under the command of Mark Antony at the battle of Actium, in 30 BC, by Octavian and the force of the Roman Empire was the death knell of ancient Egypt. Although Cleopatra VII survived for many months after the defeat, the determination of Octavian (later Augustus) Caesar, to parade her through the streets of Rome as a prisoner led to her committing suicide.

Roman domination of Egypt from 30 BC onwards was bitterly resented. Trouble erupted frequently in the country regions as increasing numbers of people were forced to work in the fields to feed Rome. The introduction of Christianity, reputedly by the evangelist Mark in the first century AD, provided a focus for anti-Roman agitation. The Egyptian Christians, called Copts (nothing more than a form of the word 'Egypt') were severely persecuted for many years by Rome. After the conversion of the Emperor Constantine, Christianity was favoured by Rome, and the pendulum swung the other way. In AD 392, Emperor Theodosius ordered all the old pagan temples to be closed down. Despite this, the temple of Isis on Philae was used as the goddess' cult centre by the local Nubians well into the fifth century.

After the split of the Roman Empire in AD 395, Egypt was controlled from Byzantium. The conquest of Egypt by Amr Ibn el-as in 641, though strongly resisted by Byzantine troops, marked the start of Arab influence in Egypt, and the triumph of Islam. The founding of Fustat (in 641), the original part of Cairo, ended the long reign of Memphis as the capital,

and saw the severing of the last links with ancient Egypt.

In 1171, Salah ad Din – the Saladin who fought the Crusaders for control of the Holy Land – built his great fortress in Cairo. This Citadel still dominates the city today. In 1250, a group of former Turkish slaves, the Mamelukes, took power and ruled Egypt themselves with great viciousness until 1517, when Sultan Selim I of Turkey conquered Egypt, making it an outpost of the Ottoman Empire.

The founding of modern Egypt

The campaigns of Napoleon Bonaparte, in 1798, briefly saw the Turkish suzereins defeated, and but for the opposition of Admiral Nelson might have left Egypt in French control. In the event, an Albanian general, Mohammed Ali, was appointed to govern Egypt in 1805. Two years later he evicted the British and destroyed any vestige of Mameluke power when he murdered the last 480 of them during a banquet in the Citadel. Mohammed Ali's reorganizations have made him generally regarded as the Father of Modern Egypt.

The accession of King Farouk, in 1937, ushered in the last era for Egyptian monarchy. The king's tolerance, even support, of British occupation of the Suez Canal zone resulted in bitter opposition. An army coup, in 1952, led to his abdication and the abolishing of the monarchy.

In 1954, Egypt's first President, Colonel Gamal Abd-el Nasser, was appointed. Under his aegis the Suez Canal was nationalized and plans were laid for the building of the Aswan High Dam eventually opened in 1971.

When Nasser died in 1970, the Egyptian people mourned him as the 'Last Pharaoh'. He was succeeded by Anwar Sadat, an army officer implacably opposed to Russian influence. He was severely troubled not only by a series of economic crises, but also by relations with Israel to the north. The defeat of Egyptian troops during the Six Day War of 1967 had been a shattering blow to Egyptian morale, and hostility towards Israel was a popular rallying point. The signing of the Camp David agreement, in 1975, by the heads of government of Egypt, Israel and the United States, was regarded by many as a great betrayal. The assassination of Sadat, in October 1981, was the culmination of growing anger towards the president by certain army factions. Today, Egypt faces a time of great challenge.

I

DISCOVERING THE PAST

'I have had to rely on the accounts given to me by the Egyptians and their priests. They have told me that 341 generations separate the first King of Egypt from the last and that there was one King and one High Priest to each generation. Reckoning three generations as a century . . . a total of 11,340 years.'
Herodotus, Book II, 142

The Egyptians themselves were the first to visit the buildings of their ancestors, followed by Classical writers who tried to explain what they saw in terms of what they knew of their own culture. The emperors of Rome began the stripping of Egypt's ancient monuments and their removal to decorate the cities of their far-flung empire. By AD 641, when the Arabs came, the hieroglyphic writing was long-forgotten and the monuments represented only strange secrets of a mysterious past.

From the 16th century onwards, responding to public demand, European merchants began to bring back quantities of mummies and coffins and innumerable small objects. The pieces found a ready market, collectors being willing to pay high prices. The trade in antiquities began to thrive.

From the 18th century, with more people visiting Egypt, there developed an almost insatiable desire for unusual pieces. The result was the plundering of many sites for things that were visually stimulating – with no thought for what other information might be destroyed in the process. The progress from tomb robbery to scientific excavation was painfully slow. Not until the end of the 19th century was there any real control over the ancient sites.

The Colossi of Memnon *now dominating a lonely plain, once stood proudly in front of the long-vanished mortuary temple of Amenhotep III on the west bank at Luxor.*

THE FIRST ARCHAEOLOGISTS

The granite rocks *in the centre of Seheil Island, near Aswan, are covered with graffiti in hieroglyphs left over centuries by officials carrying out royal commands on the Nubian frontier. Although undated, these three inscriptions were carved some 500 years apart. On the left, a scribe of the treasury, Penpasheri, left his mark; above, an official, Amenemope, a servant of the god Amun, makes an offering to Anukis, a goddess of the region; while below, a cartouche gives the name of Amenhotep II.*

The Egyptians themselves appeared to have had little interest in history for its own sake. Their myths embodied stories of the creation of the earth, with Egypt at its hub. According to these tales, in the time before the creation, the universe was filled with a watery void, formless and faceless, called Nun. From the waters of Nun, a mound of earth arose, and upon this mound first the gods and then mankind itself came into existence. According to a papyrus of Ramesside date, now in the Egyptian Museum in Turin (and known as 'the Turin papyrus'), the first rulers of Egypt were the gods themselves, ruling for incredibly long reigns of thousands of years; they were followed by demigods, and finally by a mysterious group of people called 'the followers of Horus'. This explanation of their origins seemed to satisfy the Egyptians. Where lists of kings' names did exist in the temples, they were written purely for ceremonial reasons (*see p.130*) rather than from a sense of recording facts for posterity.

Ancient Egyptologists
This does not mean, however, that the Egyptians were not fascinated by their heritage. The pyramids and temples intrigued them as

they have intrigued generations from Classical times onwards. Many of the major sites are inscribed with graffiti written by visiting ancient Egyptians. In the 'southern building' on the east side of the courtyard of the Step Pyramid complex, one such graffito, written by a tourist of the Eighteenth Dynasty, around 1400 BC, records how he spent a pleasant day walking around the monument of Djoser-Netcherikhe, already 1200 years old. On the west bank of Luxor, when Winlock (*see p. 142*) was excavating the mortuary temple of Hatshepsut in Deir el Bahri, he entered a tomb belonging to Khety (No. 311), a courtier of the Eleventh Dynasty, and found a similar graffito inscribed during the reign of Ramesses II, in the Nineteenth Dynasty, 800 years after the tomb had been built.

How many tombs, pyramids and other monuments were open to view to the later Egyptians is unclear, but the first inscription relating to the clearing of a major monument was found in Giza by T.B. Caviglia, an Italian draughtsman, in 1816. He uncovered a black granite stela, with a hieroglyphic inscription, between the paws of the Sphinx. The text related how the young King Tuthmosis IV was out hunting near the pyramids with one of his courtiers when 'the time came for taking a rest' near the Sphinx, the image of Re-Horakhte. As he sat he fell asleep, and in a dream the god appeared to him and commanded that the king clear the sand from around the Sphinx, 'because the desert has covered me up and I have been waiting a long time to inform you of my desire'. Tuthmosis clearly did all the god commanded, for the stela recording this first ever excavation stands on the bedrock!

The ancient Egyptians seldom travelled beyond the bounds of their own home towns. Those who did, either as merchant traders or leaders of royal expeditions to quarries or on campaigns of conquest, invariably left graffiti behind them, as though advising posterity of their great achievements. Many of the quarries contain small inscriptions giving the names and ranks of the commanders, and titles of the gangs they supervised. The turquoise mines of Sinai, the quarries of Wadi Hammamat and Aswan and the alabaster quarries of Hatnub are all littered with hieroglyphic graffiti from the Old Kingdom onwards. One of the largest collections of hieroglyphic graffiti is to be found on the little visited island of Seheil in the First Cataract, south of Aswan. Here, a huge mound of rocks records the visits of dignitaries to and from Nubia, from the early Old Kingdom to the Graeco-Roman period. Few of them have been studied in detail.

The first recorded interest in Egyptology belongs to one of the many sons of Ramesses II: Prince Khaemwese. He was born around 1280 BC, the fourth son of his father and the second of Queen Isinofret, one of Ramesses' favourite wives. As a child of no more than five years he accompanied his father on campaigns in Nubia, but clearly the military life did not satisfy him. By the time he reached adulthood, Prince Khaemwese was attached to the temple of Ptah in Memphis. It was in this capacity that he supervised the burial of the sacred Apis bull (see p. 121). No doubt it was while the labyrinthine underground passages of the Serapeum were being built that the prince had the opportunity to walk around Saqqara. He noted many monuments from whose walls the name of the owner had disappeared or been obliterated, and on them had a short inscription carved, labelling the tombs and pyramids for posterity.

Greek and Roman travellers

The earliest strong interest in the monuments of ancient Egypt belonged to the Greek and Roman tourists from the third century BC onwards, who travelled throughout the Nile valley, and most of the largest tombs and temples bear their marks. Some of the most remarkable are on the colossal statues that once stood before the mortuary temple of Amenhotep III on the west bank at Luxor. The northern statue, known as the Colossus of Memnon, used to 'sing' at dawn, the result, it is thought, of air whistling through the cracks in the stone as the moisture was dried when sunlight struck them. The inscriptions date from AD 20 onwards, typically: 'Servius Clemens – I heard the voice of Memnon and gave thanks.' Some visitors waxed poetic: 'Vandals have harmed your structure in vain; but still you can speak, and I heard the strain.' Yet others were not so fortunate. The Emperor Hadrian visited the site. 'On the first day we did not hear the Memnon. He kept silent to receive the husband so that beautiful Sabina (his wife) would return. At her arrival the divine cry broke out, for fear the king would be angry with you.' The delightful empress clearly charmed those ancient stones!

Around 450 BC the most celebrated visitor of all travelled in Egypt: Herodotus, called both

the 'Father of History' and 'Father of Lies.' He aimed to write an inquiry or *historia* into various contemporary nations, and in Book Two of his records, he describes Egypt as it was in the twilight of pharaonic power. Many of the stories he recorded, he frankly admitted, were told to him by priests or by tourist guides of the time. Unable to read hieroglyphs or speak the Egyptian language, he had to rely heavily on secondary sources. It is our misfortune that he did not record many details we would dearly have loved to know, while including digressions of often dubious nature. He intended in his travels solely to put his native Greece in an international context, so his writings were never meant to be an objective history. Some of the details Herodotus records, however, are incomparable eyewitness accounts. He notes how sacred, how unspeakable, was the name of Osiris – by then the great god of Egypt – and describes in some detail the festivals held for Osiris and other gods. His is the only full account of mummification to survive (see p. 153), and his comments on native customs are without equal. He found everything perplexing in terms of his own land. 'The Egyptians appear to have reversed the ordinary practices of mankind. Women attend markets and are employed in trade, while men stay at home and do the weaving! Men in Egypt carry loads on their heads, women on their shoulders. Women pass water standing up, men sitting down. To ease themselves they go indoors, but eat outside on the streets, on the theory that what is unseemly but necessary should be done in private, and what is not unseemly should be done openly.'

Information such as this enables us to get the very earliest glimpses of ancient Egypt through the eyes of near contemporaries.

The sphinx, *carved from a core of limestone, represents Re-Horakhte, or Harmachis, an aspect of the sun god. The stela between its paws was erected by Tuthmosis IV during the Eighteenth Dynasty, and records the god's visitation in a dream before Tuthmosis became king. The head and body of the sphinx are badly damaged by sand erosion and dampness, one of the problems caused directly by its being kept clear of sand. Although at many times in its history the sphinx has been almost totally covered by sand, the presence of a small temple built next to it for its veneration suggests it was kept cleared for many years during the New Kingdom.*

EARLY EXPLORERS AND TRAVELLERS

This bust *reputedly shows Herodotus, called by Cicero the 'Father of History'. Little is known of him, save that he was born in Halicarnassus in ancient Caria, now on the southwest coast of Turkey, around 485 BC. It seems likely that Herodotus began his travels in the known ancient Mediterranean world when he was in his twenties, and it is recorded that he read a report on his travels in Athens in 446 BC. How far he travelled in Egypt is uncertain, though he claims to speak as an eyewitness as far south as Aswan. Many of the stories he recorded there, however, were told to him by Greek-speaking priests, probably living in the delta.*

In 332 BC, Alexander the Great marched unopposed into Egypt and was hailed as a liberator come to free the people from Persian domination. He spent little time in Egypt; long enough to visit the Temple of Amun in the Siwa oasis where he was told by the oracle that he was of divine birth, and to find the country so attractive as to desire his body to be buried there, wherever he might die.

In June 323 BC Alexander died of a fever in Babylon. His body was embalmed with spices, loaded into a spectacular bier and dragged by 64 donkeys towards Egypt. His friend and constant companion (some say his elder half-brother), Ptolemy, met the cortège and ordered the bier to be taken to Memphis. It stood there for several years until his tomb was finished in Alexandria.

Preserving the past

After Alexander's death, his generals embarked on a power struggle to divide the new empire, but for Ptolemy there had never been a doubt in his mind. Egypt was to be his. It was his successor, Ptolemy II Philadephus, according to a letter that was recorded by the classical writer Syncellus, who appointed Manetho 'High Priest and scribe of the sacred shrines of Egypt, born at Sebennytus and living in Heliopolis' to write down for him a history of ancient Egypt.

Little is known of Manetho, but because of his work in the temple, he would have been able to read the hieroglyphic texts there for himself, including the king lists (see p. 130) written on the walls, and the library's text rolls that would have supplied him with the information that his king needed.

It was Manetho who wrote the first comprehensive list of kings of Egypt from the first king, Menes, to his own time, including the lengths of their reigns and a few of their achievements. To him we owe the dynastic division of Egyptian history. Despite some of his stranger quotations – for example, that Menes was 'carried off by a hippoptamus', and that under a King Bocchoris of the Twenty-fourth Dynasty 'a lamb spoke' – although Manethos's facts are often the subject of dispute, archaeology has shown the break points of his Dynasties to be logical. His recorded reign lengths, however, are far from accurate.

It was the writings of Manetho recorded by other classical authors, together with those of the Bible and Herodotus, that survived after all knowledge of hieroglyphs had been lost. On the words of these sources alone from the fifth century until the early 19th century all understanding of ancient Egypt derived.

When the Greek traveller Strabo visited Egypt in 25 BC, and described the sites, he found them already becoming lost under drifting sand. By the time Emperor Constantine ruled the Roman Empire in AD 306. Egypt was already considered little more than an open-air repository of curiosities. Constantine began what was to amount to centuries of pillaging and destruction by the removal of numbers of obelisks to grace Roman squares. Roman emperors after him removed more than two dozen others; to this day, 13 stand in Rome, while only five remain in Egypt. The closure of the last pagan temples in Egypt by imperial decree, in the sixth century, signified the ending of that great civilization. Knowledge of the culture slumbered.

Alchemy and ancient secrets

The arrival of the Arabs in AD 641 marked a change in attitudes towards ancient Egypt. There was a general conviction that hieroglyphs contained mystical secrets of great spiritual wisdom. Books spoke of 'the Egyptian matter' – al-Keme (from the Egyptian 'Kemet', or Black Land); and thus alchemy was born, with its emphasis on the magical transmutation of matter. Texts written at that time concerned the discovery and entering of tombs, with details of words to be spoken and offerings to be burned at salient points to ensure the revealing of great treasures. One esteemed Arab geographer, el-Masud, wrote with conviction that the heart of the Great Pyramid contained a large emerald carved in the form of 'a sheikh seated upon a divan'. During the ninth century, Caliph Miamun, son of Haroun el-Raschid, the sultan to whom Scheherazade told her stories for 1001 nights, reputedly quarried into the pyramid in search of it (*see p. 72*).

In the 12th century, an Iraqi physician called Abdul Latif arrived in Egypt and visited the major sites. The pyramids of Giza especially caught his attention; 'Time,' he wrote, 'fears the pyramids. After consideration of these pyramids, one is forced to comprehend the combined efforts of the most intelligent men ... that the most learned axioms of geometry were called upon to show in these wonders the vast extent of human ability.' Even at this early date, he wrote that for a small sum a man from a nearby village would clamber up the face of a pyramid for the amusement of tourists!

It was only after the Turkish conquest of 1517 that travellers and explorers from outside the Islamic world deemed it safe to visit Egypt. Within a few years, the first reports of the great monuments arrived in Europe. Pietro delle Valle was in Egypt in 1618–24, and brought back quantities of papyrus and mummies. 'Mummy', in fact, soon became a major export as a form of medicine. One Englishman, John Sanderson brought away 270kg (600 lb) of 'assorted mummy' in 1585 just for the London market. The arrival of papyri, meanwhile, excited scholars greatly. Athanasius Kircher, a German Jesuit scholar and Professor of Oriental languages, published the first treatise on hieroglyphs in 1643 – *Lingua Aegyptiaca Restituta*. His efforts at decipherment were ingenious although totally imaginary, since he worked on the current Arab assumption that the signs were merely symbolic.

In 1639, an English mathematician from Oxford, John Greaves, arrived in Egypt after having visited most of the countries of the Middle East. He was told strange garbled stories about the pyramids of Giza – 'they are filled with talismans and with strange things ... and a vault into which the river Nile should enter and run out into the land of Al-Said.' Greaves

did not think much of the stories. 'So much for the Arabs; their stories are no better than fairy tales,' he wrote and then proceeded to carry out the first survey of the site, drawing and measuring what he could reach and estimating the rest. This survey constitutes the first scientific approach to Egyptology.

Meanwhile, from Europe a series of groups of collectors of Egyptian antiquities had formed and set out intrepidly for the Nile in search of portable treasure. Local villagers in Upper Egypt willingly produced ancient material, including statuettes and ushabtis, or shawabtis, jars, jewellery and yet more papyri. Louis XIV himself appointed one man, Vansleb, to purchase 'old coins and manuscripts for His Majesty's collection.' The French consul in Egypt in 1692, Benoit de Maillet, travelled extensively, buying artefacts and selling them in France to increase his stipend. He wrote long accounts of his journeys to scholars in France,

This portrait *of Hans Sloane shows him holding a picture of one of the many plants he collected on his travels and brought back to England. He was born in 1660 in Ireland, and qualified as a doctor, becoming eventually personal physician to King George II. Sloane was also an avid collector of curios and antiquities, which he left to the nation on his death in 1753. It was from Sloane's bequest that the British Museum was founded.*

James Bruce was a notable 18th century explorer whose travels began as an attempt to come to terms with the grief caused by the death of his wife. After being appointed British Consul in Algiers in 1762, he became fascinated by the idea of tracing the source of the Nile – one of the great goals of adventurers and explorers. In 1769 he arrived in Cairo to start his journey south, a journey not without adventure. While in Luxor, he visited the Valley of the Kings where he cleared the tomb of Ramesses III, to this day still called Bruce's tomb. After many tribulations, Bruce arrived at what he believed to be the head of the Nile – it was, however, only the source of the Blue Nile. He died in November 1794, never aware that he had not, in fact, achieved his ambition.

describing the great temples of Upper Egypt where 'the blue and gilded ceilings are as beautiful as if they had just been finished; there are statues there of colossal size and columns too many to count.' His reports excited the recipients, and De Maillet made a stronger recommendation that 'wise people, curious but careful' should be appointed to survey Egypt scientifically, to map out the sites and measure and copy the monuments while they were still there to see. His report seems to have made a strong impression in France. Only a hundred years later his plan was brought to fruition and the science of Egyptology was born.

The Grand Tour

The second half of the 17th century saw a sudden awakening of interest in Egypt. In London, an eminent surgeon, Sir Hans Sloane, physician to King George II, amassed a large collection of curios from his travels around the Mediterranean and the Caribbean. As President of the Royal Society he was esteemed as a man of taste and great knowledge. He died just short of his hundredth birthday in 1753, and in his will offered all his books and his collection, containing some Egyptian pieces, to the nation for £20,000 – a vast sum at the time but a bargain considering the value of the material. The government was initially not too keen; but, finally, on 7 June 1753 a bill was passed through Parliament agreeing to the terms of the bequest. In this manner was the British Museum born. It was to be housed in Montague House, on the site of the present buildings, and within a short time it opened its doors to the public.

Although there were but few Egyptian objects on display they served to fascinate and

entice visitors both to the museum and to Egypt. A little earlier, a distinguished group of travellers had formed an 'Egyptian Society' in London. The founder members all knew the Nile well. Frederick Lewis Norden, a Dane, had visited Egypt on behalf of King Christian VI. He was an artist and architect by training, and produced vast numbers of paintings, sketches and plans that were published in Paris in 1751. He reported in his book that, despite the new European interest, things were not changing so quickly in Egypt itself: 'I shall never forget the people who assembled as we were mooring in Aswan to see, as they told us, expert practitioners in the arts of black magic.'

Another founder of the society was the Reverend Richard Pococke who visited Egypt in 1737, where, to his horror, he watched columns being removed from a temple to be ground into millstones for a local village. It was a work of great destruction that should be stopped, he considered. His two-volume account of his travels, published in 1745, gives excellent descriptions of the sites as they were when he saw them. His illustrations, however, are crude – if somewhat imaginative – and as reference leave much to be desired.

The Egyptian Society began enthusiastically, with financial backing from several wealthy peers. At each fortnightly meeting, the chairman brought the group to order by shaking an Egyptian sistrum; and the first paper presented to the society by William Shakeley was on the efficacy of the sistrum as an ancient bird scarer! However, after a mere 45 weeks, the initial zeal waned and the society disbanded. Many of the members later bequeathed their smaller collections of antiquities to the British Museum, while others became trustees.

Stories of adventure

It was James Bruce's adventures that really attracted the first public attention to the Nile. He was a talented young man, born into a wealthy Scottish family. After his father's death in 1758, he embarked on the Grand Tour of Europe and the Middle East. His peregrinations brought him finally to Cairo in 1769, where at last he made the decision to sail south in search of the source of the Nile. On his way through Luxor, he took time to visit the Valley of the Kings. 'It is,' he later wrote, 'a solitary place and my guides, either from a natural impatience and distaste that these people have at such employments, or that their fears of the

Lady Lucie Duff-Gordon, *a British society hostess and celebrated author of the 19th century, was advised for her health's sake to leave English winters behind. She chose Egypt, lured by tales of the beauties of the Nile. A brief return home had disastrous results and she had to reconcile herself to living permanently in Egypt, taking up residence in a house on top of the sand-filled Temple of Luxor. She came to be loved by her adopted people, being respected as a healer and widely known as 'Sitteh' – 'the Lady'. She wrote letters to her sorely-missed family, filled with enthusiastic tales of her life and her adventures on the Nile. These letters were published by her husband, inspiring a number of women to follow her example.*

robbers that live in the caverns of the mountains were real, begged to return to the boat even before I had begun my search.' But not to be deterred, he entered a tomb now known to belong to Ramesses III (still called 'Bruce's Tomb') and here found several well-preserved paintings of blind harpers. He made two hasty sketches, from which finished pictures were published in his book, *Travels to Discover the Source of the Nile*, in 1790. They excited loud criticism and derision, bearing little resemblance, it was thought, to the strict Egyptian art style.

Bruce's adventures up the Blue Nile, through the perilous land of Ethiopia, had the effect of making Egypt seem less dangerous. It was still a journey to be undertaken with a spirit of daring, however; and to meet a fellow European anywhere in the Middle East was a notable event.

The defeat of Napoleon's troops by the British (*see pp. 30–1*) and the end of hostilities in Europe at the start of the 19th century made travelling to Egypt more attractive. The strong

links that Britain and France maintained with Egypt made that country seem much less dangerous than other countries in the Levant and Middle East.

In 1812, a remarkable British eccentric, Lady Hester Stanhope, granddaughter of Pitt the elder, journeyed alone to the Middle East, making her home eventually in a half-derelict former convent in Djoun near Sidon. From here she wrote letters back to England, and many travellers called upon her. They found an irascible old lady, dressed in Turkish male costume, a heavy smoker of cheroots and more narcotic substances, who slept most of the day and frequently entertained visitors only after sunset. Among the people who met her was Henry Kinglake, a young man from Taunton, Somerset. In his highly entertaining *Eothen* he describes her with some awe tinged with disbelief – '. . . she was almost bound by the fame of her actual achievements as well as by her sublime pretensions, to look a little differently from womankind.' She was, he wrote, 'the only person in the whole of Palestine who totally disdained the overlord, Mohammed Ali in Cairo.' She had given refuge to some Albanian soldiers fleeing Mohammed Ali's wrath. 'More than once had the Pasha of Egypt commanded the Albanians delivered up to him, but this white woman of the mountain answered only with the disdainful invitation to "come and take them." Mohammed Ali used to say, I am told, that this Englishwoman had given him more trouble than all the insurgent people of Syria and Palestine.'

Kinglake's account of this redoubtable old woman enchanted his readers, and many other women felt emboldened to follow her example. Lady Lucie Duff-Gordon settled in Luxor from 1863 until her death in 1869. Although tormented with ill-health, she learned to speak Arabic and to mingle fearlessly with the native Egyptians, people she loved dearly. She would regularly administer medicines to their sick. Her reputation as a 'Sheikha', a wise woman, was widespread in Egypt, and people would travel many miles to have her examine them. Her *Letters from Egypt* published in 1865, gave the first detailed account of living in the Middle East, and was responsible for many other Victorian ladies following her example in travelling up the Nile, including the remarkable Amelia Edwards, who was to have a profound effect on the whole study of Egyptology (*see p. 39*).

THE PATAGONIAN SAMSON

This medallion bears the features of Giovanni Belzoni, whose exploits in Egypt, collecting large statues and monuments and returning them to Europe, focused attention on the plight of Egypt's vanishing heritage. The plunder of antiquities was not confined to Egypt; nor was Belzoni the only culprit. Although his methods seem crude by today's standards, he did make a great effort to record what he had seen and noted the provenance for the pieces he brought back, unlike many collectors solely motivated by greed. In his painstaking sketches and paintings of the things he found – invaluable to modern scholars – Belzoni proved himself to have an accurate eye.

Giovanni Battista Belzoni, as his name suggests, was Italian by birth. In his youth he travelled to Rome, but when Rome was invaded by Napoleon's army in 1798, Giovanni and his brother Francesco were forced to flee. For several years he appears to have learned the elements of hydraulic engineering while scraping a living as a merchant trader.

In 1802, the young Giovanni, having grown to colossal proportions, being at least 2m (6ft 7in) tall, travelled to London, where he was employed as a strongman. Billed as the 'Patagonian Samson, who presents most extraordinary specimens of the Gymnastic Art,' the highlight of his act was the lifting of a specially constructed iron frame with 12 people sitting on it, and then walking across the stage!

Belzoni's travels

In 1812, at the age of 40, Belzoni left England with his much younger wife, Sarah, to embark on a series of travels. In Malta he met a Captain Ishmail who persuaded him that Mohammed Ali, Pasha of Egypt had need of a hydraulic engineer. Belzoni at once set off for Egypt on a course that was to change not only his life but the future of Egyptology.

His arrival in Cairo depressed him. 'It was barbarous, really barbarous,' he wrote, 'and barbarous it remains to this day.' The city was torn apart by a plague, forcing the Belzonis to live for several weeks in isolation. When Belzoni finally met Mohammed Ali, the Pasha was cool and generally unenthusiastic about a plan Belzoni had drawn for a new ox-driven water pump. He was, however, awarded a tiny government allowance which permitted him to live a while longer in Egypt.

During this time, he met the renowned Swiss traveller, Jean-Louis Burckhardt. Burckhardt, by dint of adopting Arabic dress and calling himself Sheikh Ibrahim, had managed to travel in places no European could have hoped to set foot. He told Belzoni of the marvels of Egypt, of a temple in Nubia, mostly covered with sand, called Abu Simbel, and of part of a colossal statue lying in a temple on the west bank of the Nile at Luxor, known as 'Young Memnon'.

Belzoni as collector

Fired with a new enthusiasm, Belzoni applied to the British consul, Henry Salt, to move the statue to England. Salt agreed without hesitation, promising in addition to provide the

funds needed. Mere days later, Belzoni sailed south, equipped only with four poles and some locally made ropes. It took his small boat 24 days to reach Luxor, where Belzoni identified the bust with little difficulty. The moving of it proved more of a problem, and it is doubtful if anyone other than Belzoni could have accomplished it. Only three weeks later, having moved several columns that stood in the way, the bust was safely on a boat bound for the north and England.

Belzoni decided at once to move south to the temple of Abu Simbel, through the little-known waters of Lower Nubia. On more than one occasion he was threatened by 'natives with spears', but arrived safely, though appalled by the sight that faced him. He calculated that at least 9.3m (30ft) of sand covered the temple entrance. Although he remained there for several weeks, he was unable to find workmen willing to work long enough for what he could afford to pay. He had to leave without reaching the entrance.

On his return north he stopped at Philae for a short time to collect several fine pieces of sculpture and load them onto a northbound ship. He next stopped in Luxor where a brief foray to the south of the main temple of Karnak in the precinct of Mut, revealed a series of dramatic statues of the lioness goddess Sekhmet, made of black granite. Several of these joined the Philae material. Six months after he started out, Belzoni returned jubilantly to Salt, with a list of pieces he had collected, the most spectacular shopping list any archaeologist could envisage. Salt was delighted with the results of Belzoni's efforts and sponsored him a second time to return to Nubia to collect more, and finer, pieces.

Friction with the French

Belzoni, however, had antagonized the French Consul, the Italian-born Bernardino Drovetti, himself an avid collector of antiquities, by his ruthless acquisition of pieces, and his second trip was to encounter more opposition. At every place he stopped, he was to find Drovetti's men on the site rousing public opinion against him, often with justification. It was, perhaps, unfortunate for Egyptology that Drovetti's men denied him access to the temple of Karnak, leaving him to wander instead around the Valley of the Kings and the tombs of the nobles. Here, despite the pleas made to exonerate him later on the grounds of igno-

rance of archaeological method, he was to cause great damage to many potentially informative burial chambers in his avidity for saleable material (*see pp. 94–5*).

He sailed on, after some weeks, and finally arrived at Abu Simbel in July, in almost intolerable heat. He found the local people still unwilling to help and so set to work by himself, stripping to the waist to shovel sand in the heat of the midday sun. This was scarcely to be borne by the Nubians watching the mad foreigner; and thus the local people joined in. Within 10 days, a hole appeared at the top of the doorway of the temple. As Belzoni crept in on all fours, using only the light from flickering candles, he was the first man, in modern times, to set eyes on the magnificent rock-cut chambers of Ramesses II's monumental Nubian temple. He stayed only another two days, long enough to collect everything movable from inside the temple, before returning north.

On his return to Cairo, Belzoni passed a few days at Giza, where there was frantic activity. The second pyramid, that of Chephren, had remained sealed, and Drovetti had determined to enter it, using gunpowder if necessary. Belzoni walked around it, comparing it with the other pyramids, and his eye lighted on a mound of sand at the base of the pyramid. Determined to outwit Drovetti one more time, he applied to the local chief for permission to dig, rather than in Cairo where 'it would have excited great

enquiry among the Franks and in all probability I would not have obtained permission to' proceed'. After some three weeks' work, at last he found a small cavity no more than 1m (3ft) square, but it proved to be false. His work had not gone unnoticed; a party of French watched his men working and, he reports, fired a pistol in his direction.

At last on 28 February 1818, Belzoni found the entrance to the pyramid, and with a little difficulty due to his size – 'the passage being only 1.3m (4ft) high and 1m (3ft 6in) wide' – he managed to squeeze himself in and was the first person in modern times to see Chephren's sarcophagus.

Home at last

He returned to England, in 1821, where he held a great Egyptian exhibition in Piccadilly, at the end of which his prime collection was auctioned. To his great sadness, he was unable to get the backing to return to Egypt, but instead set out to trace a route to Timbuktu. Within five weeks, he was dead of dysentery in a small village in Benin, and was buried in a quiet grave that was soon lost under encroaching vegetation.

While earning himself the reputation of a plunderer, Belzoni nonetheless brought attention to the monuments lying unrecorded in Egypt. His acquisitions now form the basis of the British Museum's Egyptian collection.

Belzoni's removal *of the Young Memnon from Luxor. This statue was observed first by Jean-Louis Burckhardt, and he, together with the British consul, Henry Salt, provided Belzoni with the funds to remove it to England. The French had previously failed in their attempts to move it. But Belzoni was undeterred; as Burckhardt wrote, 'He handles masses of this kind with as much facility as others handle pebbles, and the Eygptians who see him a giant in figure, for he is over six feet and a half high, believe him to be a sorcerer'.*

NAPOLEON'S NILE CAMPAIGN

This French stamp, *issued in 1972 to commemorate the 150th anniversary of the decipherment of hieroglyphs in 1822, shows Vivant Denon, the chief artist accompanying Napoleon's expedition, with a group of French savants in front of the pyramids of Giza. The Napoleonic survey of Egypt, which recorded with plans, maps and paintings all the major monuments as they were at the time, together with Denon's brilliantly coloured paintings, inspired Europe to copy Egyptian styles in everything from architecture to furniture.*

It was inevitable, given Napoleon Bonaparte's zeal for expansion, that in 1798 his eyes should turn eastwards. To re-establish links with India – broken by the British in 1751 – he reasoned a more efficient and controllable sea route had to be created. He was therefore authorized by the French government in early 1798 to build a canal through Suez, which meant gaining control over Egypt. The British navy learnt that the French fleet was preparing to sail but was unable to discover its destination. On 20 June, when news was relayed to Admiral Nelson that Malta had fallen to the enemy fleet, the French aim was suddenly clear: to reach Alexandria and conquer Egypt.

Nelson's ships raced across the Mediterranean but when they arrived in Abukir Bay, Alexandria, on 28 June, they found the port empty. Mystified, wondering if they had misunderstood, they returned to Sicily. In fact, they missed Napoleon's fleet by hours. On 1st July the French force landed in Egypt unopposed.

The great French expedition
Napoleon's expedition was not, however, entirely militaristic. Mindful of de Maillet's recommendation (*see pp. 25–6*), a corps of 167 scholars accompanied the fleet to survey and map the country for the first time. They had been given authority to collect whatever information they could on Egypt both ancient and modern. As well as botanists, biologists, architects, geologists and chemists, there was a large body of artists, chief among whom was Domenique Vivant Denon.

Denon was a remarkable man, with a most curious background. He had been born into a family of lesser French nobility, and trained in the law. Later he abandoned this in favour of art, becoming a friend and advisor of Louis XV on whose behalf he bought antique jewellery. He was appointed diplomat at the French Embassy in St Petersburg, and in 1776, he was moved to Naples, where he became noted as a collector of art treasures. Eventually, he returned to Paris to find his estates and belongings confiscated by the revolutionary committee. Impoverished, he became a street artist, during which time he published a volume of pornographic pictures, *Oeuvre Priapique*, which, for their artistic merit attracted the attention of the painter, Jacques-Louis David. It was David who introduced Denon to Josephine Beauharnais – and thus to Napoleon.

The scholars, or savants, set off southwards along the Nile, leaving the French fleet to make ready for Nelson's expected attack. It came on 1 August. Despite the French preparations, however, the English triumphed. The French flagship *L'Orient*, containing wealth seized from Malta to fund the Egyptian expedition, was blown up in the harbour with an explosion that was heard 24km (15mi) away. Most of the crew perished, including the son of the Chief of Staff, immortalized as the boy who 'stood on the burning deck when all but he had fled'.

The scholars were now cut off, penniless and their supply line non-existent. Yet they soldiered on for almost another three years, working under intense pressure. Accompanied by a small section of the army under General Desaix, they marched between 40 and 48km (25 and 30mi) each day. Denon, however, was captivated by all he saw. 'I was treading the soil of a land covered since immemorial times with a veil of mystery,' he later wrote. The small group was in constant danger, and Denon was frequently permitted only minutes at each site to make his sketches.

The British threat
The accompanying soldiers were deeply aware of the importance of the mission, and on several occasions cases of lead bullets had to be melted down for essential but unobtainable pencils for the scholars. When, in 1799, they arrived at Luxor, the soldiers were so moved by the sight of the ancient temples that 'without an order given, they formed ranks and presented arms'.

By July 1799, things became worse for the isolated French force. Troubled by exhaustion, heat stroke, fever, flies and hunger, the savants toiled on while from the north came news that the British were regrouping to attack. Napoleon himself managed skilfully to evade a port blockade and slipped Nelson's net, leaving his forces behind to cope as best they could. While digging foundations for a fort at Raschid in the delta, a soldier uncovered a black basalt stone that was to change the face of Egyptology – the Rosetta stone (*see p. 156*). News of this discovery fascinated Europe. It was immediately realized that the key to the decipherment of hieroglyphs might have been found.

By 1801, the savants, exhausted, demoralized but academically triumphant, were back in Cairo, facing inevitable capitulation to the British. One last chance remained for them.

When Abercromby's men gathered to attack, the savants slipped away to Alexandria with their unique collection, including the Rosetta stone, to reach the French fleet. It was to be a disastrous mistake. When the city of Alexandria surrendered to the British General Hutchinson, it was under condition that the material so painfully collected by the savants was yielded in its entirety to England. The French General Menou did not give up without bitter recriminations, and an insistence that the Rosetta stone was his personal property and therefore unaffected by the capitulation, but surrender was painfully exacted.

La Description de L'Egypte

The British were only interested in the large collectors' pieces, however, so Denon and his artists brought their work home to France. Their superb paintings and sketches were published in series of 24 volumes as *La Description de L'Egypte* between 1809 and 1813. Their impact was astonishing. The brilliant colour and detail of Denon's work electrified Europe, and heralded a craze for the Egyptian style. Pottery, sculpture, furniture, paintings and even architecture of the following decade were heavily encrusted with sphinxes, pyramids and temple façades. Robert Southey, the English poet, wrote, 'Everything must now be Egyptian; the ladies wear crocodile ornaments, and one must sit on sphinxes in a room hung with mummies and the long-nosed, black hieroglyphical men who are enough to make children afraid to go bed.'

The expedition, though a military disaster, became a triumph. Of all the savants, Denon himself acquired an outstanding reputation as artist and scholar. His autobiography, *Voyage dans l'haute et basse Egypte*, became an international bestseller, bringing him fame and fortune. By 1804, he had made Paris the artistic centre of Europe, and shortly before his death, in 1825, he heard news of Champollion's triumphant decipherment of hieroglyphs from the ill-fated Rosetta stone (*see p. 157*).

Denon's own painting *of the interior of the temple of Horus at Edfu shows how much sand had accumulated in the columned hall and the outer courtyard. Against the ancient walls, a small modern village thrived. Auguste Mariette was to clear it for the first time 60 years after this picture was painted.*

AUGUSTE MARIETTE

This bronze statue (*above*) *of Auguste Mariette, founder of the Antiquities Service and the Egyptian Museum in Cairo, was made by Xavier Barthe and unveiled officially in March 1904. It stands over Mariette's tomb. His remains, in an ancient Egyptian sarcophagus, were reburied in the gardens of the present Egyptian Museum to the left of the main entrance (right) when the collection was moved here in 1900.*

Nestor L'Hôte was one of the closest friends of Champollion, to whom the decipherment of hieroglyphs is commonly attributed (*see p. 157*). On Champollion's only visit to Egypt, L'Hôte accompanied him and produced not only paintings and drawings of the highest quality but also copious notes and diaries. In 1842, when he died, all his belongings were left to his cousins, François and Eugenie Mariette; and his papers were sorted by their son, François Auguste Ferdinand, who was then 21. The papers, as he read them, enthralled him and gripped him with great excitement. For the first time in his life, he knew what he wanted to do: visit Egypt and become an archaeologist. At once he bought a full set of *La Description de L'Égypte* and Champollion's grammar, and for the next seven years pored over them in his spare time, teaching himself hieroglyphs and gleaning from the illustrations all there was to know. Nothing could deflect the course of his enthusiasm. He learned Coptic, and after writing a paper on Egyptian objects in his local museum, Boulogne, presented himself to the Louvre in Paris, asking tentatively if there might be a vacancy for an Egyptologist. The professor of Egyptology at the Collège de France, M. Lenormant, also a friend of

Champollion's, was so impressed he offered Mariette a post, provided he worked hard to add to his already thorough grasp of the subject.

Journey to Egypt

Mariette's dedication to his job impressed Lenormant to such an extent that, the following year, when some rare manuscripts appeared on the market in Egypt, and the Louvre decided to buy them, Mariette was chosen to go in person to collect them – an exciting prospect for a keen young Egyptologist longing to work in the field. When he arrived in Alexandria, however, he wrote back to Paris that the seller of the manuscripts, a Coptic priest, refused to let them go to Europe. With barely a moment's hesitation, Mariette went to Cairo and rented living quarters. Within days, he was at Saqqara conducting a dig of his own. The Louvre's reactions have not been recorded, but Mariette's discovery within a few weeks of the long-lost Serapeum, the burial place of the sacred Apis bulls (*see p. 120*), clearly placated them and reconciled them to the loss of their newest archaeologist. From this time onwards, Mariette left Egypt only with great reluctance.

Mariette's funds began to run low but his passion for his subject so impressed everyone he

The main entrance (left) of the Egyptian Museum, in Cairo. This great museum, its luxuriant gardens filled with statues and stones from antiquity, lies at the north of Tahrir Square in the bustling heart of the city. It was specially designed for the ever-increasing collection by a French architect and opened in 1900. Inside is the richest display of Egyptian antiquities in the world, while masses more remain hidden in the museum's stores. Although it is home now to the mortal remains of Egypt's greatest pharaohs, the royal mummies are no longer on public display. The treasures from many tombs, including those of Queen Hetepheres, the kings of Tanis and the boy king, Tutankhamun, attract hundreds of thousands of visitors each year.

met that both the French Consul and Pasha Abbas, son of Mohammed Ali, agreed to advance him enough money to continue. While he was working in the Serapeum, he met the German Egyptologist, Heinrich Brugsch, and the two became firm friends, a friendship that was to last the rest of their lives. Together, near the Serapeum, they cleared and explored many mastaba tombs, including that of Ti, the reliefs of whose walls are among the finest that Egyptian craftsmen ever achieved.

The young Egyptologist was indefatigable and eternally optimistic, though grieved to the heart at the plunder and damage to the monuments that he witnessed, caused by his fellow Europeans. 'Let anyone visit Ti's tomb at Saqqara,' he wrote vehemently, 'and he will be satisfied that the tomb has in fact suffered more damage by the hands of the tourists during the last 10 years than it has during the whole of the previous 6000 years of its existence.'

Early digs

Together with Brugsch, he began a whirlwind of excavations, starting digs simultaneously at innumerable sites the length of the Nile, from Bubastis in the delta to Aswan in Upper Egypt. Employing at any one time somewhere in the region of 2500 workmen, he explored a total of 35 different sites. At each of them not only did he find previously unknown monuments and tombs but also found great treasures, including the intact and rich burial of Queen Ahhotep. Ahhotep was the mother of the founder of the New Kingdom, Amosis, and the discovery of her tomb was the setting for an explosive argument. Mariette was told of the discovery of the tomb by his workmen, and while sailing south, heard that a local mayor had ordered the mummy of the queen stripped of her jewels so that he might present them to the pasha to curry favour. Mariette intercepted the mayor's boat and set about him in a fury with his bare fists. At one point, it is recorded, he even threw a crew member over the side of the boat before the jewellery was finally returned to him.

Nothing was too vast a job for him to tackle. At Edfu, finding the temple filled with sand and a whole village built on top of its walls, he evicted the inhabitants, cleared the ramshackle houses and ordered the sand dug clear. Similarly in Luxor he cleared the Temple of Luxor, revealing the foot of the obelisk and the whole of the colossal statues at its gate for the first time. In the Temple of Karnak, from the

accumulated sand and rubble he found more than 15,000 small objects, many of them ultimately sent to the Louvre Museum. Later, archaeologists would condemn his zeal, saying that he would have done better to do less more thoroughly. But time was short, as Mariette knew only too well, as more and more objects were spirited illicitly out of the country.

The first Egyptian museum

He made an influential friend, however, in the Vicomte de Lesseps, a French diplomat in Cairo. In 1854, de Lesseps persuaded Said Pasha to build a canal through Suez, an action that would change Egypt's future irrevocably. Mariette complained bitterly to de Lesseps of the problems facing Egypt's heritage, complaints which de Lesseps conveyed to Said Pasha. In 1858, Said Pasha appointed Mariette to supervise all future excavations in Egypt, and also gave him permission and the premises to set up the first ever museum of antiquities in Egypt. It was one of the finest days Egyptology was ever to know: the ending of plundering at a stroke. That day Mariette founded the Antiquities Service and the Egyptian Museum. But all was not plain sailing. The house that Said Pasha gave him in Bulaq comprised 'small filthy shacks and a house teeming with vermin,' he complained. As Director-General of the Antiquities Service, responsible for awarding concessions to all excavators, monitoring all digs and policing the export of antiquities, he naturally aroused hostility – especially among many of the English who had hitherto worked unhindered.

Yet Europe, and the Louvre in particular, first forgave him and then honoured him. On one home visit to Boulogne he was greeted by gathered crowds as a returning hero, while his stand of Egyptian exhibits at the great Paris Exposition of 1867 was the star attraction.

Although he was still short of his sixtieth birthday when he died, in 1881, Mariette achieved more in his years in Egypt than almost any other archaeologist. Single-handed, he started the control of excavations that has made Egyptology the science it is today. Yet among his less well-known achievements, besides the temples that he cleared, is the libretto to Verdi's *Aida*, which he wrote jointly with Le Socle. It was a fitting tribute to him that it was his words that were sung at the state opening of the Suez Canal. He and de Lesseps between them had ushered in a new age for Egypt.

THE ORIENTALISTS

The publication of *La Description de L'Égypte*, the records of Napoleon's scholarly survey of Egypt, alerted artists to the possibilities of depiction of Oriental scenes. Among the first to take up the challenge was a 22-year-old English architect, Charles Barry, travelling through Greece and Turkey when a friend suggested a trip up the Nile. Delighted with what he saw, he made a masterly portfolio of maps, plans and paintings of the monuments he visited. Although largely unpublished, his material is among the earliest collated by a professional architect.

The burgeoning market for pieces showing Egyptian influence encouraged other painters to employ Oriental themes, using brilliant colours and daring subjects with Islamic motifs that would otherwise have offended conservative Victorian society. Many artists, such as John Frederick Lewis and Eugene Delacroix, preferred to depict contemporary Egyptian scenes, with a fascination for clear skies, exuberant Arab costume and especially for the seraglios or harems of the Turkish rulers.

David Roberts

Many of the painters who travelled through Egypt recorded a new aspect of the country – the interplay between ancient and modern. Whether deliberately done to record the monuments or not, their pictures are often the only records that survive to show the state of Egyptian antiquities in the 19th century. The work of two artists in particular stand out in this respect: Edward Lear and David Roberts.

Edward Lear, although better known for his nonsense verses and limericks, was also a very accomplished artist. He visited Egypt and Nubia in the 1880s before he travelled through Palestine. But it is David Roberts whose paintings and sketches have most caught the atmosphere of Egypt. So accurately are they drawn that they can be used by Egyptologists as a valuable source of factual information.

David Roberts was born in Edinburgh in 1796 to a poor Scottish family. As a child he loved to paint and draw, and he remembered being permitted by his mother to draw animals on her whitewashed kitchen walls.

His parents could afford neither to have him taught fine art nor to lose the income he might bring into the house, and so he was apprenticed to a house painter called Buego. Frequently he worked 15 hours a day, from 5:00 in the morning until 8:00 at night, earning a pittance.

Roberts' first opportunity to earn money painting pictures instead of walls came at the age of 21, when a circus and theatre owner asked him to try his hand at painting scenery. He was employed in this way for the following two years; but when the troupe returned to Edinburgh, in 1818, he found himself unemployed again. Now he was quite unwilling to return to painting and decorating.

In 1820, he married, but the marriage was a failure and Roberts was left to care for his daughter, Christine. He went to London, where he was employed first at the Old Vic and then at Covent Garden. His scenery painting here for Mozart's *Il Seraglio* was declared by art critics to be 'performed in such a manner as stamps the artist as an individual of great power'. That same year not only were two of his paintings of Rouen Cathedral hung in the Society of British Artists, but he was also commissioned for the princely sum of £200 to paint *The Israelites leaving Egypt*.

Journeys

In 1832, he embarked on a visit to Spain. The works he painted there established his reputation. In 1838, he set out for Egypt, being received in person by the pasha, Mohammed Ali. Roberts hired a small dahabiyeh (sailing-boat), with a cabin only 2 by 1.5m (6 by 5ft) for himself. So infested did he find it with vermin, however, that before he would sail in it, he had it sunk in the Nile for 24 hours to cleanse it.

His cruise south into Nubia was to last three months. He found Egypt both enchanting and, in some ways, repulsive. 'You need not go far here to see a dead ass; I have seen three myself,' he recorded in his diary with disgust. But the monuments thrilled his artist's eye. 'I was struck with amazement,' he wrote from Dendera, 'at the beautiful preservation and endless labour spent upon the carving.' The Nile also fascinated him. One evening, as he sketched a scene of feluccas, he recorded in his diary, 'Nothing to a painter can exceed in beauty these craft skimming along the river with their white sails spread and shivering in the wind.'

He reached his journey's end, Abu Simbel, in November 1838 with a sense of relief. Although he admired the temples he longed to return home. 'Thank God,' he wrote, 'our vessel's prow now faces north and civilization.' He had made by then over 100 detailed sketches of the places he had seen. It was on his return to Cairo that he received a letter from

David Roberts arrived in Abu Simbel at the beginning of November 1838. The façade of Ramesses' temple had been partially cleared of sand by Belzoni only 20 years before. Roberts' painting of the colossal statues of Ramesses II shows that though the entrance was clear, sand had once again begun to drift over the northernmost figures.

his daughter informing him that he had been elected an Associate of the Royal Academy of London.

But his journey was not over. He spent several weeks in Cairo sketching contemporary scenes of markets and mosques. To achieve the latter, he had to adopt Turkish dress and shave off his beard, an act that caused him some consternation, although, 'to be the first artist who made drawings of these mosques is worth the trouble of a little inconvenience.'

He decided to travel next into Syria and Palestine by way of Mount Sinai. In February 1839, he visited the monastery of St Catherine, which he had to enter dangling from the end of a rope, 'our elbows and knees receiving sundry thumps and bumps in the course of the ascent'.

His travels took him to Jerusalem and Bethlehem and then through Lebanon to Baalbek. At each place he made drawings, later to be refined into oil paintings of great beauty.

Roberts' work

He returned to London in June 1839, nine months after he had set out, with a wealth of material on which to work. In 1842, Louis Haghe published a total of 284 lithographs based on his watercolour and oil paintings, many of which were exhibited at the Royal Academy.

David Roberts died, in 1864, aged 69. Although he painted many other subjects, his Egyptian and Nubian series are irreplaceable both for their beauty and content. To a friend, he wrote, 'Having been familiar with almost every work on Ancient Egypt previous to my coming out, I should say that those mighty remains remain yet to be done, both with regard to showing their vast magnitude and elegant formation of the architecture. Yet I think I have approached nearer the thing than anyone hitherto. To do anything nearer would take years.'

JOHN GARDNER WILKINSON

John Gardner Wilkinson's *portrait shows him as a serious gentleman, and was probably painted after he was knighted for his services to Egyptology in 1839 at the relatively young age of 42. Few Egyptologists before or after Wilkinson have showed such firmness of purpose in their work, or such a prolific knowledge of their subject. The list of aspects of Egypt that he studied in depth seems almost endless, and in return he was honoured by innumerable professional societies outside his own field for the profound knowledge he displayed in their own specialities. His book,* Manners and Customs of the Ancient Egyptians, *though written 150 years ago, is without an equal to this day.*

There are many unsung heroes in the world of Egyptology, but few have ever mastered as much with as little recognition in modern times as John Gardner Wilkinson.

He was born in 1797, the son of a clergyman, and was sent to Harrow School as a boarder. Here he was taught, among others, by his headmaster, George Butler, a close friend of Thomas Young (*see p. 156*). Butler's enthusiasm for things Egyptian and his acquired passion for hieroglyphs sparked a fire of such intensity in the young Wilkinson's mind that it lasted all his life. There was little basic material for him to study at that time. Archaeology in Egypt was almost non-existent; hieroglyphs were still unread; and despite the post-Napoleonic desire for Egyptianesque design, there had been little accurate recording of any site or monument that could satisfy a young boy's hunger for knowledge.

The spell of Egyptology

Wilkinson looked forward to a career in the army, as did most of his contemporaries, but after leaving Oxford without a degree, he was urged by his parents to travel. It was in Italy that he met Sir William Gell. Gell had moved to Rome in 1814 in the train of the future maligned Queen Caroline, with whom he had an affair that scandalized Europe. Gell was also passionately interested in archaeology, having published an account of Troy in 1804, and shortly before Wilkinson's arrival he had become embroiled in hieroglyphic decipherment. The two men became firm friends, and Gell convinced Wilkinson that he would never be contented if he were to abandon archaeology.

Wilkinson needed no second opinion. Without hesitation he wrote to his parents telling them of his change of plan and, in 1821, sailed for Egypt. He was to live there, supported by a small income from his father, for the next 12 years. At once he began to acquire the tools of his trade, learning to speak Arabic and to read and write Coptic which many scholars were certain held the key to the forgotten Egyptian language. Within days, he began to walk the ancient sites, making copious notes in the notebooks he always carried. He missed nothing, first sketching the site and making plans; then, with a meticulous eye and unfailing hand, beginning to copy the inscriptions. It was work that no one before him had considered worth the effort. Yet no inscription, no painting, no carving was too small for him to copy in the finest detail. The work was painstaking and slow, but the young man's love for his subject conquered every problem.

He did not make his home in any one place. Rather, he travelled constantly, going south by river as far as the unnavigable Second Cataract on at least two occasions. For two seasons, in 1824 and 1827, he concentrated his efforts in the region of Luxor where he sat copying the wall paintings in the tombs of the nobles (see p. 104), with an unerring eye for accuracy. As he worked, he gradually began to see patterns in the hieroglyphs. The first clue was the kings' names, conveniently enclosed in cartouches (see Glossary). Wilkinson started, very slowly, to understand the language and, quite independent of Champollion's work, using the knowledge gleaned from Thomas Young via his headmaster, he arrived at the same conclusions. Since he never wrote a grammar it is impossible to say how soon he acquired a competence in reading the material he recorded; but as Champollion's work began slowly to appear, it was Wilkinson alone who was capable of commenting upon it – frequently offering corrections. It is enlightening to realize that, while Champollion's full grammar was not published until 1836, Wilkinson succeeded not only in eliciting the names of the kings of Egypt from inscriptions, but also set them into chronological order with few mistakes, and published them and their associated titles eight years earlier, in 1828.

Royal reward

Wilkinson returned to England in 1833, with vast quantities of material that he incorporated in the first major book on Egyptology, *Manners and Customs of the Ancient Egyptians*, published in three volumes, in 1837. The deductions he made from the things he had recorded offered unique insights into the lives of the ordinary ancient Egyptians, and gave the first historically detailed account of the country readily available to the public outside the Old Testament. His scholarship was acclaimed everywhere and, in 1839, he received a knighthood from the hands of the young Queen Victoria, the only Egyptologist ever honoured in such a fashion for his work.

Yet still Egypt lured him, and Wilkinson returned in 1842, when he visited the western delta, and again in 1848. During these years, he became thoroughly acquainted with hieratic, the cursive form of the language, and consequently when, in 1849, he visited the Turin Museum, he was able to study at great length the famous 'Turin Papyrus'. Wilkinson was able to publish this comprehensive, though damaged, list of kings down to the Nineteenth Dynasty two years later.

Wilkinson moved and worked alone, without the support of colleagues. As the first man ever to walk many of the ancient sites and copy what he saw before much of the damage had been done, his notes and records are beyond price; yet to this day, vast quantities of them remain unpublished, accessible only to scholars. His method of copying exactly what he saw, without any notion of adapting it for western eyes, as others had done, or romanticizing the setting, laid the basis for Egyptian epigraphic work today.

The last years

His passion for things Egyptian so filled his life that he was almost 60 before he contemplated marriage. His wife, Caroline Lucas, was an authoress and a botanist, and with her he settled to a quieter life of semi-retirement. After his marriage, he published only one small catalogue for an exhibition of Egyptian artefacts held in the Crystal Palace, London, and virtually renounced his Egyptological research.

In his travels in Egypt Wilkinson gathered great numbers of small objects such as tools, amulets and beads, and preserved foods. Many of these things he donated regularly to the British Museum. Mindful of the impetus given to him in childhood and the source of his lifetime's work, however, after his marriage he gave the rest of his own collection of Egyptian antiquities to Harrow School, where it remains intact and almost unexamined to this day.

Few other Egyptologists have contributed so much information over so wide a field; it has been estimated that Wilkinson covered in depth no fewer than 50 separate specialized aspects of Egyptian civilization from hieroglyphs to geology, and from customs of daily life to astronomy. Even though his books refer constantly to what was considered at the time an irrefutable source of factual information, the Bible, most of his conclusions stand uncontested to this day.

KARL LEPSIUS

This illustration *from Lepsius'*
classic publication, Denkmäler
aus Ägypten und Äthiopien, *is*
from the tomb of Khnumhotep
at Beni Hasan. Khnumhotep was
a nomarch, or governor, of the
Oryx nome in Middle Egypt,
during the Twelfth Dynasty,
in the time of King Sesostris II.
Here Khnumhotep (out of the
illustration, to the right) welcomes
a group of Asiatic travellers
led by a Bedouin chief,
Abisha. The hieroglyphic
inscriptions that accompany the
colourfully dressed foreigners
records them as 'heka khaswt', a
term meaning 'foreign rulers' that
was later applied to the kings of
the Second Intermediate Period.
Lepsius' attention to detail in
recording scenes like these have
enabled scholars to study details
that have often since disappeared.

It was clear from his childhood that young Karl Lepsius was destined for an outstanding future. He was born in 1810 in Naumberg-am-Saule, the son of the procurator of Thuringia, in eastern Germany. His university training was in Classics, although he attended courses on antiquities and Eastern languages at Göttingen. He was a determined young man, with a clear and concise mind that led him constantly to criticize other scholars with little doubt of his own correctness. It was not until he was 23 that he was introduced to Egyptian material while he was in Paris; but though he regarded his instructors highly and had decided to make a career in Egyptology, he was critical enough of progress in the field to refuse absolutely to learn hieroglyphs until Champollion's definitive grammar was published. Even then, he was able to offer many constructive comments on Champollion's theories and correct many of the faults he found in Champollion's grammar.

He pursued his career with an amazing determination, deviating little from subjects he thought might be useful and wasting little time pursuing what he thought would be irrelevant.

Lepsius' expedition

He spent four full years travelling around European museum collections studying inscriptions and familiarizing himself with material from various little-known sites. Meanwhile a wealthy Prussian nobleman, Count Humboldt, had also become fascinated with ancient Egypt through the publication of Napoleon's survey. When Lepsius' professor, Bunsen, approached Humboldt to suggest a similar Prussian survey to collect antiquities, the count was delighted to agree. In consequence Kaiser Wilhelm IV

and his wife the Empress Elisabeth were persuaded to authorize an official expedition; and Lepsius, regarded as the finest living Egyptologist, was appointed to lead it.

Unlike Napoleon's expedition, which was militaristic and only part scholarly, Lepsius' team were well equipped and all of them leading experts in the field of mapping, surveying and archaeology. Their work, which lasted three years, took them to every major site in Egypt and Nubia. Around Giza and Saqqara, he and his team explored and mapped 30 pyramids unrecorded before, and drew scenes and plans of over 130 mastaba tombs, a type of monument ignored by previous travellers. While at Saqqara, he organized drawings of all the uncovered monuments, including the tombs of Horemheb and Maya, recently rediscovered (*see pp. 114–15*). Wherever they went, the Prussian team took 'squeezes' (papier-mâché casts) of inscriptions and pictures and bore them back triumphantly to Prussia.

On his return Lepsius supervised the production of the finest work on Egypt ever printed, the *Denkmäler aus Ägypten und Äthiopien*, 12 volumes as monumental in size as they were in content. From the 15,000 antiquities brought back by the survey team, the Berlin collection of Egyptian antiquities received the bulk to make that museum one of the finest outside Egypt. Lepsius himself became Professor in Egyptology at Berlin University, founding a department whose academic reputation is outstanding.

Lepsius' work makes him without peer in the world of Egyptology, and few scholars would challenge his reputation as one of the greatest Egyptologists of all time.

A THOUSAND MILES UP THE NILE

This photograph *of Amelia Edwards was taken towards the end of her life after she had seen the Egypt Exploration Fund (later Society) that she had founded, begin to flourish. She was a remarkable, tireless and immensely enthusiastic lady who remained active to the very end of her life. Some people have found this energy of hers daunting. Quentin Crewe in 1982 wrote of her: 'Amelia was one of those intrepid Victorian spinsters who is a delight to read about but who, one fears, might have been a considerable trial to know . . . a real, if mildly formidable friend'. Her record of her 1000-mile journey up the Nile inspired many others to follow her example during her lifetime, and still succeeds today. Her enthusiasm, tempered with an insatiable desire for knowledge, has been an example to many.*

It is ironic to think that the whole basis of British Egyptology today should have come about as an accident triggered by unseasonal rain, but such is the case.

Amelia Edwards was born in London, in 1831, and lived most of her life at Westbury-on-Trym, Bristol. She loved to write even as a child and her first story was published when she was only seven. She also showed an early interest in the Middle East, aroused by the *Arabian Nights* stories. She had her first novel published when she was 24, and earned enough money from it and the following seven to secure a limited financial independence. In 1873, she was travelling in Greece, when the continual rain persuaded her to flee to drier places. She arrived in Cairo in 1873, no doubt encouraged by the exploits of Ladies Stanhope and Duff-Gordon (*see p. 27*). She stayed long enough at Shepheards' Hotel, the gathering point of visiting Europeans to 'distinguish at first sight between a Cook's tourist and an independent traveller, and discover that nine-tenths of those (she is) likely to meet up with are English or American'! She therefore hired a dahabiya, the *Philae*, and sailed south in company with another boat, *The Bagstones*. On board this second vessel was Miss Marianne Brocklehurst from Macclesfield, Cheshire. The two ladies became great friends, searching around sites for antiquities while Marianne's nephew Alfred went hunting for the fearsome crocodile, which seemed continually to elude him. 'The crocodile was too clever for him, and took care never to return,' Miss Edwards remarked in amusement as Alfred returned empty-handed time after time. As they travelled up the Nile the two ladies acquired innumerable objects, some bought and some found on the sites – as Amelia Edwards recorded, 'we enjoyed it none the less because it was illegal'.

Witnesses of destruction

While they were in Luxor, they witnessed the despoliation of several monuments by the crowds of tourists, the memory of which was to stay with Miss Edwards all her life. On the other hand, they also bid against each other for an intact mummy they were offered, taken from a tomb. Although Miss Brocklehurst emerged as the victor, the mummy was to prove a problem, for its strong aromatic odour gave away its presence on board the boat even when shut tight in a locker. Fearful of being caught with an illegally acquired antiquity, with great regret Miss Brocklehurst and her nephew 'drowned the dear departed at the end of the week'.

Together they crossed the First Cataract into Nubia. Amelia Edwards remained at Abu Simbel on board the *Philae* for two weeks while *The Bagstones* sailed further south. While here, she cleaned the faces of the colossal statues of Ramesses II, 'one of the handsomest men not only of his own day but of all history,' she wrote. The statues had remains of plaster over them, left by the painter Hay when he had taken casts of them 50 years earlier. 'All we had to do,' Miss Edwards wrote, 'was remove any small lumps that might yet adhere to the surface and then tint the white patches with coffee. Ramesses' appetite for coffee was tremendous. He consumed I know not how many gallons a day.'

This short trip lasting only three months changed Amelia Edwards' life. She became devoted to Egyptology, learning hieroglyphs in her spare time and writing constantly to Maspero in Paris (*see p. 96*). Her best-selling account of the journey, *A Thousand Miles up the Nile*, brought her a comfortable income.

On her return, Miss Edwards became convinced that something should be done not only to curb illicit treasure-hunting in Egypt, but also to bring together scholars willing to excavate on behalf of an established benevolent society. She approached the Keeper of Oriental Antiquities of the British Museum, Dr Samuel Birch, who had little time for an enthusiastic amateur – and female at that! Yet Dr Birch was hardly in a position to act independently, for Mariette had set up the Antiquities Service in Cairo with this same aim almost 20 years earlier (*see pp. 32–3*).

Undeterred, and with the support of Dr Poole, the Keeper of Coins and Medals, Amelia Edwards wrote to many Egyptologists, begging their support not only to excavate various sites but also to break French control over Egyptian archaeology. Among the many who replied was Sir Erasmus Wilson, a surgeon who had recently paid £10,000 from his own pocket to bring an obelisk known as Cleopatra's Needle to England. A meeting was convened in the British Museum, and on 27 March 1882, the Egypt Exploration Fund was established. Dr Poole and Miss Edwards were appointed the joint Secretaries and Sir Erasmus Wilson, Treasurer.

FATHER OF POTS

The newly formed Egypt Exploration Fund needed an archaeologist willing to work for them and a suitable site. Approaches to Heinrich Schliemann, the newly fêted discoverer of Troy, were unfruitful, though he did suggest two sites, both in the delta – the Greek city of Naucratis and the land of Goshen, mentioned in the Old Testament. Almost immediately, letters were sent to the celebrated Swiss Egyptologist, Edouard Naville. He accepted at once and, in January 1883, conducted the fund's first dig at Tell es Maskhuta, in the delta. His success was instant. Within weeks the committee learned that two statues had been found, a falcon and a seated scribe, both of which bore the ancient name of the site – Pithom.

In search of Exodus

The news electrified England. The store-city of Pithom, mentioned in the first chapter of the Book of Exodus as having been built by the enslaved Israelites, had been found! The publication of the fund's first report, *The Store-City of Pithom and the Route of the Exodus*, assured its survival. Naville happily identified many of the mud-brick foundations he discovered as being the very ones upon which the Hebrews toiled. For an annual subscription of £1, new members of the fund would receive a free copy of the report and a genuine Hebrew-made mud brick! Unfortunately, this promise could not be kept because the bricks were far too large to be moved in the quantities demanded. Money flooded in, while Amelia Edwards' lecture tour of America recruited new members by the score.

It had been hoped that Naville would return to the site the following winter, but he declared himself too busy. Thus it was that Dr Poole introduced to the committee a young man he had known for years, who had haunted the British Museum galleries as a child – William Matthew Flinders Petrie.

Petrie was born on 3 June 1853. His mother, Anne, was the only daughter of Captain Matthew Flinders, the explorer and the first man to chart Australia. Anne was in her mid-forties when William was born, though her son was healthy and blessed, she wrote, with a fine pair of lungs. When he was four, however, he became so ill it was expected he would die. He survived, but with a chronic cough that convinced his mother that he was a weak child. As a result, he never went to school, but was

Flinders Petrie, *even in his old age, was energetic and lively. Photographed in 1922, when he was 69 years of age, at Abydos in Upper Egypt, he set a brisk walking pace over the sands that many a younger person found hard to match. Behind him, somewhat amused, stands a family friend. To Petrie's right can be seen some of the ancient sun-baked, mud-brick walls that still litter the wide desert plain behind the mortuary temple of Seti I.*

Petrie's excavation *records were exceptional in his time for their content and accuracy. The card (below, left) shows the position of a body in a predynastic burial found in Naqada, grave No. 1848, with a set of grave goods around it. Petrie's copious handwritten notes ensure that even today objects found in each grave can be readily identified. Petrie ensured that nothing was removed from the site, firstly by employing successive grades of diggers, at different stages with only the most trustworthy performing the final meticulous clearing; secondly, by remunerating each workman for every piece he found.*

Many of the objects *that Petrie found in the predynastic graves were ornamental. They may have been religious or magical, but their true purpose is unknown. These two small ivory tags (right), of Naqada II date (i.e. late predynastic) appear to represent bearded men.*

taught first by his mother, an erudite scholar who introduced him to Hebrew, Latin and Greek, and then by a governess. This governess so overworked him that the boy became ill again and for many years his official education was effectively at an end.

Early work at the Great Pyramid

However, Flinders was an inquisitive child and, unaided, developed an insatiable appetite for facts, devising chemical experiments and toying with mathematics as a hobby. He discovered geometry for himself when he was 15, devouring Euclid with joy. His father, an industrial engineer, showed him how to use a sextant and map sites accurately, so that by the time he was 18, he would spend days alone walking sites around his home making surveys. In this way he developed an unerring eye for accuracy that astounded many people in his later years. His first book, published when he was 22, *Inductive Metrology, or the Recovery of Ancient Measurements from Monuments*, was applauded by scholars as a work of supreme skill. He based much of his research on measurements made with his father at Stonehenge when he was 19.

In his youth, Petrie's father had fallen in love with a young lady called Henrietta Piazzi-Smyth, the daughter of Charles Piazzi-Smyth, the Scottish Astronomer Royal. Although his suit was rejected, the families remained friends, and thus it was, in 1867, that the Petrie family read with great interest Piazzi-Smyth's books on the Great Pyramid of Giza, a monument whose measurements, he swore, encapsulated all mathematical and astronomical knowledge, past, present and future. It naturally enthralled young Petrie, who strongly believed that these facts could not lie. It was he who wrote to Piazzi-Smyth to inform him that based on his measurements 'pi' must have been used in calculating the building of the pyramid.

Yet the book was heavily criticized and derided by scholars. In 1882, Petrie and his father went to Egypt in order to confirm Piazzi-Smyth's results. To their distress they found that virtually every measurement their friend had taken was inaccurate. Young Petrie was stunned and much wiser. His own survey of the pyramids, published in 1883, remains a standard in the field.

The publication of his work, with its scholarly accuracy, so impressed Dr Poole at the British Museum that he suggested Petrie as

the Egypt Exploration Fund's next excavator in Egypt to succeed Naville. Petrie agreed with alacrity. He was permitted the sum of £250 per month to cover not only all his, but also all the excavation's costs, and in November 1884, Petrie arrived in Egypt.

Petrie's first excavation

The two years during which Petrie excavated for the fund were tempestuous, with a violent clash of personalities. Petrie was thoroughly intolerant of the slow-acting committee, unwilling to accept any criticism of his own work, and wilfully determined that any of the allowance he saved in his work was his own to dispose of and need not be returned to the committee. He was, on the other hand, a superb excavator and supremely critical of his predecessors upon whose sites he worked. From every site he excavated, he sent back thousands of objects, most of them tiny pieces regarded as unimportant by everyone before him, but to him representing all the variety of ancient Egypt. To every workman who found anything he would give a small reward, ensuring that he

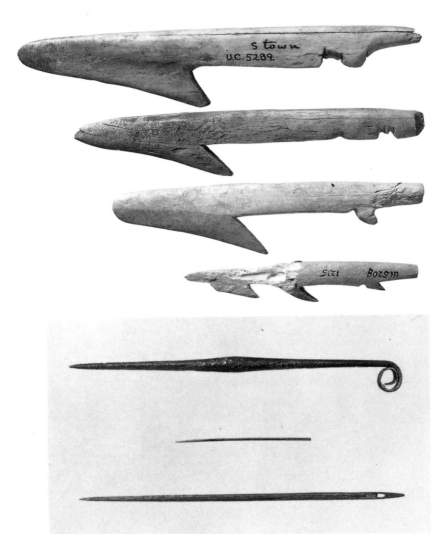

Predynastic graves *contained many objects, some personal, some practical. These four bone harpoon, or spear, heads (top) could have been used by the deceased during his life, but their inclusion in the grave suggests some belief in an afterlife where they might be useful again. The three bone needles (above) are also of Naqada II date and come from the cemetery of Naqada in Upper Egypt. Although very few specimens of cloth of such ancient date have survived, the provision of needles shows that the technique of sewing had already been mastered.*

received everything and nothing found its way on to the black market. Relations with the committee, however, deteriorated, with letters once addressed as 'My dear Petrie,' degenerating to 'Sir'. Petrie constantly criticized the committee, declaring it wasteful and mismanaging, and demanded changes or he would resign. The Chairman, Mr Newton, refused even to discuss the measures, an action which Petrie viewed as 'a declaration of war'. On 16 October 1886, Petrie tendered his resignation and the Egypt Exploration Fund was to be the poorer for it.

The eccentric archaeologist

After leaving the fund, Petrie worked independently, setting up the Egypt Research Account. Over the next 37 years, he excavated almost every major site in Egypt. Wherever he went, he insisted on rigorous discipline from his staff. One of his students wrote, 'He served a

table so excruciatingly bad that only people of iron constitutions could survive it, and even they had been known on occasion to assuage their hunger by sharing the comparatively luxurious beans of the local fellahin.' It was a habit of his to leave surplus cans of food buried on site at the end of each season; on his return the cans would be unearthed and flung against a wall – if they did not explode, they were deemed fit to eat! Another colleague wrote, 'Petrie is right in all things, from the right way to dig a temple to the only way to clean one's teeth. Further, he is full of humour and fickle to a degree that makes him delightfully quaint and a constant source of joy and amusement.'

As a true eccentric, Petrie was a sheer delight. Visitors to his sites would often find him, on hot days, immersed to his chin in the fetid water of irrigation canals. Many a lady tourist was forced to avert her eyes when they fell upon the strange bearded archaeologist working wearing nothing but vest and long-johns, 'and if pink, they serve all the better to keep the tourists away,' he averred. Despite his brilliant mind, he could never quite master Arabic, and on one occasion, by shouting 'push' instead of 'pull', watched as a stone coffin, removed from a deep shaft after hours of exertion, plummetted straight back.

As an archaeologist, however, he set a standard for every other Egyptologist to this day. His meticulous excavation, thorough analysis, and logical, careful and immediate publication have never been equalled. He was amply rewarded in his finds. He was the first scientific excavator of Egyptian sites and personally trained many students who became masters in the field. Through them, his influence is still felt by students today. He left Egypt in 1923, after the law of the division of finds was changed in the wake of the discovery of Tutankhamun's tomb, and excavated instead in the Near East. Here on many sites he traced Egyptian trade and cultural links that served to add even more information to what he had already discovered. His publications covered every field, from predynastic to Graeco-Roman material, from pottery typology through to studies of tools and toys, from analysis of art to studies in hieroglyphs and Egyptian grammar.

It was while he was working at Abydos that he earned the title 'Father of Pots.' Today, we might better call him the Father of British Egyptology.

RECORDING THE PAST

Amice Calverley *(centre) and Myrtle Broome (right), together with a younger member of the epigraphic survey, pose in a typically lighthearted way for the camera at Abydos in 1932. Their work on the mortuary temple of Seti I involved them in long hours of painstaking attention to detail. Myrtle Broome, in her diary, recorded that they usually worked from 6:00 in the morning, often until well after dark. The two ladies set up a splendid house at Abydos with a greatly admired English country garden in front of it that they fed and watered assiduously. It all made for an atmosphere that attracted many visitors and they were seldom without guests.*

Egypt has always attracted artists, lured by its clear skies, brilliant colours and unique monuments. Lepsius and Wilkinson, however, had proved that, far from such work being merely aesthetic, the accurate copying of inscriptions, paintings and reliefs could be as vitally important as excavation. The pictures thus published not only provided material for the scholar to analyze at leisure, confident of having an exact replica of distant inscriptions, but also preserved for posterity material that was fast vanishing, either removed by collectors or damaged deliberately or inadvertently by tourists. What started purely as a means of showing people what Egypt looked like acquired a new dimension: the recording of inscriptions for their own sake, or the science of epigraphy.

Excavation in the field, though vitally important, became less and less so. Many museums worldwide received far more objects than they could ever display, and, like icebergs, nine-tenths of many collections lay unseen beneath the surface. While digs were carried out primarily on desert sites safe from dampness or damage and despoilation by expanding towns and villages, other sites close to the river were being threatened before they had ever been

studied. The opening of the British dam, at Aswan, in 1901, first alerted archaeologists to the new threats. Behind the dam the rising waters engulfed several sites, including the beautiful temple of Isis on the island of Philae. Until the late 1970s, visitors to that site were only able to sail around the upper parts of the temple's columns, gazing down at the images of Isis carved on walls far below them.

The first official epigraphers
Even before this, however, in 1890, the Egypt Exploration Fund had realized the danger. Amelia Edwards wrote, 'We hope to be very shortly in a position to send out two gentlemen fully qualified as archaeologists, Egyptologists and surveyors whose duty it will be to map, plan, photograph and copy all the most important sites, sculptures, paintings and inscriptions yet extant, so as to preserve at least a record of these fast-perishing monuments!'

The Archaeological Survey was thus formed, and Francis L. Griffith was appointed as the first surveyor. Griffith, then 28, had visited Egypt several times with Flinders Petrie and even then had observed how many previously published inscriptions had been effaced. His aim, he told the fund, would be to survey Egypt completely, photographing everything, looking for previously unmarked objects and drawing maps and plans. His time scale, however, was unduly optimistic; what he envisaged as taking two years is still under way and far from complete. One of the first draughtsmen Griffith employed, Percy Newberry, realized the impossibility of the scheme within months of being asked to survey the 248km (155mi) between Minya and Assiut. He protested that the tombs of Beni Hasan alone represented 1115sq m (12,000sq ft) of paintings that had first to be analyzed for content and colour before being copied. From this time on, the survey decided to concentrate on recording individual sites accurately.

One of the finest epigraphers ever employed by the survey was Norman de Garis Davies. He was an ordained minister in the Congregational Church, where he had met Griffith's wife who introduced him to Egyptology. In 1898, he joined Petrie en route to Dendera and excavated with him for several months before branching out alone to record by copying the inscriptions of many sites. Proficient in the reading of hieroglyphs, he was able often to reconstruct with great accuracy missing or damaged scenes. As Charles Wilkinson of the Metropolitan Museum of Art, in New York, recalls, Davies was, 'not by nature a patient man,' but, 'he tackled each project with dogged determination, offset by a droll sense of humour.' In 1907, Davies married Nina McPherson, an artist trained at the Slade school and the Royal College of Art, both in London. She shared his love of Egypt, and her insistence on recording exactly what she saw, including an accurate reproduction of the extant colours, resulted in joint publications of tomb paintings for the Archaeological Survey that are masterpieces of the copyist's craft.

International copyists

Yet the Archaeological Survey was far from being the only party interested in the field. Gaston Maspero, the French head of the Antiquities Service, published between 1882 and 1893 complete copies of the pyramid texts from five separate pyramids, while Mariette's friend Brugsch had published copies of texts in the temple of Edfu in 1875. Then, in 1907, the first photographs of inscriptions were published, taken by Felix Guilmant in the Valley of the Kings. This use of photography opened up new possibilities for recording inscriptions both accurately and quickly.

The most influential and successful of all epigraphic surveys was founded in 1919. James Henry Breasted, born in 1865, in the state of Illinois, in the United States, studied Egyptology in Berlin under Erman, and in 1905 was appointed Professor at the University of Chicago – the first American chair in Egyptology. In 1919, he received an annual grant from J.D. Rockefeller, with which he established the Oriental Institute within the University. Five years later, aware of the growing pressures on Egyptian monuments, he organized the purchase of a permanent site for the institute in Egypt. With the opening of Chicago House, in Luxor, the Epigraphic Survey came into being, its aim, to record in finest detail all the monuments in the area. The recording of Medinet Habu, the mortuary temple of Ramesses III (*see p. 145*) was to take 30 years; the recording of the temples of Karnak and Luxor is still in process today. The infinitesimal care taken, a process established at the start of the survey, ensures that exact copies of the most minute details survive. From an initial photograph, an ink tracing is taken, outlining the carving on the wall and any areas of damage; the tracing and photograph are then taken back to the original where an artist marks any additional details that may have been overlooked, together with notes of any colouring that may have survived. Publication of thousands of these records has enabled scholars to reconstruct accurately both the structure and use of the buildings.

In 1925, the British Archaeological Survey, on the recommendation of Professor Blackman of Liverpool University, appointed Amice Calverly, a 31-year-old trained artist and musician from Canada, to carry out the epigraphic survey of the temple of Seti I at Abydos. Her work was painstaking and she not only quickly grasped standard epigraphic techniques but also developed new approaches that won her the admiration of scholars. Her pictures of the wonderfully preserved scenes on the walls of that temple were seen by J.D. Rockefeller when he visited Abydos in 1928, and he at once agreed to meet the cost of publication of the pictures. Thus from 1933 onwards, four volumes of her, and her assistant Myrtle Broome's work were printed as a joint Archaeological Survey/Oriental Institute venture.

With the threat to Nubian monuments raised by the High Dam, in 1955 the Egyptian Government, aided by a grant from Unesco, set up the Documentation Centre of Cairo. Using stereoscopic photographs of inscriptions on Nubian monuments, scientists applied new techniques of geographical mapping to walls. By this photogrammetry, not only the minutest details of reliefs are noted, but also contour lines of the stone's carving can be accurately recorded enabling, if need be, exact copies to be made in plaster or stone by future generations. Already a large archive of invaluable material has been established.

The erosion caused to monuments today continues unabated. Salts that would formerly have been washed away by the annual flood waters now accumulate on the walls of monuments, and the face of the stone crumbles, taking all inscriptions with it. The vibration caused by tens of thousands of visitors' feet, combined with the rumble of ever-increasing passing traffic, threatens the very foundations of the monuments. Even the fact that they have been dug out from the sand leaves them vulnerable. While excavation can, in many instances, wait a while longer, the need for epigraphers and copyists in Egypt is greater today than at any other time.

Epigraphic survey work, *here shown in progress in the temple of Amun at Karnak in Luxor, involves many hours examining and copying accurately what remains of ancient inscriptions and pictures. Unlike excavation, it brings no immediate rewards. Although there can be the pleasure of identifying a loose block in a wall, and replacing it, there is not the thrill of the unexpected discovery. It is, however, the forensic, detective side of archaeology that can be ultimately satisfying. Unlike excavation, which is usually destructive, epigraphic work is constructive and vital for future students. As the work of the Chicago House teams has shown, it can also, in the long run, reveal exciting details of Egyptian life, technology and craftsmanship that would often otherwise be missed.*

II

EGYPTIAN ORIGINS

*'I do not believe that the Egyptians came into being at the
same period as the Delta; on the contrary, they have existed
ever since Mankind appeared on earth, and as the Delta
increased with the passage of time, many of them moved into
the new territory and many remained where they originally
were.'*
Herodotus, Book II, 16

The aim of every archaeologist is to understand our earliest
ancestors – how they lived, and how we developed from them
– and the Egyptologist is well-placed to examine such
questions very closely, for Egypt's climatic mixture of heat
and dryness has preserved even the most fragile material for
thousands of years. The first point to be answered is where
did the Egyptians come from?

In 1900, almost nothing was known either of Stone Age
Egypt, or of the first settlers of the Nile Valley, nor even of
the first generations of kings who ruled in Egypt before the
pyramids were built. By 1960, not only had a firm sequence of
progress during prehistoric times been established by excavation of ancient cemetery sites and geological context,
but also the names and a little of the background of the kings
of the first two dynasties had been discovered. But with the
constant irony of archaeology, not one, but two 'tombs' for
each of the earliest kings were found 480km (300mi) apart.
Scholars still argue as to which, if either, of the two tombs
was the genuine resting place for the pharaohs' forefathers.

The search for human origins in Egypt is still in its infancy.
The answer to that most baffling of questions – how did
humankind begin? – still awaits a firm answer.

Part of the wall scene *from the remarkable Painted Tomb 100 at
Hieraconpolis – possibly that of an early king – one of the most
ancient painted scenes ever found in Egypt.*

FROM HUNTER TO FARMER

**Dr Fred Wendorf
(1924 –   )**

Dr Wendorf was born in Texas and received his doctorate from Harvard in 1953. Specializing in the study of early humans, he headed a combined expedition of Egyptian, American, British, French, Belgian and Polish archaeologists in Nubia in 1962 which examined the sites used by the earliest Egyptian settlers in terms of archaeology and geology. With his colleagues, he was able to divide the Palaeolithic era of Egyptian history into distinct periods, making prehistory, for the first time, a major aspect of Egyptology. Today, he holds the Henderson-Morrison Chair in Prehistory at Southern Methodist University, Dallas.

Human origins are constantly being pushed farther back in time. Since Egyptian civilization is one of the earliest in the world, it comes as no surprise that the skeletal remains of a pre-human primate should have been found in Egypt. Remains of Aegyptopithecus, described as a small cat-like ape weighing around 4.1 kg (9 lb), were found in the Faiyum Oasis. Dr E. Simmons of Duke University, in the United States, has recently dated them to around 33 million years ago, 'the oldest creature we know that is in direct ancestry of Man'.

Early remains in Egypt

It is all the more strange, therefore, not only that nothing more is known of our predecessors until 4 million years ago but also that no remains whatever of even these ancestors are found in Egypt. The earliest human skeletal material found in an Egyptian context, in Gebel Sahaba in Nubia, is no more than 12,000 years old.

This absence of human skeletal remains is all the more surprising in the context of the plethora of material discovered in Africa. The Leakey family alone, working in east Africa since 1929, has succeeded in tracing many groups of early humans. The earliest, almost complete, skeleton yet found, nicknamed Lucy, was discovered, in 1974, by Dr D. Johanson in Ethiopia. This 20-year-old female belonged to a group called Australopithecus (literally) 'southern ape', believed by many to be the direct ancestor of Homo erectus and thus Homo sapiens. This has led scholars to propose a northern dispersion route for mankind from Africa by way of the Nile Valley. The lack of any remains of the Australopithecus family in Egypt is thus all the more surprising.

Palaeoarchaeology in Egypt is, in fact, a little studied area. So great is the volume and content of historical evidence from predynastic (Neolithic) times onwards that few scholars have ventured into the less informative prehistoric times. Much of the information that has been gathered comes from geological, ecological and palaeological areas of study rather than Egyptological, something that is to be greatly regretted.

New perspective

In 1976, Karl Butzer, Professor of Anthropology and Geology at the Oriental Institute of Chicago, published the results of an ecological survey of Egypt that showed many earlier scholars' suppositions to be 'wildly inaccurate'. The climate of ancient north Africa was not as mild as once had been thought, nor was the Nile Valley an inhospitable swamp hostile to humans. On the contrary, for much of its history Egypt's climate appears to have been little different from today's. Only around 17,000 years ago was there a significant increase in rainfall that turned the Sahara temporarily into savannah grassland, roamed by such large game as elephants, rhinoceroses and huge wild oxen, tempting the river-bank settlers to move away from the Nile to hunt game.

Before this, little is known of the settlement of Egypt. Although early human remains have yet to be found, evidence for the activities of what was probably Homo erectus was discovered, in 1926, by K. Sandford and W.J. Arkell, two archaeologists specializing in prehistory and geology. They had been appointed to survey Egypt as best they could for early remains. In Abu Simbel they discovered early Palaeolithic hand axes that could be dated to around 700,000 years ago.

The threatened drowning of Nubia by the High Dam resulted in a great increase in international investment in archaeology in the 1960s. One team, led by Drs Fred Wendorf, of Dallas, and Rushdi Said, of Cairo University, specifically searched for prehistoric sites and, as a result, quantities of new information came to light. Near Wadi Halfa (at the Second Cataract) and in the western desert at the Dungul Oasis, southwest of Aswan, two early Palaeolithic sites were found that contained (other than evidence from Olduvai Gorge found by the Leakeys), the oldest hut-circles, dating to around 250,000 years ago. The stone circles of Dungul, lined with sandstone blocks and covered with a scatter of Acheulian (i.e. Lower Palaeolithic) tools, are approximately 11m (12yd) in diameter, a compound large enough to house many people.

Dr Wendorf's forays into the western desert also took him to Bir Sahara – 'one of the most desolate and isolated places on earth,' as he described it. Here he found the earliest animal remains yet known from Egypt in a human context – bones of antelope and wild ass, dating to around 100,000 years ago. A covering of ostrich eggshells reminded him strongly of a habit adopted by Kalahari bushmen of using eggshells as water carriers when out hunting in the desert. This led him to propose that this

A selection of small *figurines, now in the Cairo Museum, that represent some of the earliest examples of sculpture ever found in Egypt. Figures such as these, made of faience, ivory and a variety of stones, were found in many late predynastic graves. Their significance is much discussed. Suggestions for their use range from votive objects for primitive gods, and amulets, to toys, or even gaming pieces for the board games so loved by Egyptians from the very earliest times. These pieces come from a variety of sites: the crocodile, falcon, hippopotamus, frog and baboon, all faience, were found by Petrie in Abydos; the limestone baboon by Möller at Abusir; the rock-crystal lion was found in the tomb of one of Aha's wives at Naqada. Since the creatures these carvings represent were, a thousand years after they were made, identified with various Egyptian deities, it is tempting to see them as amulets or fetishes, worn by local people to attract the good will of their god.*

was not a settlement site, but rather a camp site used by palaeolithic hunter-gatherers.

Early experiments in agriculture

Crop cultivation, linked with permanent settled sites and domestication of animals, has usually been regarded as having been developed later in Egypt than in other parts of the world – around 5500 BC, a thousand years later than in southwestern Asia. However, excavation of prehistoric sites along the Nile Valley has revealed many settlements of late Palaeolithic date, around 12,000 years ago, that challenge this. It was in 1920 that the French archaeologist Edmund Vignard found the first such site at Kom Ombo, with a profusion of slender, finely-worked flint tools, bone needles and tiny barbed harpoons – lightweight flints that he called 'Sebilian' but which we now term microlithic. These tiny, beautifully worked tools indicate the first true settling of hunter-gatherers into communities as hunting for large game became less reliable than local foraging. Other sites were found – Edfu, Esna, Naqada and Tushka in Nubia, 160km (100mi) south of Aswan, all told the same story. At Tushka, excavated by Dr Wendorf in the late 1960s, not only were over 100 distinct hearths or hut areas found, but together with the microlithic tools were remains of cooked fish and small animals. Many sickles were also uncovered – wooden and bone handles inset with tiny flints, used for reaping grain – and quern stones used for grinding grain into flour. Organic remains have

been carbon-dated and revealed dates around 12,500 BC. Another survey at Esna, carried out by Dr Hassan, of Washington State University, has revealed pollens and grains belonging to an early cultivated barley.

Return to hunting

It is clear, then, that around 12,000 BC, the Nile Valley settlers developed a form of agriculture, although primitive, well in advance of other cultures. Yet from around 10,500 BC onwards, cemetery sites show no more sickles and microliths, but a return to larger and heavier hunting weapons, including spearheads and arrowheads. Clearly the agricultural experiment that lasted a thousand years failed. Perhaps it was a change in climate that forced the large game to leave Egypt for several hundred years, so that the valley settlers had to adapt to foraging what they could to survive. Yet the reappearance of game around 10,500 BC resulted in the abandoning of what were obviously harder and poorer methods of survival.

Excavations in 1968 near El Kab by Dr Paul Vermeersch uncovered a site of around 6000 BC. Here a cemetery yielded over 4000 artefacts that showed the Egyptian settlers were still hunters and fishermen. It seems probable that yet another climatic change around 5500 BC did indeed encourage the introduction of agriculture from neighbouring countries. By 5500 BC, Egypt was already beginning to emerge as a nation that had to depend on cultivating the land to survive.

Work at Naqada

In 1894, Flinders Petrie arrived at the site of Naqada on the west bank of the Nile, about 33km (20mi) north of Luxor. As companion and assistant he took James Quibell, a 26-year-old Oxford graduate; workmen were recruited from the east bank town of Quft.

Over the next few months, more than 2200 shallow pit graves were discovered, the occupant of each curled in foetal position and accompanied by lavish grave goods, from ivory figurines and combs to simple slate palettes, used for grinding green malachite (copper ore), and a bewildering variety of pots and jars. Not a single inscription showed who the people might have been, and for some time Petrie believed he had found the graves of foreigners who had invaded Egypt during the First Intermediate Period (c. 2134–2040 BC). Quibell disagreed, though not in print. These were, he considered, the cemeteries of the earliest settlers in Egypt.

The Sequence Dating System

By 1899, after examining more cemetery sites at Hu and Abydos, Petrie had come to the same conclusion. But the Naqada cemetery, now identified as the necropolis of the settlement of Nubt, a town devoted to the god Seth, revealed many problems, not least of which was the pottery. Petrie began to analyze the grave goods methodically. Grave A might contain certain types of pot in common with Grave B; Grave B also contained a later style of pot; and this was the only type of pot found in Grave C. In time,

by writing cards for each grave and filing them in logical order, Petrie established a full sequence for the cemetery, concluding that the last graves on the site were probably contemporary with the beginning of the First Dynasty. For the first time, evidence of the slow human development along the Nile was revealed, from the earliest settler to the accomplished farmer, and then the politically aware generations at whose time Egypt was united. Yet Petrie was unable to establish fixed dates for his sequence, and thus gave them numbers: sequence date 30, he marked as the earliest material, leaving allowance for earlier finds; SD 80 he made the First Dynasty with unification occurring, he thought, around SD 76.

Later excavations showed that these dates needed some adjustment; that the unification of Egypt happened around SD 63, while the settlement pattern seemed to have changed quite noticeably, around SD 37. As more sites were examined and parallel cemeteries were found to match those of Naqada, it was clear that Petrie's dating system could stand any test. Petrie's technique of seriation has led him to be regarded as 'one of the greatest applied mathematicians of the 19th century'.

Early settlements

By around 5000 BC, settlements were growing all along the Nile Valley, with fields of grain being cultivated successfully for the first time (since the first experiments with agriculture some 7500 years before (*see p. 49*), while the

A selection of *pottery of Naqada II (Gerzean) date, around 3400 BC. These pots were found as a complete group in Luxor, in a cache inside the temple of Karnak. Nothing is known, however, of Luxor during this very early period. So it is possible that they were brought to the temple at a much later date. The painted vessels are all decorated with a buff slip and brown-red pattern applied before firing. The pierced lug handles on the two jars on the right would be for ropes from which to suspend them. The tall vessel on the left (back row) is painted to resemble a net in which, presumably, jars of this kind were carried. The jars with the black tops were common just before and after unification, approximately 3100 BC. They are not painted. The clay pot was burnished with a pebble before firing to achieve the polished red base, and then upturned in ashes afterwards to give the black top. The small pot in the centre (front) is a mystery. Of early Aegean or Cypriot style, it is about 2000 years younger than the others, though found with them.*

unaccustomed farmer also attempted to domesticate groups of wild animals. It seems likely that there were three distinct areas in Egypt at this time: from Assiut southwards through Nubia; from Assiut northwards to the foot of the delta; and the delta itself. Each area was fundamentally different in its customs. This earliest group of settlers were typified at two sites: El Badari, in Upper Egypt, and Merimde Beni Salama in the delta.

El Badari

No trace of houses was found on this Upper Egyptian site, although the cemetery was extensive. It seems likely that these people would have lived in tents or temporary shacks. Their graves were oval, shallow and large. The people already wore woven linen clothes, although bone needles used for sewing them were only found in men's graves. Both sexes wore jewellery in the form of belts of beads and amulets many of which were faience.

Merimde Beni Salama

When Junker excavated here, 60km (37mi) north of Cairo, on behalf of the German Archaeological Institute, he discovered one of the largest early predynastic sites in Egypt, dating to 5000 BC. Unlike El Badari, these settlers built houses over a wide area. The dead were buried in the town rather than outside it. The occupants had virtually no grave goods with them other than a reed mat on which the body lay. The houses were oval or round, and built of mats or wickerwork stretched around posts, with mud floors. Hearths showed that the settlers cooked their food, and almost every house had a quern stone for grinding grain. Thousands of potsherds were found, hand-raised and plain, although many bowls and jars had tiny human feet of fired clay on which to stand.

Naqada I (SD. 30-37)

Because, in 1899, a site of the same period was excavated by Randall-McIver and A. C. Mace at El-Amra this period is also often referred to as Amratian. These sites were considerably more prosperous than those of Badarian date. The first house settlements in Upper Egypt were found in El Hammamiya, by Gertrude Caton-Thompson, and Armant, by Oliver Myers. Some of the graves that Petrie investigated at Naqada of this date contained carefully arranged piles of human bones rather than

skeletons, some with more or fewer bones than there should be. This led early scholars to suggest the settlers could have been cannibalistic. It seems more likely, however, that these were reburials, either the bodies of families being moved later to a common grave, or bones from bodies that had been left exposed for some time being collected and buried.

Among the finest grave goods were finely carved small ivory combs, and red polished jars and bowls decorated with patterns of cream lines. Although these patterns are usually geometric, some show crudely drawn figures of men, animals and birds. Flint tools of this date are superbly knapped (i.e. their edges are finely chipped) on both sides, and are of almost transparent fineness.

Naqada II (SD. 38-63)

The site of El Gerzeh south of Cairo, when excavated by Gerald Wainwright in 1910, revealed graves of similar date. As a result this period is alternatively called Gerzean.

Around 3800 BC, contacts between Egypt and neighbouring countries suddenly leapt forward. In Naqada II sites, including Maadi and El Ballas, large numbers of objects demonstrate strong Mesopotamian and Syrian influences, and craftsmanship is so fine and different from Naqada I pieces that it has been inferred that Egypt was actually invaded. As more sites are analyzed, it is clear that the numbers of foreign, imported objects do not suddenly appear, as would have been the case if invaders were the cause, but become increasingly common, a more certain indication of trade.

The graves of this period are lavishly equipped, often 'lined with wooden planking, and the first coffins, for use with contracted burials, are found. Copper, silver and gold are now plentiful. It is the pottery, however, that shows how great a leap forward had been made. Much of it is wheel-turned; many pieces have a buff slip, and are decorated in red/brown lines with finely drawn pictures of men, animals, birds, trees and stylized boats with banks of oars. Spouts are found on them for the first time.

The impetus given to Egypt's development by the Naqada II settlers raised society from primitive settlers to superb farmers and craftsmen. In the 700 years from the first appearance of these people to the time of the unification, greater progress, in every cultural field, was made than at any other time. By 3100 BC, Egypt was ready to enter into a new age.

DAWN OF THE TWO LANDS

Among the smaller objects found by Quibell and Green in Hieraconpolis were a number of ivory labels, probably used as seals placed on royal belongings. This example, only 4.5cm (1¾in) high, shows King Den wearing the royal uraeus on top of a simple nemes headcloth, in the act of smiting an Asiatic with his mace. The rectangular serekh in front of the king's face, surmounted by Horus, the god of Hieraconpolis, contains Den's name in hieroglyphs. The hieroglyphs on the right say the piece commemorated 'the first occasion of striking the East'.

The appearance of very fine goods in the graves of Naqada II date signifies new interests in the lives of the Nile dwellers. Contact with Mesopotamia and the lands to the north of Egypt, as evidenced in architectural devices such as the introduction of niched brick façades on buildings and the use of cylinder-seals bearing names and titles of officials, was probably achieved by increasingly sophisticated trade, with all the administration that entails. The beautiful and delicate pottery of the period also suggests greater leisure time on the part of some members of society, resulting in an awareness of objects that were attractive and not simply utilitarian. Moreover, the spread of all these wares, native and imported, throughout Egypt, implies national and local trade routes and presumably the establishment of marketplaces.

In Upper Egypt, the town of Nubt near Naqada, dedicated to the god Seth (see p. 134), was ideally placed as a market centre, standing as it did on the Nile bank at the edge of the Wadi Hammamat, one of the few routes across the eastern desert to the Red Sea. The name Nubt itself, the Egyptian word for 'gold', suggests that gold was the main trading commodity. Meanwhile to the south of Luxor, another major town developed on the west bank of the Nile across from modern El Kab, known to ancient Egyptians as Nekhen. Its local god was the falcon Horus, giving rise to the Greek name for the site: Hieraconpolis (Falcon-city).

It was inevitable, given the new ambitions and the increasing wealth of Egypt, that these major centres should clash. According to many scholars, the very ancient story of the battles of Horus and Seth, later adapted into the myth of Osiris (see p. 134), was a folk-memory of the war that waged between these two towns. The victory of Horus over Seth – that is, Hieraconpolis over Nubt – gave the prince of Hieraconpolis authority over the whole of Upper Egypt, and the power to extend and consolidate his territory until finally all Egypt was united under one king.

According to legend and myth, the king who united Egypt, at approximately 3100 BC, was called Menes. Archaeological evidence suggests that the triumph of Hieraconpolis and the move to establish an administrative system under one rule, could have occurred 50 years before Menes' victory. When, finally, Menes did succeed in joining Lower and Upper Egypt together, he established a brand new admin-

istrative city at the neck of the delta and the Nile Valley. This city, called originally 'Inbuhedj' or 'White Walls', later became known as Mennefer – Memphis, the capital of Egypt for over 3500 years.

Excavations at Hieraconpolis

In 1897, James Quibell moved away from Petrie's supervision and turned his attention to an area on the west bank of the Nile dominated by massive ancient mud-brick walls. He was accompanied by another English archaeologist, Frederick Green, who had read Egyptology at Cambridge and had also studied excavation techniques with Petrie. The area west of the walls, a wadi or dried riverbed, was liberally scattered with potsherds and flints of Palaeolithic date and was certain to reveal information about the earliest Egyptians that both men sought. To the east of the great walled enclosure, the plain was clearly scarred with markings, and it was to this area that Quibell and Green turned. Immediately below the surface of the sand lay the remains of an Old and early Middle Kingdom town, the mud-brick houses packed in streets and once surrounded by an outer enclosure wall. In the centre, a much earlier mud-brick gateway was uncovered that appeared to have been incorporated into the later town.

The town had clearly fallen into disuse towards the Middle Kingdom, and it was known that it had fallen under the domination of El Kab on the opposite bank, ancient Nekheb. Yet the two settlements had flourished in predynastic times as the twin towns of Pe and Dep, and it was this town that Quibell and Green sought. To the southwest of the Old Kingdom town, they then uncovered more brick walls that surrounded a temple site. Under the Middle and Old Kingdom levels, in his second season on the site, Green found a low stone wall filled with a large mound of pure, clean white sand almost 3.1m (10ft) high. He was convinced that this was the site of the first ever temple on the site, the Perwer, the most important shrine of predynastic Egypt. It was here, surrounded by reed matting in a flimsy shelter, that the god Horus was venerated, and as conqueror of Seth of Nubt became identified with the King of Egypt himself.

Green's conclusions were heavily criticized by many scholars who believed this mound must have been of later date, but excavations from 1969 onwards, undertaken by Professor

Fairservis for the American Museum of Natural History, in New York, confirmed the dating. Parallel trenches were found in the mound, together with post-holes and what appeared to be the remains of an ancient doorway. Here indeed was the birthplace of the Egyptian monarchy.

The painted tomb

In 1898–99, to the south of the ancient Perwer temple site, Frederick Green excavated the cemetery site of Hieraconpolis. From his notes, it is clear that he opened more than 200 graves of late predynastic date, but none of them matched Tomb 100. This rock-cut tomb, subdivided into two chambers, measured in total approximately 3.7 by 2.5m (12 by 8ft). The walls were lined with mud bricks, and over the top of that, in the larger chamber, the four faces had been smoothed and painted with unique scenes. The paintings of Hieraconpolis Tomb 100 resemble some of the scenes on pots of Naqada II date. Over a buff-coloured background, a series of river-going ships were painted in white. Dominating them all was a great papyriform black-painted boat with raised prow. On all of the ships were cabins, their rounded roofs indicating they were of reed matting, while in front of each stood a pennant on a mast. Around the ships cluster people and animals; soldiers carrying rectangular shields of animal skins fight with clubs; another soldier fights two lions with his bare hands; while in one corner is drawn the earliest-known representation of one of the commonest scenes of Egyptian kingship – a man grasps three enemies and holds his mace aloft, ready to club them. Above the ships, domesticated animals, including ibex, roam in groups, while a hunter with a bow and arrow pursues lions. Over one ship with two cabins, three figures stand with arms outstretched in a posture of mourning.

This, the earliest decorated tomb ever found in Egypt, was surely the grave of one of the princes of the ancient city, its incomparable information proving how later generations of kings merely followed the examples of the great, late predynastic warriors. The tomb did not stand alone, however, but was one of a group of five; and reference to Petrie's unpublished notes from Naqada shows tombs of equal size and similar date were found there. But the location of Painted Tomb 100 was never clearly noted; today it is lost again beneath the drifting sand.

This superb gold hawk's head, 37.5cm (15in) tall, was found in the Main Deposit of Hieraconpolis. It was originally mounted on a wooden body sheathed with plates of copper, although these were too badly damaged to survive. It is difficult to give it an exact date. Because it was found near two fine copper statues, one bearing the name of King Pepi I, it is generally believed to be of late Old Kingdom date. It is possible, though, that it was made much later in the New Kingdom. The remarkable piercing eyes of the head are formed from a single rod of obsidian which runs from side to side, each end being shaped and polished.

Treasures of Hieraconpolis

The ancient town site of Hieraconpolis revealed more than simply information about the early Egyptian settlers. As Green was excavating the ancient temple site of Horus, he was fortunate in locating several treasures which proved to be of vital archaeological and historical importance.

The first group appeared once to have lain in underground stone chambers below a later building on the site, perhaps a temple of early Middle Kingdom date. Among a selection of

Slate palettes *are common in graves of the late Predynastic period, but around the time of the unification (i.e. 3100 BC) several exceptionally large ones were made with fine carved reliefs. The Narmer palette is not only a superb piece of craftsmanship, but also historically important, showing for the first time a king wearing the separate crowns of Upper and Lower Egypt. The circular indentation on the first side (above) would have been used for the grinding of malachite, probably for technological rather than cosmetic use.*

fine stone and calcite jars of the Sixth Dynasty, Green found two remarkable copper statues, one life-size and the other smaller, standing on one base. The inscription on this names the subject as King Pepi I, and the smaller figure is generally taken to be that of Pepi's son, Merenre. This pair of statues, made of plates of copper hammered to shape over a wooden base and riveted together, are a unique find, though the Palermo stone (*see p. 15*) does record the creation of a similar statue for King Khasekhem of the Second Dynasty.

Together with the statues was found a falcon's head surmounted by two 'plumes' of solid gold. This, now one of the great treasures held by the Cairo Museum, may possibly have formed the head of the ancient cult statue of the god Horus that once stood in the Perwer shrine.

The Main Deposit

It is unfortunate that Green's discovery of the second cache, which turned out to contain some of the most important historical pieces ever found in Egypt, is badly documented.

Although the exact circumstances of the find are unknown, it is certain that as he excavated the area between the foundations of the Old and Middle Kingdom temples, Green came upon true buried treasure. The pieces, comprising huge decorated slate palettes, mace heads, ivory figures and jars, appear to have been treasured possessions of the predynastic temple, but once discarded were collected together by later priests and buried en masse. The most important piece of all, the Narmer palette, was apparently not found with the rest but at a distance of 1 to 2m (3 to 6ft) away. It may indeed have been found upon the site of the first temple itself. It is forever to be regretted that the origins and purpose of this most famous of all Egyptian palettes, so vital to the reconstruction of the dynastic age, should be so unclear.

The Scorpion mace head

Two full mace heads and two fragments were found in the Main Deposit. Despite their name, none of them were actual mace heads, being far too large, from 25 to 30cm (10 to 12in) in height. It is possible that they were bases for shafts bearing fetishes or banners similar to ones found in Tutankhamun's tomb; or they may simply have been ceremonial or commemorative.

One fragmentary mace head, made of limestone, is carved in raised relief and depicts a king in the crown of Upper Egypt holding a mattock, standing near a canal. Below him, workers appear to be busy building a wall from within which a palm tree rises. Behind the king two courtiers hold fans of wickerwork. Above him, a panel bears a series of nome flags (see Glossary) with figures of gods mounted over them. From each of them, a lapwing hangs by a cord around its neck. The lapwing, the 'rekhyt' bird in hieroglyphs, is the symbol for the peasants, or common people, of Egypt, and in this instance probably represents the ability of each nome to control its own area.

The scene is variously interpreted by scholars as the founding of a temple or the opening of an irrigation canal, though the former seems more likely. The identity of the king is unknown. The 'scorpion' near his face, which is often said to be his name, is in fact surmounted by a flower. The two symbols are probably to be read as a title. This king must be one of the last predynastic rulers of Hieraconpolis, perhaps even Narmer himself. The mace head is in the Ashmolean Museum, Oxford.

The Narmer palette

This large slate ceremonial palette is carved on both sides. On the front, two lions twist their elongated necks to form an indentation which, on smaller palettes, served as a place for the grinding of green malachite. On the top of the palette, two human heads with bulls' horns flank a rectangular panel bearing two hieroglyphs that give the king's name – Narmer. On the register below, Narmer, wearing the red crown of Lower Egypt inspects two rows of decapitated enemies on the battlefield. He is preceded by flag-bearers – each carrying a nome standard – and a scribe, while behind him walks his sandal bearer. At the foot of the palette the king, depicted as a powerful bull, breaks down a town wall and tramples over an enemy.

On the reverse, a large-scale figure of Narmer, now wearing the white crown of Upper Egypt, holds a defeated enemy by the scalp and prepares to slay him with a mace. Below him, two dead enemies appear to represent conquered towns. To the front of the

king, a neat picture shows Horus (both the king and god of Hieraconpolis, capital of Upper Egypt) dominating the plants and the marshes (representing the area of the delta), and leading its inhabitants captive by the nose.

This is the earliest piece ever to show a King of Egypt wearing the crowns of both Upper and Lower Egypt. The victory it commemorates appears to be the unification of the two disparate parts of Egypt.

The identity of Menes

With Nubt and Hieraconpolis united under one powerful king, only victory over the delta remained to make Egypt a united country. The king who achieved this, the legendary Menes, is not attested by archaeology. No object bearing the image and name of a King Menes exists, but since every king bore several names, could we without realizing it have found Menes under a different name?

The Narmer palette, showing the victory of the king over the delta, is regarded by many as positive proof that Narmer was Menes. However, it should be noted that the king is not shown wearing the double crown – he wears the crown of Lower Egypt as he surveys his defeated enemy. This could be interpreted as pure propaganda. An ivory label found at Naqada, on the contrary, shows the name of Narmer's successor, Aha, and alongside it the symbol 'Men', seeming to imply that Aha may have been Menes.

The Main Deposit pieces thus help to deepen, rather than solve, the mystery. Who is the king on the so-called 'Scorpion' mace head? Could it perhaps actually record the founding of Memphis? Herodotus records that Menes diverted the Nile and built a dam to reclaim land upon which the city of Memphis was built. Did Narmer ever unite Egypt or merely inflict a crushing defeat over the delta in a single battle? The one thing for which Menes was historically renowned was the founding of Memphis, and it is interesting that no tomb has been discovered at Saqqara for Narmer, the earliest tomb found to date in that necropolis being for Aha. One suggestion about Narmer's significance is that he started the military campaign which Aha actually finished.

Perhaps Menes, was based on the legendary victories of several kings and cannot be identified with any one of them, but there is no doubt that, whether with Narmer or Aha, the first dynasty of Egyptian kings had begun.

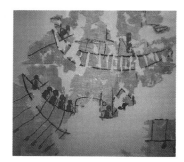

Textiles survive *well in Egypt's hot, dry climate. This small fragment of linen found at Gebelein about 32km (20mi) north of Hieraconpolis is one of the earliest decorated pieces to survive. Although 5000 years old and very delicate, it shows two Nile boats, typical of the Predynastic period. The fragment, now in the Turin Museum, took several years to conserve and restore to its present condition.*

THE FIRST KINGS

In March 1899, the French archaeologist Emile Amélineau was walking away from his excavation site at Abydos on the last day of the season's work when he passed a couple going in the opposite direction. A young woman was riding a donkey, with a bearded and bronzed man walking by her side. Amélineau took little notice at the time, but when later, at his hotel, he was told that Flinders and Hilda Petrie had arrived in Abydos, he realized whom he had seen. He must have felt uneasy, for he knew that Petrie had already requested the Antiquities Service to give him permission to dig that very site.

As a result of that evening visit, Petrie informed Gaston Maspero, Director-General of the Antiquities Service, that the irreplaceable site of Abydos was being systematically vandalized through Amélineau's incompetence. Without being consulted, or even informed, Amélineau later complained, Maspero handed Petrie the concession that he had held for three years.

Petrie's justification in doing this is still debatable, but there seems little doubt that Amélineau's main interest was in the retrieval of large or inscribed objects. Petrie's relatively new approach to excavating Egyptian sites by investigating even the tiniest pieces was not generally valued by others who were accustomed to working in their own ways.

But differences in methodology aside, Petrie's own interest in the site can be appreciated. Having excavated several predynastic and Old Kingdom sites, there remained a gap in his knowledge – the period of the first two royal dynasties. The site of Amélineau's excavations lay about 1.6km (1mi) west of the mortuary temple of Seti I at Abydos. The large cliff-encircled plain here was so liberally covered with ancient potsherds that the local villagers called it 'Umm el Qa'ab'– or 'Mother of pots'. In this area, Amélineau had discovered burial chambers in the sand, with objects in them bearing the names of a number of First Dynasty kings.

Petrie arrived on the site in the winter of 1899, and prepared himself for several seasons' work. Within a matter of days he began to retrieve vast numbers of small objects, including mud-jar seals impressed with names of Archaic period kings. Each piece had to be copied meticulously for his records, a time-consuming job that occupied him every evening.

The royal tombs

Over two seasons' excavations, Petrie found 10 major royal tombs, eight representing all the kings of the First Dynasty and two of the Second. They were clustered within one area, and marked with stone stelae bearing the kings' names. The burial chambers were cut into the rock, lined with sun-baked mud bricks and originally had been faced with wooden boards. Within many of the chambers, other brick walls separated side rooms within which were found innumerable jars and other small objects, including the traditional offerings of food and drink.

The principal surprise was that many of the tombs were surrounded by subsidiary graves, often in very large numbers. In them, bodies were found flexed and lying on their sides, many of them named on small stone stelae. The vast majority of the occupants of these graves were women and several were dwarves. It seems that these were servants of the king, probably sacrificed at the time of their master's death to serve him in his afterlife. Although no superstructure remains over the tombs, it has been suggested that the whole area of each, including the subsidiary graves, was covered with sand and rubble retained by an outer mud-brick wall that has since disappeared.

Another tomb, that of Merneith, examined by Petrie in 1900, offered even greater interest. Merneith was not a king at all, but a queen, although the size of her burial chamber and the surrounding 41 subsidiary burials equalled and often exceeded that of many of the kings. Hers was one of the best-preserved tombs in the

Although nothing *remains of a superstructure over the royal tombs at Abydos, it is possible that it would have appeared as the hypothetical reconstruction shown below. The two stelae in front of the mastaba, either side of an offering table, would have recorded the king's name. The small mounds around the outside would have contained subsidiary burials.*

TOMBS AT ABYDOS		
Name	Overall Size	Subsidiary Burials
Dynasty I		
Narmer	11 × 9.4m	—
Aha	11.7 × 9.4m	—
Djer	21.5 × 20m	338
Merneith	19.2 × 16.3m	41 plus 77
Djet	19 × 15m	174 plus 161
Den	23.5 × 16.4m	136
Adjib	16.4 × 9m	64
Semerkhe	29.2 × 20.8m	—
Qa'a	30 × 23m	26
Dynasty II		
Peribsen	21 × 18.5m	—
Khasekhem	68.97 × 17.6m	—

area. In one part of it, Petrie discovered objects bearing the name of Den. These he later discounted as being of no relevance, since the tomb of Den lay alongside the tomb of Merneith and both had been found by Amélineau. The objects, he decided, were probably just part of the spoil discarded by his careless predecessor.

In a lower part of the site, Petrie came across two large rectangular areas flanked by yet more subsidiary graves, one marked with the name of Djet and the other, again with that of Merneith. In total, 118 courtiers had accompanied this lady at her death. There seems little escaping the conclusion that Merneith was not simply a king's consort, but a reigning monarch in her own right. If this is correct, not only is she the earliest attested female ruler, but also it suggests an interesting lack of discrimination between male and female rulers on the part of these earliest Egyptians.

The treasure of King Djer

Within many of the tombs, Petrie had found precious objects including, in the huge complex of the Second Dynasty King Khasekhem, a stone rod with carnelian and gold that he considered was a royal mace.

In February 1901, however, one of his workmen discovered what, at first sight, appeared to be a bundle of rags thrust into a

hole in the mud-brick wall. Thanks to Petrie's insistence on rewarding each man for his finds, the pile of linen was taken to him. It was revealed to be a human arm, apparently not mummified, but simply swathed in linen. Around the wrist were four intact bracelets of gold, lapis lazuli and turquoise, one of which comprised 13 plaques in the form of a serekh surrounded by a Horus-falcon, within which was carved the name of King Djer. It seems likely that robbers in antiquity had dismembered the King's body. One-and-a-half-thousand years later, during the reign of Amenhotep III in the New Kingdom, officials had regarded this tomb as having once belonged to the god Osiris. In order that pilgrims could visit the sacred site they had thrust the arm out of the way into a hole.

The arm was considered, at the time, to be of no interest and was discarded unexamined once it reached the museum. The bracelets, however, are on display in the Cairo Museum – the oldest pieces of royal jewellery found in Egypt. Their most remarkable feature is the use of lapis lazuli, the sole known source for which is northern Afghanistan. For these stones to have arrived in Egypt at the time of the third king of the First Dynasty, around 3000 BC, indicates the sophisticated administration that must have existed in order to exploit such distant trade routes.

This small disc (top) was probably used as a playing piece for one of the board games that were popular in Egypt from Predynastic times. Although barely 7.5cm (3in) across, the black steatite base is inlaid with two beautifully detailed hunting dogs, one black, one light brown, bringing down an oryx. The details on the animals show what fine craftsmen the early Egyptians were.

These four bracelets (above) were found on a bandaged arm in the tomb of King Djer at Abydos, in 1901. The stones – lapis lazuli, turquoise and amethyst – are set in gold. The bracelet second from the bottom is formed with plaques in the shape of a serekh, showing the king's name within. Petrie wrote of them: 'There is not a single bead in any one bracelet that would be interchangeable with those in another bracelet. Each is independent in design, fresh and free of all convention.' Considering their date, around 3000 BC, they are masterpieces of the ancient jeweller's art.

THE MYSTERY OF SAQQARA

**Walter B. Emery
(1903–1971)**

Although interested from the age of 13 in becoming an Egyptologist, Emery's parents were opposed and persuaded him to train as a marine engineer. At 18, he was finally free to study his chosen subject at Liverpool University and, while there, he was appointed director of an excavation at Luxor. In 1935, after a period heading the Archaeological Survey of Nubia, he began working at Saqqara on the First Dynasty tombs. In 1951, while still continuing his work in Nubia and at Saqqara, he was elected to the chair in Egyptology at University College, London. He collapsed and died while working at Saqqara and was buried in Cairo.

In 1912, James Quibell examined an area of Saqqara to the north of the Step Pyramid complex and found several massive mud-brick tombs. The shape of these long rectangular buildings reminded the Egyptian workmen of the low mud-brick benches that stood against the outside walls of their houses, and thus they called them 'benches' or, in Arabic, 'mastabas.'

In 1931, Cecil Frith, who had been working for some time on the Step Pyramid complex itself, returned to the area of the mastabas with the intention of excavating them thoroughly but, unfortunately, within days of his arrival, contracted pneumonia and died. It was clear that more work was required and, in 1935, Walter Emery was appointed by the Antiquities Service to take over the task. With a gap of four years during the Second World War, Emery worked continuously at the site until 1956. He uncovered 12 huge mastaba tombs that all dated to the First Dynasty. More information on this earliest part of Egypt's history was vitally needed; but to everyone's astonishment, Emery found the names of kings on objects within the mastabas that duplicated the names found on the tombs of Abydos (*see p. 56–7*). He claimed, as a result, that these, and not the tombs at Abydos, were the actual burial places of Egypt's first monarchs.

The Saqqara tombs

The mastabas comprised vast mud-brick buildings with their outer faces decorated with niches reminiscent of Mesopotamian palace façades, and sometimes impressed with a pattern of reed mats.

The mastabas were built over a chamber that was cut underground in the bedrock. This long, thin room was subdivided by brick walls into smaller chambers – either five or seven, the central one being the burial chamber. Inside the superstructure, overlying the burial chamber and surrounding area, more internal brick walls divided the mastaba into store chambers that could only be entered from the roof, because none of them had interconnecting doorways. In many of these chambers, burial goods were found intact.

Two of the mastabas, found with the names of Aha and Merneith, had boat pits cut into the rock on the outside of the structure. Although both were empty, the boat pit belonging to the mastaba of Merneith was 17.8m (58ft 7in) long, large enough to have held a boat of considerable proportions. In addition, many of the store chambers within the mastaba of Merneith were discovered intact and richly provisioned, while around the perimeter of the walls, 20 subsidiary graves were uncovered containing the bodies and burial goods of craftsmen – an artist and a boat builder among them. The mastaba of Djer, the largest in area on the site, contained a central burial chamber that was once lined with wood and decorated with strips of gold. Around its outer wall, a low bench on each side had had bulls' heads mounted on it in mud, their horns intact, while in front of them 62 subsidiary burials were found. The later mastabas of Den and Adjib were more elaborate than earlier ones; they had deep burial chambers approached by a staircase in the superstructure, and sealed with a granite monolith.

It is clear that the basic structure of the mastaba was unstable, for the roofs of all of them had either caved in or been broken through by robbers. Over the underground burial chambers of the earlier ones, a simple pile of rubble had been placed over wooden beams. However, in the mastaba of Adjib, this mound had been reinforced on all sides with a mud-brick wall inside the outer face. This had been built not vertically, but in the form of a low stepped pyramid and, Emery believed, probably gave later architects the notion of building the Step Pyramid itself.

Where were the kings buried?

The mystery of the two tombs for each king of the First Dynasty has still to be satisfactorily resolved. Emery was quite adamant that the massive size of the Saqqara mastabas so dwarfed the shallow chambers at Abydos that the kings must have been buried at Saqqara. Several of the mastabas, however, contained the names of officials, while for some kings, more than one mastaba was found. Other scholars refuted his theory. The Saqqara tombs must have belonged to powerful administrators, they claimed, for only in the Abydos tombs were stelae, or gravestones, found with the kings' name carved on them. The surrounding subsidiary burials of Abydos, moreover, with the predominance of women, suggested that the kings had been accompanied by their wives and concubines at their death. Emery disagreed, and insisted that the Abydos chambers discovered by Petrie were cenotaphs (*see Glossary*), never intended to hold a king's body but simply to symbolize his political hold over Upper Egypt.

TOMBS AT SAQQARA

Name	Sizes of Mastabas
Narmer	(No tomb)
Aha	48.2 × 22m
Djer	41.3 × 15.15m
Merneith	42.6 × 16m
Djet	56.45 × 25.45m
Den	Three tombs, largest: 57.3 × 26m
Adjib	37 × 13.85m
Semerkhe	(No tomb)
Qa'a	Two tombs, largest: 65 × 37m

The inside *of the mastaba was subdivided into numerous store chambers, whose walls were undecorated. Many were found intact. The roof structure, especially over the burial chamber, was inherently unstable and in every case collapsed. It may have been barrel-vaulted.*

The underground *burial shafts of the Saqqara mastabas were robbed but clearly once contained interments. As such, they could not have been cenotaphs, but since the names of officials were found, these shafts could have been used for Egypt's earliest administrators.*

Low mud-brick *mounds covered each subsidiary burial around the main mastaba tomb. In these, were found the bodies of courtiers, placed in a fetal position and surrounded by grave goods.*

Although the remaining *mastaba walls stand at a height of around 4m (12ft), the sand is burying them again very quickly. On the northern horizon, far in the distance, the pyramids of Abusir (right) can just be seen.*

The argument raged on. In 1966, Barry Kemp, of Cambridge University, added a new dimension to the dilemma. To the north of Umm el Qa'ab stand massive mud-brick wall enclosures, still some 12.2m (40ft) high, that date to the Archaic period. These enclosures are generally described as the 'fortresses' of Shunet es Zebib. Yet these enclosure walls, a series of them, many still unexamined, stand in close proximity to each other. There are no signs of other buildings or walls inside them to explain their purpose. Kemp reasoned that they could scarcely be considered fortresses – why should successive kings build forts in this isolated desert position, and so closely together? Nor could they be reasonably described as mortuary complexes since they contained no offering chapels. Mindful of the structure of the Step Pyramid complex, he suggested these could be courtyards built for the ruler's Sed festival (*see p. 66*). Each year, it is known, the king had to prove his fitness to rule by running a set course. The word 'sed', meaning 'to destroy', seems to imply that a king who failed could be killed or replaced by a fitter person. The large number of subsidiary burials at Abydos contemporary with the main chamber shows that these First Dynasty Egyptians had no compunction in sacrificing large numbers of people at one time. These courtyards, then, appear to have been built at Abydos as an integral part of each funerary complex. If the size of these is taken into account and added to the size of the graves themselves, then, in sheer size, it exceeds the total area of the Saqqara mastabas.

In the face of this evidence, it seems likely that the kings of the First Dynasty were, indeed, buried at Abydos, while the mastabas of Saqqara were built for the powerful administrators who established the government in the new capital city of Memphis. But we cannot be certain, and the opinion of scholars on the subject is still divided.

III

PYRAMIDS: HOUSES FOR ETERNITY

'Cheops closed all the temples, then compelled everyone
without exception to serve as slaves to his own end. Some were
forced to drag stones from the quarries in the Arabian hills to
the Nile . . . a hundred-thousand men in a shift. To build it
took 10 years – including the underground burial chamber.'
Herodotus, Book II, 126

Inscriptions in hieroglyphs on stone and papyrus survive in
large numbers from 2650 BC onwards, making Egyptian
history a little easier to understand. From then until the end
of the Old Kingdom, approximately 2134 BC, the King of
Egypt was no less than a living god, inspiring such terror in
those around him that one courtier, Washptah, having been
permitted to kiss the feet of Neferirkare, in the Fifth
Dynasty, instead of the ground on which he walked, actually
died in the king's presence.

These gods incarnate were buried in tombs as monumental
as their personalities – the pyramids. More than 87 are
known today, many surviving as little more than unim-
pressive heaps of rubble. The pyramids are not lone monuments either, for they provide the focal points for whole
cities of the dead, whose inhabitants are the ordinary people
whose small tombs cluster together, as if seeking to be as close
to their sovereign in death as they had hoped to be in life.

The three great pyramids of the Giza plateau. Behind the three
subsidiary pyramids stand, in succession, the pyramids of Mycerinus,
Chephren and Cheops.

THE TRADITIONAL PYRAMID COMPLEX

Pyramids were built as the monumental burial places of the kings of Egypt between 2700 and 1640 BC. The shape did not just appear, but the transition from mastaba tomb (*see p. 59*) through step pyramid to true pyramid was slow. It is not known what initially made the pyramid shape so attractive although, with its large square base, it is very stable and long-lasting. It has been calculated that approximately 80 per cent of the building material used in a pyramid lies in its lower half, hence significantly smaller quantities of stone needed to be dragged up to the higher levels than would be required with other shapes.

The complex

Pyramids do not stand alone, but form the hub of a mortuary complex surrounded by avenues of mastaba tombs built for the king's relatives and courtiers. The site for the complex was chosen on a sound rocky hillside, almost always on the west bank of the Nile. Although little is known about the initial marking out of the site, undoubtedly the king himself would have inspected the area and chosen the spot. The pyramids align almost exactly with a true north/south axis, which could have been achieved by the architect fixing two poles in the sand to line up with two separate observations of a star from a set sighting point. By running lines from these markers to the observer and bisecting the angle thus formed, true north would have been found.

Although the perimeter of the pyramid base, once laid out, would be smoothed with exactitude, the central area would not necessarily be flattened; rather outcrops of rock could be incorporated into the design, presumably to save time and effort, as was the case with the Great Pyramid at Giza. The exact levelling of the perimeter was achieved by a network of trenches cut into the surface and flooded. Such a series of trenches can still be seen to the north of Chephren's pyramid at Giza.

While preparations were under way on the pyramid site, gangs of workers would simultaneously be cutting a canal from the river to the foot of the desert plateau, and smoothing a wide causeway from a quayside to the pyramid itself. In this way, blocks of stone could be shipped close to the building site and dragged into position along a clearly defined route. For the pyramids of the Third and Fourth Dynasties, a core of limestone blocks, cut locally, would be built in tiers and then faced with gleaming white limestone cut at the Tura quarries on the opposite bank of the Nile.

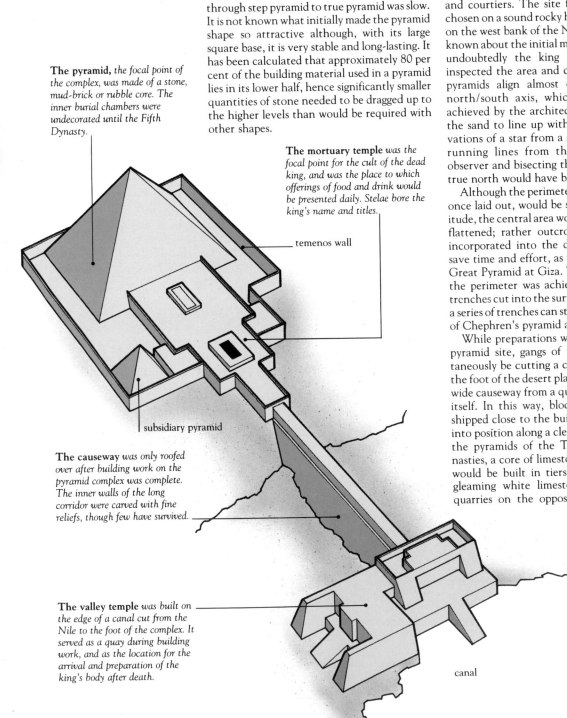

The pyramid, *the focal point of the complex, was made of a stone, mud-brick or rubble core. The inner burial chambers were undecorated until the Fifth Dynasty.*

The mortuary temple *was the focal point for the cult of the dead king, and was the place to which offerings of food and drink would be presented daily. Stelae bore the king's name and titles.*

temenos wall

subsidiary pyramid

The causeway *was only roofed over after building work on the pyramid complex was complete. The inner walls of the long corridor were carved with fine reliefs, though few have survived.*

The valley temple *was built on the edge of a canal cut from the Nile to the foot of the complex. It served as a quay during building work, and as the location for the arrival and preparation of the king's body after death.*

canal

Internal passages and chambers were lined with pink granite blocks, cut 900km (570mi) south in the quarries of Aswan. These stones were fitted with great precision and polished to a fine smoothness once they were in position. Later pyramids of the Old Kingdom were of a more modest size, with a core, often of unshaped rubble. When the fine outer covering of these pyramids was removed by later generations, the inner core collapsed, leaving little but rough mounds. During the Middle Kingdom, the Twelfth Dynasty, pyramids built at Illahun and Hawara, southeast of the Faiyum, were of sun-baked mud brick formed locally by workmen.

The construction process

Stones used for building the pyramids would be dragged up the causeway on sledges, their path being eased by a substance being poured under the sledge, as a lubricant. Once the first layer of stone was in place, a mud-brick ramp would be erected, increasing in height as the pyramid grew. The building of this ramp alone would have required vast quantities of material. It has been suggested by some scholars that such a ramp would have been impractical, and that the same end might be achieved by coiling the ramp around the pyramid walls as it grew higher.

Once at the top of the ramp, stones would have to be moved into position. The precise means of doing this is unclear. Wooden rockers found on pyramid sites could have been used to tilt and slide the stones into position. Although it is often asserted that pulleys were not invented by this date, they are, in fact, clearly depicted being used in the rigging of ships on contemporary reliefs. The use of fulcrums was also well-known. Either of these methods could conceivably have been used in pyramid building.

The internal corridors and chambers of the pyramids, with their security precautions, were established as the pyramid was being built, rather than being quarried through the stone later and lined. This is evident because the granite sarcophagus provided for the reception of the king's body, and cut from one solid piece of stone, was too large to fit through the outer passages after the pyramid was finished.

The building of the Great Pyramid, Herodotus was told, took 20 years; lesser ones obviously were finished more quickly. Although vast work gangs are generally envisaged as having been necessary, in fact the average stone block at Giza, weighing 2.6t (2 ½ tons),

can be dragged on a sledge, without too much difficulty, by as few as 10 men.

According to the depiction of pyramids in hieroglyphic inscriptions used in early texts, the outer surfaces of the completed pyramid could have been either painted or carved with inscriptions. Unhappily, none of these survive.

The pyramid as a tomb

Once the pyramid was finished, the approach ramp would be dismantled and the site made ready for the king's eventual funeral. Stone walls would be built along the causeway to form a covered corridor to the pyramid. Though only a few loose blocks of such causeways survive, the inner faces were evidently carved with fine reliefs. Small buildings were erected at either end of this corridor, to serve as chapels for use during the funeral of the king.

On the king's death, his body would be taken by boat to the foot of the pyramid complex. Within the Valley Temple, built where once the quayside stood, the remains would be preserved by mummification. Although no mortal remains of the kings buried in these pyramids have been discovered to date, the granite sarcophagi show that the body must have been laid in the extended position, ideal for the mummification process (see p. 152–55), and not (as in the mastabas) in the foetal position. The body would then be carried along the causeway corridor, hidden from the gaze of casual onlookers, to a chapel usually built against the east face of the pyramid. Here the mortuary ceremonies would be enacted before the body was placed within the pyramid and the pyramid sealed.

The 'queens' pyramids'

In addition to the mortuary buildings and the surrounding tombs, there were invariably subsidiary pyramids – between one and three. These are often called 'queens' pyramids', although the internal chambers are too small to take an extended body in a sarcophagus; on the contrary, mastaba tombs in the outlying necropolis areas have been discovered for many kings' wives. One suggestion is that these subsidiary pyramids were used to house the viscera removed from the king's body and placed in canopic chests (see p. 154), but there is no archaeological proof for this idea. Alternatively, as some German scholars have suggested, these pyramids could have served a ritual purpose.

This valley temple of Chephren at Giza is one of the few to remain intact from the Old Kingdom. Its columns are made of polished monoliths of granite, completely undecorated. In front of each a statue of the king once stood. Fragments of one of these statues, made of diorite, were found in a pit in the valley temple in 1860 by Auguste Mariette. Reassembled, the statue is one of the masterpieces of Egyptian sculpture, depicting the king seated on a throne, his head protected by the wings of a mantling falcon.

THE STEP PYRAMID

**Jean-Philippe Lauer
(1902–)**

In late 1926, Professor Lauer arrived at Saqqara as an architect employed by the government in order to assist C.M. Firth in the surveying of the Step Pyramid complex. After Firth's sudden death five years later, Lauer found himself working alone and has continued to do so ever since, devoting virtually the whole of his life to the painstaking reconstruction of this great monument of the Third Dynasty.

During the First and Second Dynasties, the kings of Egypt had been buried in underground chambers at the foot of shafts with the flat, rectangular superstructure of a mastaba tomb over them, either at Abydos or Saqqara (*see pp. 56–9*). Throughout this Archaic period intense squabbling had reduced Egypt virtually to a state of civil war. Only with the accession of the first king of the Third Dynasty was there established a powerful centralized administration based in the city of Memphis that was strong enough to subdue all opposition. The name of this king, inscriptions record, was Netcherikhe; almost a thousand years later, during the Middle Kingdom, another inscription gives him the name of Djoser.

Djoser-Netcherikhe was able to appoint many loyal and able men to serve him. Chief among them, inscriptions record, was a wise man and scholar called Imhotep. So beloved was he that his memory was revered by succeeding generations as an architect, astronomer, mathematician, doctor and writer; in Greek times he was deified and identified with the god of medicine, Aesculapius. But of all the things Imhotep did, none proclaims his ability more than the tomb he designed and built for his king – the Step Pyramid at Saqqara.

Building the pyramid

It was about 3.2km (2mi) to the west of Memphis that Imhotep chose a rocky plateau on which to build the tomb. Previously all tombs had been built of sunbaked mud brick, but from the start, Imhotep chose stone as his medium. He first designed it as a rectangular mastaba tomb, solid stone to cover a vertical shaft, leading to a subterranean burial chamber. This was hewn out of the rock and located directly under the centre of the mastaba. The sides of the mastaba were about 62.5m (205ft) in length and it rose to a height of 7.9m (26ft).

After this stage had been completed and the sides finished with polished white Tura (a site to the east of what is now Cairo) limestone, the plan was amended with the addition of an outer wall 4.3m (14ft) wide, slightly lower than the original. A third alteration changed it into a longer rectangular shape. This third stage was never completed, but a new revolutionary design allowed for the building of three more mastaba blocks on top of the first to form a four-step pyramid. Finally the whole base was extended, north and west, adding a further 60.9m (200ft) in both directions to form the base for the final, six-step pyramid. When finished, it was faced with a smooth outer covering of limestone to form a true pyramid, though on a rectangular and not a square base.

While the pyramid was being built, the original underground chamber was also being supplemented by a whole labyrinth of corridors and siderooms of great complexity. The burial chamber was lined entirely in pink granite casing slabs to form a solid box, with a hole quarried into one end barely large enough to admit the king's body, thus forming a huge sarcophagus that was an integral part of the overall structure. After the burial, the chamber was sealed with a granite plug, 1.8m (6ft) long that by itself weighed more than 3.1t (3 tons). The burial chamber, when entered, was found to have been robbed in antiquity. When Lauer cleared it in 1934, however, the foot of a mummy was found, perhaps the only part of the king's remains to have survived.

Passages led away from the burial chamber in every direction, and many of their walls bore relief carvings of the king, and brief inscriptions in hieroglyphs recording his name. In several small rooms, the walls were lined with rectangular blue faience tiles to emulate the mats which decorated the walls of houses.

Underneath the third alteration to the original design, a series of 11 entrances in a row under the eastern face of the pyramid opened onto immensely deep vertical shafts, cut about 33.5m (110ft) down into the rock of the plateau. Each of these led to a horizontal corridor under the pyramid, all of them, presumably, intended to house a beloved wife or child of the king. When these shafts were excavated in 1932–33 by Lauer and James Quibell, two fine alabaster sarcophagi were found, one containing the intact burial of an eight-year-old boy, probably a young prince. The body had been enclosed within a coffin made of six-ply wood, fine layers glued and dowelled in alternate directions, the oldest plywood in the world. The outer coffin casing, originally of gold, had been stripped by robbers.

Another shaft led to a gallery stacked high with stone vessels of superb craftsmanship, each made of stone polished to a glossy sheen. More than 40,000 were found, cups, goblets, bowls, dishes and plates, many of calcite (alabaster), and some carved with infinite care to resemble woven baskets or the subtle curves of worked metal. Many of them bore the names and titles, not of Djoser-Netcherikhe but of his

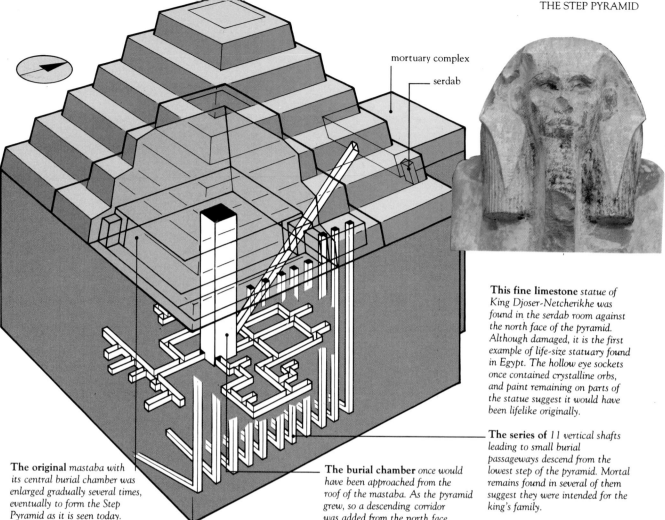

mortuary complex

serdab

This fine limestone *statue of King Djoser-Netcherikhe was found in the serdab room against the north face of the pyramid. Although damaged, it is the first example of life-size statuary found in Egypt. The hollow eye sockets once contained crystalline orbs, and paint remaining on parts of the statue suggest it would have been lifelike originally.*

The series of *11 vertical shafts leading to small burial passageways descend from the lowest step of the pyramid. Mortal remains found in several of them suggest they were intended for the king's family.*

The original *mastaba with its central burial chamber was enlarged gradually several times, eventually to form the Step Pyramid as it is seen today.*

The burial chamber *once would have been approached from the roof of the mastaba. As the pyramid grew, so a descending corridor was added from the north face.*

ancestors of the First and Second Dynasties. However the impression of a seal in the plaster in the corridor bore the name 'Netcherikhe', so clearly the vessels had been placed there by him, though the reason is unknown.

The mortuary temple and serdab

Against the northern face of the completed pyramid a small mortuary temple was built. An entrance door in its east wall led to two small open courtyards, from the western of which a tunnel descended under the pyramid and led to the burial chamber. Other small rooms within the temple against the face of the pyramid itself were designed for the daily food and drink offerings brought to the complex by mortuary' priests. The design for the mortuary temple is unusual, in that all the rooms, courts and even columns are duplicated, perhaps to symbolize the king's authority over both Upper and Lower Egypt.

By the entrance to the chapel in 1924, the excavations of Cecil Firth uncovered a small stone-built chamber without any door, and with only two small holes drilled through the stone at eye level. Inside this chamber (called a serdab, the Arabic for 'cellar') he saw what must have been a startling sight – a life-size seated statue of the king himself. The king was depicted wrapped in a long cloak of a style like that worn during the Sed festival, and wearing a striped 'nemes' headcloth placed over a heavy wig. The statue had once been painted, but time had removed all but a few traces of colour. The face of the statue had been damaged, with the eyes, in which once rock-crystal orbs had been set, ripped out, leaving only empty sockets facing the holes in the serdab walls. The original statue is now in the Cairo Museum, but a duplicate is in its place, so Djoser-Netcherikhe continues to look out as it has done for 4700 years.

The chambers below *the pyramid and the southern tomb seem to be copies in stone of the king's palace, its walls carved to resemble wooden structures faced with mats. The 'mats' in these chambers comprise a series of rectangular faience tiles set into plaster. In the niches they appear to have been 'rolled up' to reveal a finely carved relief underneath. All these passages are now closed to the public because the ceilings are in a dangerous condition.*

The complex

Although the outer walls of the Step Pyramid complex tower over the visitor to the site, extending 545m (1790ft) from north to south and 270m (910ft) from east to west, it is difficult to realize that only 60 years ago, virtually nothing could be seen but sand. Even when the Prussian epigraphic survey of Lepsius had visited Saqqara (*see p. 38*) they had failed to appreciate the mass of buildings and walls that cluster around the pyramid. The remains of the outer wall were excavated in 1924 by Cecil Firth. Two years later he was joined by an indefatigable French architect, Jean-Philippe Lauer. It is almost solely thanks to Lauer's vision of what the site once was, and his determination to restore it, that the great colonnade entrance has been rebuilt, giving some inkling of what the plateau of Saqqara looked like when the pyramid was first erected.

The southern tomb

The huge courtyard to the south of the pyramid was first cleared of sand in 1925. At the foot of this courtyard, the outer wall was revealed and at its southwestern corner, was a tall building topped with a frieze of stone cobras. The building contained two rooms that gave the impression of being a mortuary chapel, and behind it, actually within the width of the boundary wall, a deep shaft-entrance to a hidden subterranean chamber was revealed. Forty-six metres (50yd) to the west of this a second, robbers', entrance was found.

A series of shallow steps led first to a tunnel and then to a rubble-filled chamber, the floor of which was solid granite and had a hole at one end. Through this Cecil Firth entered a small burial chamber which was identical to that found below the pyramid except that it was too small to contain a body.

Beyond the upper chamber a small gallery was found, the walls decorated with three fine reliefs of King Djoser-Netcherikhe shown celebrating his Sed festival, while between the reliefs were panels of brilliant blue faience tiles in the form of reed matting.

Clearly this tomb, known as the southern tomb, was built by and for the king, almost a duplicate of the chambers below the pyramid itself. Yet since a part of the king's mummy had been found in the pyramid chamber, this secondary tomb could hardly have been intended for the king. Despite various speculations, its purpose is unknown.

The Sed court

To the east of the main courtyard in front of the pyramid lies a smaller enclosed courtyard faced with a series of small rectangular buildings that proved, when excavated, to be dummies constructed of solid stone, 13 on the west side and 13 on the east. These buildings appear to be stone copies of the first Egyptian temple built in Nekhen (Hieraconpolis), the Perwer (*see p. 52*). All the buildings have a façade with four slender columns joined to the front face, and a curved roof. At the head of each of the columns was a large round hole, probably designed to hold a flagpole, each flagpole bearing the banner of a different political area, or nome, of Upper and Lower Egypt. While the northern end of the courtyard had curved corners, the southern end had a small square stone dais about .8m (2½ft) high in the centre of it.

The purpose of the courtyard appears to have been the celebration of a Sed festival. On these occasions the king was required to prove his physical fitness to rule Egypt by running a set course on behalf of each nome area. Provided he completed the course successfully, he would re-enact his coronation, the crowns of Egypt and the regalia being presented to him while he was seated under a canopy on a dais.

The word 'sed' in ancient Egyptian means 'to slay' or 'to slaughter', and there seems little doubt that in predynastic times, should the king have failed to run the course he would have been killed and replaced. By the time the Step Pyramid was built, during the Third Dynasty, this primitive ritual had been turned into a ceremonial jubilee festival and no such barbaric royal sacrifice would be made.

It has been suggested that this courtyard was either used by King Djoser-Netcherikhe during his lifetime, or was an exact replica of another in Memphis. Since the aim of the ceremony was to re-invigorate the king by means of ritual, part of the ceremony involved the king's casting aside his old self in a purely symbolic way by attending its 'burial' in the southern tomb (i.e. making it a cenotaph).

The design of the complex

The outer façade wall, when traced by Lauer, proved to have had 14 doorways at intervals around it. Only one was a genuine doorway, however; the others were all false, with hinges and 'wooden planks' carved onto the surface of the solid stone wall. The only true entrance, via the colonnade in the south-eastern corner of the complex, led into the large courtyard. The columns of the colonnade and those of the inner courtyard were all joined to the walls behind them like those of the dummy buildings of the Sed court, rather than being free-standing. Moreover, all were carved to resemble natural features. The columns in the courtyard bear capitals in the form of lotus blossoms, buds and papyrus heads while those of the colonnade resemble bundles of reeds.

Some archaeologists have theorized that the Egyptians, who had constructed large-scale works previously only in wood, placed their confidence as much in the design – i.e. the natural forms of reed bundles, lotus and papyrus, and so on – as in the inherent strength of the material. There was, however, no example on which to assess the strength of stone, so as a safeguard Imhotep used all the design features he would have employed with the old medium. Alternatively, it is possible that Imhotep's purpose in copying wooden features in stone was not purely structural, but simply an attempt to reproduce faithfully everything that had surrounded the king during his life.

The design of the complex itself is quite different from any before or after it. It has been suggested that the whole area was designed to be an eternal stone copy of the king's palace and surrounding buildings in Memphis, the capital of Egypt. The name of Memphis at this time was 'Ineb-hedj', or 'white walls', and without doubt the most dominant feature of the necropolis plateau of Saqqara would have been the white limestone walls of Djoser's complex.

Within the outer walls of the complex many of the buildings are dummies while others, such as the so-called House of the North and House of the South lying to the north of the Sed court, have no clear purpose within the funerary complex, although they too may represent part of the ceremonies by which the king retook control of the Two Lands.

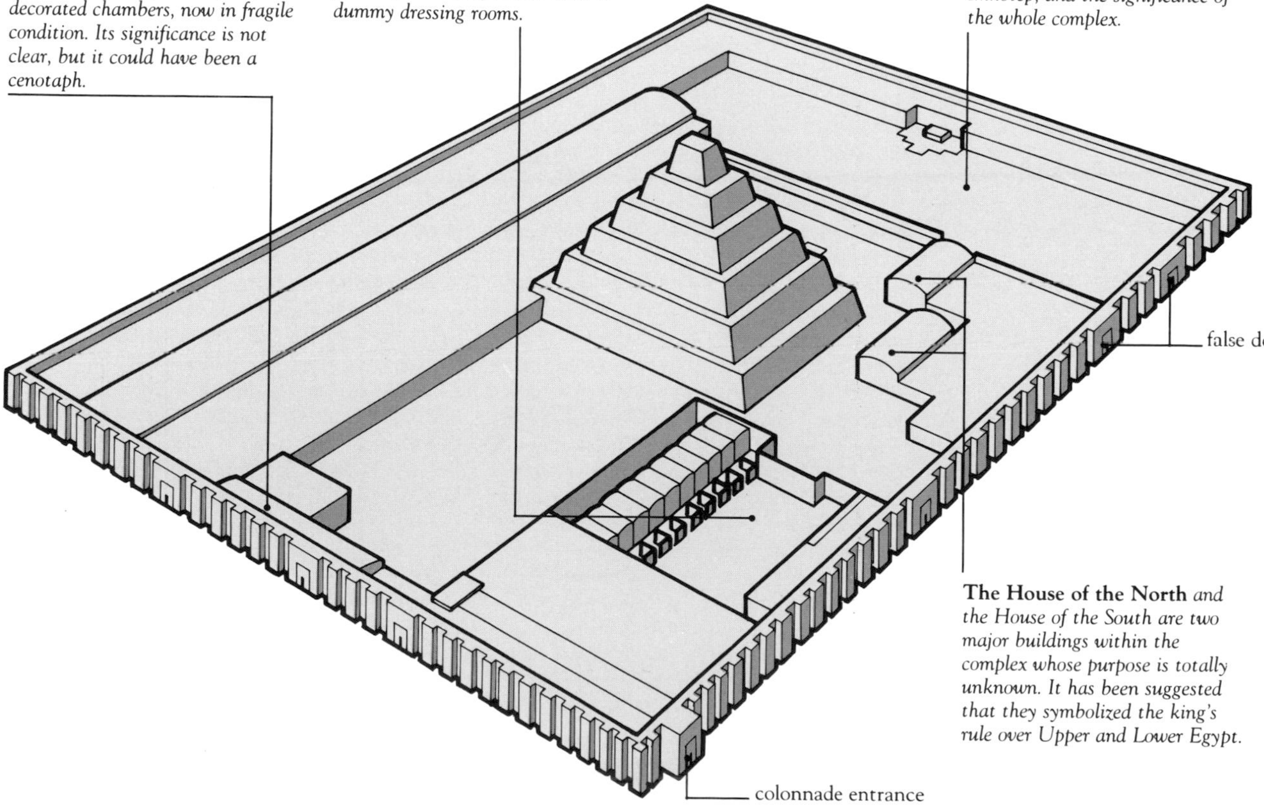

The area *to the north of the Step Pyramid still awaits clearing. It is apparent that many more rooms lie under rubble and accumulated sand. They may contain more information about the architect, Imhotep, and the significance of the whole complex.*

The southern tomb *is approached by a steeply sloping shaft to a series of small, finely decorated chambers, now in fragile condition. Its significance is not clear, but it could have been a cenotaph.*

The Sed court, *used for the jubilee festivals of the king, is faced by a series of barrel-vaulted dummy dressing rooms.*

false doors

The House of the North *and the House of the South are two major buildings within the complex whose purpose is totally unknown. It has been suggested that they symbolized the king's rule over Upper and Lower Egypt.*

colonnade entrance

THE LOST PYRAMID

The entrance *to the lost pyramid of Sekhemkhe was found unexpectedly under banks of sand. It is still covered with sand today and inaccessible to the general public. The doorway leads to a gently descending corridor and the burial chamber with its empty sarcophagus.*

The sands of Saqqara may hide many chambers and tombs, but few of them could ever match the discovery made by the Egyptian Egyptologist Mohammed Zacharia Goneim during his excavations there between 1951 and 1955.

Patterns in the sand to the southwest of the Step Pyramid complex had intrigued him. A huge rectangular shape almost as long as the outer walls of the Step Pyramid could be natural rock formations, but might have been man-made. Goneim excavated on behalf of the Antiquities Service, and soon uncovered a brilliant white, palace-façaded wall almost identical to that of the Step Pyramid, some 550m (600yd) long and 190m (207yd) wide. To one end of this enclosure, the base of a previously unknown step pyramid, 65m sq (365 ft sq), was discovered. Although only 7.2m (23ft) in height of the lowest level had been completed, had it been finished, it would have matched the Step Pyramid itself in dominating the necropolis of Saqqara.

Surprises are revealed

It was hardly to be expected that such an incomplete pyramid would contain anything of importance and certainly not a burial. However, a shallow trench in the bedrock cut to the north of the pyramid descended slowly into the ground, and opened into an underground tunnel. Part way along its length, a vertical shaft rose upwards some 12.5m (41ft) into the core of the pyramid; this would presumably have been intended to meet an entrance passage in the face of the pyramid. The shaft was blocked with loose shale that had to be cleared, and it was here that Goneim met his first surprise. At the top of the shale, animal remains were found, later analyzed and found to be parts of oxen, sheep and antelopes. These presumably represented offerings of food for the tomb. Below this, however, some 60 fragments of papyrus were uncovered, dating from the Late period, around 700 BC. Towards the foot of the shaft infill, a series of stone jars had been placed in neat rows and here, for the first time, the name of the owner and builder of the pyramid was discovered – Sekhemkhe.

Little was known about Sekhemkhe. Relief carvings showing a king of this name in the Wadi Maghara, in the Sinai, had long been assumed to be a mistaken writing of an earlier king's name – Semerkhe of the Second Dynasty. Here was the first proof of a king who had ruled Egypt during the Third Dynasty at the start of the Old Kingdom. He had lived after Djoser and before Snofru, the first king of the brilliant Fourth Dynasty, a period about which virtually nothing was known. But who was this Sekhemkhe? The name did not appear in any lists of kings inscribed on the walls of the temples. In them, the successor of Djoser was one Djoser-Teti, whom Manetho recorded as ruling Egypt for only six years. If, as seems reasonable, Sekhemkhe is to be identified as Djoser-Teti, the state of the unfinished pyramid can be explained by the king's dying soon after building work on his pyramid had begun. The question that faced Goneim was whether the king had been buried in his unfinished pyramid. The papyri of a much later date found in the shaft showed that at least part of the pyramid had once been open, but the stone jars suggested that the base of the shaft might never have been disturbed.

As excavation continued, against the wall of the corridor, leading from the base of the shaft, a pile of hundreds of beads, covered with gold, was found lying among 21 gold bracelets. Was this all that would remain of the burial?

The burial

Beneath the shaft, a corridor led under the pyramid, and off this, a doorway led into a labyrinthine series of 132 storerooms. At the end of the corridor, blocks of stone filled the entrance to what proved to be the burial chamber. Like the pyramid itself the chamber had never been completed, and the walls, floor and ceiling were only roughly chiselled. But here Goneim found the answer to his question. In the centre of the chamber stood a fine, rectangular sarcophagus. It had been cut from one single block of alabaster, with the opening, not on the top in the form of the usual lid, but at one end, where a T-shaped alabaster block fitted tightly into a vertical slot. On the top of the sarcophagus lay what appeared to be a funerary wreath.

With high expectations of finding the remains of one of the earliest kings of Egypt intact, arrangements were made for a public opening of the sarcophagus. On 26 June 1954, in front of an invited audience of scholars and pressmen, Goneim attached ropes to the cover of the sarcophagus, fixed them to a pulley and gave the order for it to be lifted while another helper used a wooden lever to ease it free. In stunned disbelief, all present saw that the sarcophagus was completely empty.

Some archaeologists believe that the burial chamber had never been used and that the body of the king had been placed elsewhere in a completed tomb. Analysis of the 'wreath' on top of the sarcophagus, however, showed that it was ancient decayed wood. It seems likely, then, that robbers had indeed broken into the sarcophagus and removed the body of the king. Only the gold jewellery in the outer corridor remained.

A tragic end

For Goneim a brilliant future in Egyptology beckoned, and he worked hard to publish his findings as speedily as he could. Then, on 9 January 1959, his body was found floating in the Nile in Cairo. The true story of what brought about his unexpected death has never been fully understood. Some newspapers, naturally, put the death down to the 'Curse of the Pharaohs', a suggestion Goneim himself would have derided. Those who knew him well thought it was purely the pressure of work that may have depressed him.

Whatever the truth of his mysterious death, the unfinished pyramid he discovered is quite unique. A lot of work still remains to be done on the enclosure – to this day it remains virtually unexcavated. Lauer (*see p. 64*) cleared a mastaba tomb that lay to the south of the pyramid. Like the pyramid, the mastaba had been robbed in antiquity. All that was found at the foot of the 30.5m (100ft) shaft under it were fragments of wood and gold leaf that had once formed a small coffin. Inside, the remains of a young child were found – perhaps those of a young prince. Alternatively, it may have been a later burial placed in a conveniently empty shaft.

Many problems on the site remain to be solved. Aerial photographs of the area have revealed the clear outline of what may prove to be yet another uncompleted pyramid complex lying to the west of that of Sekhemkhe. From the lines in the sand, it appears to be even larger in area than the Step Pyramid complex itself. Future excavation may well bring knowledge of yet another king of the unknown years at the end of the Third Dynasty.

Zacharia Goneim, *on the left, points out details on some blocks to a worker at the site of the lost pyramid of Sekhemkhe. Goneim was a shy man and intensely private. Few people knew him well, but what was clear was that he possessed the potential to be one of the truly great Egyptologists. His tragic death in 1959 shocked his friends and colleagues – and cost the world a fine archaeologist.*

MEIDUM

For a king of the Old Kingdom, the building of a pyramid complex to ensure safe passage of his soul to join the gods after death should have been the apogee of his reign. Yet Snofru, father of Cheops, reputedly built not one, but three pyramids.

Eight kilometres (5mi) south of Saqqara, among the pyramids of Dahshur is the so-called Bent pyramid and, nearby, the gently sloping Northern pyramid; 45km (28mi) south of that, stands the tower-like pyramid of Meidum. Inside the Bent pyramid, a graffito written on a block by a workman records Snofru's name, while a stela found alongside the nearly subsidiary pyramid depicts him taking part in a Sed festival. Moreover, the Northern pyramid also contains several examples of Snofru's name. A stela, found nearby and published in 1905, records that the villages lying in the vicinity of the 'Two Pyramids of Snofru' should be exempt from taxation. Obviously Snofru had two pyramids – the question is which. Structurally, the pyramid of Meidum and the Bent pyramid are earlier than the Northern pyramid. Could the stela have referred to the earlier two? Is it likely that two pyramids 45km (28mi) apart should be covered by the one stela?

So what of the Meidum pyramid? A graffito left there by an Eighteenth Dynasty tourist in the mortuary temple records that, having come to visit the temple of the King Snofru, he found it 'as though heaven were in it' – in other words, it was undamaged. The thought of any king building not two, but three pyramids appears on the face of it to be out of the question. Given the long passage of time that had elapsed between the building of the pyramid and the visit of the tourist – over a thousand years – archaeologists suspect that the tourist may have been misinformed. Meidum may have belonged to Snofru's predecessor, of whom little is known save his name. A Middle Kingdom papyrus records: 'The Majesty of King Huni died, and the Majesty of King Snofru was raised up as a benevolent King in this entire land.' One possiblity is that Meidum could have been started by Huni and completed by Snofru.

The Meidum pyramid

Unlike the Step Pyramid which grew slowly from a mastaba to a pyramid (see p. 64–5), the Meidum structure appears to have been conceived from the start as a pyramid. A central square-based core was built that was to form the nucleus and peak of the pyramid. Around it, a succession of six more layers was added, each sloping at an angle of 75 degrees towards the core, the face of each layer covered with fine white limestone. Each succeeding layer was shorter than the previous one, with the exposed limestone faces trimmed and polished. The whole thus formed a step pyramid on the outside that was then entirely faced with stone to form a true pyramid. Today, with the three outer layers having become reduced to rubble in antiquity it scarcely resembles a pyramid.

On the north face, a steeply descending passage drops below the bedrock and levels out into a short passage, from which a short vertical shaft leads up into the burial chamber. This, with its corbelled roof, stands slightly under the bedrock, such that the floor and lower parts of the wall were quarried out and the rest built over it. The surfaces are all left roughly hewn, with a depression in the floor, probably intended for a sarcophagus, left unfinished. A hole in the west wall of the chamber, probably intended as a so-called air shaft (see p. 73) had been abandoned after being cut barely 45.7cm (18in) into the stone.

The Dahshur pyramids

The Bent pyramid is so named because the angle of the outer walls alters abruptly part way up. The lower part is a steep 54 degrees, while the upper part of 43 degrees has the same shallow angle as the sides of the Northern pyramid. From this evidence, it seems reasonable to suggest that the Northern pyramid was started when the Bent pyramid was almost complete.

The Bent pyramid is unique also in that it is the only pyramid to have two entrances: the usual north face entrance leads to a subterranean chamber, while the other, from the west face, leads to a corbelled chamber within the pyramid itself. When Perring entered the chambers in 1838, both were empty.

The Northern pyramid is entered through a descending passage cut into the usual northern face. It leads to two chambers lying side by side in the heart of the pyramid. The burial chamber, above these two rooms, entered by Perring, was reported as containing no remains at all.

Although both these pyramids were true, i.e. with sloping exterior faces, and not step pyramids, it is probable that both were built, like Meidum, around an extended inner core.

The core of *the Meidum pyramid is made up of layers that slope gently inwards. Each layer was covered with fine white Tura limestone, but only the section that could be seen above the succeeding layers could be smoothed to a fine polish.*

The entrance on *the north face of the pyramid slopes downwards at an angle of almost 45°. The walls of the passage were never smoothed. At the foot, a short horizontal corridor leads to a small upward shaft and the unfinished burial chamber.*

The theory of collapse

In 1974, Professor Kurt Mendelssohn, of Oxford University, attempted to apply his knowledge as a physicist to unravel the problems of the three alleged pyramids of Snofru. The accumulation of sand and rubble at the foot of the Meidum pyramid persuaded him that at some point it had been subjected to such vigorous earth tremors that it collapsed, leaving only the centre core standing. Similar tremors would certainly have convinced ancient builders of the inherent instability of building a pyramid angled at 54 degrees, causing them to change their design part-way through construction of the Bent pyramid. Later, a third pyramid, at the safe, lesser angle of 43 degrees was started. It was this pyramid, the Northern pyramid at Dahshur, Mendelssohn reasoned, in which the king would have been buried.

Yet archaeologically there is little proof for these theories. There is no structural cracking either in the core of the Meidum pyramid, or in the lower levels of the Bent pyramid which might be expected had earth movements strong enough to cause a pyramid to collapse occurred. More significantly, the mortuary temple attached to the Meidum pyramid is unfinished, its twin stelae uninscribed and the burial chamber left only roughly hewn. If the pyramid was abandoned because it had col-lapsed before it was finished, it is hard to understand why the tombs of several courtiers were completed and used in the vicinity. In 1871, the mastaba of Nefermaat and Itet, and that of Rahotep and Nofret were explored. Both were finely decorated and well equipped, the former yielding not only panels of pictures utilizing colour-infill of solid pigment (*see p. 149*), but also the famous scene of the 'Meidum Geese'; and the latter, the famous statues of Rahotep and his wife (*see p. 151*).

Another puzzle, should this theory be correct, is that the lesser – so-called safer – angle of 43 degrees was not adopted by any later king in the building of his pyramid; on the contrary, a universal 51 degrees was used, implying that a steeper angle was not considered unstable.

The complexes surrounding the Meidum and the Dahshur pyramids have never been excavated more than cursorily, and undulations in the sand around all three indicate that many tomb superstructures still await discovery. No doubt inscriptions in some of them may provide conclusive evidence as to the ownership of the pyramids. Somewhere in the neighbourhood of one of them must lie the original burial place of Queen Hetepheres, wife of Snofru and mother of Cheops (*see pp. 78–79*). This tomb alone would surely pinpoint the final resting place of Snofru.

Little excavation *has been done at Meidum. The causeway was cleared of sand, but it has already begun to fill, though the line of the causeway to the mortuary temple at its head, is still clearly visible.*

71

THE PYRAMIDS OF GIZA

This superb *diorite statue of Chephren, builder of the second of the three Giza pyramids, was found smashed in a pit in the valley temple of the King at Giza by Mariette's men in 1860, and has since been reconstructed. Originally a whole series of these statues filled the main hall of the valley temple, as the empty emplacements in the floor show. This statue is unquestionably one of the sculptural masterpieces of ancient Egypt, showing Chephren seated upon his throne – with its front and back legs those of lions – as the embodiment of majesty, his expression aloof and impenetrable. At the back of his head, a Horus falcon spreads its wings, mantling the pharaoh as the birds, in life, mantle their young to protect them from heat and predators. Carved in high relief on the side of Chephren's throne is the symbol for the union of the Two Lands: the hieroglyph 'sma' ('join' or 'union'), around which are wound the plants of Upper and Lower Egypt.*

No words or pictures can ever prepare you for your first sight of the pyramids of Giza – the last surviving of the seven wonders of the ancient world. Their size can scarcely be conceived until, standing before one of them, the sky filled with stone blocks, the immensity of the project can suddenly be realized.

Cheops, great king of the Fourth Dynasty, whom the Egyptians called Khufu, chose to build his monumental tomb on a high rocky ridge on the west bank of the Nile, lying about 24km (15mi) north of the ancient capital of Memphis. When the spot was chosen it must have been visible for miles around. Today, the sprawling suburbs of Cairo spread to the very foot of the plateau, and a coach or taxi can drive to within 90m (100yd) of the pyramid.

Chephren, or Khaefre, the son who succeeded Cheops, almost matched his father's example. The pyramid of Chephren, lying just south of the Great Pyramid, was only 3m (10ft) lower than that of Cheops, but since he chose a higher place on which to build, it is his pyramid, the centre one of the three, that appears to dominate the plateau of Giza.

The third, and most southerly pyramid, was built by Mycerinus (Menkaure), who was probably one of Chephren's brothers. Although no mean monument, standing 61m (204ft) tall, it is dwarfed by the other two pyramids, being approximately only a quarter of their bulk.

Around all three pyramids cluster the mastaba tombs of the kings' families and courtiers, laid out in neat streets. The mortuary temples of all three pyramids survive in outline against the east faces; while of their causeways that once led to canals from the Nile, that of Mycerinus was never finished and that of Cheops is covered with sand. The causeway of Chephren's pyramid is one of the finest to have survived, leading, as it does, to an almost intact valley temple. Alongside this granite-faced temple stands the Sphinx.

The Great Pyramid

This pyramid stood 146.6m (481ft) tall, its base 230.3m (756ft) square, and it comprises an estimated 2.5 million limestone blocks, each weighing approximately 2.5t (2½ tons). It has been measured more times than virtually any other building in the world, the measurements often being misrepresented as having some sort of mystical significance.

It was first entered, according to legend, by Caliph Siamun, the son of Harun al Raschid,

the Sultan to whom Scheherazade told her stories for 1001 nights, in the ninth century. Believing the myth that an emerald of stupendous size was hidden inside, he ordered his men to find the entrance. While they were probing the north face, the falling of a loose stone inside the pyramid indicated the location of passages within. They tunnelled through the stone walls, and after a short distance, met the original outer passage, still sealed with granite blocks. The burial chambers, when reached, were empty. Today, tourists enter not through the original entrance, which remains sealed, but through the robbers' entrance.

The inner structure

The pyramid was originally planned to have a subterranean burial chamber, approached via a descending passage from the northern face. Photographs of this underground chamber published in 1910 show that it was left incomplete, with a sunken rectangular pit, probably cut to contain a sarcophagus, that was abandoned when only half excavated. The entrance to the descending passage is about 16.8m (55ft) above the plateau, and its walls were lined with finely fitted and polished stone slabs as the pyramid rose in height. It is clear that this plan was changed to incorporate a chamber within the pyramid itself after this passage had been built and lined. So, an ascending passage had to be cut through the blocks that had already been laid, before levelling out to a second burial chamber, called 'the Queen's Chamber' by early Arab visitors on account of its pointed roof, a feature of contemporary women's tombs. Like the subterranean burial chamber, however, this too had been abandoned by its builders before it was completed.

The third and final design called for the cutting of what is called the Grand Gallery, an upward sloping extension of the ascending corridor on a large scale. The walls of this corridor, faced with slabs of polished limestone, are corbelled, each section jutting about 7.5cm (3in) beyond the course beneath to form a vaulted passage 8.5m (28ft) high and 46.6m (153ft) long. At the lower end of the passage, a narrow vertical shaft was cut that emerged on the descending passage. At the upper end, a series of two portcullises led into the burial chamber. Faced entirely with pink granite, this chamber measures 10.4m (34ft) × 5.2m (17ft) and still contains a sarcophagus. When Petrie first

The central chamber (*above*) in the Great Pyramid of Cheops (*left*) is faced with polished granite slabs; those of the ceiling alone are estimated to weigh in excess of 400 tons. The granite sarcophagus, on the west side of the chamber, was empty when first examined in modern times. When Flinders Petrie – the Father of Egyptology – worked here, in 1882, he noted saw marks on the underside of the sarcophagus, suggesting it had not been split from the bedrock with wedges as marks in the granite quarries in Aswan suggest. Interestingly he also noted that there were greater discrepancies in the measurements and levels of this chamber than in the whole of the rest of the Great Pyramid.

measured the sarcophagus, in 1881, he discovered it was too large to fit through the approach corridors and thus must have been put in place as the pyramid was being built. The flat roof of the chamber has over it a series of five shallow compartments, apparently built to relieve the pressure of the weight of stone above the burial chamber. In 1837, Col. Howard Vyse discovered a red painted graffito in the uppermost compartment left by a workman that named the builder of the pyramid as Khufu – Cheops. It is the only instance of the king's name in the pyramid.

In the walls of the burial chamber, two narrow shafts lead to the outside of the pyramid. Piazzi-Smyth (*see p. 41*), regarded these as air shafts that maintained the temperature inside the chamber at a steady 20°C (68°F). This, as any visitor can affirm, is clearly false; nor is there any practical justification for such air channels because the burial chamber was completed as the pyramid was being built and was thus open to the air. In fact, references in the later Pyramid Texts (*see p. 168*) affirm that at the time of Cheops' burial his soul was expected to join not the sun but the stars.

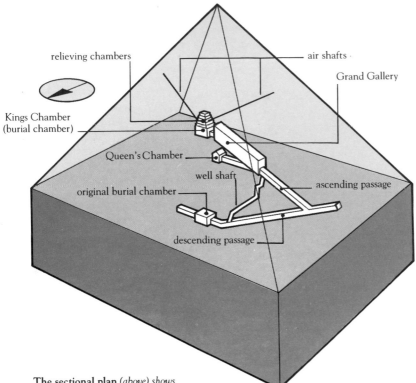

relieving chambers

air shafts

Grand Gallery

Kings Chamber
(burial chamber)

Queen's Chamber

well shaft

original burial chamber

ascending passage

descending passage

The sectional plan (above) shows the passages and chambers within the Great Pyramid. Although perspective can be slightly distorting, the pyramid itself is on a square base. The original entrance shaft was intended at first to lead to an underground burial chamber. Before it was completed, two successive changes in design were made. Initially, a burial chamber was built in the heart of the pyramid. Then the final King's Chamber was added at the head of the imposing Grand Gallery. The two narrow shafts from the King's Chamber were cut to align with the stars with which the king's eternity was linked. The modern entrance is below the original one, but joins up with the original passages on the ascending corridor.

These two shafts would have aligned exactly with Orion and the Dog Star, Sirius, serving to guide the king's soul.

After burial, the ascending passage was filled with granite stones to block the pyramid. Because these stones are too large to have fitted through the descending corridor, they must have been stored inside the pyramid itself. Petrie discovered that they were too large, also, to have fitted into the Queen's chamber. Thus they must have been stored in the Grand Gallery. Borchardt noticed holes cut at regular intervals in the walls of this gallery, and suggested that once wooden beams held the blocks clear of the ground. After the burial of the king, workmen remaining inside the pyramid would have the unenviable task of loosing the blocks which would then have slid down the ascending passage and sealed it. The men then effected their escape by means of the vertical shaft. The drama of this climb, in total darkness via a chimney less than .9m (3ft) square, can only be imagined.

Once the descending corridor had been blocked, the facing stone of the pyramid could be completed – the pyramid was sealed solid.

Recent work

It has long been considered a possibility that more chambers may yet be hidden within the pyramid. Sonar tests carried out early in 1987 revealed the possibility of a hollow behind the limestone facing of the ascending passage. Trial drillings have revealed an infill of about .3m (1 ft) of dry sand behind the facing slabs, a totally unexpected feature, and behind that, blocks of white Tura limestone. It has been suggested that this may be a doorway to yet another chamber. Work is continuing at the spot by a Japanese team and soon a sort of miniaturized camera is going to be inserted into the wall to assess the true situation.

However, Borchardt noted in an article in 1932 that the method of using an inner core surrounded by outer layers to build a pyramid, as used at Meidum (see p. 70–1), was also used in the building of the Fifth Dynasty pyramids at Abusir and could, thus, conceivably have been used in the construction of the Great Pyramid. If this were the case, then the Tura limestone encountered behind the facing blocks of the internal corridors could well be the external facing stone habitually used over each succeeding layer.

The pyramid of Chephren

The base of Chephren's pyramid is 215.2m (708ft) square, its height 143.5m (471ft), the faces rising slightly more steeply than those of the Great Pyramid. It is easily distinguished from the Great Pyramid by its 'cap', the intact layers of limestone covering at its peak.

The pyramid was entered, in 1818, by Belzoni (see p. 29), and was found to have been robbed in antiquity. It has, in fact, two entrances, one above the other, leading to a single horizontal corridor at the surface of the underlying bedrock. The burial chamber is also cut in the face of the rock, the whole lined with pink granite. As in the Great Pyramid, shafts were cut into the walls of the burial chamber to align with the stars but were never completed. The intact sarcophagus stands inside a pit and the lid would have been level with the floor. No trace of the king's body has been found.

In 1881, outside the pyramid against its western enclosure wall, Petrie found the foundations of a series of terraced chambers that appear to have housed workers on the Giza complex. There would seem to have been 91 small houses, offering shelter to far fewer than the 400,000 men proposed by Herodotus.

The pyramid of Mycerinus

When Reisner excavated on behalf of the Harvard-Boston Project, between 1905 and 1926, he discovered that the complex had never been completed, even though Mycerinus ruled for approximately 28 years, probably longer than his brother Chephren. It is possible that the much smaller scale of his pyramid complex reflects the dreadful drain on manpower that the monuments of his brother and father must have been. In addition, this pyramid, unlike the others, was to have been encased in red granite on its lower courses – but this idea was abandoned.

Inside, as in the Great Pyramid, the design had been changed. The first entrance and descending passage, had to be abandoned when the pyramid was enlarged. The second, and final entrance led to the same burial chamber, but below it two more chambers were added. When Howard Vyse entered the pyramid in the 1840s, using gunpowder, he found a black basalt sarcophagus containing wood from a coffin and some human remains. He removed all three, to be shipped to England, but unfortunately the ship carrying the sarcophagus was sunk during a violent storm in the Bay of Biscay, north of Spain. The sarcophagus itself was lost at sea, but the other remains from the burial chamber found their way to the British Museum in London, where detailed analysis has dated the wooden coffin fragments to the Twenty-sixth Dynasty.

The subsidiary pyramids

Both Cheops' and Mycerinus' pyramids have three smaller pyramids built alongside; Chephren's only has one. Their purpose is unknown, although they are commonly called 'Queens' pyramids'. Certainly in the central pyramid of the three of Mycerinus' complex, Howard Vyse found a sarcophagus and some human remains said to be of a young woman. There is no evidence to show that this was not a burial of a later period, like that within the main pyramid. On the contrary, mastaba tombs have been found in all three complexes that belonged to the royal women.

Another suggestion, that they were intended to hold the viscera of the mummified kings, is also unproven. There is a striking parallel, however, between the provision of a subsidiary pyramid and the southern tomb of the Step Pyramid at Saqqara (see p. 66). It is possible, therefore, that they were intended purely as cenotaphs either for religious reasons (for use after Sed festivals), or for political reasons (signifying the king's supremacy over various parts of Egypt).

The Sphinx

The man-headed lion statue crouches at the foot of Chephren's causeway, and stands 19.8m (65ft) high and 73.2m (240ft) long. It is cut from a natural outcrop of limestone that appears to have been left after stone blocks used for building the pyramids had been removed. It represents one aspect of the sun god, Re-Horakhte, sometimes called Hor-m-akhet, or Harmachis, the sun as it stands above the horizon. The origin of the term 'sphinx' is unknown, but it is possible that it is derived from the Egyptian words 'shesep ankh', meaning 'living image'.

It was cut with the face of a king of the Fourth Dynasty, generally said to be that of Chephren since it stands alongside Chephren's causeway. The features, however, bear a far more striking resemblance to Chephren's older brother, Radjedef, who ruled Egypt for a short time after Cheops' death before, in all probability being usurped by Chephren. Radjedef's tomb, an unfinished pyramid, is at Abu Roash about 8km (5mi) from Giza, and was badly smashed.

Between the paws of the Sphinx, a granite stela records a dream in which the god himself visited a sleeping prince, later Tuthmosis IV, and requested the sand cleared around him. The stela, standing on bedrock, proves that the prince complied with the god's request. A temple built alongside, probably of the same Eighteenth Dynasty date, appears to have been built for the veneration of the Sphinx after this revelation.

The head of the Sphinx, still bearing some traces of red and yellow paint, has been badly battered. Both the nose and the beard have been broken away, fragments of the former being in the Cairo Museum and a small fragment of the latter in the British Museum. Restoration work undertaken by the American Research Centre in Egypt, under the direction of Mark Lehner, has shown that an accumulation of salts in ancient mortar used around the Sphinx, is causing further severe erosion when dissolved in water rising through the bedrock and then dried by wind and sun action. The Egyptian Antiquities Service is presently adding a new covering of limestone blocks in order to conserve the core of this great ancient monument, while more major work has been proposed to deal with the problems which are being caused by the rising dampness under the plateau of Giza.

Although Cheops' pyramid is the largest stone building in Egypt and a wonder of the ancient world, this tiny ivory figurine, 7.5cm (3in) tall, is the only surviving image of its owner. The body of a headless figure, with the king's name in a cartouche by its legs identifying it as Cheops-Khufu, was found by Petrie's workmen at Abydos in 1903. It says much for Petrie's meticulous methods that he stopped all other excavation at the site until the head was found. Sieving and minute examination of every basket of sand resulted in the only image of the king's face being found after three weeks' searching.

75

BOAT OF THE SUN

Despite the seemingly *fragile structure of the Cheops boat, it resembles paintings and models of other Egyptian vessels, suggesting it was typical of the design they favoured. The papyriform shape is emphasized by the removable bow and stern posts. The closed cabin, amidships, is made from a number of small panels interspersed with graceful palm-form columns. The open canopy was once probably hung with mats or linen cloths to provide a cooling breeze for the king and his entourage. The small cabin towards the prow would have been intended for the use of the captain and pilot.*

The ripples caused in Egyptian government circles, following the revolution of 1952, spread wide and had repercussions in the sedate world of archaeology. Numbers of Egyptian archaeologists were appointed to work with the Antiquities Service and among them one, Kamal el Mallakh, found himself, in 1954, working at Giza at the foot of the Great Pyramid.

The great German archaeologist Hermann Junker of Giza worked on the plateau for 15 years, cleaning and excavating the whole area. In his work he showed how a boundary wall had once surrounded the Great Pyramid. One stretch of it still lay under sand, and it was this section of wall that Mallakh was examining. Despite the ancient Egyptians' love of order, for some reason the wall that was appearing from beneath the sand stood 4.9m (16ft) closer to the pyramid than on the other sides. Mallakh was perplexed. Wondering if it hid something, he gave orders to clear the wall down to the bedrock.

Under the wall, a flat, smooth area of plastered mud lay like a great pavement. The workmen cut away one section of it, to reveal the corner of a huge limestone block and next to it, gypsum plaster sealing a cavity. Several days later, with the mud removed, two huge panels of limestone blocks were revealed, one with 40 and the other with 41 giant stones sealed with plaster. Into this had been pressed a royal seal bearing the name Radjedef, the heir and successor of Cheops.

It seemed likely that what Mallakh had discovered was two boat pits; others existed around several pyramids, but all were empty. Arrangements were made to open one pit and, on 26 May 1954, a group gathered while Mallakh chipped away one small area of stone to peer inside. A rush of hot air assailed him, followed immediately by a reaction to the smell. 'I closed my eyes,' he wrote , 'and I smelt incense . . . I smelt time . . . I smelt centuries . . . I

smelt history itself, and then I knew there was a boat there.' As the first sunlight broke into the darkness of a pit sealed more than 4800 years ago, it illuminated an oar and the unmistakable shape of the prow of a great boat.

The removal of the sealing blocks was done slowly, each stage being checked by the outstanding conservator Dr Zaki Iskander. Slivers of wood carefully removed proved that the anaerobic conditions had preserved the wood so completely that it looked 'fresh and new', redolent of pine oil, though it was almost completely dry of natural moisture.

The stones, each weighing 16 tons and wedged on a shoulder inside the pit, took more than six months to remove. In the meantime, a shed was built over and around the pit to stabilize the atmosphere and ensure that there was no accidental fall of debris into the pit. It was finally revealed that the pit contained not a complete boat, but 1224 individual pieces of wood, laid carefully in 13 layers, together with ropes for rigging, baskets and matting. Some parts, such as oars and slender cabin poles, were recognizable, but the majority were not. The overwhelming sense of confusion can be imagined as archaeologists saw for the first time a huge kit-form boat, with no indication of how to put it together.

The reassembly, after a great number of false starts, took more than 10 years. Even then it was destined to be dismantled and rebuilt four more times before it found its final resting place in the huge purpose-built museum where it lies today at the foot of the Great Pyramid. It is a truly breathtaking sight, and a great privilege to be able to see in its entirety a vessel in which the builder of the Great Pyramid may once have sailed.

The construction of the boat

The boat is 5.9m (19ft 6in) wide at its centre, and 43.6m (143ft) long, and when afloat is

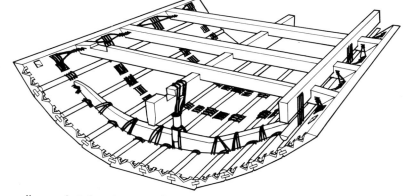

calculated to have a displacement of 45 tons, so that she would have floated 38cm (15in) clear of the water amidships. She had no keel but the hull boards were first pegged roughly together and then 'sewn' through holes that only pierce the inside of each plank. This 'stitching' was done with rope made of twisted hemp, or with leather thongs, with slender battens lashed underneath to seal each crack. As the lashings tightened in water, these strips made caulking unnecessary.

Once the hull had been built, the 16 ribs were cut; they were made exactly to shape, and were not interchangeable. On each side of these rested a narrow beam which supported the main deck joist. Lashed to the centre of these was the spine of the boat, a timber running from prow to stern.

Over the main joists, the decking was laid as a series of hatches, each of which could be easily lifted aside to put stores, for example, into the hull. On the prow and stern, huge pegs locate into sockets in the distinctive posts that give the boat its shape. Towards the bow, a captain or pilot's cabin stands – a simple canopy made of 10 slender poles. Amidships and running to the stern is a large cabin, its roof supported inside by three posts with palm-form capitals. In front of the closed cabin stands another open canopy that is supported by 12 more posts.

There are six pairs of oars, the shortest 6.5m (21ft 6in), the longest 8.5m (28ft) long. Five pairs were lashed with rope row-locks next to the fore canopy, while the sixth pair served as rudder oars by the stern post. Their length, design and position would make them relatively ineffective for rowing, and it has been suggested that all 12 were used for steering, the boat being towed either by a tug or by ropes on land.

It is usually stated that this boat was made of cedar of Lebanon, but there is no clear proof. Timber was readily available in Egypt, as recent

pollen analysis has shown, with native pines, junipers, hardwoods and ornamental woods such as cherry and plum. The straight graining suggests some variety of pine, and it is probable that the wood was not imported at all, but in fact native to Egypt.

The boat's purpose

The papyriform boat shape generally is linked in illustrations with the 'wia' or state boat of the sun god, in which the sun was believed to traverse the heavens. As a result, the Cheops boat is frequently called 'the solar boat', implying that it was provided purely for ceremonial reasons to ferry the soul of the dead king daily across the sky.

There are several problems with this theory. The caulking strips all bore the rope markings where the ropes had tightened into place, showing clearly that the boat had been used in the water. The boat did not fit into the boat pit whole, but had to be dismantled, showing that the pit was not constructed specifically for the boat. Finally, there were no ritual objects or inscriptions found in the pit to support a religious use.

The implications are that the boat had been functional, but its unwieldiness suggests it was not for travelling long distances. It may have been used as a state boat during the king's lifetime and perhaps it even carried Cheops' body to the plateau of Giza prior to its embalming and burial in the pyramid.

The planks on the Cheops boat were lashed together internally over narrow caulking strips, making a watertight seal that needed no external filling. The hull was proportionately wide and shallow, and probably of little use for storage. The rope lashings that held everything in place, including the huge oars, all survived intact in the boat pit, some 195mm 7¾ in) in diameter.

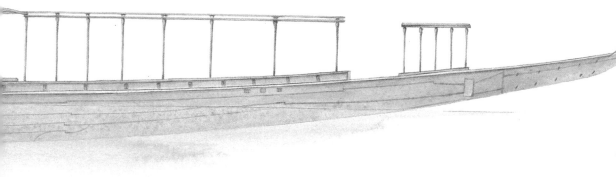

A QUEEN'S TREASURE

As with all the best stories of archaeology, the discovery of the only almost intact burial dating from the Old Kingdom, and contemporary with the building of the pyramids at Giza, was a complete accident.

In 1925, an American team of archaeologists of the Harvard-Boston Museum of Fine Arts' expedition, led by George Reisner, was working at Giza surveying, mapping and exploring the tombs that lay at the foot of the Great Pyramid. A photographer on the site was trying, with great difficulty, to set up his tripod near the three subsidiary pyramids to the southeast of the pyramid of Cheops. Suddenly, one of the legs of the tripod slipped into a hole and he discovered that he had accidentally disturbed some ancient plaster.

Below the plaster-sealed block of limestone was a vertical shaft 30.5m (100ft) deep, filled with rubble. The clearing of the shaft took some time, but at the foot of it, Reisner managed to enter a small chamber that was in total disarray. The floor was littered with mounds of crumbling wood interspersed with fragments of gold leaf. In the entrance to the chamber stood a large rectangular sarcophagus made of alabaster on top of which was what appeared to be a series of gilded tubes.

The excavation and recording of that small chamber was a triumph for Reisner. So meticulously was every fragment photographed, with the exact position in which it was found clearly marked, that it was possible to reconstruct everything precisely. What might at an earlier time have been swept aside as rotting sawdust proved to be the remains of magnificent furniture made for Queen Hetepheres, wife of Snofru and mother of Cheops.

Along one side of the chamber there had been a carrying-chair, the poles of which terminated in gold-covered palm capitals. It lay on top of a bed which had been put upside-down on the floor. In front of the bed had stood two armchairs. When reconstructed, the bed and armchairs – among the oldest extant chairs in the world – were seen to be light in design and masterpieces of the carpenter's craft.

Although the wood of the original furniture was too badly decayed to be analyzed, similar objects of later date were made of native acacia and tamarisk wood. The inlays of ebony strips overlaid with gold were glued into place using animal-based glue. The principal joints used for the furniture, however, are identical to those still in use today – mortice and tenon, dove-tailing and dowelling. The corners of the bed canopy had originally been lashed together with leather thongs, though the leather had rotted away over the centuries.

The treasure

Inside a box found between the sarcophagus and the bed was a smaller box containing two tapered wooden shafts on which were placed 20 silver bracelets each inlaid with pieces of lapis lazuli and carnelian in the form of butterflies.

The tubes on the sarcophagus, when combined with gilded wooden beams lying on the floor, proved to form a bed-canopy. The slender rods, like tent poles terminating in lotus buds, had been carved by hand and not turned on a lathe, and were probably once hung with reed mats or light curtains to give the queen cool shelter; the door frames were covered in gold. The inlaid inscriptions, in beautifully worked hieroglyphs, gave the name of her royal husband, King Snofru.

The sarcophagus

With the furniture fragments removed, attention could be focused on the sarcophagus. Since the tomb had clearly lain undisturbed since antiquity, the anticipation of finding the remains of the queen was great. Arrangements were made for an official opening, but when the lid was finally lifted, to the dismay of all present, the sarcophagus was found to be completely empty. It was removed and the empty chamber examined. It was only now that a plastered area of the wall was noticed and, when this plaster was removed, a niche was found containing a small alabaster chest. Inside this, suspended in a brine solution were the embalmed viscera of the queen – all that survived of her mortal remains.

The empty sarcophagus, together with the canopic chest, perplexed Reisner, lying as they did in what was an unviolated tomb. The layout of the objects proved two things to him: that the furniture had been pushed in hastily; and that the sarcophagus, standing next to the entrance of the chamber, had been lowered inside after the rest of the funerary equipment, a most unusual procedure.

Reisner reasoned that this was not an original burial at all, but a reburial, presumably done on the orders of the queen's son Cheops. Reisner surmised that the queen must originally have been buried near her husband Snofru, whose pyramids, at Dahshur (see p. 88–9) lie nearly

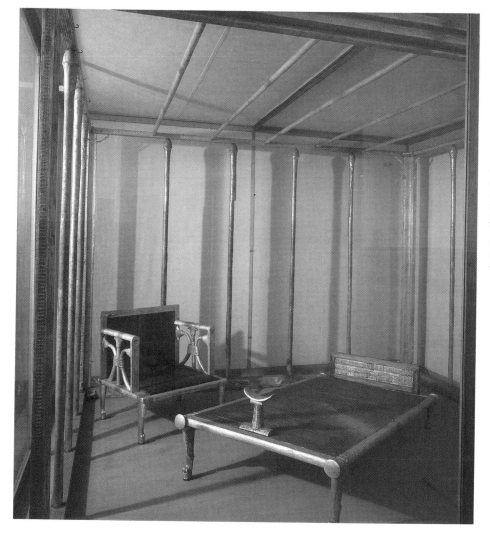

The reconstructed *furniture of Queen Hetepheres (left) stands inside a delicate wooden canopy which bears the name and titles of her husband, King Snofru. The bed, like most of those found from ancient Egypt, slopes down towards a decorated floorboard. The headrest, perhaps the most common item of household furniture, is made of gilded wood. The sleeper rested his or her cheek on the headrest; the height of the supporting stand was equal to the width of the owner's shoulder.*

48km (30mi) to the south. Reisner suggested that the original burial had been violated by robbers who, in their hurried search for jewels, had torn the queen's body from the sarcophagus, perhaps throwing it out into the desert. When the robbery was discovered, the court officials must have been too afraid to inform the king that the body of his mother had been destroyed and they had then enacted a macabre charade: an empty sarcophagus was lowered into the shaft at Giza. The king, he considered, would probably never have known that his mother's body was not within its sarcophagus, though no doubt he would have witnessed the funeral ceremonies. His intention in burying her close to his own resting place must have been so that she might share his eternity.

Whether this is the truth of what happened will probably never be known, although Reisner's romantic explanation does fit the mysterious circumstances. What is certain is

that at the time of the reburial, elaborate precautions were taken to conceal the burial, with no superstructure at all being built over the shaft to mark its location.

From the inscriptions on the objects recovered from the tomb, Hetepheres was a royal princess, the 'daughter of the God', i.e. the previous king Huni and, it is believed, one of his minor wives, Meresankh. She married her half-brother, Snofru, and gave him at least one son, Cheops, thus ensuring a wholly royal succession to the throne. Since the crown in ancient Egypt was never automatically inherited by the oldest son, her royal birth no doubt made Cheops' succession all the smoother. Clearly in the position of her reburial, close to her son's pyramid, Cheops was acknowledging the debt he owed her, while obeying one of the most important tenets of ancient Egyptian wisdom – 'Honour your mother above all other women.'

THE PYRAMIDS OF ABUSIR

The pyramids *of the Fifth Dynasty kings, Neferirkare, Niuserre and Sahure, are surrounded by buildings that are yet to be excavated. The rubble which can be seen in the foreground is part of another pyramid complex, probably that of Raneferef, also of the Fifth Dynasty.*

The Westcar Papyrus, in the Berlin Museum, records that the first three kings of the Fifth Dynasty were triplets born to the wife of an insignificant priest of Re. Archaeological evidence, in fact, suggests that what at first sight appears to be little more than legend may reflect an element of truth.

The first king of the Fifth Dynasty, Userkaf, was probably the grandson of Radjedef, the son who succeeded Cheops (*see p. 72*). His wife, Khentkawes, who may have been a daughter of Mycerinus, was the mother of two of Userkaf's successors, Sahure and Neferirkare. The sudden rise to prominence of the cult of Re during the reigns of these two kings and the other kings of the Fifth Dynasty could well have given rise to the legend.

The pyramid of Userkaf

Userkaf chose to build his pyramid at Saqqara, to the east of the Step Pyramid. To the south of it, a courtyard contained a small temple within which a superb greywacke head of the king was found. Reliefs that once embellished the walls have yet to be published, although an Australian team from McQuairie University, Sydney, has once again begun to explore the area in the hope of finding a Fifth Dynasty cemetery nearby.

Userkaf also built a sun temple, however, dedicated to the worship of Re, some 3.2km (2mi) north of his pyramid at Abusir. It was here, rather than at Saqqara, that his successors chose to build their pyramids. The site was first excavated by Ludwig Borchardt and Heinrich Schäfer between 1898 and 1902, on behalf of the Deutsche Orientgesellschaft. They ex-

amined three pyramids: those of Sahure and Neferirkare; and that of the next king, Niuserre, a little to the north of Abusir at Abu Ghurab. Associated with each of these pyramids was not only the standard causeway with valley and mortuary temples, but also a solar temple. A cache of papyri found here in 1893, the daily administrative and accounts records dealing with the organization of Neferirkare's temple, suggests that there were originally six of these sun-temples in the area, but only two – those of Userkaf and Niuserre – have been located.

The Abusir pyramids

The kings of the Fifth Dynasty chose to build their pyramids of a rubble and mud-brick core faced with limestone. When the limestone was later removed, the core collapsed. The pyramids, once around 48.8m (160ft) high, are now little more than piles of debris, and the corridors and chambers under them are blocked and too dangerous to enter.

The three pyramids of Sahure, Neferirkare and Niuserre, however, are all furnished with funerary complexes of unequalled magnificence. Borchardt estimated that the mortuary and valley temples of Sahure alone once had more than 2787sq m (30,000sq ft) of fine reliefs carved upon their walls. Most of it has been removed over the centuries to be burnt to provide lime for fertilizer.

The valley building of Sahure was once paved with polished basalt blocks, and granite columns in the form of date palms supported a ceiling painted dark blue and studded with reliefs of stars. On the walls painted reliefs showed Sahure as a sphinx trampling his enemies in the north. The causeway, long since vanished, led to a mortuary temple which, in its original state, must have had no equal in Egypt. An open courtyard, also paved with basalt, was faced with walls bearing reliefs of Sahure conquering his enemies, the Libyans and Asiatics, while his victorious army take captives, including animals. One fragmentary scene alone records the seizure of almost a million animals – sheep, gazelles, cattle and onagers (wild asses). Around the outer walls of this court, a corridor was also finely decorated with animals driven into enclosures by courtiers for the king and the crown prince to kill with their deadly arrows. On the western wall of the corridor, a sea-going expedition was depicted, with 12 ships leaving, and then returning heavily laden with cargo.

The most remarkable feature of the whole complex, however, was its drainage system. Rainwater from the roof of the mortuary temple was spat out by lion-headed gargoyles into channels below which led to an elaborate underground pipe system. Copper pipes run over 320m (350yd), the full length of the causeway, before emerging where the canal was once cut at the foot of the complex. Since all copper had to be imported from Sinai, this drainage system alone shows how effective and wealthy a ruler Sahure must have been.

The solar temples

The complex of Niuserre, excavated by Borchardt and Schäfer in 1898, shows how large and striking the solar temples once were.

In layout the solar temple of Niuserre very much resembled a pyramid complex. On the river bank, a small valley temple surrounded by houses for temple officials, led to a rising causeway. This in turn led to an open walled courtyard 100.5m (330ft) long and 76.2m (250ft) wide and dominated by a dais. On top of this stood the prototype obelisk, a pyramidal tower built up of smaller stones (later ones were made of single stones). Called the 'Benben' stone in Egyptian, it symbolized the plant that grew on the Island of Creation (see p. 128), from which the sun emerged. An altar in front of the benben stone comprised five separate alabaster slabs, each cut in the shape of an offering table, their surfaces cut in relief with loaves of bread, jars of beer and pieces of meat. A covered corridor around the inside of the enclosure wall contained scenes of Niuserre celebrating his Sed festival (see p. 66). The most

unusual reliefs came from a tiny chapel attached to the south of the base of the benben stone. Here, in superbly painted and lightly carved scenes, were depicted the three Egyptian seasons, with plants and animals flourishing under the gifts of Re, the sun god. Blocks now in Cairo and Berlin show the rotation of the agricultural year, with animals mating, giving birth and then being hunted, and plants and trees being sown, fruiting and then being harvested and pruned.

Although the pyramids of the kings of the Fifth Dynasty are badly damaged and even when complete, scarcely compared in size to those of the Fourth Dynasty kings of Giza, the complexes attached to them show that Egypt still was a power to be reckoned with at the onset of the Fifth Dynasty. The cult temples of Re are unique for the period. So closely do they resemble pyramid complexes, and evidently so closely allied were they to the pyramids of Abusir, that it is hard to say whether they are typical of temples of the Old Kingdom.

An artist's reconstruction (right) of a Fifth Dynasty solar temple complex. The main courtyard, open to the sky, where the passage of Re, the sun god, could be freely observed, was dominated by a podium and squat pyramidal altar in front of the Benben. The causeway, valley temple and buildings clustered around the Benben stone are modelled directly on the funerary pyramid complexes of earlier dynasties – even to the presence of a solar boat.

This superbly *styled head, in greywacke (a dark sandstone, with a compressed clay base), was found in the solar temple of Userkaf, first king of the Fifth Dynasty, and is generally taken to depict that ruler. It is, however, unnamed, and the lack of a royal beard and uraeus has led many scholars to suggest it is not even masculine, but perhaps depicts Neith. This ancient goddess is often associated with war – her name, in hieroglyphs, being written with a pair of crossed arrows. The headdress worn by this figure, too tall and outwardly sloping to be satisfactorily identified with the crown of Lower Egypt, is one regularly depicted worn by Neith.*

Benben stone

House of the Seasons

solar boat

causeway

valley temple

THE END OF THE OLD KINGDOM

A view of *the badly damaged Fifth Dynasty pyramid of Unas, which lies at the end of the decorated causeway. The remains of the mortuary temple can still be seen, attached to the face of the pyramid itself.*

The last two kings of the Fifth Dynasty, Isesi and Unas, chose not to build their pyramids alongside their predecessors at Abusir, but further north in the old Memphis necropolis site of Saqqara. Although the pyramid of Isesi was excavated in 1945, reports were never published and little is known of the site which today is once more covered with sand.

The pyramid of Unas, however, stands at the southwestern corner of the Step Pyramid complex, adjacent to the southern tomb (*see p. 66*). The site of the Step Pyramid it seems, was already decaying and abandoned, with sand covering the mastabas built outside the enclosure walls. The small pyramid of Unas, only 18.9m (62ft) in height when complete, and the associated buildings around it, were all constructed with re-used limestone blocks taken from the Step Pyramid.

The kings of the Sixth Dynasty built their pyramids in the same area. Today all of them are badly damaged, for the core of rubble held together by mortar of Nile mud collapsed after the outer covering of limestone was removed in antiquity. Many of them would be barely recognizable as pyramids at all were it not for the entrance shafts and passages that stand alongside them. The size and dilapidation of these pyramids has led many scholars to conjecture that the monarchy at this period was impoverished, the combined result of vast expenditures of manpower and resources on generations of huge pyramids, increased foreign pressure requiring army expeditions to be sent constantly from Egypt, and diminution in royal estates as tracts of land were given as reward to the king's faithful courtiers. This land, many believed, never returned to the Crown.

It is now understood, however, that none of this has much substance archaeologically. Estates were awarded by the king to vassals on condition that only the produce of the land could be disposed of, and not the land itself. The land reverted to the king when use for it had died out along with the mortuary cult of its new 'owner'. Foreign pressure was little greater during this period than it had been earlier in the Old Kingdom, especially when the massive foreign campaigns of Snofru (recorded on the Palermo stone annals) are taken into consideration. There seems to have been, on the contrary, a general decline in Egyptian wealth and status which affected king and nobleman alike. Some of the increasing poverty may have been the result of a series of poor Nile inundations, or possibly even a minor change in the climate, but it was also undoubtedly due in part to generations of administrators having abandoned their home towns to live, serve the king and die in Memphis.

The pyramid of Unas

The identity of the owner of this pyramid was noted on a small inscription carved on its south face by Prince Khaemwese, son of Ramesses II (*see p. 23*). Maspero found the entrance shaft in 1881 and, unlike previous pyramids, the entrance was not in the face of the pyramid but under the limestone paved courtyard north of it. A descending passage led to a square chamber, off which were three small storerooms. A stone portcullis once sealed the entrance to the adjacent burial chamber, which still contains a stone sarcophagus. When opened by Maspero, this was found to contain the remains of a mummy whose location is now unknown. For the first time ever, the walls of both chambers were decorated. Around the dais on which the sarcophagus stands, fine alabaster (calcite) panels are carved in relief to resemble elaborately niched palace-façading with a false door, all infilled with red and blue paint. More importantly, the other walls are totally covered with hieroglyphic inscriptions, the first occurrence of the Pyramid Texts (see p. 168).

These comprise a total of 228 magical spells all aimed at speeding the king's soul through to his afterlife. Some of them contain ideas and sentence structures that are very old indeed, probably predynastic, while others were probably contemporary with the building of the pyramid. They were deeply cut into the walls and then infilled with blue paste, making them easily legible. It is clear that the hieroglyphic signs themselves were considered a magical threat to the king's soul, however, for some of the potentially dangerous ones – lions, reptiles and armed human figures – are shown either cut in half or deliberately damaged in some way, to render them harmless.

Outside the pyramid, a mortuary temple on the east wall led to a long causeway, the finest to survive on any pyramid complex. This was excavated first by Selim, and then Abdessalam Hassan, from 1937 onwards, and was found to be 685.8m (750yd) long. It originally took the form of an enclosed passage, the inside faces of the side walls covered in delicate raised relief with scenes recording events from the king's life and reign. Many of the scenes, besides being among the earliest royal autobiographical records, are unique in their own right. One scene records the shipping of ready-carved granite columns from Aswan to the site; another shows the smelting of gold and silver, and the hammering of precious vessels; a third, a hunting scene, depicts the varieties of animals probably common in Egypt at this early date, from hyenas, wild dogs, leopards and giraffes to the humble hedgehog! The most remarkable scene of all, though, is the depiction on one loose block of the emaciated victims of famine,

their bodies reduced almost to skeletons. Unfortunately, the context of the block has been lost, so it is unclear whether they were Egyptians or foreigners. In any case, the scene appears to confirm other inscriptions of the same period which refer to starvation throughout Egypt and, presumably, neighbouring countries. In the light of the misery and suffering famine has brought in modern times to the people of Africa, the relief reflects some of the severe problems Unas had to face.

The tomb of Nefer

While restoring the causeway in 1964 the Inspector of Antiquities, Ahmed Moussa, discovered an earlier tomb that had been covered with sand at the time the causeway was built. Unas' builders, it is believed, found the tomb by chance and rifled through it before covering it over and building the causeway over the top of it. It is the tomb of a singer named Nefer and his wife Kahai. The walls are carved in superb reliefs, one of which depicts Kahai seated with a child on her knee watching dancers; another shows Nefer at work in his own vegetable garden, sowing and tending onions, radishes and lettuces. Under the stone superstructure were several shafts, one of which had collapsed in antiquity. When emptied in 1966, this was found to contain an intact mummy. Although often referred to as that of Nefer, a wooden box lying next to the body was inscribed for 'the Chief of weavers, Watay'. The mummy still lies in the tomb which is rarely open to the public.

The mummy of Watay has survived by chance, giving us one of the earliest examples of mummification. Within the shell of painted plaster, little remains of the body. It seems likely that at this date the body was not desiccated by being buried in natron, but was simply bandaged. The impression of Watay's face is most striking, however, with its faintly smiling lips. Moustaches, in this instance painted on the shell, were commonly worn by men during the Old Kingdom.

Among the more unusual scenes to be found on the walls of mastaba tombs at Saqqara is this illustration of the performing of a circumcision. It is in the tomb of Ankhmahor, a physician, and is opposite the entrance to the pyramid of Teti. Ankhmahor is depicted performing the operation on a grown man using a flint knife while a friend restrains the arms of the unfortunate patient. Herodotus comments that Egyptian men were circumcised for cleanliness' sake. This operation probably took place at puberty.

Mastaba tombs

Clustered around all the pyramids of the kings of the Old Kingdom are streets of stone tombs in which the courtiers and families of the monarchs chose to be buried. These low, rectangular tombs are smaller copies of those used for the kings of the First and Second Dynasties at Saqqara. Although only the earliest ones are solid stone superstructures with sealed inner stone chambers, and the later ones are a complex series of rooms and passages, they are generally all still known as mastaba tombs (see p. 59).

The mastabas around the pyramids of Giza have been excavated and reasonably well documented, but in this they are exceptional. The vast necropolis of Saqqara is virtually unexcavated. A sonar survey of the plateau was undertaken in 1980 by a Californian research team, and they confirmed that below the sands lie hundreds of hidden chambers. Most of these, from experience of the area, will have superstructures of stone that are decorated. Little is known of the areas of Dahshur, now a military zone and thus prohibited to visitors, and Abusir (see p. 80). Around the Meidum pyramid, undulations in the surface of the sand indicate numerous tombs.

Towards the end of the Old Kingdom with the gradual separation of courtiers from the king's orbit, many nobles had their tombs cut in their own home areas. Among the best examples of these, though little visited, are the Sixth Dynasty tombs at Qubbet el Hawa on the west bank at Aswan.

Purpose of the mastaba

The aim of the mastaba tomb was to ensure the eternal well-being of the deceased. It is clear both from the Pyramid Texts (see p. 168) and from inscriptions on the walls of the mastaba that the soul of everyone except the king was to be excluded from an afterlife with the gods. Instead it was to continue to inhabit the tomb and thus needed to return to it daily for offerings of food and drink. The undecorated burial chamber was cut into the rock often at the foot of very deep vertical shafts. Close to the shaft entrance, a nearby wall would be decorated with a false door carved in raised relief. Often the centre of this false door would be filled with a carving of the deceased, as though it enticed the ka (see Glossary) to enter through it. In some cases, as in the tomb of Mereruka, this would be made into a statue.

In order that the soul had something to identify with to encourage its return, it was vital that the body should be preserved if at all possible. To meet all exigencies, however, other representations of the deceased person would be placed in the tomb, including relief carving, figures and statues. Often the latter would be enclosed in a walled-up side chamber called a serdab (Arabic for cellar) with only a small hole from which the statue could peer. In some tombs a smaller serdab was built into the foot of the burial shaft as well, and within this was a stone portrait head of the dead person; these have come to be known as 'reserve heads'.

The scenes carved on the walls of the chambers of these mastaba tombs are among the finest ever executed by the ancient sculptor. They are so finely detailed and perceptively styled that often they achieve a liveliness rarely found in stone carving. They depict scenes of the production of food, drink and material goods, from initial stages through to the preparation and offering of meals to the deceased. As a result of the magical importance of all the scenes, the hieroglyphs and the reliefs all orientate towards the focal point of the tomb, the false door. The finest mastaba tomb reliefs are to be seen at Saqqara.

The tomb of Ti

This tomb contains some of the finest scenes in any mastaba. Ti was a scribe whose job involved supervising building works that included the pyramids and sun temples of Abusir for kings of the Fifth Dynasty (about 2200 BC). The entrance door leads to an open courtyard with the remains of 12 square pillars, in the centre of which is the open entrance to the underground burial chamber. In the southwest corner of this court, a narrow passage leads to two chambers and the serdab.

The corridor is decorated with finely preserved scenes that are still brightly coloured. On the left, beside the usual scenes of food preparation, workmen are shown moving statues on sledges while Ti oversees them. Opposite this, ships are shown in full sail, presumably bringing stone for use in the king's building works.

The larger of the rooms has two central pillars made of limestone though painted to resemble granite. The walls around them are full of life, with farming and fishing scenes. To the left of the door a famous relief shows cattle being driven through a stream, their legs, indi-

A scene of hunting *in the marshes from the tomb of Mereruka at Saqqara. Five men punt a papyrus raft along a verdant Nile bank, packed with reeds and teeming with wildlife. Nesting lapwings protect their young from a marauding ichneumon – a type of mongoose – either by spreading their wings over their chicks, or by mobbing the intruder. In the river, one adult hippopotamus seizes and kills a basking crocodile, while behind it another crocodile turns the tables, waiting to devour a newborn hippopotamus.*

cated behind zigzag lines, appearing distorted as if behind water. At the front of the scene, a boy carries a calf on his back to encourage its mother to follow. This cow, though reluctant to walk through the water, raises her head, her eyes and mouth wide open as she tries to reach her offspring.

One of the finest scenes in the room shows Ti on a papyrus skiff hunting for birds along the marshy banks of the river. Hidden among the reeds are hippopotami, one of which has caught a baby crocodile in its mouth.

The tomb of Mereruka

Mereruka married the daughter of King Teti of the early Sixth Dynasty, and his mastaba lies facing the pyramid of his father-in-law. Unlike that of Ti, this is a highly elaborate complex of 33 rooms, one section dedicated to himself, the second to his wife, Heret-waketkhet, and the third to their son Meryteti. Although the reliefs are not as well preserved as Ti's, the mastaba has several unique features.

Walking into the entrance, the visitor enters Mereruka's own complex. Walking a little to the right and straight ahead, the principal chamber is approached with its false door. Through this, the figure of Mereruka himself emerges, the standing statue with its left foot forwards appearing to stride out of the wall. Most of the paint on this life-size figure is preserved, so that it appears startlingly real.

The princess's complex at the left of the entrance shows her receiving offerings due to a king's daughter, including a selection of finely carved furniture , while she herself relaxes and watches dancing girls.

The rock-cut tombs of Aswan

Qubbet el Hawa – Arabic for 'Dome of the Winds' – stands on the west bank at Aswan, and the terrace of the rock-cut chambers can be seen easily from the town. Long ramps in front of several of them slope steeply down to the river; these are coffin slides up which the funeral goods were hauled. Several of the tombs date from the Sixth Dynasty.

Although the climb is hard and steep, the tombs are well worth the visit. Of particular interest is the tomb of Sabni, whose father was murdered on a visit to Nubia. Sabni went south to retrieve his father's body and punish the killers. That he was successful is proved by the next-door tomb of Mekhu, his father.

The tomb of Harkhuf, a merchant trader, bears a long autobiographical text on the façade relating how he journeyed to Nubia where he obtained a 'dancing dwarf'. The King, Pepi II, only a little boy, wrote to Harkhuf to congratulate him on his acquisition, and to beseech him to guard the dwarf well, 'for My Majesty wishes to see him more than all the produce from the land of Punt'. The letter is carved, in full, on the front face of the tomb.

TREASURE OF THE PRINCESSES

This gold diadem *belonged to Princess Sit-Hathor-Yunet, a daughter of King Sesostris II of the Twelfth Dynasty, and was found with other jewels near her father's pyramid in 1914 by Flinders Petrie and Guy Brunton. A narrow band of plain gold is studded with 15 rosettes inlaid with carnelian and blue and green frit. Three of the rosettes have tiny hinges below them, also of gold, to which are fixed twin streamers of gold made to resemble ribbons. The uraeus-serpent at the front, signifying her royal birth, is inlaid also with frit, the head being of lapis lazuli and the eyes, carnelian. The uraeus is detachable, being mounted on a flat square of gold that slides between bars fixed to the diadem.*

Although the security precautions of the pyramids had been taken in vain, some treasure did survive, by accident. It belonged not to the kings, however, whose great funerary monuments could scarcely be overlooked by robbers, but to their wives and daughters.

In 1894, the French archaeologist, Jacques de Morgan, excavated in the vicinity of the Twelfth Dynasty mud-brick pyramids of Dahshur (*see p. 88–9*). In several tombs he found a number of items of jewellery of exquisite workmanship, many pieces, it is believed, actually on and around the mummies of their owners. De Morgan, unfortunately, retrieved the pieces in great haste, recording virtually nothing of their original appearance or position. Even the elementary sketches he made were of little help when it came to their reconstruction in the Cairo Museum.

De Morgan had found jewellery belonging to two royal women: Princess Itaweret, probably a daughter of Amenemhet II; and her sister, Princess Khnumet, who later may have been associated on the throne with her father or her brother. The jewellery of both women showed many unusual non-Egyptian features, with elements that were common in the art of Syria and the Aegean islands.

Several months later, De Morgan found a second cache, belonging this time to Princess Sit-Hathor, daughter of Sesostris II, and Queen Mereret. Both were probably wives of Sesostris III. Again, however, details of the discovery of these pieces was virtually unrecorded.

In 1914, however, working in the same area, Flinders Petrie and Guy Brunton had the great fortune to find yet more pieces of jewellery belonging to ladies of the Middle Kingdom. They lay in a hidden corner of a robbed tomb. The tomb had been flooded in antiquity, and the jewellery, lying originally in a wooden casket, had fallen on to the floor – probably dropped by robbers – and mingled in the mud. The excavation was a daunting prospect, and Petrie and Brunton worked with infinite caution, marking the location of each tiny bead before removing it from the solidified mud, washing and photographing it. Brunton ate and slept in the tomb for almost two weeks, frequently working late into the night, using a pin to separate each delicate fragment. The pieces belonged to yet another princess, Sit-Hathor-Yunet, another daughter of Sesostris II. When the jewellery was later meticulously reconstructed by H. E. Winlock, in the Metropolitan Museum of Art, New York, using Brunton and Petrie's notes, their caution was fully repaid. From these reconstructions, the Cairo Museum was able to look at De Morgan's finds with a new eye, and re-thread its own pieces in a more accurate fashion.

The jewels found in the Twelfth Dynasty caches are rightly considered the finest ever found in Egypt, beside which those of Tutankhamun (*see p. 112–13*) appear heavy and crudely fashioned. Their delicacy and craftsmanship have scarcely been equalled to this day.

The place of jewellery
The Egyptians loved jewellery and, if they could afford it, both men and women wore it in profusion. Tomb pictures show that even the poorest members of society would fashion neckbands of simple wild flowers; and much Egyptian jewellery, in fact, was created in imitation of these natural motifs.

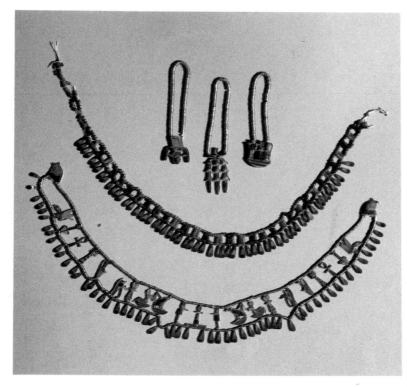

Some of the jewellery that belonged to Queen Khnumet, a wife of Amenemhet II, who was buried at Dahshur. Her tomb was found by De Morgan in 1894, though the jewellery was badly excavated, and has had to be reconstructed by deduction. The falcon collar (bottom) is of gold, inlaid with tiny pieces of lapis lazuli, carnelian and turquoise. The symbols are hieroglyphs representing life, prosperity, stability, kingship and unity. The three jewels shown at the top have been described as 'motto clasps' or armlets, but they could also have been ornaments for hanging over the ears. The jewels in them, like the collar, are hieroglyphs for joy, birth, life and protection.

Gold was found in Egypt from earliest times, the first pieces probably being nuggets either washed downstream by the Nile or picked up in the eastern desert. The first indication of a gold trading place was found in predynastic Nubt, or Naqada (see p. 51). From the start of the Old Kingdom, army expeditions were sent to Nubia to mine quartz lodes for gold. The mines there are approached via extraordinarily narrow and deep shafts. The quartz was apparently shattered by fires lit around it and the gold extracted on the surface by crushing the debris. When the mines finally failed around the middle of the New Kingdom, gold was brought instead from the Eastern desert. Here it was not so plentiful, and its extraction from rocks was harsh. Many prisoners, condemned to working in these regions, never returned alive.

The gold could be worked cold, by hammering it into shape, or melted and cast. Goldsmiths' workshops were strictly controlled by the vizier on the king's behalf, and the gold objects manufactured there belonged to the king and were his to bestow as he pleased.

Precious stones used as inlay for jewellery or for beads were admired for the brilliance and deepness of their colour rather than their translucence. Favourite stones were lapis lazuli, which had to be imported along trade routes from the mines of what would now be Afghanistan; turquoise, imported from the Sinai Peninsula, and red carnelian from the eastern desert. Green stones, either malachite (copper ore) or beryl, were used less frequently. All these stones were cabochon-cut and polished, rather than faceted.

Transparent gems, such as amethyst and garnet, were occasionally used but seem to have been regarded as poor substitutes for the more valued stones. Often they were used alone, as though they could not stand close proximity to brighter coloured stones. Rock crystal, used frequently as eye inserts (see p. 151), was sometimes mounted over a coloured paste base in a gold setting.

Favourite pieces of jewellery included chokers, bracelets, armlets and anklets in the Old Kingdom; and broad collars and earrings from the Middle Kingdom onwards. Pectorals (pendants suspended from bead necklaces) grew heavier and more elaborate from the New Kingdom onwards. From the reign of Amenhotep II in the Eighteenth Dynasty, men as well as women wore earrings. These were stud-mounted for use in pierced ear lobes. The holes made in the ears were stretched using a series of larger and larger studs until quite large discs, up to 19mm (³⁄₄in) in diameter could be worn.

The mounting of stones in gold settings was frequently employed. So scarce were the favoured lapis lazuli and turquoise that even in the late predynastic period, substitutes were sought. From this time onwards, glass was made, with silica sand fired with malachite to produce a blue/green friable material called frit. This, when ground into powder, could be used as a pigment base for paint, or could be sprinkled into prepared gold settings and fired at a low temperature a second time. This glass inlay, used as enamelling or cloisonné work, was highly regarded as a cheaper alternative to the rarer stones.

When the glass glaze was applied either to a carved steatite piece or a fired quartz-clay base, using natron as a fixative, the resulting material, incorrectly called 'faience' by excavators in the 19th century, was also often used as a substitute for real stones. Faience was frequently used for beads, earrings, amulets and multi-coloured inlays, especially during the New Kingdom.

DAHSHUR: THE LAST PYRAMIDS

The area of Dahshur, *above, is dominated by the Bent Pyramid of early Old Kingdom date. In the foreground, the heap of rubble topped by some mud bricks is all that remains of the Middle Kingdom pyramid of Amenemhet III.*

After the collapse of the Old Kingdom and the chaos of the First Intermediate Period, a family of soldiers from Luxor succeeded in restoring some order and founded the Eleventh Dynasty. The tombs of these kings all lie in their home town, cut into the cliffs of the west bank, with one exception, arguably that of the finest king of the dynasty, Mentuhotep Nebhepetre. He, in a revolutionary design never to be repeated, was buried under a small pyramid that stood on top of his mortuary temple at Deir el Bahri (*see p. 142*). The last king of the Eleventh Dynasty reigned but briefly and apparently died without heir. His successor, Amenemhet I, appears to have been a vizier of noble southern extraction who took the throne by default.

Early Middle Kingdom pyramids

Amenemhet I came from a different village from that of the kings of the Eleventh Dynasty, a village where the little-known god Amun was venerated. In taking the throne, he not only elevated Amun to national status, but decided to establish control from a new city. Slightly south of Memphis, which was probably still functioning as an administrative centre independent of the monarch, he founded a city called 'Amenemhet-Itj-tawy' – 'Amenemhet who seizes the two lands'. This town, although still not located exactly, clearly lay between the Nile and the Faiyum oasis. Here, in the vicinity of Lisht, Dahshur, Illahun and Hawara, the kings built their pyramids, the last pyramids created on such a grand scale in Egypt.

The area of Lisht was first excavated, though cursorily, by the Swiss archaeologists Gustave Jequier and J. Gautier in 1894. They identified the pyramids of the first two kings of the dynasty, Amenemhet I and Sesostris I. New York's Metropolitan Museum of Art re-excavated the pyramid complex of Sesostris I between 1908 and 1934, finding two splendid painted wooden statues of a king bricked up in a nearby tomb. Like previous pyramids, a subsidiary pyramid lay within the enclosure wall; but uniquely another nine smaller pyramids, belonging to the king's wives and daughters, encircle the whole complex. The main burial chambers of the pyramids of both Amenemhet I and Sesostris I have never been able to be fully explored because they are completely flooded.

It is clear by this time that the architects of the pyramids had been playing a losing game with tomb robbers. Seven hundred years of pyramid building utilizing almost every conceivable type of ruse to mislead intruders had been to no avail. The tombs had all been entered and plundered. The next three pyramids, built in Dahshur and Hawara, show how desperate the designers had become in their desire to foil the thieves.

The Dahshur pyramid of Sesostris II has its entrance, unusually, on the south face, a ploy which exasperated Petrie for two full seasons. The architect had also made use of a natural outcrop of rock to form the core of the pyramid, overlaying it first with mud brick and then adding a fine limestone outer covering. The pyramids of Sesostris III and Amenemhet II, flanking that of Sesostris II, were also built around a mud-brick core, with underground passages and chambers of labyrinthine complexity. De Morgan, who excavated here in 1894, spent more than six months trying to find a way in, though he did succeed in finding a cache of treasure (*see p. 86–7*) and two wooden boats in pits.

The pyramid of Hawara

But it is the pyramid of Amenemhet III at Hawara that demonstrates the lengths to which the architects were prepared to go. Petrie's excavations here took him many months of hard labour. The mud-brick pyramid stands 58m (190ft) high. Its entrance, on the south face like the other Twelfth Dynasty pyramids, leads apparently to a small empty chamber; a narrow passage beyond that leads nowhere at all. In the roof of this passage, however, Petrie discovered that a huge stone, weighing in excess of 22 tons, had been made to slide sideways, giving access to an upper corridor. This, again, seemed to lead nowhere; but a hidden brick door in one wall finally led to a third passage, with two more sliding roof blocks to be encountered before an ante-chamber was reached. Here again measures were taken to mislead the robber. Two vertical shafts on the floor were filled with rubble. They, like the passages before them, led no-where, but were simply built to frustrate thieves. One of the walls was also clearly bricked up; beyond it lay nothing but a solid wall. Even the burial chamber itself was cunn-ingly devised. A solid block of quartzite 6.7m (22ft) long and 2.4m (8ft) wide was lowered into the pyramid as it was being built, and then excavated to form a hollow chamber. Inside this a granite sarcophagus was placed. On top of this solid chamber large roofing slabs, each more than 1m (3ft) thick, were laid. The King's body had to be lowered under these and laid in the sarcophagus before the roof slabs were dropped, effectively sealing it inside a solid stone.

Yet still the pyramid was plundered. Probably out of sheer frustration the thieves had simply dropped a lighted torch into the chamber and incinerated everything.

The labyrinth

While Petrie worked at the pyramid of Amene-mhet III, in 1888, he also took the opportunity to excavate the surrounding area. Here to his delight he uncovered the foundations of a huge building, 305m (1000ft) long and 244m (800ft) wide. It was the remains of a mortuary building

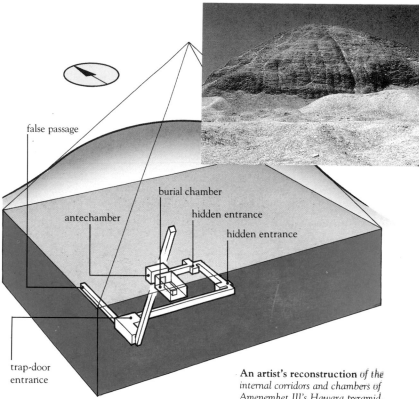

false passage

burial chamber

antechamber

hidden entrance

hidden entrance

trap-door entrance

An artist's reconstruction *of the internal corridors and chambers of Amenemhet III's Hawara pyramid. Although it appears simple in its design, it was deceptively complex, with many hidden doorways and false leads. The inset shows the external remains, still standing to a height of around 45m (150ft). The entrance was at the foot of this, the south face, and is now blocked.*

and palace built by Amenemhet III that still stood intact in Graeco-Roman times. Visitors to Egypt, including Herodotus, flocked to see it. 'The pyramids,' he wrote, 'are astonishing structures . . . but the labyrinth surpasses them all . . . Inside, the building is of two stories and contains 3000 rooms, of which half are under-ground and the other half above them... It is hard to believe they are all the work of men. The baffling and winding corridors from room to room and courtyard to courtyard were an endless wonder to me . . . The walls are covered with carved figures and each courtyard is faced with superb white marble, surrounded by a colonnade.'

Even Petrie was impressed with the outline of what he found. Yet little remained to be seen, and most of his reconstruction had to be based on the accounts of classical visitors.

By the close of the Middle Kingdom, around 1650 BC, despite every initiative and trick employed in their building, pyramids had failed in their sole objective – to house a mortal king's remains throughout eternity. So complex are the methods used in some that one is forced to speculate that the pyramids must have been robbed by the very people who placed the king's remains inside them. Future kings would have to devise new ways to build their tombs if they were to achieve eternal peace.

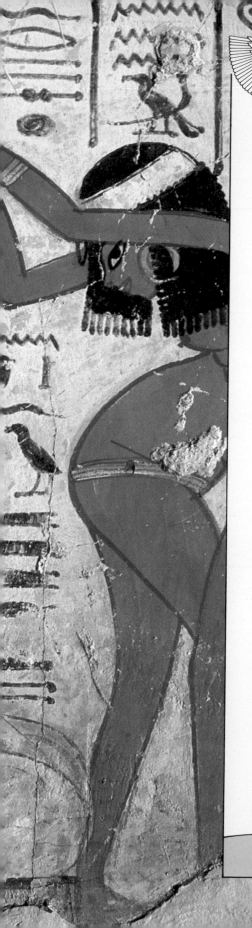

THE SHIFTING SANDS

IV

'The people of Sais buried all the Kings that came from the country inside the temple precinct . . . The tomb of Amasis is in the temple court, a great cloistered building of stone decorated with pillars in imitation of palm trees and other costly ornaments. Within the courtyard is a room with double doors, and behind those doors is the burial chamber.'
Herodotus, Book II, 172

From earliest times, the severe limitations of fertile land in Egypt meant that the dead were placed in shallow graves and tombs cut into the rock in the desert. The desert sand, fine and dry, moves at the slightest whisper of breeze, uncovering the entrances to some tombs and covering others. Sometimes travellers or archaeologists find these tombs, only to lose them again to the shifting sand.

Like the kings in their pyramids, the Egyptian dead went to their eternity with their precious belongings gathered around them, and these almost unfailingly attracted the robber. Very few tombs discovered have survived intact. In some cases, it is clear that the gravediggers themselves often broke into neighbouring burial chambers to rob them, while others that did survive early depredation were discovered and emptied by thieves over thousands of years. But even though the burial chambers are often found empty, their wonderfully preserved painted walls gives the archaeologist more information than treasure ever could.

In this wall painting from the tomb of Nebamun at Luxor, female musicians, one of whom plays a double flute, accompany dancers at a banquet – an entertainment intended to continue for eternity.

THE ROCK TOMBS OF BENI HASAN

**John Garstang
(1876–1956)**

While studying mathematics at Oxford, Garstang became interested in archaeology. His first experience of actual excavation was on Roman sites in Britain, and it was not until 1900 that he visited Egypt. Liverpool University created an honorary post for him, and the recognition this afforded allowed Garstang to raise enough money to found the Liverpool Institute of Archaeology, on whose behalf he excavated many sites, including Beni Hasan, and from 1909–14, Meröe in Nubia. From 1920 onwards, his attention was directed to sites in Palestine; he died in Beirut.

As a schoolboy of only 14 years of age, Percy Newberry, born in London, visited the British Museum so often that his enthusiasm attracted the attention of Dr Poole, head of the Coins and Medals department and founder member of the Egyptian Exploration Fund (see p. 39). Poole introduced the boy to Flinders Petrie who took an instant liking to him, allowing him to assist with the unpacking of Egyptian objects freshly arrived from excavations. From this auspicious start, Newberry's future as an Egyptologist was almost assured and when, in 1890, Newberry was appointed to record the tombs of Beni Hasan for the archaeological survey, it was Petrie who not only advised him on things as varied as how to work and what to take with him, but also accompanied the young man, and personally introduced him to Egypt.

The tombs of Beni Hasan, rock-cut 'caves' that stand side by side in a row on the cliff face on the east side of the Nile in Middle Egypt, had been open for many years; all had been robbed in antiquity and were visited regularly by those who sailed past them. Yet they had never been copied before; and over the following four years, Newberry meticulously recorded every scene on their walls, the results being published in two volumes in 1893.

Less than 10 years later, another young English archaeologist, John Garstang, arrived at Beni Hasan, not to work upon the large tombs so admirably recorded by Newberry, but to investigate the hillside below them. Within two seasons he had uncovered and investigated hundreds of tomb shafts cut vertically into the rock belonging not to the nobles of the area, but to the ordinary people who had served them. At the foot of the shafts he found many intact burials, from which a reconstruction of life and death in provincial Egypt could be made, a part of Egyptian history little known before this time.

The work of Newberry and Garstang, later Brunner Professor and Reader in Egyptology at Liverpool University, established Beni Hasan as a site that yielded fundamental information about life in Egypt during the early years of the Middle Kingdom.

The history of Beni Hasan

Following the decline in the effectiveness of the monarchy at the end of the Old Kingdom, many powerful nobles left the court of Memphis and returned to their own home towns. Beni Hasan had been an important town in Middle Egypt since at least the Old Kingdom, being the head of the Oryx Nome (i.e. capital of its province). From the end of the Old Kingdom to the reign of Sesostris III, the monarchs had wielded great influence locally. Choosing to have rock-cut chambers for tombs, they employed local workmen to decorate them, and they established their own ranks of administration. When the power of the local governors was curtailed by Sesostris III, burials in the region ceased.

The rock-cut tombs

The façades of several of the tombs have columned entrances, with the columns cut from the face of the rock. Inside, the single chamber often has columns cut into it. The walls of the tombs are painted in horizontal registers, or bands, that run right around the walls. The themes of the paintings were those used in the mastabas of the end of the Old Kingdom (see p. 84–5) – scenes such as the provision of food and hunting in the marshes – but because the work at Beni Hasan was carried out by local, untrained craftsmen, often the execution is odd. Figures are often disproportionate, with long, stick-like limbs, and are painted in unusual colours, with pinks, greys and oranges used instead of the bold primary colours that are more recognizably Egyptian.

Other events represented appear to be specifically of local interest. Whole lines of wrestling scenes, dancers and children playing games, if followed quickly with the eye, appear almost to move because the artists painted series of consecutive movements. In one of the finest tombs, that of Khnumhotep, a governor in the early Twelfth Dynasty, the visit of a group of nomads is recorded. This caravan, bearing quantities of eye paint to trade, shows the nomads dressed in brightly coloured fringed robes. In 1974, Dr Ahmed Fakhry noted that these were identical to those shown in later scenes in Bahriya Oasis. Two children of the Bedouin merchants are also shown unusually riding in baskets that are slung over the back of a donkey.

The shaft tombs

Unlike the 30.5m (100ft) shafts cut in the rock at Memphis, the courtiers and families of the governors of Beni Hasan utilized chambers only 3 to 9m (10 to 30ft) deep. The entrances, only .9m sq (3ft sq), are scattered all over the hillside below the rock-cut tombs, some very close to

their neighbours. The chamber at the foot of the shaft was invariably very small and undecorated; barely large enough to hold a coffin. Garstang excavated hundreds of these chambers, registered by number from 1 to at least 888. In some cases the workers who cut the shafts had availed themselves of the proximity of other shafts to break through into the next-door chamber to rob it.

The ownership of these tombs was recorded not on the surface (only 10 stelae were found on the site altogether) nor in the wall paintings, but on the brilliantly painted wooden coffins. These coffins usually were inscribed with prayers to Osiris or Anubis (see p. 134–35), while a pair of eyes were painted on the side through which the deceased, by magic, could see out. Spells painted on the inside ensured the passage of the deceased through to the afterlife (see p. 169), while often on the floor of the coffin a 'map' of the underworld was painted to direct the soul on its journey.

Many of the coffins contained multiple burials, often of what appeared to be entire families. Many of the bodies were badly mummified or simply swathed hastily in linen bandages. It has never been established satisfactorily whether they were all buried at the same time, or whether they could have been placed together at later dates.

The most remarkable features of these tombs, however, were the hundreds of brilliantly painted wooden models that were placed in virtually every chamber. Since the walls of the tombs were unpainted, the needs of the de-

ceased would be supplied eternally by hundreds of tiny figures busily occupied in model bakeries, granaries, butchers' shops, carpenters' workshops and any number of other industries. In most of the tombs, model boats were found, with rigging and sails intact, manned by crews of small wooden sailors. The tiny human figures, generally no more than 15cm (6in) tall and often about 7.5cm (3in), are perfectly formed, complete with painted wigs, jointed arms and often real linen kilts. The information regarding the organization of crafts and industries that these models have supplied, together with evidence from the burials themselves, has enabled archaeologists to reconstruct details of a period and a group of people about which very little had previously been known.

The tombs of *the governors of the First Intermediate Period and early Middle Kingdom, and those of the courtiers around them, were lavishly provided with tiny painted wooden models to 'work' for them in the afterlife. The picture above shows a complete set of models as they were found on top of a wooden coffin in Tomb 366 in Beni Hasan. The beautifully painted group (top) demonstrates a range of daily activities: a butcher slaughtering an ox, a brewer soaking barley bread for beer, a water carrier bringing jars of water, a woman rolling grain in a saddle quern to make flour, and a couple pounding dough.*

VALLEY OF THE KINGS: BELZONI'S EXPLOITS

The paintings *in the tomb of Prince Mentuhirkhopeshef, discovered by Belzoni, are some of the best preserved in the Valley of the Kings. Here the young prince, wearing an elaborate costume of diaphanous linen over an underskirt bound by a coloured sash, offers a leg of beef – considered by the Egyptians the prime cut – to an image of Ptah, the god of Memphis.*

While staying in Luxor, in 1816, Belzoni visited the Valley of the Kings where he admired the wall paintings in the tomb of Ramesses III. He had his attention drawn to the royal sarcophagus and marked it down for removal. But it was no doubt his accidental discovery there of the sarcophagus lid in accumulated flood water in the tomb that excited his curiosity as to what else might remain concealed in the valley. He started by walking through the valley noting dark and light patterns in the accumulations of rubble, paying special attention to depressions that might indicate other tomb entrances.

Early successes
Belzoni was rewarded almost at once. In the west valley, little explored to this day, he observed a gap between some stones, 'I happened to have a stick with me and thrust it into the hole . . . I found it to penetrate very deep . . . In less than two hours all the stones were taken away, and I went in.'

Since hieroglyphic inscriptions could not at the time be read, Belzoni was unable to identify the owner of the tomb. The structure was badly damaged and contained little to excite Belzoni's interest, except for one wall painting of 12 baboons, from which he called it 'the tomb of the 12 monkeys'. We now know that the tomb had belonged to King Ay, successor to Tutankhamun. The tomb had perhaps been begun for the boy king himself, but was incomplete at his sudden death and had been used by Ay.

Belzoni initially stayed in Luxor for only a few weeks, moving southwards to Abu Simbel (*see p. 176–77*). The following August, 1817, however, he returned, and immediately made an agreement with local people to be allowed to dig uninterrupted in the Valley of the Kings. He went back, at once, to where he had discovered Ay's tomb and immediately chose a nearby depression to investigate. After only two days clearing rubble, his workmen came upon an ancient wall, whereupon, with great panache, he commanded them to create a battering ram, the more speedily to effect an entrance. It was his recording of this crude method of exploration that was later to blacken his reputation as an archaeologist.

Inside this tomb (No. 25), he recorded finding eight mummies in coffins 'all painted, and one with a large covering thrown upon it'. Whose these mummies were is today completely unknown, although from their isolated position in the west valley and his description

of them, they must have belonged to high-ranking people rather than royalty – possibly high priests from the temple of Karnak. The tomb was not rich enough to give him cause for delay, and he moved at once to the main valley, the eastern section.

Within three days he was clambering into yet another tomb, that of Prince Mentuhirkhopeshef of the Twentieth Dynasty. Although it too was unfinished, the paintings on the wall were the finest he had yet seen. 'This first success,' he wrote, 'gave me much encouragement, as it assured me that I was correct in my idea of discovering tombs.' Undaunted, he moved his men to another area, and later that very same day, entered yet another tomb. Although completely unpainted, he did find two mummies, which he described as 'females, and their hair pretty, long and well preserved, though it was easily separated from the body by pulling it a little'. Comments of this sort have inevitably served to anger many scholars.

The following day, a party of English visitors requested Belzoni to show them what he had found. As he was talking to them, a workman ran up in great excitement, to inform him that yet another tomb had been found. It was to prove to be the tomb of Ramesses I, the first ruler of the Nineteenth Dynasty, and quite beautifully painted. Once again the sarcophagus was intact, and the visitors were treated to the first sight of two mummies lying within it, although they were from later burials. Two statues, 2m (6ft 6in) tall, stood to one side, now recognized to be the painted and gilded 'guardian' statues of the kind later found in Tutankhamun's tomb. These statues were later bought by the British Museum.

A tomb 'of the first rate'
Four days later, his 'excavations' delayed by sandstorms, Belzoni returned to the valley. Close by the tomb of Ramesses I, there was a large hole filled with rubble, which he decided to investigate at once. The workmen found the tomb entrance 6.1m (20ft) lower down. The painted walls he saw through it suggested 'that the tomb was of the first rate'. Within hours, a passageway had been cleared and a corridor uncovered. The paintings and reliefs along it were without equal in the whole of the valley. Today it is known to have been the tomb of Seti I of the Nineteenth Dynasty and the finest tomb ever found in the Valley of the Kings. Although now deteriorating rapidly, when

Belzoni first entered it he could scarcely believe its antiquity: the walls appeared freshly painted. A columned hall led them into another chamber 'covered with figures which, though only outlined, are so fine and perfect one would think they had been drawn only the day before'. To one side, stones blocked another entrance, and it was through this, finally, that the burial chamber was entered, a great barrel-vaulted room whose perfect astronomical ceiling of deepest blue, marked with gold stellar constellations is a triumph of the ancient artists. Here he found the royal sarcophagus which 'merits the most particular attention, not having an equal anywhere in the world. It is of finest ornamental alabaster, 9 feet 5 inches long and 3 feet 7 inches wide. Its thickness is only 2 inches, and it is transparent when a light is placed inside. It is sculpted within and without with 700 figures which do not exceed 2 inches in height.' Although the mummy had been removed in antiquity to be placed eventually in the small cache tomb where it was later discovered (see p. 97), the sarcophagus was so beautiful that Belzoni was well pleased. It was, without a doubt, the finest and richest tomb ever discovered to date.

Farewell to Egypt

Dispirited and finding themselves embroiled in local arguments, Belzoni and his wife decided to leave Egypt. In 1819, they set sail for London, little realizing they would never return.

The splendid objects he retrieved were displayed in a great Egyptian exhibition in London which drew vast crowds of admirers. In one of the halls he recreated a full-size replica of the burial chamber of Seti I, 60.9m (200ft) long. The sarcophagus, however, was denied him. It was claimed by the British Museum who refused to let Belzoni put it on display. However, when Salt (for whom Belzoni had excavated in the valley) put the sarcophagus up for sale, to everyone's dismay the Government were unwilling to pay the price, having been exposed in previous weeks to intense public censure for the money they had recently paid Lord Elgin for his Greek marbles. Thus it was sold to Sir John Soane, and can be seen in his collection.

Belzoni's exploits in the valley were cataclysmic even by the standards of his day. To uncover six previously unknown tombs was remarkable, but his methods were so strongly criticized that never again would anyone be permitted to scavenge so wildly on any site in Egypt.

The hall *of the magnificently painted tomb of Seti I in the Valley of the Kings, shows some of the vibrancy of the colours and scenes that impressed Belzoni when he first entered it. Belzoni and his wife, Sarah, so loved this tomb that they lived in it for several weeks. A sudden flash flood in the valley at this time allowed rainwater to enter the tomb and caused immense damage to the paintwork that still continues to this day. The scaffolding supports shown in this picture prevent any immediate collapse. The tomb is, however, too badly damaged to permit tourists to enter today.*

VALLEY OF THE KINGS: ROYAL MUMMIES

In the 1870s, the Antiquities Service was alarmed by the appearance on the European market of a number of magnificent illustrated funerary papyri. What disturbed the Service was that the papyri seemed to have come from royal burials of the New Kingdom (in fact, they are from what is now referred to as the Third Intermediate Period), and were of such size and condition that they could only have come from a recently discovered tomb. Since all the pieces must historically have derived from Luxor, it was to be there that Gaston Maspero, the Service's Director General, turned his attention in 1881. He enlisted the aid of a wealthy American collector, Charles Wilbour, who was known on the local grapevine to be willing to pay highly for authentic pieces.

When Wilbour arrived in Luxor, he found the town full of rumours about the discovery of a new tomb. Within a matter of days, he had

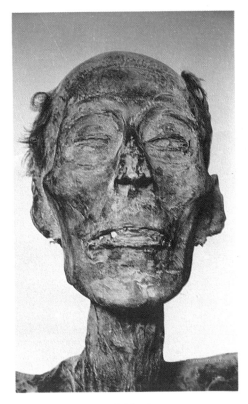

The face of Ramesses II (above) is that of a man in serene old age, probably in his late eighties when he died. His large, hooked nose is typical of all the Ramesside kings of the Nineteenth Dynasty. Examination of his mummy has shown that he suffered badly from arthritis in his hip, advanced heart disease and bad teeth. This, nevertheless, is the face of the man who oversaw the building of the temples of Karnak and Abu Simbel. He was also husband to more than 90 wives and father of over 100 sons. The lid of the coffin (left) in which his body was found at Deir el Bahri would once have been gilded and inlaid with precious stones like the outer coffins of Tutankhamun. The gilding and stones were removed by robbers in antiquity.

made contact with a local guide who directed him to the house of one Ahmed Abd er Rassul in the village of Abd el Qurna, close to the Ramesseum on the west bank. He was shown a quantity of red leather, stamped with the titles of a king of the Eighteenth Dynasty, 'so fresh that they must have been opened lately'. Immediately he telegraphed Maspero who set out without hestitation to Luxor.

Meanwhile, news of the imminent arrival of the Head of the Antiquities Service spread like wildfire through the village of Qurna, making the villagers unusually wary. When Wilbour asked them to show him the tomb from which the newly found pieces had come, they showed him a small tomb which had clearly been open for a long time. Wilbour was unconvinced and asked them questions, as a result of which one of the guides whispered a mention of a 'wonderful tomb' that they had discovered.

Maspero's arrival produced gloom among the villagers of the west bank, with the certain anticipation that he would take their find from them – a find that had provided them with wealth for almost 10 years. Naturally, Maspero found no one willing to talk to him, though the Abd er Rassul family, still not suspecting Wilbour's part in the affair, continued to confide in Wilbour, hoping his willingness to buy from them would bear fruit before Maspero discovered their trail.

Within days, Maspero issued a warrant for the arrest of two brothers, Ahmed and Hussein Abd er Rassul, yet despite the thorough questioning they were subjected to, neither of them would speak of their find. After three months Maspero had to return empty-handed to Cairo, warning the Abd er Rassul family that he was giving them but a brief respite, and that he would be back.

The first cache

The tension within the family from Qurna was almost unbearable and bitter quarrels ensued. It was then that the head of the family, Mohammed, went to the governor of the province and told him all he knew. He had discovered a small tomb that contained many mummies, most of them bearing the symbols of ancient kingship. The Antiquities Service was informed, and although Maspero had left Egypt temporarily, his assistant Emile Brugsch raced south to Luxor.

Three days later the crestfallen family took the archaeologist towards the mortuary temple

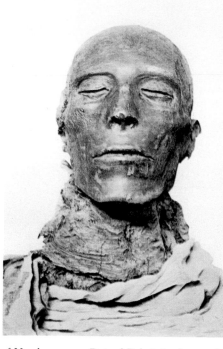

The mummy of Seti I, *father of Ramesses II (opposite) is one of the best preserved of all the kings of Egypt. It was found in the Deir el Bahri cache. Seti was about 1.7m (5½ft) tall, and had pierced ears. His face is that of a man just sleeping, although he died almost 3300 years ago – a triumph of the embalmer's art. His cartouche, shown above, contains his coronation name, Menmaatre. Reading the signs right to left: men – a game board; maat – the goddess; Re – the sun. Menmaatre Seti was the builder of the beautiful temple of Abydos where his cartouche can be seen in many locations.*

of Hatshepsut, at Deir el Bahri. In the north face of the cliffs, a path twisted upwards. Along this route, the carcass of a donkey lay decaying in the hot sun, the stink guaranteed to dissuade even the strongest willed passerby from closer investigation. Beyond lay a small entrance in the rock, about 2.4m sq (8ft sq). Inside, a vertical shaft plummeted some 15m (50ft) below them. Tentatively Brugsch clambered down a rope and at the foot of the shaft, a corridor only 1.2m (4ft) high disappeared into the rock. At once, a wooden coffin lay before him, the name on it that of a high priest.

Some 21m (70ft) further along, the corridor gradually became larger and here, to Brugsch's astonishment, a tiny chamber was seen stacked high with coffins of gigantic proportions. By the light of the candle held in shaking hands, Brugsch read the names on the coffins: Tuthmosis III, the great pharaoh of the Eighteenth Dynasty; Amenhotep I, the founder of the workman's village of Deir el Medina; Amosis, the king who freed Egypt from Hyksos domination at the start of the New Kingdom; Seti I, the builder of the great Osiride temple of Abydos; and Ramesses II, arguably the greatest pharaoh ever to rule Egypt. Brugsch was staggered. 'Their gold covering,' he said, 'and their polished surfaces reflected on my own excited face so that it seemed as though I was looking into the faces of my own ancestors.' One of them, that of a queen, smiled on me like an old friend'.

Yet the story was still not ended. Beyond the tiny chamber, another corridor 4.9m (16ft) long led further into the cliff to a second room where the intact burial of the original occupants of the tomb had been found – the family of the High Priest Pinedjem of the Twenty-first Dynasty. For 10 years, the Abd er Rassul family had rifled through the treasures, and the floor was littered with a mêlée of beautiful funerary objects – statuettes, vases and among them, bundles of long-dried flowers. In one corner, a pile of leather gleamed: a large tent, made of red, blue and green leather squares, ornamented with a frieze of lotus flowers; a unique object, used during the funeral of Pinedjem's family. It was from here that the leather straps, shown to Wilbour, had been taken.

As Brugsch emerged dumbfounded, he found the entire area suddenly alert. He knew the contents must be moved immediately for their own security. Three hundred local men were summoned, and without pause the coffins and objects were carried down to the boats moored on the Nile, ready to take them to Cairo. It took almost two full days. On 15 June 1881, the cortège of ships bearing the mortal remains of Egypt's greatest kings sailed slowly northwards. But the people had not forgotten their heritage, and the news travelled fast. As the boats sailed, the banks of the Nile were lined with crowds, shrieking and wailing as they mourned once again their ancient dead. 'At every village,' a report stated, 'the cry of mourners was heard as we passed by.'

The second cache
In 1898, Victor Loret took over the post of Director-General of the Antiquities Service. Trained by Maspero, he had a wide knowledge

of the area of Luxor, and especially the towns of the west bank. Suspecting other undiscovered tombs in the Valley of the Kings, he made trial diggings, or 'sondages', in the loose soil of the valley in the hope of discovering tomb entrances. At the beginning of March, one of his workmen uncovered the entrance to a tomb shaft, filled with rubble, in the floor of the Valley of the Kings at the foot of a cliff. The rubble contained many fragments of broken objects, including ushabti figures which had been provided for the burial of King Amenhotep II. It was obvious that the tomb had been robbed in antiquity and little could be expected to be discovered.

The rubble cleared away, the sealed tomb entrance to a corridor was found, and in the evening Loret and his workmen entered the tomb, crossing over a pit at the foot of a staircase to enter into a great chamber beyond. They found themselves surrounded by broken furniture and several huge painted model boats in one of which lay a mummy. It was that of a young boy – perhaps a prince. He had been carelessly unwrapped by tomb robbers – no doubt in haste to strip the corpse – while the resins on his bandages were still soft, with the result that his frail body had stuck to the boat.

Further into the tomb, a passage led into a huge burial chamber, the walls and ceiling of which were painted in bright, fresh colours with hieratic (see p. 158) characters. At one end, surrounded by debris of yet more smashed objects, stood the giant granite sarcophagus bearing the name and title of Amenhotep II, its lid thrown to one side. Scarcely expecting to see anything, Loret peered in. To his astonishment, the king's coffin – actually a replacement cartonnage coffin of late New Kingdom date – wreathed with floral tributes, lay intact. This was indeed a stunning discovery in the world of Egyptology: the first royal burial ever to be found in its own tomb.

Elated, he looked further. In side chambers were stacked the usual funerary offerings: jars for meat, wine and beer, statuettes and small pieces of furniture. Suddenly a macabre sight met his eyes. Lying on the floor of one chamber were three unwrapped mummies side by side; a man, a boy of about 15, and a woman with long, luxuriant, blackened, auburn hair. Tests carried out in 1984, by the University of Michigan, have shown that this lady was none other than Queen Tiye, the wife of Amenhotep II's grandson Amenhotep III, and mother of the in-

famous Akhenaten. One more side chamber remained, this last blocked with limestone. As the stones were removed, a small chamber no more than 3 by 3.6m (10 by 12ft) was revealed, containing nine coffins, in two rows. As Loret blew away the dust from one of them, he read a royal cartouche – that of Ramesses IV. Behind, the coffin bore the titles of Seti II. Yet another group of royal mummies had been discovered. Together with the mummies found in the Deir el Bahri cache, virtually every king of the Eighteenth and Nineteenth Dynasties had now been accounted for.

The fate of a king

As Brugsch had done before him, the order was given to empty the tomb and the mummies were placed in crates. As they were being carried to the river a letter was brought to Loret from the Government of Egypt. The mummies and all the objects were to be replaced in the tomb, an honourable reburial. Antagonism against these 'foreigners' who were seen to be looting the ancient dead had mounted until it was regarded as a public outrage. Loret carried out the instructions in the letter, and the body of Amenhotep II was taken back, the only royal mummy permitted to remain where it had lain for 3500 years.

In 1902, when Howard Carter was Inspector of Antiquities for Luxor, word was brought to him that the tomb of Amenhotep II had been robbed. He arrived to find it lying open, pillaged for a second time. The boat with the boy's mummy on it had vanished, and the mummy of the king had been stripped of its linen, torn apart and thrown on the floor. A determined Carter employed detective tactics. He followed footprints and other signs left by the robbers; they led him straight to the door of the Abd er Rassul family! Though charged and brought to trial, they denied the charges and were later freed by the authorities.

It was not until 1931 that the pathetic human remains of Amenhotep II were finally removed from the gaze of the casual tourist and taken to the quieter, more sanctified atmosphere of the Cairo Museum, so that they might regain their dignity.

The royal mummies still lie together in the Cairo Museum. They are in a room sealed by presidential decree in 1982, out of respect for the mortal remains of the ancient royal kings and queens.

The exquisitely carved red quartzite sarcophagus of the Eighteenth Dynasty ruler, Amenhotep II, was found in the burial chamber of the king's tomb by Loret in 1898. To his amazement, the body of the king lay inside it, though in a wooden coffin of a later date, the first king ever found still lying in his own tomb. The mummy was that of a man in his mid-forties, exceptionally tall and strongly built, which reinforced his proud boast, found on many inscriptions, that no man could pull his bow. The remark remains true for eternity for his bow lay beside his body, neatly sawn in two.

VALLEY OF THE KINGS: THE TOMBS

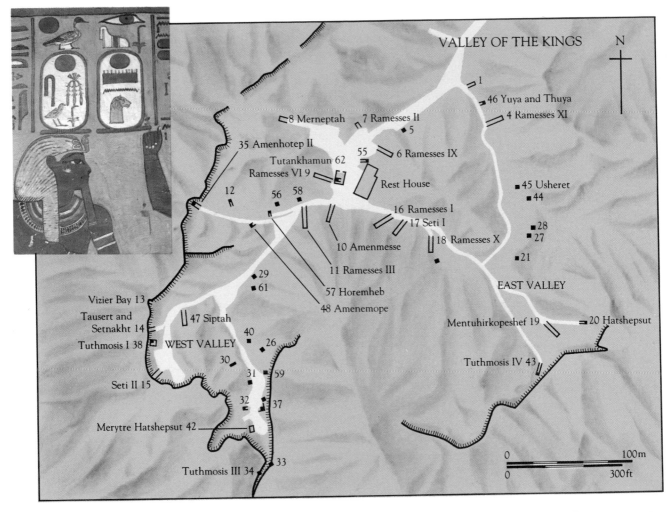

VALLEY OF THE KINGS   N

1
46 Yuya and Thuya
4 Ramesses XI
8 Merneptah   7 Ramesses II
5
35 Amenhotep II
55   6 Ramesses IX
Tutankhamun 62
Ramesses VI 9   Rest House
45 Usheret
12   56   58   44
16 Ramesses I
17 Seti I
28
18 Ramesses X   27
10 Amenmesse
11 Ramesses III   21
29   EAST VALLEY
61
57 Horemheb
48 Amenemope
Vizier Bay 13   Mentuhirkopeshef 19   20 Hatshepsut
Tausert and
Setnakht 14   47 Siptah
Tuthmosis I 38   WEST VALLEY   40   26   Tuthmosis IV 43
30
31   59
Seti II 15   32   37
Merytre Hatshepsut 42
Tuthmosis III 34   33

0   100m
0   300ft

This plan of *the Valley of the*
Kings demonstrates how almost
every natural cranny and crevice
was exploited. The inset shows the
head of Ramesses I, painted on the
wall of his tomb – No. 16 on the
plan. Above it are his names and
titles: 'Son of Re, Ramesses, the
Osiris, the King Menpekhtyre'.
The first name was his from birth;
the second he received when he
was crowned. Ramesses was a
soldier who served and later
succeeded Horemheb as the first
king of the Nineteenth Dynasty.

In the years following Belzoni's escapades in the
Valley of the Kings, emphasis was placed by
scholars on recording and studying what had
been found, rather than on searching for yet
more tombs. When John Gardner Wilkinson
(*see p. 36–7*) visited the valley in 1827, he
recorded that there were 21 tombs open to
view. He assiduously copied scenes and inscriptions and, in 1830, published the first accurate
account of them in his book, *Topography of*
Thebes. In a brilliant analysis of the material, he
put the 21 tombs in chronological order.

In 1844, Lepsius' Prussian epigraphic survey
team visited the valley and measured accurately
the tombs they found open. Their publication
of the scenes in the tombs in the mammoth
Denkmäler (*see p. 38*) established a new
standard of copying.

By the middle of the 19th century, tourists
began to arrive in Egypt in large numbers. The
hiring of cruise boats for travellers between
Cairo and Luxor by an English gentleman,
Thomas Cook, from 1845 onwards ensured a
steady stream of feet in this hitherto little-
frequented valley.

Although the Antiquities Service had been
set up by Mariette in 1856, the time of their
inspectors was devoted principally to the clearing of many major monuments in Upper Egypt
from the encroaching sand. The discovery of
the first cache of royal mummies (*see pp. 97–8*),
in 1881, focused world attention on the quiet
valley in the hills of Luxor's west bank, and
heralded the arrival of more archaeologists, and
the beginning of the first new excavations in
the area for 70 years.

A new tomb

Victor Loret arrived in Luxor from Paris in 1898, and at once selected a likely area to dig, below the cliffs under the Qurn (the 'Horn') mountain that dominates the valley. The entrance to a tomb was discovered there only five days later. A shaft descended steeply into the darkness below. Loret slithered down the accumulations of rubble, until by the light of a torch, 12m (40ft) down, he came into a deep well. The powerful scent of cedar wood filled his nostrils, he later remembered.

The light from his torch illuminated a great columned hall covered with fragments of burial equipment including a life-size standing statue. The walls were painted in a manner not seen before, with a buff background that resembled papyrus encircling the room, with stick figures and hieratic texts written hastily but beautifully on them. In one corner of this chamber, a black hole gaped in the floor. A short staircase led down to the burial chamber, painted in the same strange fashion as the upper room, but in a unique cartouche shape. The sarcophagus was intact, and upon it was the name of the tomb's owner – Tuthmosis III, greatest warrior and empire builder of the Eighteenth Dynasty. The mummy of the king had already been removed in antiquity to a cache and only his burial equipment surrounded Loret.

While Loret worked on this tomb, his workmen had already discovered yet another, that of Tuthmosis' son, Amenhotep II, with its second cache of royal mummies (see p. 98). It was decorated in the same unusual style as that of Tuthmosis III. It is ironic that these two tombs, the only ones yet found with the curious hieratic texts, should have been found almost simultaneously after 3000 years.

Loret returned to the valley the following year, and turned his attention to the area of the cliff below the tomb of Tuthmosis III. Yet again he was lucky, for the entrance to a tomb was uncovered. The tomb was badly damaged by water, and little remained other than the sarcophagus bearing the name of Tuthmosis I.

Despite Loret's excellent work and great success, he was little liked either by his fellows or by those who worked for him. He was asked to resign and Maspero, who had actually retired some years before, was reinstated. Maspero's first task was to appoint new and younger men to be trained in fieldwork. As a result, in 1899 Howard Carter was appointed Antiquities Inspector for the monuments of Upper Egypt.

A new generation

It was as a portrait painter that Carter had come to the attention of a wealthy patron, Lord Amherst, who recommended the eager 17-year-old to the newly founded Archaeological Survey. Carter had already worked as a copyist on various sites when he was seconded to the irascible Flinders Petrie in 1892. Petrie was not overly impressed. 'He is a good natured lad whose only interest is entirely in painting,' he wrote. 'It is of no use to me to work him up as an excavator!'

Carter had spent six of the intervening seven years working on the mortuary temple of Hatshepsut at Deir el Bahri. He spent his spare time walking the hills and valleys behind the temple, and came to know the area intimately. His new post, however, required him to maintain all the sites of Upper Egypt and to grant concessions for others to dig, rather than to dig solely on his own account.

Carter's work in the valley for the following two years was occupied with more mundane matters, though of great urgency. Maspero had been concerned that the burning of torches, or more often rags or wood, to light the tourists' view of the tombs, was causing smoke damage to the paintings. Many visitors were also in danger of injury from falling stones and the frequently hazardous descent into the open tombs. One of Carter's less frequently cited claims to fame is that he installed the first electric lighting, handrails, staircases and running boards in royal tombs, elements often taken for granted by tourists today!

The question of patronage

The cost of these improvements was high, draining the Antiquities Service of funds it felt it should be spending on excavation, and Maspero had to seek out new and willing investors. With the enticement of an officially recognized excavation and the acquisition of provenanced and authentic antiquities as a reward, Maspero was able to catch the attention of a wealthy American businessman, Theodore Davis. What attraction Davis boasted in his willingness to invest dollars, he lacked, however, in charm. He was abrupt in his dealings, and often frank with people to the point of causing offence. He had few friends, and he and Carter found little in common. As they worked together, they fought bitterly about who had the right to dictate how the excavation should be carried out.

Two of the finest *surviving mummies of commoners found in Egypt: Yuya (top), master of the king's chariots and Thuya (above), his blond-haired wife, were found in their intact tomb in 1903 by Egyptologists who were working under the patronage of Theodore Davis. Yuya and Thuya were the parents of Queen Tiye, the wife of Amenhotep III – and thus the grandparents of Akhenaten and great-grandparents of Tutankhamun.*

Davis eventually sailed south on his regular cruise to Aswan, leaving Carter alone to excavate. The new Inspector knew that his patron expected a return for his investment, but his first season was disappointing, yielding only two fine canopic jars and a painted box from the tomb of Amenhotep II.

The following season was to be more fortunate. Close to the tomb of Seti I, an entrance was found under rubble, with a staircase leading steeply underground. Objects scattered in the infill showed it was a royal tomb, that of Tuthmosis IV. When the burial chamber was entered, although devastated by robbers, the floor was deeply embedded with fragments of superb furniture and pottery vessels. Carter's careful recording of what was found enabled many objects to be restored, including a wonderful royal chariot, complete with leather trappings and weapons of war. Davis was delighted with this, his first royal tomb.

Almost simultaneously another tomb was being cleared. Its site known since antiquity, it had never been fully cleared, and when Carter discovered nearby, objects naming Queen Hatshepsut, Davis, who had a great and enduring love for ancient Egyptian queens, was delighted to see it excavated. It proved indeed to belong to Hatshepsut, and also to be the longest and deepest tomb in the valley. So little air penetrated the 243m (800ft) long corridors that pumps had to be installed after several of Carter's workmen collapsed. Although a burial chamber was found containing the queen's sarcophagus and that of her father Tuthmosis I, little else remained. A tunnel that led from there even deeper into the rock was never entered and remains unexplored to this day.

Carter is replaced

In 1903, Davis persuaded Maspero that he could work no longer with Carter, leaving the Director General (i.e. Maspero) little choice but to move him. As a result, Carter found himself promoted to the Inspectorate of Saqqara in the north, an area for which he had little liking. Six weeks later, Carter was forced to resign and never worked for the Antiquities Service again.

Meanwhile, in Luxor another Englishman, James Quibell, was made Chief Inspector by Maspero. Quibell, unlike Carter, was a brilliant academic and a highly qualified Egyptologist. Davis, so impatient for more tombs of the calibre of Tuthmosis IV, and Quibell, slow and

scholarly, liked each other as little as had Davis and Carter, and within days clashed over the speed with which one area of ground was cleared. Quibell at once asked Maspero for a transfer. While Maspero made arrangements for Arthur Weigall to take his place, Quibell continued to work in the valley, and almost immediately found an entrance to a tomb. It was Weigall, however, who finally broke through into what was to prove a small, but very rich burial. The first object to be picked from the rubble of the short entrance corridor was a gold encrusted chariot yoke. The excavation had to cease when dusk fell, but Weigall slept over the entrance to ensure the safety of the tomb. The following morning, Maspero, Davis and Weigall came upon a sealed doorway. 'Imagine a stuffy room,' Weigall wrote, 'the feeling that some ghostly occupants of the vacant chairs have just been disturbed... That was the sensation as we stood, dumbfounded, and stared at the relics of life of over 3000 years ago, all of which were as new as when they graced the palace.'

It was an intact burial whose magnificence was only later overshadowed by that of Tutankhamun. The owner was one Yuya, Master of the King's Horse, and his wife Thuya. They were the parents of Queen Tiye, wife of Amenhotep III and mother of the heretic king Akhenaten. The mummies were intact, and as Weigall looked down on them after their wrappings had been removed, he recorded, 'there was almost a feeling that they would presently open their eyes and blink at the light'. These two remain among the finest of Egyptian mummies. The furniture that stood around them was without equal from the ancient world; gold-covered chairs and stools, beds 'with springy string mattresses and decorated with charming designs in gold'. In one corner stood a wig belonging to Thuya, with a wreath of apparently fresh flowers over it, though they had been gathered millennia before; in another, was a light chariot of Yuya's, looking ready to be mounted. Weigall and Davis were astounded. 'These were the things of yesterday,' Weigall wrote. 'One looked from one article to another with the feeling that the whole human conception of time was wrong.'

When Quibell arrived in the Valley of the Kings the following morning, he was aghast to find the tomb already almost cleared on Davis' orders, with no record having been made of the contents. It was a sign of what would follow.

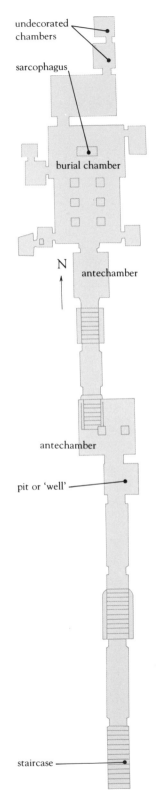

undecorated chambers

sarcophagus

burial chamber

N

antechamber

antechamber

pit or 'well'

staircase

The plan of *the tomb of Horemheb (left), No. 57 in the Valley of the Kings, is typical of the layout of the royal tombs, with long corridors leading to a series of chambers, often with columns cut from the rock, and the burial chamber at the rear. Small side chambers would once have contained great treasures that would have eclipsed those of Tutankhamun.*

The tombs of *the valley have yielded fine examples of the work of ancient craftsmen. This superb chair (right) belonged to Princess Sitamun, one of the daughters of Amenhotep III and Queen Tiye, and a sister of Akhenaten. She gave it as a funerary gift to her grandparents, Yuya and Thuya, in whose tomb it was found. The heads at the front of the arms probably bear her features. On the back, necklaces are being presented to the princess, while on the arms, the demigods Bes and Beset are shown dancing, holding knives and cymbals. The reliefs are plated in gold. The fine gilded wooden chariot of Tuthmosis IV (above, far right), now in the Cairo Museum, was found in his tomb in 1902 by Theodore Davis. It bears images of the king, both inside and out, as a mighty victor slaughtering his foes in battle. There is no evidence for these battles historically, so we can only assume that it records an Egyptian ideal of a king during the New Kingdom.*

The mystery of Tomb 55

In the early weeks of 1907, Davis, working with a new assistant, Edward Ayrton, discovered the entrance to a small tomb near that of Ramesses IX. The doorway, sealed with mud and bearing several cartouches, including that of Tutankhamun, had been opened several times. Behind the doorway, lying over rubble was what appeared to be a wall of gold, now recognized, thanks to Tutankhamun's tomb, to be the outer wall of a gilded wooden shrine that once covered a sarcophagus. It was badly damaged by water, causing the gold to flake and flutter off as the archaeologists moved past. On the panel, Ayrton noted, was the name of Queen Tiye. In the small burial chamber, a collapsed coffin lay partly shattered on the ground. The lid had slipped to one side, revealing the mummy.

Since there appeared to be little recoverable wealth in the tomb, orders were given for it to be cleared quickly. By the time a photographer had arrived, most of the floor had been swept clean. A few of the objects were briefly sketched, including the unique shrine panel; but none of the wooden material survived.

The mummy from the tomb (known to this day as Tomb 55) was removed to Cairo for examination. But even this was badly done; many of the outer bands wrapped around the mummy, said to have been inscribed, were inexplicably lost. The mummy was so mis-

handled that, as Davis wrote, 'the front teeth fell into the dust when touched, showing it could not have been well preserved.' Only later – too late – did the anatomists' report state that the body was not that of the elderly queen, but may have been that of a young man aged between 20 and 30 though the arms were folded in the manner more usual for a woman's burial. The identity of the occupant of Tomb 55 remains a mystery – and a source of controversy. The inscriptions that would once have borne a name on the coffin had been deliberately hacked away. Many wondered if it could not have been Akhenaten himself. But the body appeared to be too young; Akhenaten had ruled 17 years, and he fathered two daughters very soon after his coronation. Only later, with evidence gleaned from excavations at the site of Akhenaten's city, Akhetaten, modern Tell el Amarna, did another name appear – Smenkhare, the mysterious 'brother' of the little-known Tutankhamun.

Much of the material excavated on Davis' behalf lies in the Cairo Museum, for many years standing in a gallery known as 'Salle Théodore Davis.' Davis sponsored the publication of many volumes recounting details of the tombs he was responsible for reopening; today they are a fine memorial to him. Only the mystery of Tomb 55 and its hasty clearance remains a cloud on an otherwise distinguished reputation.

TOMBS OF THE NOBLES

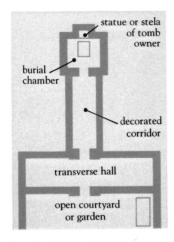

Tombs of New Kingdom *nobles follow typical ground plans (top). The chapel at the front leads to a narrow corridor, where the small back chamber often held a statue of the deceased. The burial shaft lay below the ground. One such tomb is that of Huya (above), the ruler of Kush, or southern Nubia, during the reign of Tutankhamun.*

The limestone hills on the west bank at Luxor are deeply scarred with the entrances of hundreds of tomb chambers cut into the rock. The kings of the Middle Kingdom, although coming from this area, often chose to be buried in pyramids to the north. But an independent spirit of mind had come to predominate by the beginning of the Middle Kingdom and the nobility often preferred to be buried near their ancestors in Luxor. During the New Kingdom, with the development of royal rock-cut shafts in the Valley of the Kings, courtiers chose to be buried in those hills, both to live eternally in their home area and to be close to the monarchs they served. Many people who were particularly close to the king, either by marriage or by bonds of friendship, were permitted to be buried within the Valley of the Kings itself. In fact, almost half the tombs in the valley belong to commoners.

The tombs

Many of the burial chambers of the nobles have lain open to visitors for hundreds of years. During the reign of Ramesses IX, the vizier of the time sat in judgment upon tomb robbers in the area who declared that they had entered and robbed many of the smaller tombs, apparently with impunity.

The tombs are generally very small, shaped like the letter T, with the transverse chamber opening each side of the entrance. At the rear of the tomb was either a false door or a carved image of the tomb owner, or sometimes both. The false door was painted on the wall so that, as in the mastaba tombs of the nobles of the Old Kingdom, the ka of the deceased could enter and leave the tomb at will by magic to partake of food and drink brought by relatives. The undecorated burial shaft was cut into the floor of the chamber.

The mortuary cult of these tombs was fixed during the man's lifetime, with priests appointed and endowed with parcels of land from which to supply food. Yet the tomb owners realized this would one day be forgotten. Unlike the earlier mastaba tombs that reflected an eternal life associated with the tomb and Egypt, however, these tomb owners envisaged an afterlife primarily spent in the company of the gods. Images of the judgment of the dead, the admission of the deceased to the land of eternity and the welcome by the gods are, therefore, frequently included. Scenes from the life of the tomb owner are also shown, as are

pictures of relatives – from parents, wives, brothers and sisters, to children and grandchildren. Sometimes relatives might have tombs of their own, but these images undoubtedly allowed families to stay together through eternity.

The tomb of Sennefer

This small tomb, lying in a small group of Eighteenth Dynasty tombs at the top of a slope, is one of the finest and most charming in the area. Sennefer was the Mayor of Luxor during the reign of Amenhotep II, at about 1425 BC. His brother Amenemopet, nicknamed Pairy, was the Vizier of Egypt, and was granted burial in a tomb in the Valley of the Kings. Another tomb nearby in the valley contained many objects with Sennefer's name on. It is possible, since this tomb, among those of other nobles, was found empty, that it was never used.

A short, steep staircase leads first into a small chamber and then into a larger one with four square pillars cut from the rock. When the tomb was being built the workmen encountered problems with a particularly hard outcrop of rock, and the ceiling was not flattened but left undulating. This was plastered and then painted with vines that seem to grow from the floor of the tomb. Bunches of grapes hang thickly among the leaves and are so realistic that they seem to be waiting to be harvested.

The walls and pillars, painted in brilliant colours, show Sennefer with his two wives, Sentnay and Sentnofret, receiving offerings of food and drink, often brought by his daughter Muttui. In one scene, Sennefer himself offers gifts to the king, shown seated under a canopy. Another scene depicts his funeral, and shows him being presented to Osiris, as his wife, Sentnofret waits for him in the afterlife.

The tomb of Rekhmire

Rekhmire served Tuthmosis III as Vizier, and since the king was often absent from Egypt fighting campaigns in the north, much of the day-to-day administration must have been left in Rekhmire's hands. In consequence his tomb reflects his high status. It is one of the largest, most finely decorated and informative in the whole necropolis. Although only a standard T-shaped tomb, the long chamber at the rear increases in height, with walls rising from 2.7m (9ft) near the entrance to 7.6m (25ft) at the rear of the tomb. The scenes on these walls, showing the duties of a vizier, are unique.

To the left of the entrance a side chamber is painted with an autobiographical text telling how Rekhmire was appointed Vizier. It records the king's own words at the time of the investiture: 'His Majesty said to him, fill the post of Vizier! Supervise every task, for it is the foundation block of the whole land. Being Vizier is not easy; it is as bitter as gall.' The king continues by insisting on Rekhmire's impartiality as a judge, and pointing out his duty to hear everyone who comes to him. He is to be held responsible for the economy, and must supervise every department. Rekhmire is then shown receiving and preparing to record foreign tribute for the king.

To the right of the entrance, the new Vizier collects taxes from Upper and Lower Egypt, assessing such diverse products as honey from hives, statues from a sculptor's workshop and corn and flax from farmers' fields. In one section Rekhmire is also shown visiting the garrison forts that stood on Egypt's northeastern frontier, inspecting fishing and winemaking in the area.

The inner corridor, directly in front of the entrance, is crammed on the left with pictures of trades and crafts for which Rekhmire was responsible: stoneworkers, some of whom work on colossal statues; leather workers and jewellers; brickmakers and bricklayers (many of whom are foreign workers); ropemakers; metal workers and goldsmiths; and dock workers. Their produce is shown being admitted to royal warehouses under Rekhmire's supervision, and then being redistributed throughout Egypt. On the right wall, Rekhmire is shown taking much needed relaxation with his wife Merit and their sons and daughters. He attends a banquet, listening to musicians and watching dancers. Among the famous scenes here is one group of musicians that includes a lutist; another shows a serving-girl in semi-transparent sheath dress depicted in a unique back view. Finally, to the rear of the tomb, the funeral of Rekhmire is depicted, with the coffin being carried to the tomb, the 'Opening of the Mouth' ceremony being performed, the deceased receiving food and drink offerings from his children.

THE ENIGMA OF AKHENATEN

The brooding *limestone colossal statue of Akhenaten shows the distorted features so commonly used in artistic depiction during the early years of the king's reign. Although Sir Alan Gardiner described them as 'frankly hideous portraits, the general fidelity of which cannot be doubted,' few would doubt today that these are no more than an artistic idiosyncratic style of the times. The names carved on the king's bracelets and on his chest bear the titles of his god, the Aten, and not those of the king at all. There thus remains a doubt as to whom these statues do represent.*

At the height of the Eighteenth Dynasty, Prince Tuthmosis, the eldest son of King Amenhotep III and his strong-willed common-born wife, Queen Tiye, died unexpectedly thrusting his younger brother, Amenhotep, into the limelight.

Of the young Amenhotep we know little, except that he spent much of his time either in Memphis or in his father's new palace-city of Malkata, on the west bank of Luxor about 1.6km (1mi) south of the mortuary palace of Medinet Habu. A strong companion, and probably an influential one, was his mother's brother, Ay. From the evidence, it appears that Ay and his wife Teye had two daughters, Mutnodjme (*see p. 114*) and Nefertiti, and the latter daughter was chosen to be the wife of the young prince.

The rise of the Aten
Amenhotep seems to have been an idealist, who rejected virtually every old Egyptian tradition. We know that when the young Amenhotep became king he was already married to Nefertiti and probably the father of a daughter, Meritaten. The name chosen for this princess, meaning 'Beloved of Aten,' reflects Amenhotep's increasing preoccupation with the new god. In his early years as king, portrayed on the third pylon in the temple of Karnak, his god, the Aten, was identified with Re-Horakhte, shown as a falcon with a sun-disc on his head, while in the Nubian town of Sesebi where the young king founded a temple, the Aten in falcon form is depicted in the company of the old, traditional Egyptian gods.

In his fourth or fifth year of rule the young king changed his name to Akhenaten and appears to have openly expressed his dissatisfaction with Egyptian traditions. His artists depicted him and his wife in a grossly distorted manner, with swollen thighs, pendulous breasts and bellies, and elongated skulls. In the tomb of the Vizier Ramose, No. 55 on the west bank of Luxor, the images of the king and queen were sketched on one wall in this fashion. King Amenhotep III celebrated a jubilee festival in his thirtieth year, which Ramose organized; in his next jubilee, held in his thirty-fourth year, Ramose was not even present and presumably was dead. The distorted images of Akhenaten and Nefertiti adopted only around their fifth regnal year, found in Ramose's tomb, gives some idea of the length of the co-regency between Akhenaten and his father.

A new city
In his fourth year, Akhenaten sought a place to build a new city devoted to the Aten. This god he now ordered depicted as an image of the sun with rays radiating from it, terminating in hands holding the hieroglyphic symbols for life and power, with himself, his wife and two daughters receiving benefit. This image is frequently described as being the 'sun-disc', yet the inscriptions make it clear that the Aten was regarded by the king as being the creative force of the universe that was manifested by the sun. The god itself had no image.

The young king sailed north in his sixth year from Luxor and 370km (230mi) away on the east bank of the Nile, near modern Ashmunein, found a cliff-encircled plain that belonged to no man and owed allegiance to no god. The following morning he rode around the cliffs of the west bank and the east bank and ordered 14 boundary stelae erected to show the limits of his new city. He called it Akhetaten – 'The Horizon of the Aten,' and ordered building work to commence.

Two years later it appears that both the king's palace and the Great Temple of the Aten had been built, so that the royal family could move into their own city, together with their loyal courtiers. First citizen of the new city was Nefertiti's father, Ay. For him and for other prominent citizens, rock-cut tombs were started high in the cliffs to the north and south. All the buildings in the city itself were carved with scenes of everyday life, with a unique frank portrayal of the royal family. The king and queen and their daughters evidently walked and rode freely around the town, and were shown openly embracing each other.

Nefertiti's 'disappearance'
Inscriptions bearing the name of the king's eldest daughter, Meritaten, have been found on the walls of small ruined shrines, in the southern part of the city, near the pleasure palace called the Maruaten. But it was obvious that Meritaten's name had been carved over that of someone else. These underlying inscriptions have, in the past, been wrongly recorded as having borne the name of Nefertiti. They are now known, however, to have been inscriptions bearing the name of Kiya, a minor queen of Akhenaten. As a result of this misunderstanding, many archaeologists have spoken of the downfall of the beloved queen, and her possible replacement in the affections of

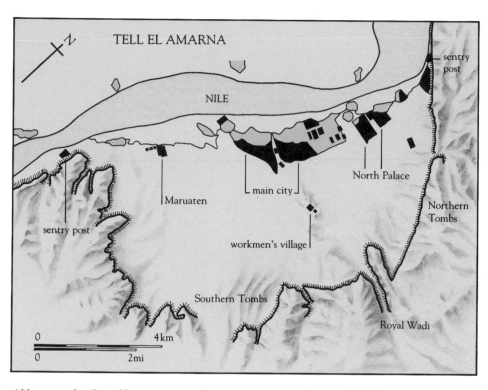

TELL EL AMARNA

NILE

sentry post

North Palace

Northern Tombs

Maruaten

main city

sentry post

workmen's village

Southern Tombs

Royal Wadi

0   4km

0   2mi

The map *of the plain of Tell el Amarna (left) shows the original plan for Akhenaten's city. Only the bare outlines of walls remain today on the flat expanse of sand.*

This magnificent *painted bust (above), unnamed but generally taken to show Akhenaten's queen, Nefertiti, was found in a sculptor's workshop north of the royal palace. Though the left eye appears unfinished, modern analysis has revealed minute traces of paint that have flaked away. The bust, therefore, may have been completed and perfect when the city was abandoned.*

Akhenaten by Smenkhare, a young homosexual. There is, however, no strong archaeological evidence for the existence of any such person. As Julia Samson and Professor J.R. Harris have recently shown, many portraits reputed to be those of Smenkhare, in fact, bear one of Nefertiti's names, Nefernefruaten. That leaves the distinct possibility that Nefertiti did not 'disappear', but that the king took his much loved wife as his heir. From this time, the succession after his death was to pass to his daughters – of whom there were now six – the Great Heiress being the eldest, Meritaten.

Shortly before the death of Amenhotep III, according to inscriptions found on fragments of a sarcophagus, the second of the princesses, Meketaten, died. In the royal tomb that was cut in a wadi (dried riverbed) behind the city, one chamber depicted a uniquely frank mourning scene, showing Akhenaten and Nefertiti openly weeping over her body.

The city's closing years

Akhenaten died during his seventeenth year as king, and was apparently buried in the tomb that had been prepared for him. It seems that Nefertiti may have taken the throne for a short time as Smenkhare, taking the coronation name of Ankh(et)kheprure, but neither she nor Meritaten survived for long. Within a year, Tutankhaten, later Tutankhamun, took the

crown and married Akhenaten's surviving daughter, Ankhesenpaaten.

In the early years of this century the British Assyriologist, Reverend A.H. Sayce, travelled widely in Egypt and, while moored near the ancient city of Akhetaten, reported seeing a procession leaving the royal tomb, carrying bodies which they burned on a funeral pyre. Whether there is any basis in this is unclear, but when the tomb was finally entered, the bodies of Akhenaten, Nefertiti and the other members of the royal family had been removed.

The city was deserted within three years of Tutankhamun's coronation. When the young king returned to Luxor and reopened the temples of the old gods, courtiers left Akhetaten with him. The city that should never have existed in the first place, in so isolated and waterless a plain, died. Later, stones from the city were removed and used in the building of Ashmunein. For the archaeologist the foundations form a time capsule depicting urban life in the Eighteenth Dynasty.

The plain of Akhetaten is now dotted with small villages – Hawata, El Hag Kandil, Et Till and El Amran. The last two have given their names to form the name by which the site is now known – Tell el Amarna. From this, the time of the city's flowering is called the Amarna Age. It has been and remains one of the most contentious periods in all of Egyptian history.

CITY OF THE ATEN

Thomas Eric Peet
(1882–1934)

Born in Liverpool, Peet took his degree in Mathematics and Classics at Oxford. While travelling in Italy, he first studied archaeology and experienced fieldwork. After being introduced to Egyptology, he worked under Garstang at Abydos. In 1913 he was appointed lecturer at Manchester University and, while there, taught himself hieroglyphs, in addition to Coptic and Demotic. After 1918, he became Director of Excavations for the Egypt Exploration Society. From 1920 to 1933 he was Professor of Egyptology at Liverpool. Tragically, having just been designated Professor at Oxford, he died unexpectedly.

The city built by Akhenaten was divided into several distinct areas. In the centre of the plain, a main highway, running parallel with the river, divided the royal palace. To the west were the official apartments, comprising halls and great open courtyards flanked with colossal statues of the king and queen. A bridge formed a balcony where the royal family often appeared in public, and connected with the private apartments on the other side of the road. Attached on the south side of the private apartments was a small temple to the Aten, probably for the king's own use. To the north, a series of storehouses separated the palace from the Great Temple that dominated the city. This huge open courtyard was filled with stone altar tables at which everyone could make offerings of food and drink each day to the Aten. At the east end of this courtyard, a small sanctuary was built, presumably for the sole use of Akhenaten and the high priest. At a later date, near the entrance on the west side of the court, a smaller closed structure was added called the Gem-aten ('Aten is found'), with a columned hall, the Perhai, or House of Rejoicing.

To the east of the palace and temple stood the main administrative buildings, among which was the Foreign Office. Here, in 1887, baked clay tablets were found upon which were copies of letters sent from Amenhotep III, Queen Tiye, Akhenaten and Tutankhamun to Egypt's northern vassal states. According to these, the princes of the north were being attacked by the expanding Hittite nation, and they beseeched the kings of Egypt for aid. They had, they pleaded, sent tribute regularly to Egypt; in return, they demanded troops and military aid. It seems that none was sent – whether, as is often claimed, Akhenaten was too preoccupied with his god, the Aten, to care about the rest of the world is unclear. But as a result of these years of inaction, Egypt's empire began its inexorable decline.

North of the temple, the so-called northern suburbs were packed with private houses. Many of the larger houses were equipped with every luxury, including gardens, pools surrounded by trees, kitchen blocks and even private bathrooms. Between the larger houses, whose position was presumably chosen by prominent

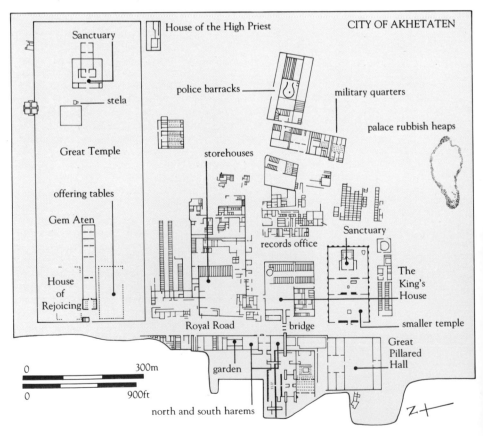

This small *though well-preserved and brightly coloured fragment of plaster, above, once formed part of the wall decoration of Akhenaten's palace at Tell el Amarna. The white robe at the top is part of the garb of either the king or Queen Nefertiti seated on a painted floor on a carpet, while two of their daughters, probably Meritaten and Meketaten, sit on a cushion at their side. The distorted features of the princesses, like those of their parents elsewhere, are typical of the art conventions of the period.*

The plan of the central city *of Tell el Amarna (left) shows the extent of excavations to date. The main road, or Royal Road, divides the palace, with the official rooms on the west and private apartments to the east. But it was the Aten's great temple that dominated the area.*

courtiers when the town was founded, were crammed the poorer houses, often utilizing other people's house walls to form supports for their own.

On the northern edge of the town, beyond a ditch that ran to the Nile and probably carried away the town's waste water, stood a northern palace that appears to have belonged to Queen Nefertiti.

On the southern edge of the plain stood another palace, the Maruaten. When excavated, it was shown to be a large and delightfully airy building, with brightly painted rooms and surrounded (according to representations of it on blocks from the city) by plants and trees. Behind this palace a number of red quartzite shrines stood now commonly called 'sunshades'. Although smashed into tiny pieces after the city was abandoned, inscriptions show that they belonged to the royal ladies. It all suggests that this palace was used by the royal ladies as a pleasant place away from the central city.

The tombs of the nobles

In the rock faces of the curving cliffs at the east of the plain small tombs were cut for the king's courtiers. Most of them were never finished. The tombs all show scenes not of an afterlife but of life around the city, with depictions of

the houses, palace and temple, and everywhere the images of the royal family.

In the southern group, a large tomb was cut for the king's uncle and closest confidant, Ay. In this tomb was carved the famous 'Hymn to the Aten', a declaration of Akhenaten's belief in a universal god who created all mankind, not just Egypt, and reputedly written by the king.

The royal tombs

At the head of the wadi that cuts into the centre of the cliffs at the rear of the plain is the entrance to the tomb of the royal family.

An entrance shaft in the floor of the valley leads via a staircase to a passage. On the right, a doorway leads into a curving corridor, which terminates in a large burial chamber. Here, several side rooms were apparently made for the burials of the six royal daughters. The main corridor descends past another small chamber on the right, to a main burial chamber. Here fragments of a sarcophagus and several ushabti figures were found with Akhenaten's name inscribed on them. Professor Geoffrey Martin has pointed out that the two corridors and principal burial chambers are virtually of equal dimensions, and must have been intended to hold the burials of two rulers: Akhenaten and Nefertiti.

THE DISCOVERY OF TUTANKHAMUN

**Howard Carter
(1874–1939)**

*After a boyhood during which he
was educated at home – his
constitution being considered weak
and rendering him unsuitable for
normal schooling – Carter met
Percy Newberry and then trained
under Flinders Petrie. Petrie's
comment was that 'Carter's
interest is only in painting . . . it is
of no use to me to work him up as
an excavator.' Carter worked as a
draughtsman at Deir el Bahri for
nine years, having been appointed
Chief Inspector of Upper Egypt in
1899. He developed a detailed
knowledge of the hills of the west
bank of Luxor, including the
Valley of the Kings. In 1903, he
was moved to Saqqara, but after a
disagreement, he left the
Antiquities Service entirely. From
1907, he worked for the Earl of
Carnarvon, for whom he found six
royal tombs. But it was Carter's
1922 discovery of the tomb of
Tutankhamun that electrified the
world and guaranteed his fame as
an Egyptologist. The 10-year
clearance of the tomb yielded great
quantities of material – much of
which still awaits study and
publication. Carter died in London
in 1939, aged 65.*

In 1907, work in the Valley of the Kings was
interrupted when archaeologists digging on
behalf of Theodore Davis (*see p. 102*) discovered
a rectangular pit in the foothills of a small
side-cutting near the tomb of Seti I. The
shallow pit, around 1m (3ft) deep, contained a
variety of large pots together with piles of
linen, some of it tied in small bundles. On the
side of one of the pots was found a seal
impression bearing the coronation name of
Tutankhamun.

Davis was jubilant. Few pharaohs' tombs
remained to be found in the valley. He himself
had accounted for the discovery of many royal
tombs, and of those that were missing, that of
Tutankhamun was at the head of his list. The
jars, when opened, contained only the remains
of food and a number of broad collars made of
papyrus and decorated with layers of flower
petals, seeds and berries stitched on to resemble
jewels. It was, he was sure, all that remained of
the burial equipment of this most insignificant
king. He had little use for the objects, and after
a few months, willingly gave the entire find to
the Metropolitan Museum of Art in New York.
He later published his find under the title of
'The Tombs of Harmhabi and Touatânkhan-
amanou'.

When H.E. Winlock, of the Metropolitan
Museum, examined the collection of material
later in New York, he found it was not tomb
equipment at all, but rather the remains of a
banquet for eight people. The bundles of linen,
some stained and some containing natron, were
all that remained of a mummification, perhaps
carried out in or near that small pit. The tomb
of Tutankhamun, he declared, was still to be
found. Davis never accepted this, and remained
convinced, to his death in 1915, that he had
found the tomb of the boy king. When, in
1914, he gave up his concession to dig in the
valley, he declared, 'I fear that the Valley of the
Kings is now exhausted.'

Carter and Carnarvon
After his resignation from the Antiquities
Service in 1903 (*see p. 102*), Howard Carter set
up a small shop in Luxor as an artist and it was
here that he first met Lord Carnarvon.

George Herbert, Fifth Earl of Carnarvon,
came to Egypt in 1903 to convalesce. Since a
motoring accident several years previously in
which he had narrowly escaped death, he had
been constantly ill and in pain. He was only 37
at the time, but wealthy enough to have

amassed a large collection of antiquities out of
genuine love for the pieces and what they
represented. Carnarvon quickly became fascinated by Egypt's past. He applied to Gaston
Maspero, the Director of the Antiquities
Service, and was given a concession to dig at his
own expense near Deir el Bahri on the west
bank of Luxor. After only a few exhausting days
of digging to no avail, it became clear that he
would get nowhere without help, and it was
thus that he was introduced to Howard Carter
– and one of the most famous partnerships in
the history of Egyptology was formed.

The announcement that Davis' much pub-
licized 'tomb' of Tutankhamun was no more
than a cache, persuaded Carter that the tomb
must still lie somewhere in the Valley of the
Kings. Research soon indicated to him a likely
spot, a triangle of ground in front of the tomb
of Ramesses VI. The cache of embalming
equipment, and the small Tomb 55, sealed with
Tutankhamun's name, both lay within a short
distance. He readily convinced Carnarvon of
the likelihood of finding more tombs in the
valley, and when Davis relinquished his concession in 1914 – a year before his death –
Carter and Carnarvon took it up in 1915.

For the next few years, Carter dug in the
Valley of the Kings. He was requested by the
Antiquities Service to leave his chosen triangle
alone, after his digging interrupted the passage
of tourists into the popular tomb of Ramesses
VI. On Lord Carnarvon's behalf, he excavated
many tombs. But the sought-after tomb of
Tutankhamun still eluded him.

The discovery
'Hardly had I arrived on the work next morning,
4th November 1922, than the unusual silence
. . . made me realize that something out of the
ordinary had happened; and I was greeted by
the announcement that a step cut in the rock
had been discovered.'

So Carter described the fateful morning. His
men had been excavating deep in the floor of
the Valley of the Kings, where they had found
the foundations of several houses used by
workmen who had decorated the ancient tomb
of Ramesses VI. By chance, the houses had
been built on top of the entrance to another
tomb that sand, rubble and time had conveniently conspired to hide.

Carter was jubilant. Only months before,
Lord Carnarvon had informed him that his
patronage had to come to an end, and that this

would have to be Carter's last season's work in the valley. Carter ordered his men to clear the step, and by the following afternoon, a staircase of 16 shallow steps had been revealed. The upper part of a mud-sealed doorway was uncovered, bearing the seals of the ancient necropolis guard.

That afternoon, in a fever of excitement, Carter sent Carnarvon a cable: 'At last have made wonderful discovery in the valley; a magnificent tomb with seals intact; recovered same for your arrival. Congratulations!' Carter, at this point, was being unduly optimistic, for he had already observed that the tomb door had been broken and resealed. Moreover, although he had seen the necropolis seal, he had not seen any royal seal on the door. Seventeen days later, however, with Lord Carnarvon and his daughter, Lady Evelyn Herbert, present on the site, the staircase, which had been filled again as a security measure, was cleared again. This time the base of the door was uncovered, and there, at last, was the seal impression both men had waited 10 years to see – 'Nebkheprure' (Tutankhamun).

The tomb is entered

Two days later, in the presence of the Inspector of the Antiquities Service, R. Engelbach, the door was broken away. Beyond it lay a passage, gradually sloping downwards and filled with rubble. At one upper corner, a narrow passage had been cut through the rubble, along which a robber had entered the tomb. If Carter felt any disquiet, he did not show it. The presence of the workmen's huts over the entrance proved it had been intact and unentered since the time of the Twentieth Dynasty, during the reign of Ramesses VI.

'The following day, November 26th,' wrote Carter, 'was the day of days, the most wonderful I have ever lived through and certainly one whose like I can never hope to see again.' Beyond the rubble, at the end of the passage 9.1m (30ft) long, another door was reached. This, too, had been opened and resealed, and Carter's expectations of finding anything at all inside the tomb (an intact burial being a miracle) were, by now, not high.

'Slowly, desperately slowly, it seemed to us, the remains of the passage debris that encumbered the lower part of the door was removed, until at last we had the whole door before us. The decisive moment had arrived. With trembling hands, I made a tiny breach in the

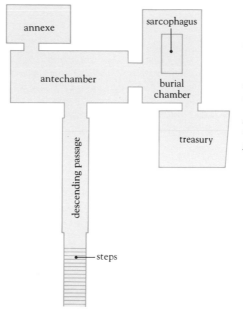

The tomb of Tutankhamun is the smallest royal tomb in the Valley of the Kings. The antechamber contained the large beds and chariots; the annexe and the treasury contained the smaller, more precious objects. Only the burial chamber was finished, its walls hastily painted.

upper left-hand corner . . . Candle tests were applied as a precaution against foul gases and then, widening the hole a little, I inserted the candle and peered in. At first I could see nothing, the hot air escaping from the chamber, causing the candle flame to flicker but presently, as my eyes grew accustomed to the light, details of the room within emerged slowly from the mist; strange animals, statues and gold – everywhere the glint of gold. For the moment I was struck dumb with amazement, and when Lord Carnarvon, unable to stand the suspense any longer, inquired anxiously, "Can you see anything?" it was all I could do to get the words, "Yes, wonderful things!" '

The entrance to Tutankhamun's small tomb lies in the floor of the valley at the foot of the later, and much larger, tomb of Ramesses VI. The huts of the workmen who built this tomb were erected over the entrance of the forgotten tomb of the boy king, effectively sealing it from robbers until Howard Carter found it in 1922.

This small coffin *of solid gold, inlaid with lapis lazuli, turquoise and carnelian, is one of four that contained the mummified viscera of Tutankhamun. They were placed inside an alabaster chest divided into four compartments and then into a gilded wooden shrine. The coffins are miniature copies of the large, third coffin of gold which held the king's body and show him in the form of Osiris. Inside, the coffins are engraved with spells from the Book of the Dead.*

The treasure of Tutankhamun

When Carter and Carnarvon first entered the antechamber in March 1922, it was evident that robbers had ransacked the small tomb in antiquity. The tiny space was packed to the ceiling with an unbelievable array of furniture, boxes and vases that were simply thrown one on top of another. The robbers, it appeared, had been apprehended in the act, and priests or the necropolis guard had returned to the tomb and thrust objects away wherever they could find space. Clothes more than 3000 years old were bundled together in boxes like rags. How were they to be separated? Conserved? To Carter, it must have been both a dream and a nightmare, as the realization of his find slowly dawned on him.

As a partially robbed tomb, under Egyptian law, Carter and Carnarvon could expect to retain many of the objects to repay the expense and time incurred in its discovery. But the government and the people of Egypt were appalled that any of Tutankhamun's treasure should leave the country. As a result, the law of Egypt was changed, and from that time onwards, objects found in Egypt had to remain there unless specifically given to the excavator.

With 10 years' searching behind them, and 10 years' hard work facing them, and no direct financial reward at the end of it, Carter and Carnarvon's triumph must have seemed hollow. Carnarvon, for years an ill man, was never to see the culmination of his search – the richness of the contents and the mummy of the young king – for only three months later he contracted pneumonia and died in Cairo. But for Carter, as an archaeologist, the value of the tomb far exceeded the material wealth spread out before him. There were questions posed and answers to be found. Who was Tutankhamun? Why did he become king? What had it been like to live under the rule of Akhenaten? Surely, in the mass of material that faced him, somewhere he would find those answers. That information would outweigh all the gold.

The tomb

The tomb of Tutankhamun comprises four chambers, and is the smallest royal tomb in the Valley of the Kings, occupying only 83.6sq m (900sq ft) of floor space. It had been hastily cut and never finished, with all but one room, the burial chamber, unlevelled and undecorated. Yet within it lay the greatest treasure ever found by any archaeologist.

The antechamber, 8 × 3.7m (26½ × 12ft) was dominated by three gilded wooden beds with carved animal heads. In front and on top of them were crammed chairs, stools and assorted boxes, mixed with bows and arrows, throwing-sticks and walking sticks, and flowers that seemed freshly picked. One of the walking sticks, a simple reed with an inscribed gold ferrule and knob, recorded that it had been cut by the little king's own hand. Under one of the beds, a long decorated box contained a trumpet, one of two discovered in the tomb. (In 1939, it was sounded once again, fittingly in the Cairo Museum.)

To the left of the entrance lay a confused pile that proved to be two golden chariots, while to the right, two black and gold life-size statues enshrouded in tattered linen stood sentry against a plastered wall.

Under one of the beds, a low doorway could be seen. 'Cautiously we crept under the couch, inserted our torch, and there before us lay another chamber, smaller than the first, but even more crowded with objects. The state of this room (afterwards called the annexe) simply defies description,' Carter wrote.' Not a single square inch of floor remains vacant.' Among the objects he found were low beds, used by the king in life, more chairs, and several superb gaming boards, inlaid in ivory and gold.

Clearing the tomb

Within days, the nearby tomb of Seti II was turned into a makeshift laboratory and storehouse for the objects, and the clearing of the tomb began. With the antechamber emptied,

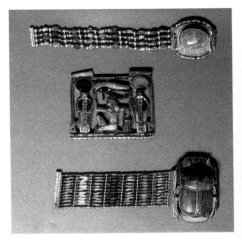

The unusual *heavy gold pendant, above, takes the form of Re-Horakhte as a falcon, with the sun disc on its head. The Re-Horakhte falcon was the earliest form of the Aten, the god served by Tutankhamun's father, Akhenaten. The falcon's wings are inlaid with coloured glass; the sun disc is a cabochon-cut carnelian.*

Two bracelets *bearing scarabs (left), some of many similar ones found in Tutankhamun's tomb. The upper bracelet, with its fine amethyst set on a granulated gold background, is not typical of Egyptian design and may have been a gift from another country, probably to the north of Egypt. The lower bracelet is a design based on the king's name: the basket – 'neb'; the scarab – 'kheper'; and the cartouche bearing the full name in place of the sun sign – 'Re'. The beads of the bracelet are made of glass, calcite, lapis lazuli and electrum. In the centre, is a counterweight, used at the back of heavy necklaces to keep them in place. The piece, of inferior design, shows the symbol of a god with upraised hands, meaning, in hieroglyphs 'million', while the vertical 'bars' at each side are symbols for 'years'. It is thus a wish for the king's long life encapsulated in gold.*

attention was turned to the plastered wall between the wooden sentry statues. On 17 February 1923, an invited audience of dignitaries entered the tomb and sat watching as Carter chipped away some of the plaster. 'I inserted an electric torch. An astonishing sight its light revealed, for there, within a yard of the doorway, stood what to all appearances was a solid wall of gold.'

The 'wall' proved to be the outer of a series of four shrines nesting one inside the other, covered with heavy gold leaf and inscribed with spells to ensure the king's passage through eternity. So large was the shrine that only a small passage remained between it and the walls, which, when the visitors squeezed through, were seen to be painted. To the right of the shrine, an open doorway in the wall revealed yet another small room. Later called the treasury, it contained the most valuable jewels and objects in the tomb. The entrance was guarded by a disquietingly lifelike statue of Anubis (*see p. 133*), crouching like a guard-dog ready to spring.

Examination of the shrines was to take some time. To separate them was extremely difficult. Between each shrine, even more unique treasures were found. It was another year before the last shrine was removed, and inside it a yellow quartzite sarcophagus was seen, its lid of pink granite painted to match the base and cracked from side to side. Once again, an invited audience was present to witness the lifting of the lid. 'The contents were completely covered with linen shrouds,' Carter wrote. 'As

the last shroud was removed a gasp of wonderment escaped our lips, so gorgeous was the sight that met our eyes; a golden effigy of the young boy-king of most magnificent workmanship, filled the whole interior of the sarcophagus!'

The king's mummy

Examination of the contents was to wait until 1926. The coffin proved to be the outer of three, and so tight a fit that its extrication was a problem. Moreover, it seemed unbelievably heavy. At last, a hoist was fixed in place, and ropes attached to silver handles in the coffin lid. When the first coffin was clear of the sarcophagus, its lid was lifted to reveal a second coffin. Over this, a tiny wreath of blue lotus flowers and cornflowers had been placed. It was on 17 October 1926 that the second coffin lid was opened and the cause of the great weight was at last discovered. The third and final coffin was 110.4kg (296 lb) of solid gold!

The mummy of the king lay within the gold coffin, a mask of superb craftsmanship of gold, inlaid with glass and lapis lazuli, covering his face. Unguents poured liberally over the mummy had interacted chemically, carbonizing most of the body. Only the face, protected by the magnificent mask, escaped the worst damage. A postmortem later suggested that the king had been between 16 and 17 years of age when he died. A thinning of the skull behind the left ear, found years later in an X-ray, suggested that he may have died as the result of an accident – perhaps a blow to the head.

Who was Tutankhamun?

The vital information Carter wanted was never found. In all the material packed into that small tomb, not one papyrus nor one single historical inscription was ever found. Although scholars still dispute Tutankhamun's right to the throne, it seems likely that he was, in fact, a son of the infamous Akhenaten, possibly by the little-known minor wife, Queen Kiya, who vanished from Amarna at about the same time Tutankhamun must have been born (*see p. 107*). The identity of the body in nearby Tomb 55, sealed with Tutankhamun's name, also remains a mystery; but the postmortem examination of the body from that tomb and that of Tutankhamun showed that the two were related. The excavation of Tomb 55 (*see p. 103*) was so badly handled that even the sex of the occupant is in doubt. There remains the intriguing possibility that it is the body of Queen Kiya.

NEW KINGDOM FINDS: HOREMHEB AND MAYA

**Geoffrey T. Martin
(1934-)**

*After studying Ancient History,
Geoffrey Martin turned to
Egyptology, assisting on the
Nubian rescue expedition
excavating at Buhen. He then
pursued the subject academically,
and after completing his doctorate,
spent a short period as Wilbour
Fellow at the Brooklyn Museum,
in New York. Dr. Martin returned
to Britain to take up a post as
lecturer at University College,
London. In 1980, he directed the
epigraphic survey at the royal
tomb in Tell el Amarna. His
connection with the Saqqara
necropolis began in 1964, but he
has been directing excavations
there since 1971, the first at the
necropolis of sacred animals. The
discovery of the tomb of Maya at
the end of the 1986 season is only
the latest in a series of remarkable
discoveries.*

The announcement in the world's press, in February 1986, that the tomb of Maya, a treasury official who served under Tutankhamun, had been rediscovered, excited public reaction in a way scarcely seen since the discovery of Tutankhamun's tomb. It was not a chance discovery, as many reports suggested, but the culmination of painstaking detective work lasting more than a decade.

The area of Saqqara south of the pyramid and causeway of Unas had never been scientifically examined. Lepsius (*see p. 38*), on his expedition there from 1842 to 1845, had recorded parts of several tombs that at that time stood open to view. By 1975, encroaching sand covered them completely, leaving only curious rectangular depressions that alerted the attention of Professor Geoffrey Martin of University College, London, and the Egypt Exploration Society. The Leiden Museum, in the Netherlands, which possesses several loose blocks from the area, together with fine statues of Maya and his wife Meryt, declared their interest and so, in 1975, a joint EES-Leiden team, with Professor Martin as Field Director, was granted permission to excavate.

The tomb of Horemheb

Using the sketch map made by Lepsius' architect, one of the rectangular depressions, after a detailed survey, was chosen as the spot to excavate. Within minutes of the opening of the work mud-brick walls emerged forming a courtyard. Inside them the top of a limestone column was inscribed, not with the name of Maya as they had hoped, but that of Horemheb. An army general, Horemheb had taken the throne as pharaoh after the deaths of Tutankhamun and his successor, Ay, at the end of the Eighteenth Dynasty. At his accession, Horemheb had had a royal tomb hewn for himself in the Valley of the Kings at Luxor. No kingly burial was, therefore, to be expected at Saqqara, but since Horemheb had married at least twice, there was hope that one of his wives may have been buried there.

Work on clearing the tomb lasted for four seasons. Much of the stone for the superstructure was found to have been removed from the nearby Step Pyramid complex (*see p. 64–7*), built over 1200 years earlier. Under the floor of courtyards, entrance shafts to four deep chambers were excavated and investigated. Through the bedrock, a complex series of passages, chambers and halls of truly royal

proportion was discovered. Dampness had caused all the wooden coffins to rot, but some bones, in fragile condition, did survive. An examination of one of the burials revealed clues that indicated it might be that of Mutnodjme, the second wife of Horemheb and probably the sister of Nefertiti. The remains were those of a woman in her forties who had had numerous pregnancies. Since we know that Horemheb died without an heir, we can only presume that his and Mutnodjmet's children must have been miscarried or died in infancy.

The tomb of Tia

In 1982, work directly to the north of Horemheb's tomb revealed another stone superstructure which was shown to be the tomb complex of Princess Tia, one of the two sisters of King Ramesses II, and her husband also called Tia. The complex was slightly smaller than Horemheb's, and had been hastily executed. The tomb yielded two surprises. First, and most unexpected, the base and lower part of a small pyramid, originally about 6m (20ft) high, was found in the rear courtyard. Second, a burial shaft under the stone-flagged forecourt led to a series of chambers belonging to Iurudef, a loyal retainer of the princess. The original burial had been put to the torch, but lying over the charred remains were 75 intact and virtually undisturbed burials, many of them children. This cache clearly dates from the very late Ramesside period, a far earlier date than was anticipated, since most intrusive (i.e. material of a later period that has been found in an older site) caches so far found at Saqqara have been of Late, or even Graeco-Roman, date.

The tomb of Maya

In 1986, to the west of the tomb of Tia and Tia, a tomb was discovered belonging to another Eighteenth Dynasty army officer, Ramose. An entrance shaft cut into the rock led to a burial chamber. At the foot of the shaft an ancient robbers' tunnel was found. At the foot of the shaft beyond it, some 18m (60ft) below the surface, a door could be seen. On 6 February 1986, at the end of the season's dig, and to ensure everything was checked before the tomb was resealed until the following season's excavation, Professor Martin, together with Dr Van Dijk representing the Leiden Museum, descended the shaft, with little expectation of what awaited them.

Maya

Tia

Horemheb

Ramose

The superstructures *of these New Kingdom tombs at Saqqara form a small section of a probable 'street' that will be extended in future excavations. The original search for Maya's tomb resulted in the discovery of that of General (later King) Horemheb. Subsequently,* *the tomb of Tia was uncovered. In 1986, while exploring a shaft belonging to a soldier, Ramose, the underground chambers of Maya's tomb were found totally by chance. Above is an artist's impression of what Maya's super- and substructure will look like.*

'We were in total darkness for about 15 minutes,' Professor Martin reported. 'Suddenly we glimpsed wonderful reliefs and were extremely startled to find ourselves in the antechamber leading to a burial chamber. My colleague looked across at an inscribed wall and said, "My God, it's Maya".'

The chamber they discovered is unique for its period at Saqqara, its walls covered with almost life-size representations of the deceased, his wife, and various gods and goddesses, all painted in a monochrome yellow. The passage that leads from it is filled with rubble, and has already afforded the Egyptologists glimpses of painted chambers beyond.

The first full season's work on the tomb, in early 1987, centred on the clearance of the superstructure. Evidence indicates that the tomb is a slightly smaller, abbreviated version of Horemheb's. An open courtyard has a colonnade on its west side and doors leading to three vaulted chapels. An inner courtyard has been found to contain reliefs of very fine quality and a statue of Maya and his wife. It is interesting to note that, as in the nearby tomb of Horemheb, some of the blocks used in the building were re-used from Old Kingdom monuments. When the superstructure has been completely cleared, evacuation of the chambers below will begin.

Archaeologists of the *joint EES-Leiden expedition examined with amazement the decorated chamber that lay at the foot of the burial shaft. The brightly painted walls around them, here illuminated by a local assistant, are so far unique at Saqqara. More chambers could be seen lying beyond this room, as yet still unexplored. Inscriptions in them may reveal more information about not only Maya, but the kings he served – Tutankhamun, Ay and Horemheb.*

THE WORKERS OF PHARAOH

The walled village *of Deir el Medina nestles in a waterless valley on the west bank of Luxor about a kilometre from the limits of vegetation and 3km (2mi) from the river. The lower parts of the walls, built of stone cemented with mud and plaster, stand to a height of around 1.2m (4ft). Above this height, the houses were probably made of mud brick. Around the perimeter of the village, the outer wall is thicker than those of the houses and would probably have been higher, with only one point of entry at the north end of the village. The whole area was securely controlled, with vigilant Medjay guards – a regiment that policed Egypt – keeping close watch on the workmen.*

Around 1550 BC the Hyksos invaders who had ruled Egypt were vanquished and driven out of their delta capital by two brothers from Luxor – Kamose and Amosis. After the death of Amosis, his son Amenhotep I relied heavily on the help of his mother, Queen Ahmose-Nefertari, while he attempted to re-establish central control. Together, the young king and his mother looked to their own town of Luxor in which to spend their eternity instead of the area around Memphis. It is most likely to have been Amenhotep I and his mother who founded a village in which the tomb craftsmen could live.

Deir el Medina in history

This village, known today as Deir el Medina, served to house the craftsmen and artists who decorated royal tombs for almost 500 years before it was finally abandoned. It is one of the few town sites in Egypt to have been systematically excavated and recorded. The site yielded vast quantities of inscribed material, giving those interested today not only the chance to walk through streets once occupied by some of the finest artists Egypt ever produced, but also the opportunity to read stories of individuals, reconstructed from the letters and documents that were found there.

The village, abandoned during the reign of Ramesses XI sometime around 1080 BC, lay covered with sand for hundreds of years. None of Luxor's early visitors mention its existence.

Even Napoleon's team of surveyors, though they drew a plan of the Ptolemaic temple that stands at the north of the village, did not suspect a whole town beneath their feet.

It was only in 1815 that the first antiquities were found around the site, gathered together by local villagers and sold to passing tourists. Among these tourists was Sir William Bankes, and the splendid pieces he bought from the village can be seen today in his family home, Kingston Lacey in Dorset. The British consul, Henry Salt, for whom Giovanni Belzoni (*see p. 28*) collected antiquities throughout Egypt, similarly came into possession of large numbers of objects from Deir el Medina, while his great rival, the French consul Drovetti, was a keen bidder against him. After their deaths, their collections were distributed throughout Europe, with Salt's material going principally to the British Museum and Drovetti's to the Turin Museum. It is probable that the remarkable Turin Papyrus with its Ramesside Canon of Kings came from the village.

It was the tireless copyist, John Gardner Wilkinson, who first excavated in the area, opening several tombs in order to record the remarkable information they contained. Attention having been drawn to the potential of the area, it was inevitable that some illicit digging should follow – in the 1850s a large collection of papyri was found, many of the larger pieces being cut in half to increase their value on the black market. Quite by chance, in 1935, the Belgian Egyptologist Jean Capart was able to reunite two of these pieces, when he found a papyrus rolled inside a wooden statue that matched another well-known papyrus in the Pierpoint Morgan Library in New York.

Although scientific excavation was carried out by Schiaparelli from Turin, in 1905, the village was finally systematically cleared by Bernard Bruyère of the French Institute of Oriental Archaeology between 1922 and 1951 with the aid and support of Georges Posener and the Czech, Jaroslav Černỳ.

The houses

The village was built in an isolated, waterless valley on the west bank of Luxor. Inside an outer mud-brick enclosure wall, 18.3m (20ft) in height, a mass of stone foundations were laid for houses standing side by side. It seems that sometime during the Eighteenth Dynasty, a fire destroyed many workmen's possessions, and that at the start of the Nineteenth Dynasty houses were rebuilt and the whole village was extended.

The village could only be entered via one doorway at the north end. Here, janitors guarded the gate, not only protecting the warehouses that stored pigments and precious tools, but also controlling the activities of the workmen themselves. Since all the materials they used were issued by the king's own order, any theft of even the pettiest nature would be seen as an offence against the throne itself and therefore a state crime amounting to treason. The janitors were responsible for the issue and accounting of all village stores, from copper tools weighed against a stone marked with the workman's name, to bundles of firewood and jars of water.

The village comprised one central street, running north to south, with narrow houses all running off it. Excavation suggests this street was probably covered over, making the village one solid roofed community that was doubtless airless and dark. The floors of the houses and the main street were found to be covered with layers of accumulated and well-trodden animal droppings of goats, sheep and pigs. Life in the village must, therefore, have been far from pleasant, especially during the intensely hot summer months.

The houses are narrow and usually have four small rooms, one behind the other. The front room usually contained a mud-brick raised dais

in one corner about 1m (3ft) in height and approached by steps. When originally found, these daises were plastered and painted with figures of the jolly demigod Bes and his female counterpart Beset (*see p. 132*). This has led many scholars to suggest that this was perhaps a birth-bed. It is just as possible, however, that it was purely a place for visitors to sit clear of the debris on the floor. The second room, often with one or two wooden columns mounted on stone bases, was slightly larger, with a small raised plinth about 15cm (6in) high in one corner that probably served as a bed. Under the floor of this room there was a cellar where jars of food and drink and family valuables could be stored. The third room, sometimes divided into two, served as a storage area, while the fourth, at the rear of the house, may well have been open to the sky, serving as a small courtyard in which the cooking was done. From this area, a narrow staircase led up onto the roof.

The houses were sparsely furnished, as wooden furniture was beyond the means of even these highly paid craftsmen. Most Egyptian households would contain little other than the wooden headrests everyone used.

There are few town sites available to Egyptologists to study. With limited land available in Egypt, most sites have been used and reused for thousands of years, with new houses being constructed on the levelled foundations of older ones. The workmen's village of Deir el Medina is almost a unique source of information about the everyday lives of ordinary people.

This small *painted ostracon, depicting two girls scouring a pot, is the ancient equivalent of a doodle or cartoon. The highly trained artists and craftsmen who occupied Deir el Medina continuously for around 500 years obviously had some free moments. In a 10-day week, eight days would be spent away from home, sleeping overnight in local shacks, near the tomb in which they were working. On the ninth and tenth days, they returned home to organize local affairs and take their ease. But it is shown from work registers and inscriptions found in the village that the cutting and decorating of a tomb did not take more than about five years, so if a king survived to reign for a long time, the workmen must have found themselves with some leisure time. In these idle moments, it appears, they doodled, or practised aspects of their art which they found problematic. Many hundreds of these delightfully frank and natural pieces have survived.*

DEIR EL MEDINA: THE PAINTED TOMBS

A lavishly filled *offering table, painted on the walls of the tomb of Sennedjem (No. 1), an overseer of works in the village of Deir el Medina, offers eternal fresh food for the spirit of the dead man. The fresh meats – a leg of beef, trussed ducks and geese – mingle with loaves of bread, bunches of grapes and various vegetables. Under the table, the tops of sealed jars indicate an everlasting supply of beer to wash it all down. A feast for a nobleman, which has lasted on the walls of a tomb for over 3000 years, yet still looks as fresh as when it was painted.*

The workmen who lived with their families in the craftsmen's village on the west bank of Luxor were invariably buried in tombs in the locality. Directly to the west of the village, shallow terraces contain the entrance shafts to more than 60 burial chambers. Like the royal tombs the craftsmen worked on for their masters, their own tombs are all brightly painted. However, since many of these tombs remained undiscovered until recent years, unlike the royal tombs that stood open to visitors and received consequent damage, their preservation is far better.

These tombs, though often tiny, glow with colour, freshness and a vitality that is missing from the royal tombs. All of them were built to a standard design, though some were larger than others. A vertical shaft into the rock led often to a small chamber from which a short staircase descended to a barrel-vaulted room measuring little more than 3.7 × 2.4m (12 × 8ft). The entrance to the shaft was located in a small courtyard which also contained a small mortuary chapel. The chapel, either of stone or mud brick, was surrounded by a small, deeply angled pyramid within which was a T-shaped room, the outer section often with a vaulted ceiling. The pyramid had stelae, or gravestones, carved with the image, name and titles of the dead man and his family, attached to each side. Since the burial shafts were usually rubble-filled and outside the pyramidion-topped chapel, they were often difficult for robbers to find. As a result of this, several fine tombs in an excellent state of preservation have been discovered with their burials intact.

The tomb of Sennedjem
On 6 February 1886, Gaston Maspero, head of the Antiquities Service, entered a small tomb in the workmen's village, later numbered 1, and found it intact. The small burial chamber, with its curved roof, contained the mummies of Sennedjem, an overseer in the village at the start of the Nineteenth Dynasty, his wife Iyneferty, their son Khons and daughter-in-law Tamakhet and the Lady Isis, wife of their second son Khabekhnet, together with most of their funerary objects. Sennedjem and his wife lived to a venerable old age. Iyneferty's mummy, now in the Metropolitan Museum of Art, New York, is that of a woman aged approximately 75; but her coffins are wonderfully preserved, and depict her as beautiful, slim, lithe and eternally young.

The tomb was badly recorded, unfortunately, and the objects in it dispersed to museums around the world. It is a sad reflection that this family who had intended to spend eternity together now lies thousands of miles apart, with Sennedjem in Cairo, his wife in New York and one of his daughters-in-law in Berlin.

The burial chamber remains a wonder to visitors, however, who are free to admire its immaculately preserved paintings. The walls and ceiling of the tiny room are alive with colour and vigour. On a yellow background, scenes of the eternal life of the old couple are depicted. On one side wall, the mummy of Sennedjem lies on a bier, with the two goddesses Isis and Nephthys, depicted as falcons, wings opened protectively around the dead man. The other walls reflect a little of the post-Amarna preoccupation with the gods, for several registers show Sennedjem and Iyneferty facing panels of them, all tribunals listening to their pleas for admittance. The god of the dead, Osiris, stands waiting under a canopy as Anubis ushers Sennedjem forward, to be judged for the correctness of his life on earth. The eastern end wall shows that the trials and tribulations were successfully faced, for Sennedjem and Iyneferty, with their sons and daughters-in-law, spend eternity in the lush fields of Iaru, the land of cool streams where palm trees hang heavy with ripe dates, and where the fields, as quickly as the couple sow them, yield heavy crops of grain and flax. Above them, free from worry, their son Khons stands behind the gods Re and Ptah and waits to greet his parents – this clearly demonstrates that this son died before his parents, and is eager to welcome their company in the afterlife.

The tomb of Kha and Meryt
The Italian Egyptologist Ernesto Schiaparelli came to Deir el Medina for his second season in 1906, to excavate on behalf of the Italian Archaeological Mission. It was a season that was to prove lucky, for Schiaparelli found an intact tomb.

The pyramid-chapel of the foreman Kha and his wife, Meryt, had been known for some years, and the scenes in it had been copied by various archaeologists including Wilkinson (*see p. 36*) and Lepsius (*see p. 38*). It was already known that Kha had worked in Deir el Medina in the early years of the village, serving the Eighteenth Dynasty kings Amenhotep II, Tuthmosis IV and Amenhotep III. He and his

In the tomb of Sennedjem, the body of the deceased man is embalmed and prepared for the tomb by Anubis, protector of the dead. The picture shows Sennedjem's mummy, complete with a painted and gilded mask, lying on a lion-headed bier, a fine example of which was found in the tomb of Tutankhamun. The height of the base of the actual example suggests it was used not for the embalming, a messy affair, but rather for the final funerary rites. Here the mortuary priest, wearing a mask to represent Anubis, performs some of those rites. The patterning to the rear of this priest (from his waist upwards) is strongly reminiscent of tomb ceilings of the period. It is possible that these rites took place in the tomb itself.

wife were shown with an unnamed daughter and son making offerings to Osiris. The pyramidion of the chapel had already been removed by an earlier traveller, and was taken away to the Louvre.

It was a surprise, then, that the burial chamber should be in the cliffs surrounding the village and not in the proximity of the chapel. The outer doorway had been blocked with stones and buried under loose rubble. With the removal of the door, an unfinished corridor was found running horizontally for about 9.1m (30ft) into the cliff, its walls and ceiling rough-hewn. It was obvious to the excavators that this burial had been hasty, for the tools of the workmen who had helped at the funeral were still stacked up against one wall where they had been left thousands of years ago, while a stool and a low wooden bed had been simply left in the corridor.

A second, sealed doorway led Schiaparelli into the burial chamber which had never been disturbed. Here, stacked against one wall, stood another bed piled high with bed linen, with stools and a finely carved chair leaning against it. On the chair, whose back was inlaid with a delicate frieze of lotus flowers, stood a statue of Kha himself made of wood, a cape of elaborate plaited linen threads hanging around its

shoulders. Most touching of all, two wooden coffins stood against another wall still hung about with garlands of flowers placed there by ancient mourners. The mummies still lie in their coffins in the Turin Museum. An X-ray taken in recent years shows that the mummy of Kha was adorned with a gold necklace and heavy earrings, one of the earliest examples yet found of men wearing earrings. Inscriptions of some of the objects found in the tomb show that their son, Userhet, was a priest who served Queen Mutnofret, the wife of Amenhotep II, and also Queen Sitamun, the daughter-wife of Amenhotep III. It is clear that Kha's position in the village brought him and his family great honours, as well as proximity to the royal family.

The objects from the intact tomb were all removed and, except for two small articles, taken to Turin where they can be seen today. The workmen's tombs that cluster around the village are all full of life, leaving the visitor not only amazed at the colour and the preservation but also frequently amused by the pervading and unexpected sense of humour shown in them – where pet cats steal fish from piles of painted funerary offerings, and sailors in boats hang forlornly over the side suffering, one imagines, from seasickness.

RESTING PLACE OF THE APIS BULLS

This stela was found by Mariette with the only intact burial of an Apis bull that had survived in the Serapeum. It shows the sacred bull standing upright – artistic licence, since they were mummified in the crouching position – standing on a sledge-base inside a sarcophagus. The barrel-vaulted lid of the sarcophagus is surmounted by a Horus falcon. The stela itself is now in the Louvre.

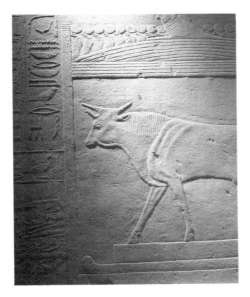

'The Apis Bull,' wrote Herodotus, 'is the calf of a cow which is never able after to have another. The Egyptians believe that a flash of lightning strikes the cow from heaven, and thus causes her to conceive the Apis. It has distinctive marks. It is black, with a white diamond on its forehead, the image of an eagle on its back, two white hairs on its tail and a scarab-beetle mark under its tongue.'

Such a remarkable creature as this could scarcely be expected to work in the fields! In fact, the Apis bull was considered sacred by the ancient Egyptians, along with its 'cousins' the Mnevis bull and the Buchis bull. All were considered to be the earthly incarnation of a god. Unlike other animals who merely interceded on humans' behalf with a deity (*see p. 135*), the bulls were believed to be the very god himself living among humans. Apis was the manifestation of Osiris, Mnevis, of Re-Atum and Buchis of Re in Memphis. All three were chosen for their special markings, were accorded the lives of a god on earth, and were mourned, mummified and buried after their death with all the pomp and magnificence accompanying the burial of a pharaoh.

Despite the universal veneration of Osiris as god of the dead from the end of the Old Kingdom onwards, his incarnation as the Apis bull is much older. The first mention of one such is on two historic documents, the Palermo stone and the Cairo annals. They record the festival held to celebrate the appearance of an Apis bull in the First Dynasty. The predominance of the king's image at this time on ceremonial slate palettes as a mighty bull (*see p. 55*), and the inclusion of the bulls' horns around the First Dynasty mastaba of King Djer at Saqqara (*see p. 58*), suggest that veneration of bulls was firmly established by then and could even go back to early predynastic times.

There could only ever be one Apis bull alive at any one time, and at its death, it was believed to be reincarnated in the form of another calf. This notion of resurrection and the eternal recycling of the soul naturally applied especially to Osiris. The Egyptian name of that god, 'User', linked with the name 'Apis', resulted in a conjoint god, Serapis who, in the Graeco-Roman period, was venerated along with Isis throughout the classical world.

Strabo, the Greek geographer (63 BC–AD 22) noted when he visited Egypt that the Apis bulls were buried in an underground chamber called the Serapeum, at the end of a paved avenue flanked by stone sphinxes. It was, he recorded, constantly being covered with sand and thus was sometimes difficult to visit even in his day.

The rediscovery of the Serapeum

When Mariette arrived in Egypt on the Louvre's business in 1851 (*see p. 32*), he observed large numbers of stone sphinxes of identical design embellishing the gardens of many large houses in Cairo. When he enquired as to where they came from, he received vague directions to the ancient necropolis site of Saqqara. Walking, therefore, around the Step Pyramid complex, he came upon another sphinx lying in the sand, its head and paws standing clear. He was told that it was nothing exciting, and that many lay here under the sand. Remembering the words of Strabo, in great excitement Mariette summoned workmen to dig for him. In all, over 140 sphinxes were found in a wide avenue and, at the head of it as Mariette had guessed, a quarter of a mile into the desert, the stepped entrance was revealed which led to an underground chamber.

'When I first entered the tombs of the Apis,' he wrote, 'I was so overwhelmed with astonishment that even now, five years later, the feeling is still vivid in my mind.' The feeling is understandable even today as the visitor enters what appears to be a huge, dimly lit cavern. On the wall facing the entrance, regular-shaped niches in a mud base show where once votive stelae were placed by pilgrims visiting the site.

The gently sloping *staircase descends below the surface of the sand at Saqqara towards the entrance of the Serapeum. It was down this slope that the bull sarcophagi, huge granite blocks hollowed out and weighing in excess of 80 tons, would be slowly drawn. Sarcophagi found in the chambers within the Serapeum dated from the New Kingdom, though the Apis cult goes back to the Archaic period. Just as Mariette followed this staircase, no doubt some future archaeologist will be faced with a similar entrance to older vaults when the necropolis is more fully excavated.*

The galleries to left and right, are almost 7.6m (25ft) high, and cut from them on both sides are vast side-chambers, their floors some 1.5m (5ft) lower than the main corridor. In these stand the huge sarcophagi in which the mummified bulls once lay. Each of them, carved from a single block of granite or diorite, weighs more than 80 tons, its lid more than 30cm (12in) thick. In all there were 28 sarcophagi of Apis bulls from the time of Ramesses II to the Twenty-sixth Dynasty. The last sarcophagus was not moved into place; it was abandoned together with its lid in one of the passages.

When Mariette first entered the Serapeum, all but one of the sarcophagi had been robbed in antiquity, their lids pushed to one side as if gently moved. In one wall, however, Mariette found a bricked-up gap – 'Three thousand years had had no effect upon it. The fingermarks of the last Egyptian who put the last stone in place, were still visible in the mud plaster. In a corner, bare feet had left their mark in soft sand; nothing was disturbed.' Unlike the ancient robbers, all Mariette's efforts to move the lid were to no avail; he had to use dynamite to blow it off! Within the sarcophagus he found the mummy of the bull, together with several alabaster jars. This, the only mummy to survive intact from seven centuries of bull-burials, is now in the Agricultural Museum in Cairo.

The chambers of the Serapeum that Mariette discovered were constructed on the orders of Prince Khaemwese, the son of Ramesses II (*see p. 23*). The prince died during the fifty-fifth year of his father's reign and chose to be buried with the Apis bulls he had spent so much of his life serving. Here, behind the burial of the Apis bull, the ceiling collapsed, hiding his sarcophagus; and here in 1852, Mariette found his mummy intact. The elderly prince lay in a wooden coffin, a gold mask over his face and jewels about his body.

Although it is clear that Apis bulls had been venerated for thousands of years before Prince Khaemwese built this labyrinth, their burial places have never been found. They presumably still lie hidden under the sands of Saqqara.

The embalming house

Although little remains today of what was once the vast city of Memphis, about 4.8km (3mi) east of Saqqara, near the village of Mit Rahina, is an open-air museum in which assorted statues, blocks and other objects now lie. Most of them were discovered in the precinct of what was once the largest temple in Egypt – that of Ptah. To the south of this lay the Apis enclosure, where the Apis bull once lived in splendour with its equally divine mother. Strabo described this as being, 'a sort of temple'. In 1941, the Antiquities Service excavated the area and found several huge beds of calcite. A depression ran around the edge of each and sloped to one end, where a container set on the floor collected fluid. It was here that the dead bulls were mummified and then bandaged. From 1982 onwards, the Institute of Fine Arts in New York has re-excavated the area and more tables have been discovered, together with the foundations of several buildings, one upon the other. In future years, more of the story concerning the sacred bulls is almost certain to be revealed.

THE LAST GREAT KINGS

This splendid mask, made of a single sheet of gold hammered to shape, covered the face of King Sheshonk, whose mummy and sarcophagus lay in the entrance chamber of the tomb of Psusennes I. The body in the coffin was that of an elderly man. This king, given the title today of Sheshonk II, seems not to have ruled Egypt at all in his own right. He served as co-regent to his father, Osorkon II at the start of the Twenty-second Dynasty, but died before him.

The Valley of the Kings and the workmen's village of Deir el Medina were finally abandoned at the end of the Twentieth Dynasty. The tomb of the last king cut in the valley, that of Ramesses XI, was never finished. Once the ringing of the blows of stonecutters' chisels on rock had died away, the valley stood empty. By this time, some of the tombs had already been robbed, not, as is often thought, by workmen but perhaps as Cyril Aldred pointed out in 1979, by a marauding army.

A time of unrest
At the end of the reign of Ramesses VI, a priest in the temple of Karnak by the name of Amenhotep dared to aspire to the throne. He had himself depicted in the temple with a pseudo-royal cartouche. A Nubian army, under Panehesy, was summoned to suppress him.

In the Valley of the Kings, the granite sarcophagus of Ramesses VI lies smashed, part of it lying on its side. Upon this, black lines of the unguents poured over the king's body drip vertically downwards, showing that the sarcophagus was smashed and upturned, probably with great violence – possibly within days of the burial. Meanwhile, work registers from the workmen's village show that foreigners were causing disruption in the area that affected their attendance in the valley.

Later, during the reign of Ramesses IX, tomb-robbery trials were held in Luxor and several workmen were called before the vizier to account for what amounted to petty pilfering. In every case but one, the defendants protested that the tombs they were accused of violating were already open. Only in one case, that of King Sobekemsaf of the Seventeenth Dynasty (a tomb that has still not been found, although the British Museum possesses jewellery and a statue from his burial) did the robbers admit to breaking into the tomb. From it, they took the mummy of the king, 'covered in gold, his coffins inlaid with gold and silver inside and out and decorated with jewels. We took the gold and jewels, and the precious metals of his coffins. Then we found the queen, and took everything that was hers, and set fire to (both) the coffins.'

The rich tombs of the greatest pharaohs were thus apparently plundered not by workmen, who were so closely supervised that even one gold ring illicitly acquired would be instantly observed, but by a great body of dissatisfied men (i.e. Nubians) summoned into the area to suppress one upstart priest. Nor were the tombs entered secretly and silently by night, but as the tomb of Ramesses VI proves, with great commotion and violence. All the priests of the area could do afterwards was to gather together the mummies of the kings and put them, together, in a more secure place (*see p. 96–9*).

After the Valley of the Kings
As early as the Nineteenth Dynasty, moves had been made by the kings of Egypt to distance themselves from Luxor. Ramesses I, was born in the delta. His son, Seti I, had established a summer residence in the old Hyksos capital of Tanis. It was Ramesses II, Seti's son, who decided to build a great permanent palace there called Per-Ramesses. Around the luxurious palace that he built, inlaid, it was recorded, with gold and silver, lapis lazuli and turquoise, a city grew. By the end of the Twentieth Dynasty, all links with Luxor had been broken. The kings of the Twenty-first Dynasty had to find a new site for their tombs.

The location of Ramesses' palace-city was first noted in 1798 by Napoleon's soldiers, as being near the delta town of San el Hagar. Although several people excavated there, confirming the connection, including Naville and Petrie (see p. 40), little was known of the actual layout of the site until the arrival, in 1939, of Pierre Montet.

The foundations of a huge temple dominated the site, and it was to this that Montet turned. Within the original great enclosure walls of the temple, around 372 by 210m (407 by 230yd) wide, built by Ramesses II, Psusennes I, second king of the Twenty-first Dynasty, had built a much smaller temple. Though little remained, the foundations of the enclosure wall showed that it was carelessly laid out, with unequal sides and its corners not square.

It was soon after his arrival, in 1939, while excavating the south-western corner of this area, that Montet discovered a tomb. Within the next months, another five were discovered, two of which were intact. All were royal tombs, belonging to kings of the Twenty-first and Twenty-second Dynasties. Montet's discovery of the largest group of intact royal burials ever found in Egypt was hailed, at the time, as even more spectacular than that of Carter's discovery of the tomb of Tutankhamun and yet, today, it is little known.

The royal tombs

Within the six tombs were discovered the burials of Psusennes I, his mother Queen Mutnodjme, one of his sons, Ramesses Ankhenefmut, a fellow soldier, Wendebawended; Siamun; and Kings Osorkon II, Takelot II, Sheshonk III and a Prince Hornakht of the Twenty-second Dynasty.

The burial chambers are all small rooms clustered together, cut into the bedrock below the temple courtyard. They were lined with an assortment of granite and limestone blocks and

mud bricks. If there had originally been a superstructure, it had vanished. Many of the stones, and even the sarcophagi and burial equipment had been re-used. In the chamber of Psusennes, the body of the king lay inside a sarcophagus cut for Merenptah, son and successor of Ramesses II, while his viscera were placed in alabaster canopic jars bearing the assorted names of Tuthmosis, Amenmose, Amenhotep and Osiris. It also seems that the chambers within the tombs had been reorganized several times, as none of the royal burials were found in the rooms that bore their names.

Despite this, the burials were lavish. The coffin and mask of Psusennes I were of solid silver, overlaid with gold, while the body of Sheshonk II was enclosed in a curious black and silver coffin with the face of a falcon. The burial of Psusennes I, the founder of the temple, was the most richly endowed. The king's body was weighed down with numerous necklaces, bracelets and amulets of gold and lapis lazuli; one pendant was uniquely inscribed in cuneiform, stating that it had been brought to Egypt from Assyria. Even the king's fingers and toes were covered with gold caps, and sandals of pure gold were on his feet. Around him were found 18 vases of gold and silver, many of them of Syrian design.

The objects from the royal burials are all to be seen today in the Cairo Museum, in a room alongside those of Tutankhamun. Although there were fewer pieces found than in the tomb of the more illustrious boy king, their quality is superb. Montet completed his excavations at Tanis in 1951, but he remained dissatisfied. In his account of the excavations, *Les Énigmes de Tanis*, he wrote, 'we remain convinced that there are still more royal tombs in the tell of San el Hagar.' Many of the burials of the kings of the Twenty-first and Twenty-second Dynasties are still missing. If Montet is correct, the site of Tanis holds yet more secrets.

The inner silver coffin, inlaid with gold, of Psusennes I, king during the Twenty-first Dynasty, whose burial was found intact at Tanis. The base of the coffin was found in pieces and has had to be restored. Since silver was considerably rarer in Egypt than gold (it being impossible for Egyptian craftsmen to cupellate silver from the gold that bore it), this coffin represents a sumptuous burial of great wealth during Egypt's declining years. The tomb in which Pierre Montet found all the royal burials was constructed originally for Psusennes I.

THE SHIFTING SANDS
AFTER THE PHARAOHS

This fragment *of textile of Coptic date shows a woven design of dyed wool laid over linen. Dating, perhaps from around the fourth century AD, it shows a hunter in a Phrygian cap holding a staff in his hands. During the period of the introduction and spread of Christianity many people were buried unmummified, dressed in their ordinary clothes. Thousands of pieces of such textiles have survived, but because of disinterest in what, in Egyptian terms, are 'modern' pieces, and careless excavation, it is still difficult to date fragments even on grounds of style, context and colour.*

The founding of Alexandria on the Mediterranean coast soon after the Greek conquest marked the beginning of the end of ancient Egypt. The chosen site had never been of major importance before, being the location of a small fishing village called Rakote. Although it was isolated from Egypt, it was convenient for the new Greek overlords. Many wealthy Greeks settled in the delta, forming tightly-knit communities. Their interests were served intellectually by the founding of a new university and library, which incorporated much ancient Egyptian knowledge (acquired over thousands of years), and economically, by a large Jewish quarter. Virtually nothing that might bear witness to this early Alexandria remains to be seen today.

The Greeks built many temples along the Nile Valley, but with the exception of a few isolated places, seem seldom to have lived there. Burial sites and towns of this period are remarkably few. In Middle Egypt, however, about 290km (180mi) south of Cairo is the town of Hermopolis – the city of Hermes, the name by which they knew Thoth. Nearby, at Tuna el Gebel, is the necropolis for the Greek settlement, with several unique tombs. These, though built in Egyptian style with small, temple-like stone superstructures, show how rapidly things changed in Egypt after the Greeks arrived. The tomb of Petosiris, a priest who lived during the reign of Ptolemy I, though decorated with Egyptianesque scenes, contain curiously Greek-attired figures in non-Egyptian poses. The transition to Classical styles of art, dress and language clearly spread rapidly southwards from the delta.

When Petrie excavated the delta site of Naucratis at the start of his career in Egyptology in 1894, he found the foundations of a large Greek trading city that spanned the end of native Egyptian rule and the Greek conquest. Yet although many objects were recovered, they were primarily of Greek design, confirming the view that Greek attitudes soon overcame Egyptian ones. Nothing remains to be seen on the site today.

Greek quickly became the language of the administration. Many Greek words entered the native language through local administrators and priests. Fewer and fewer Egyptians could read hieroglyphs and within the temples the priesthood made the script increasingly complicated, excluding even the few secular folk who were able to read it.

Roman Egypt
Although relatively little is known of burial customs of the Greek period save that mummification continued much as before, more evidence is available from the time of the Roman conquest. When Rome took command of Egypt in 30 BC, the Greek community continued to flourish and Greek remained the official language of the government. Many Roman soliders were rewarded for their valour with parcels of land in Egypt, some of them in the fertile area of the Faiyum.

While Flinders Petrie was excavating the pyramid of Amenemhet III in Haward in 1888 and 1911, he examined the nearby cemetery of the Roman town of Arsinoe. The 146 bodies he found were all mummified and most elaborately bandaged. Over the face instead of a mask, as had previously been found on mummies, a painted portrait board was inserted. This appears to have been painted from life and perhaps even hung within the owner's house until his or her death, when the corners would have been trimmed in order for it to fit the mummy.

Similar portraits were found in Middle Egypt near El Sheikh Ibada, the necropolis site of ancient Antinoöpolis. Since this town was founded in AD 130 by the Emperor Hadrian in memory of his favourite, Antinous, who had been drowned in the Nile, these striking portraits would appear to date from the time of the Roman occupation, perhaps to the first three or four centuries AD. The boards give individualistic portraits of Roman citizens painted in coloured, melted wax paint called 'encaustic'. Although they are strongly reminiscent of portraits found in Pompeii and Herculaneum, many of the sitters nevertheless had Egyptian attributes, including jewellery and clothing. Several of the boards show a vertical dripping of paint that indicates easels were used during the painting, if so this is the first attested use of them.

Although bodies were still being mummified and bandaged Egyptian-style in the Faiyum and Middle Egypt, in the delta town of Kom Abu Billo, anciently known as Terenuthis, F.L. Griffith in 1887 found another Romano-Egyptian cemetery that, from coins found in the area, dated to the first four centuries AD. Here stelae or gravestones show the deceased reclining on a Roman triclinium, or dining couch, and dressed in Roman fashion, sometimes under an Egyptian portico supported by

Egyptian columns at each side, and with Greek or Coptic inscriptions. There seems to have been a strong cultural intermixing at this time.

Many aspects of Egyptian life influenced Roman artists throughout the empire. Nilotic scenes showing classical buildings alongside rivers teeming with Egyptian fish, birds and crocodiles became favourites, while temples to Serapis and Isis are found in many Roman towns. Horus, one of the oldest of all the ancient Egyptian gods, is frequently depicted in statues battling with his old adversary Seth, who is often shown in the form of a crocodile, while Horus, dressed as a Roman centurion, rides on horseback.

Christian Egypt

Word of the teachings of Christ and his Crucifixion spread quickly around the Mediterranean wherever there were settlements of Jews. It was natural, then, that word should reach Egypt very quickly, and legend has it that it arrived in the person of St Mark. Filled with resentment against their Roman overlords, the Egyptians welcomed Christianity, which spread rapidly the length of the Nile. Although little is recorded of these early years – the Christians probably being regarded by the Romans as another, and more troublesome, sect of Jews – there can be no doubt of its effect. From AD 66 onwards, there are records of Jewish riots in Egypt, which attest to tens of thousands having been killed or martyred.

By the second century, Christian communities apparently flourished in Egypt. In many places ancient temples were adapted for purposes of Christian worship, while the 'ankh', the hieroglyphic sign that meant 'life' or 'to live', was adopted by them as a looped cross, the crux ansata.

The Christians vehemently rejected the old pagan traditions, including mummification. Instead, their dead were buried simply clad in everyday garments. Although many Coptic sites have been found, most of them were unfortunately quickly cleared, unremarked, in the hasty search for more ancient, and by definition, more interesting, material. Many fine Coptic textiles have survived, though usually undated and unprovenanced. It seems that the people of the time wore simple linen and cotton tunics, with bands and 'medallions' of tapestry stitched on, often transferred from one garment to another as the clothes were outgrown or became worn. These tapestries show such interesting mixtures of Egyptian, Greek, Roman and Christian elements that it is often impossible to separate them and assign them to a definite period.

The birth of monasticism

The first hermits moved out into the desert, occupying ancient tombs and turning them into anchorite's cells. The first acknowledged monk was St Antony. It is recorded that he was an Egyptian by birth, and raised as an indifferent Christian until shortly before his parents' deaths. At this time, when he was '18 or 20', he left his little sister in the care of Christian women, gave away everything he owned and moved into the desert. Though sorely tormented by the Devil in many forms, Antony overcame every trial, and other hermits gathered about him to learn from him, forming a small community. A contemporary of Antony's, St Pachom, laid down the first rules for monastic life. From the end of the fourth century, many monasteries were built in Egypt, and it was from this Egyptian seed that monasticism spread to Europe.

Today several of these early monasteries can still be visited. In the Wadi Natrun' in the western delta, monks still live in the ancient buildings and follow the rules of Pachom to this day. In Aswan, on the west bank, the long deserted monastery of St Simeon dates back to the sixth century, and after all these hundreds of years, some of the earliest examples of Christian paintings can still be seen on the walls.

In 1945, in Nag Hammadi in Middle Egypt, a local farmer accidentally found a large earthenware jar. Inside were 13 codices, sheets of papyrus and vellum stitched into leather bindings as primitive books. Ten years later, when scholars finally examined them, they were found to be episodes from the New Testament declared heretical by Church Councils and buried by local priests. These Gnostic Gospels, Epistles and Acts – Gnostic being an heretical Christian sect which flourished in Egypt from the third to the fifth centuries AD – revealed for the first time details of many early Christian beliefs long since lost and forgotten.

Although the culture of ancient Egypt died during this Christian era, in the Coptic language and through the art and literature of the early Egyptian church, hints of its influences and traditions can still be felt.

These two small *mummies of children who died some time in the Graeco-Roman period represent the closing stages of mummification in Egypt. Over their faces, a portrait board, worked in melted wax paint, was inserted in the elaborately folded bandages. Inside, the bodies were hastily and carelessly mummified. The portraits, which frequently bear great resemblance to Roman paintings found in Pompeii and Herculaneum, enable us to fix dates on the mummies of between the first and the fourth centuries* AD, *with the majority dating to the second and third centuries.*

V

TEMPLES: MANSIONS OF THE GODS

'The Egyptians are religious to excess, beyond any other nation in the world, and here are some of their customs that illustrate the point. They all wear linen clothes which they make a point of continually washing . . . The priests shave their bodies all over every other day to guard against the presence of lice or anything else equally unpleasant while they are about their duties.'
Herodotus, Book II, 37

The colossal temples that flank the Nile have, by and large, been restored and made safe, the accumulations of sand built up over the centuries swept away, and today tourists flock in their thousands to see them. The visitor might be forgiven for thinking that the temples alone represent the whole history of Egypt. Yet virtually nothing remains of temple structures for the first half of Egyptian civilization – almost 1500 years. The majority that do date from the Graeco-Roman occupation.

The impact of Egyptian temples, with their multi-columned hypostyle halls and massive pylon gateways, is such that people often feel overwhelmed. In addition, temples outnumber every other kind of monument along the Nile, and the similarity of their design tends to make them indistinguishable from each other. In fact, all the temples are different in various ways – some mortuary temples belonging to great kings, other cult temples of local or national gods and goddesses – and each adds its own small contribution to our knowledge of the temple and its functions.

The Temple of Amun *at Karnak. This view shows the renowned great hypostyle hall as it appears from the outside.*

TEMPLE STRUCTURE AND RITUAL

Standing inside one of the massively columned inner walls of an Egyptian temple dwarfed by stone pillars fixed like trunks of trees in a dense forest, one could be forgiven for wondering if the ancient architects ever came to terms with considerations of the strength and stresses of stone. Compared with the ethereal and graceful columns of a Greek temple that supported roofs with the minimum of effort, Egyptian temples appear at first sight clumsy and ill-conceived.

Yet, as innumerable texts carved on temple walls prove, the structure of an Egyptian temple had little to do with the vagaries of aesthetic design. On the contrary, their very form was intended to represent the concrete reality of an old and, to the Egyptians, a powerful belief.

The First Occasion

There was once a time, Egyptian legend said, when the earth was filled with a watery emptiness, without shape. From these waters, called Nun, there emerged a mound of land, and upon this mound, all that exists came into being. According to which group of priests told the story, either a plant emerged that served as a perch for the first life, the falcon Horus; or a lotus plant grew and blossomed, from which the sun emerged. The outpouring of energy that created Mankind on this, called the First Occasion, was revered by the Egyptians as the tangible manifestation of divine power. The first temple came into existence on this mound in the form of an outer enclosure wall, designed to separate the god and its power from everything outside. Inside, a reed-mat shelter was placed over the very source of creation – the perch or plant – to protect it and mark it as being sacred.

The form of this first temple, according to texts in the temple of Horus at Edfu, was strictly laid down by the gods themselves, even to the dimensions of all its walls. As time went on, courtyards in front of the reed shelter further separated those who might enter the sacred areas from those who might not.

Every Egyptian temple, then, was built as a copy of the first temple, with the aim of encouraging the god to return to earth, lured by the familiarity of the structure. Every town or settlement area in Egypt had its own temple, dedicated to the needs of its own local god or family of gods; and each temple was built to the same design.

According to Egyptian legend, before humans existed, the gods ruled and filled the earth. These gods were born, lived their allotted life span (usually an incredible length of time, often measured in thousands of years) and then died and were buried. Each Egyptian temple recalled the life and often the burial location of a specific god. In Egyptian belief, the spirits of the dead – their kas – required food and drink daily if they were to survive eternally. The ka was summoned via the medium of a statue or painted picture. The cult temple represented the spot to which the ka of each god was recalled. In a parallel manner, a mortuary temple or chapel served the ka of a dead man, whether king or wealthy commoner.

The First Servant of the God

The temple formed the focus of a great cluster of buildings and estates at the centre of each community, employing many local people. The lands, often permitted by royal decree to be free of payment of taxes, yielded grain, fruit and vegetables, and supported livestock for the upkeep of the god and the temple personnel. In theory, only the king could ever come into the presence of a god. In practice, however, since the king could not be everywhere at once, he appointed a deputy – often a relative or a member of his household – to serve in his place. These deputies, usually referred to as 'high priests', were called the 'First Servant of the God' by the Egyptians.

Under him served ranks of full-time priests, some supervising the workshops, some studying the ancient writings stored on scrolls within each temple as a library, some organizing the copying of scripts (often for inclusion in burials), some educating future generations of scholars, and some arranging the day-to-day routine of the temple. All priests had to be ritually purified, their heads and bodies shaven, washed twice a day and twice a night and dressed only in gowns or kilts of fine, pure white linen.

The great mass of the people who worked on the temple estates were purely labourers and not priests at all, but were counted as temple workers. The Great Harris Papyrus in the British Museum, London, records that during the reign of Ramesses II, around 1150 BC, 81,322 men worked in the temple of Karnak, tending over 400,000 livestock.

The function of the high priest was to furnish the god with its daily needs, just as the chamberlain within the court served the king.

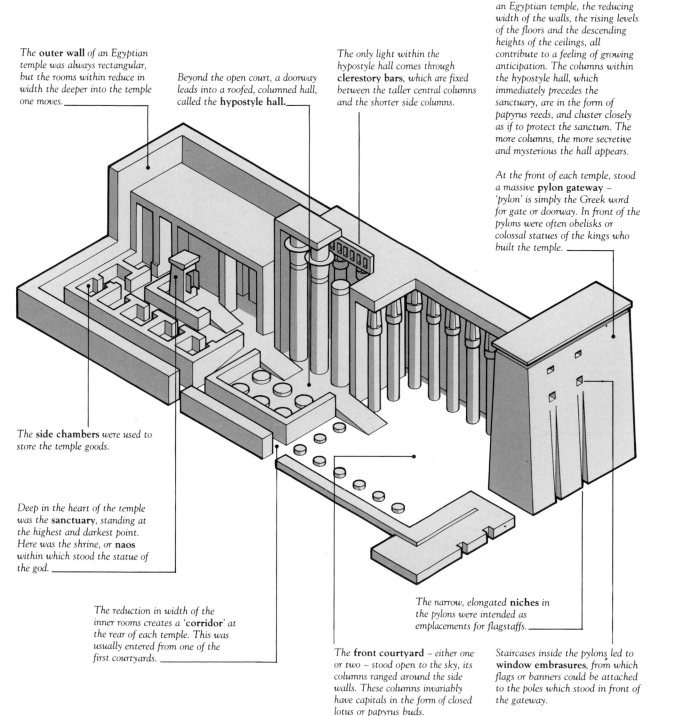

The **outer wall** of an Egyptian temple was always rectangular, but the rooms within reduce in width the deeper into the temple one moves.

Beyond the open court, a doorway leads into a roofed, columned hall, called the **hypostyle hall.**

The only light within the hypostyle hall comes through **clerestory bars**, which are fixed between the taller central columns and the shorter side columns.

As one walks towards the naos of an Egyptian temple, the reducing width of the walls, the rising levels of the floors and the descending heights of the ceilings, all contribute to a feeling of growing anticipation. The columns within the hypostyle hall, which immediately precedes the sanctuary, are in the form of papyrus reeds, and cluster closely as if to protect the sanctum. The more columns, the more secretive and mysterious the hall appears.

At the front of each temple, stood a massive **pylon gateway** – 'pylon' is simply the Greek word for gate or doorway. In front of the pylons were often obelisks or colossal statues of the kings who built the temple.

The **side chambers** were used to store the temple goods.

Deep in the heart of the temple was the **sanctuary**, standing at the highest and darkest point. Here was the shrine, or **naos** within which stood the statue of the god.

The reduction in width of the inner rooms creates a 'corridor' at the rear of each temple. This was usually entered from one of the first courtyards.

The narrow, elongated **niches** in the pylons were intended as emplacements for flagstaffs.

The **front courtyard** – either one or two – stood open to the sky, its columns ranged around the side walls. These columns invariably have capitals in the form of closed lotus or papyrus buds.

Staircases inside the pylons led to **window embrasures**, from which flags or banners could be attached to the poles which stood in front of the gateway.

Three times a day, in the morning, at dusk and in the evening, the priests would carry dishes of prepared food and drink into the temple. The high priest, or the king if he were present, would walk through the temple to the sanctuary. There he would draw back the bolts on the door and enter it alone, taking portions of food and drink with him. As he opened the doors of the shrine, the figure of the god, cast in gold or silver, or perhaps wood covered with gold or silver, would be revealed, and the spirit, or ka, of the god was summoned to eat and drink. Before the meal, however, the high priest would carefully remove the clothing wrapped around the statue and clean the statue using water and natron. When this was completed,

he would gently apply eye paint to the god's face, and reclothe the statue in layers of fresh linen. Using the correct spoken formulae, he would then present the figure with jewellery and royal regalia, before finally offering up the food and drink for the divine repast.

The ceremony ended, the shrine's shutters would be closed once more, and secured with a mud seal until the time of the next meal. The high priest withdrew still facing the shrine, sweeping the floor carefully in front of him as he went to erase all trace of human presence.

In the major temples, once the god's meal was ended, a procession of food- and drink-bearers would move into a side corridor at the rear of the temple, where one wall was carved with a list of the ancient kings' names. By uttering the names of all the kings who had ever ruled Egypt (omitting those likely to offend the gods, such as the female king Hatshepsut and the 'Great Enemy' Akhenaten), the kas of these pharaohs would also be summoned in order to partake of the essence of the food being offered.

The temple and the ordinary man

On several occasions each year, when the major feast days were celebrated, instead of being replaced in its shrine the statue of the god would be placed inside the cabin of a ceremonial gilded wooden boat that stood permanently on a plinth in the sanctuary. Carried shoulder-high by the priests, the god in its boat, or barque, would travel the perimeter of the temple walls. On these occasions, the ordinary person would be permitted to consult the god over matters that troubled him. A scribe would write alternative questions on two sherds of pottery or stone: for example, 'The man should plant his field with wheat', and 'The man

On the outer, *northern wall of the temple of Karnak, the fine reliefs show Seti I, who reigned during the Nineteenth Dynasty, making offerings to the god Amun in his ithyphallic form, that in which he presided in the temple of Luxor a very short distance to the south. Seti fought a great campaign in the north, and on his return, made offerings to the god who had 'made strong his arm in battle'.*

should not plant his field with wheat'. The sherds would be placed in the path of the divine procession and, as it approached, the god would 'nod' before the alternative it preferred. (Presumably, the priests bearing the barque would bend their knees and dip, as though the god had become heavier.) This consultation of the oracle became increasingly important from the Nineteenth Dynasty onwards, until eventually the god's procession took place frequently.

A wealthy man might make an endowment of land or a percentage of annual produce from his land to the temple. In return for this, a statue of him could be placed in the open forecourt of the temple, and occasionally it too could partake of the offering of food and drink for the god. In Tomb 1 at Assiut, dating from the Middle Kingdom, the owner Hapdjefa carved such an endowment contract on one

wall, stipulating the exact quantities of beer and bread that were to be offered to his statue. The statue, it appears, was to be kept in his tomb, but carried to the temple for the major festivals of the year. In return, Hapdjefa endowed the temple with land inherited from his father, and produce from his official estates.

After each daily ceremony or festival, the food and drink that had been prepared for the god would be divided between all the temple workers in strictly ordained proportions. The greater part of this reversion-offering was bread, but from time to time, everyone would receive a few vegetables and some meat.

On the whole, except during the great festivals, the ordinary people would have little contact with the temple, and would never, in any case, be permitted to go beyond the front open courtyards.

The colonnade *of the temple of Luxor marked the start of the processional route through the temple designed by Amenhotep III. On the side walls, reliefs from Tutankhamun's reign show the celebration of the Opet festival held here once a year.*

GODS OF ANCIENT EGYPT

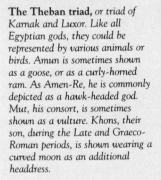

Bes, the ugly little *dwarf god, was probably not Egyptian in origin but adopted from another country, possibly to the north of Egypt. From the New Kingdom onwards, he is to be found often in paintings and reliefs and in the form of amulets. He was thought to be present in every Egyptian household at times of feasting, gaiety and music. With his female counterpart, Beset, he was also thought to assist women at the time of childbirth.*

To understand the system of Egyptian gods, it is necessary to realize that various deities were important during some periods, but not at others; and that a god who was revered in one town would scarcely have been recognized in a neighbouring town even a short distance away. An ancient Egyptian, then, would probably recognize only one local god.

The local god

This god was regarded as a superhuman who had lived and died in that area in a time long forgotten. During his lifetime, the god had often had a wife and a child (i.e. together they consituted a triad). The spirits of these three individual gods would be served by the local people of each area just as the soul of any dead person was served with food and drink.

Every Egyptian would address his prayers to 'the god'. These prayers could be written – by the supplicant or a scribe and left in a temple. The god was often left unnamed. Whoever read the prayer at a later date could insert the name of any god he pleased – the name was not so important as the certainty that a god listened.

In reality, then, the average Egyptian did not worships hundreds of gods. On the contrary, religious devotion was focused on only one small group, or triad, of local deities. The national god had barely any effect at all on the life of the ordinary Egyptian.

The national god

When, as happened from time to time, someone rose so high in society as to become king, his own local triad would be elevated by him to national status. As national deities, only the king or his appointed representative could come into their presence (*see p. 128*). In return for the best of food and drink offered by a leader of men, the god would be expected to grant bountiful food to the whole land, contentment to the people and victory in war to the king. Much of the wealth seized in any campaign would thus go either to building or enhancing the mansion of the god (temple), or into the temple's storehouses. This constant source of wealth naturally increased the influence of the temple – and increased the status of that god's priesthood.

In response to this, the stories told by the priesthood relating to the lifetime of that god – especially with regard to his creation of the world and humankind – would try to show how much more effective that god was than the ones that came before. A later god, such as Amun who was elevated during the Twelfth Dynasty, but reigned supreme during the New Kingdom, would not only dominate earlier gods such as Ptah by taking the title of 'King of the gods', but also might take upon himself some of their characteristics. So by amalgamating with Re, the sun-god, Amun also took charge of the

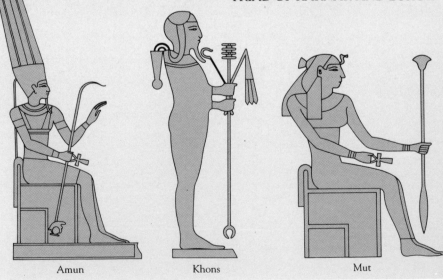

The Theban triad, *or triad of Karnak and Luxor. Like all Egyptian gods, they could be represented by various animals or birds. Amun is sometimes shown as a goose, or as a curly-horned ram. As Amen-Re, he is commonly depicted as a hawk-headed god. Mut, his consort, is sometimes shown as a vulture. Khons, their son, during the Late and Graeco-Roman periods, is shown wearing a curved moon as an additional headdress.*

TRIAD OF KARNAK AND LUXOR

Amun

Khons

Mut

course of the sun, in his form Amen-Re. This did not in any way, however, affect the existence, power and nature of either Amun or Re! This adaptability permitted other gods and goddesses to be introduced at any time.

Gods of the dead

It is clear from the pyramid texts that at the start of Egyptian history the king alone was entitled to an afterlife spent in the company of the gods. But with the demise of the autocratic, semi-divine king of the Old Kingdom, people looked to an afterlife of their own, in the company of the gods in a land free from problems.

From the start of the Middle Kingdom onwards, Osiris, previously mentioned in the pyramid texts as one of the gods of the king's afterlife, took upon himself many of the characteristics of Andjety, an ancient local god of Abydos. Andjety, and henceforth Osiris, was always shown mummiform, with a green skin, and was believed to take care of the regrowth of vegetation. The new Osiris was also seen as a god of resurrection, but of the dead, being regarded as the king of the land of the dead.

Yet another god, Anubis, mentioned in the pyramid texts as a dog who protected the king, took to himself some of the aspects of Wepwawet of Assiut – 'the opener of the ways' who protected the paths of the king into

When Reisner excavated the Giza pyramids between 1899 and 1905, in the valley temple of the smallest pyramid, that of Mycerinus, he found four of these triad statues, each showing the king with the goddess Hathor on his right and a local goddess on his left. In this statue, the local goddess wears on her head the symbol of a wild dog recumbent on a flagstaff or totem. It is the image of Oxyrhynchus (modern El Bahnasa). The statue, which is only 93cm (37in) tall, is made of finely polished greywacke.

TRIAD OF ASWAN

Khnum

Satis

Anukis

The triad of *Elephantine and the region of the first cataract. Khnum, shown as a straight-horned ram-headed god, was of very ancient origin, thought to be a potter who created the human race on his wheel. He was also associated closely with the inundation. Satis and Anukis both appear to have been his consorts. The curious headdress of Anukis seems to point to a Nubian origin. However, she was also a much-favoured goddess in Egypt, closely linked with Hathor.*

Although Horus, Thoth and Anubis were among the most ancient local gods, from the end of the Old Kingdom onwards they were more commonly associated with the West – in other words, the land of the dead. Anubis, guard dog of the West, was seen as responsible not only for the mummification and bandaging of the body but also the supervision of the weighing of the heart. Thoth, either an ibis or a baboon, was the scribe god responsible for recording the verdict on a soul. Horus guided the deceased through the chambers of the underworld. His consort, Hathor, local goddess of Dendera, was one of the best-loved Egyptian deities. She was especially associated with music and the seductive side of woman.

foreign countries (seen in this guise in an inscription at Sinai). As a result, Anubis became the guardian and protector of the dead, sitting 'upon his mountain' of the west bank, between the land of the living and that of the dead, as 'foremost' or 'in front of' 'the westerners'. In company with Thoth, the ancient god of Hermopolis (modern Ashmunein), who, as the wisest of gods, recorded the verdict of the king of the dead, Osiris and Anubis offered a new form of existence for the souls of the dead.

The legend of Osiris and Isis

The story of Osiris was recorded in full by Plutarch and temple inscriptions in Egypt confirm the details. Osiris was once a living king of Egypt, married to his sister Isis, 'Great of Magic'. Their brother Seth, the evil one, married to another sister, Nephthys, murdered Osiris by tricking him into stepping into a golden coffin. With his cronies, Seth slammed the lid shut and threw the body into the Nile. While Seth took the throne, Isis rescued the body of her husband from Byblos, where it had been carried by the Nile, and brought it back to Egypt. Seth, however, seized the body once more, ripped it into 14 pieces and threw them into the Nile. Wherever a piece of his body was found by Isis, there, in what would be considered a sacred burial place, a temple could be built. Thus temples to Osiris were built in Abydos

(i.e. the Osireion), in Busiris in the delta and Biggeh near the island of Philae at Aswan among other places.

Once Isis had collected all the pieces of Osiris' body together, she turned into a kite, wheeling and screeching, and with the breeze from her wings, breathed life back into the body of Osiris. The protective wings of Isis are thus to be seen enfolded around many coffins and sarcophagi, that they too may breathe new life into the soul of the dead.

From the resurrected soul of her husband, she conceived a son, Horus. Osiris's soul was relegated to kingship of the land of the dead, while the child Horus was brought up by Isis to avenge his father's murder. After years of fighting against Seth, Horus was victorious and became King of Egypt. In his honour, every successive king was seen as the embodiment of Horus, seated on the Horus throne.

Many temples were built to Horus in his different roles. Horus, the child of Isis (Harpocrates), was venerated in Edfu, while Horus the elder (Haroeris), the grown avenger of Seth, had a sanctuary in Kom Ombo. As a local god as well as a god associated with his dead father, he took many distinctive characteristics in each place he had a temple. Although invariably portrayed as a falcon, the stories concerning Horus of Buhen were different from those of Horus of Ausim in the delta.

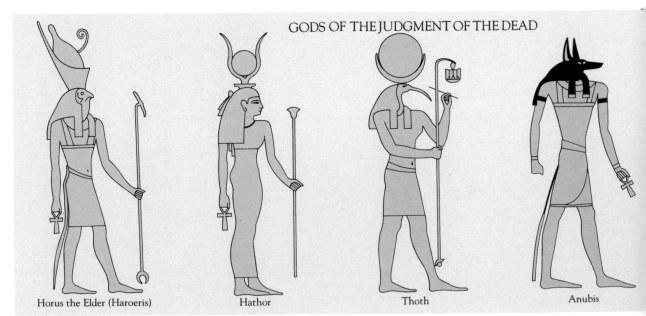

GODS OF THE JUDGMENT OF THE DEAD

Horus the Elder (Haroeris)   Hathor   Thoth   Anubis

The consort of Horus was Hathor, a curious goddess who may be said to have been deliberately created. According to the legend of Osiris, during the battles between Horus and Seth, Horus became angry that his mother Isis would not help him, and while she slept decapitated her. When the goddess awakened she took the first head she could find – that of a cow. This cow-headed goddess is called Hathor, though in fact she was merely one aspect of Isis. The name 'Hathor' in Egyptian means simply 'Mansion of Horus' – the name of Horus' temple.

Domestic gods

Often the local god was considered too remote or powerful to be consulted on personal matters. Therefore, the domestic or demigods who offered protection within the house were probably more real to the individual Egyptian than any other god. They were not worshipped but, rather like protective saints, their images, worn as amulets or painted on walls as icons, ensured some degree of safety or assistance.

Many domestic gods were concerned especially with childbearing and illness, since the home was predominantly the woman's concern. Thoueris (Egyptian Ta-weret – the Great Lady), in the form of a pregnant hippopotamus, protected the pregnant woman and assisted at childbirth. The Seven Hathors, rather like the fates, wove around the child protection for life.

Meskhent, or the birth stool, which was the first thing a newborn baby encountered, was revered as giving the child its destiny and was kept within the household. Hekat, a little frog, was a protection device used against miscarriage and stillbirth and probably, inversely, as a contraceptive aid.

Cults

Unlike the gods of the Classical civilizations, Egyptian gods did not embody abstract ideas; for instance, there was no god of wisdom, no god of storms. However, each god with its own characteristics had specific strengths and weaknesses, and specific powers and inclinations. During the Graeco-Roman period many of these aspects were emphasized, so that Hathor, for example, instead of being a local goddess, was revered nationally as representing youthful sexual love and beauty, while Isis became the great Mother-Goddess.

The identification of the gods with animals, birds, reptiles and insects appears to go back to most ancient times when each local area adopted an animal as their token or fetish. As a result, a god might be identified with different animals in different areas. Thoth, for example, manifested himself as either an ibis or a baboon. In the Late Period, especially, these creatures were believed to have the ear of the deity, and acted as intercessors with the god.

Through the life and death of Osiris, from the Middle Kingdom onwards, every Egyptian expected a life eternal. The four deities here – Osiris, Isis, Seth and Nephthys – were siblings. Osiris typified goodness and life; Seth, evil, storms and darkness. Isis, 'Great of Magic', was revered as the great mother-goddess, often shown suckling her offspring, Horus. As a Kite, with her sister, Nephthys, she represented mourning women, and was the protector of the deceased.

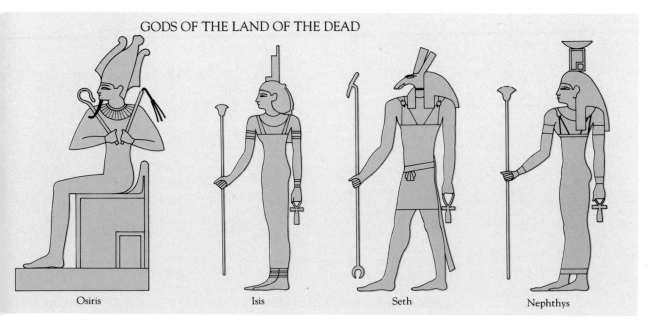

GODS OF THE LAND OF THE DEAD

Osiris   Isis   Seth   Nephthys

CULT TEMPLES

The central columns of Karnak's hypostyle hall, with their lotus-flower capitals, rise 22m (73ft) above the temple floor. To each side of them stand smaller columns with the bars of clerestory window-embrasures above them. This was the only source of light to what was otherwise a dark and secret place in which only the king and his priests once trod.

The cult temple dominated the village that clustered around it both physically and politically. It housed the statue of the god to whom offerings were made daily (see p. 130), managed great estates of land and employed many of the local people.

Although mention is made of many gods in the pyramid texts of the Old Kingdom, no cult temple at all has survived from that period. Among the temples that existed and may one day be fully excavated was that of Ptah in Memphis and of Re in Heliopolis, the influence of the latter lasting throughout Egyptian history. The sun temples of the Fifth Dynasty in Abusir (see p. 81), seem to have been associated with the pyramids of their builders and it is impossible to say how typical of an Old Kingdom cult temple they were.

In fact, there are very few remaining temples that date before the New Kingdom; the majority that are visited today date from the Graeco-Roman period.

The temple of Karnak
It is virtually impossible in a single visit to come to terms with the vastness of this temple that stands on the northern edge of the town of Luxor. It was home to the king of the gods, Amen-Re, and every king from the start of the New Kingdom onwards added to it until today its ruins cover 2 hectares (5 acres).

As king succeeded king, many added to the temple of Karnak by building on a great pylon gateway. In all six gateways separate the front of the temple from the sanctuary; and then, when space at the front of the temple ran out, the kings built sideways, and yet another four gateways were added. For the rubble infill for each of these pylons, many of them standing originally over 30.5m (100ft) high, the builders pillaged and reused earlier structures. One pylon alone, the third, though it now stands barely 6m (20ft) high, contained the blocks of 10 earlier buildings inside it.

The front pylon is approached by an avenue of sphinxes, the curly-horned ram's head representing one form of the god Amen-Re. They originally fronted the building of Ramesses II, the tiny figure of whom stands between the paws of each sphinx. The pylon, unfinished, was built during the Twenty-fifty Dynasty. On the right wall of the doorway as you enter is an inscription carved by Napoleon's soldiers. The entrance leads into an open courtyard of the same date. The king who built it had to incorporate two earlier temples that had stood in his way – to the right, a temple to Amun, built by Ramesses III and, on the left, one to Amun, Mut and Khons built by Seti II.

A large red granite Osiriform statue bears the face of Ramesses II, though the inscription on the kilt is that of the High Priest Pinnedjem of the Twenty-first Dynasty.

The hypostyle hall
The second pylon was built by Ramesses II from blocks removed from Akhenaten's temple to the Aten (see p. 106–09) which was built here. This pylon leads to the famous hypostyle hall, a triumph of Egyptian architecture, with central columns flanking the processional way standing 21m (70ft) tall. Another 122 columns 13m (43ft) tall, stand in 7 rows on either side, the innermost rows containing 7 columns and the remainder each with 9. The capitals of the central columns, in the form of open papyrus heads, have been recorded as holding 100 men standing on them at the same time. This hall was begun by Ramesses I, completed by Seti I and usurped by Ramesses II. The names of the kings in cartouches can be seen carved one over the other on the central columns.

The third pylon, built by Amenhotep III, was once, it is recorded, inlaid from head to foot in gold and silver; it is hard to imagine it by its condition today.

The fourth pylon was built by Tuthmosis I around 1500 BC, and stands before the only 2 remaining obelisks in the temple. The one on the right was cut by the architect Ineni (the builder of the first tomb in the Valley of the Kings) for Tuthmosis I, while that on the left was erected for the female king, Hatshepsut. The inscription on the base records that it took only 7 months to cut it in Aswan and erect it here, and that it was once covered from tip to base in electrum, an alloy of gold and silver.

The fifth pylon marks the original heart of the temple built by Tuthmosis I, behind which the sanctuary stood. This was altered by his grandson, Tuthmosis III, who built the small sixth pylon, carved with the names of the towns and villages he conquered in Palestine, Syria and Lebanon.

The sanctuary made of fine pink granite blocks, was added by Philip Arrhidaeus, brother of Alexander the Great, around 330 BC, and on the outside walls can be seen carved the coronation of Philip and the festival of Opet (see p. 139).

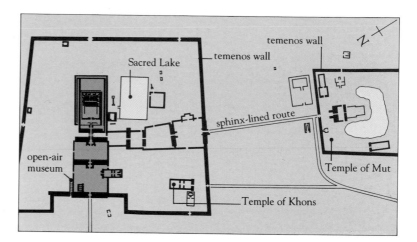

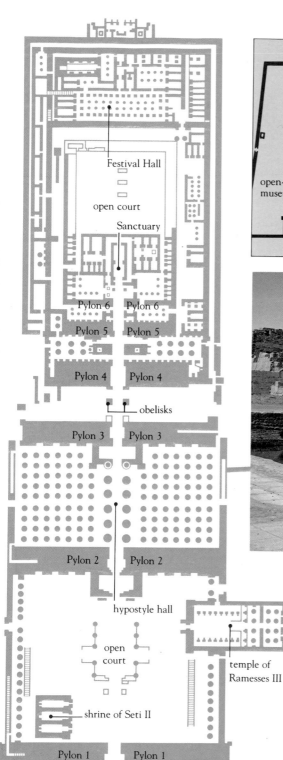

Festival Hall

open court

Sanctuary

Pylon 6   Pylon 6

Pylon 5   Pylon 5

Pylon 4   Pylon 4

obelisks

Pylon 3   Pylon 3

Pylon 2   Pylon 2

hypostyle hall

open
court

temple of
Ramesses III

shrine of Seti II

Pylon 1   Pylon 1

0 ——————————— 50m

0 ——————————— 150ft

TEMPLE OF AMUN, KARNAK

temenos wall

Sacred Lake

temenos wall

sphinx-lined route

open-air
museum

Temple of Mut

Temple of Khons

The plan of *the temple of Karnak (left) gives some idea of the complexity of the structure with its large numbers of columns and side chambers. Kings added continually to its size, extending it further and further to the east. The map (top) of the 5-acre site of Karnak shows how a second processional way led at right angles to the main temple towards the separate enclosure in which Amun's wife, Mut, resided.*

The remains of *the temple of Karnak are mirrored in the sacred lake (above), where once the priests came daily to purify themselves. Today, visitors sit every night in their hundreds beside the lake to witness the son-et-lumière re-enactment of the life of the temple.*

Beautifully carved *reliefs on the northern outer wall of the Great Hypostyle Hall of the Temple of Karnak depict some of the battle campaigns of King Seti I during the 19th Dynasty. Both Seti and his son, Ramesses II, fought valiantly in Syria, Lebanon and what is now Israel to maintain Egypt's empire. Here, the king drives his own two-horse chariot while firing arrows at his enemies.*

Across the courtyard behind the sanctuary lies a low building packed with columns. This is the Festival Hall, built by Tuthmosis III to celebrate his victories in the north. Although most of the rooms here are ruined, at the rear, a series of low steps leads into a rear chamber, and to the left of this is a small room whose walls are covered with representations of the strange and exotic plants, seeds, birds and animals brought back to Egypt by Tuthmosis III. The skill of the sculptors is evident in the light, raised reliefs in which the various species of animal can be clearly recognized, in what appears to be the world's first zoo.

To the right of the Festival Hall is the sacred lake, where once, three times a day, the priests would come to purify themselves. Today, the banks of seats to the rear of the lake nightly hold the hundreds of vistors who attend the Son-et-Lumière performance. By the side of the sacred lake lies a fallen obelisk, on the tip of which is depicted the coronation of Hatshepsut by the god Amen-Re. The nearby granite sculpture of a scarab beetle on a polished base was placed here around 1380 BC by Amenhotep III, and still bears the strange local superstition that any childless woman who runs around it three times in a clockwise direction will afterwards bear a child.

The Kadesh relief
A return to the hypostyle hall and exit through the left (south) door, brings the visitor to the outer wall of the temple on which is carved representations of Ramesses II's battle against the Hittites, around 1285 BC, fought at Kadesh, a town standing on a hill between two streams of the river Orontes. A long rectangular panel bearing slightly damaged hieroglyphs is a copy of the peace treaty between Ramesses and the Hittite king, purporting to celebrate a great Egyptian victory. Unfortunately for Ramesses, another version of the same treaty found in the Hittite capital Boghazköy declared it a win for the Hittites!

The pylon gateways extend southwards at right angles to the main temple, although these are currently being rebuilt and are now closed to visitors. It was here in 1902–03, at the corner of the main temple and the southern pylons, that Gaston Maspero conducted excavations on behalf of the Antiquities Service. Noticing pieces of statues hidden in the soil, he dug out of the ground first 15 colossal statues, and then a series of finely carved blocks from

the temple of Amenhotep I. By this time, the hole he ordered dug was full of water because the Nile was high. Maspero's assistant noticed 'vague outlines of statues in the mud at the bottom of the cavity'. First one statue, then another was pulled clear; and as fast as one was removed, another appeared. It was, Maspero recorded, simply 'fishing for statues' while tourists 'came in crowds every day . . . and if they were quiet and orderly were willingly admitted to the spectacle.' In all, over 2000 statues were found, together with more than 17,000 bronze figures. It appeared that at some late period a king had ordered the great temple tidied, and that a great mass of older objects were simply thrown into a pit and buried.

The temple of Mut can only be approached by walking around the outer walls of the temple of Karnak. Few people go there, yet the remains of the small temple, surrounded by a horseshoe-shaped lake and packed with broken black granite statues of the lioness goddess Sekhmet, all peering through high grasses, have a charm and air of mystery that other cult temples, including the temple of Karnak, lack.

To the north of the main temple, walking into the front pylon and through the left of the open courtyard, stands an open-air museum. Here, among numerous blocks found during excavations at Karnak, can be seen the oldest part of the temple, the Kiosk of Sesostris I. The blocks for this kiosk, dating to approximately 1950 BC, were found used as infill in the third pylon of the great temple. The reliefs on the walls of the small building are outstanding, with some of the finest detail to be seen on any relief work in Egypt.

Also here are the dark red quartzite blocks that once made up another small building, the Red Chapel of Queen Hatshepsut. Examination of the scenes will reveal not only the queen's coronation ritual, with a series of crowns being presented by a number of goddesses, but also depictions of a Sed festival that Hatshepsut shared with her stepson, Tuthmosis III.

The temple of Luxor
In ancient times a limestone-paved road led south from the temple of Karnak flanked on both sides by an avenue of stone sphinxes. A mile away, at the other end of the route, lay the temple of Luxor. The Egyptian name of the temple, 'the Southern Harem' – 'ta ipet resy' – was heard by the Greeks as 'Thebes', a name frequently used for the whole area.

The temple of Luxor, *looking northwards towards the front pylons appears sadly dilapidated, although from ground level it is one of the most charming and unspoilt of all Egyptian temples. The tall and graceful colonnade once formed the approach to this temple, which was built by Amenhotep III, at the foot of a causeway 1.6km (1mi) long, leading from the great temple of Amun at Karnak. More than a century later, Ramesses II enlarged it by adding a forecourt and two massive pylons. The mosque of Abu l'Haggag, built on sand that once filled the temple, now can be seen some 6m (20ft) above ground level.*

The present temple was built on the site of a Middle Kingdom building by Amenhotep III, approximately 1380 BC. Of the old temple only a few stray blocks survive. About a hundred years later Ramesses II extended it northwards, adding the great pylon gateway and an open courtyard. Unlike Karnak, however, the temple of Luxor was not added to by later kings, giving it a charm and simplicity that Karnak lacks.

Over the centuries, sand accumulated in the temple of Luxor and covered the processional way. The modern main street of Luxor now stands over the middle portion of the route, and the heads of sphinxes that appear from time to time during building work in the town are continuing evidence of its presence. The temple itself had an entire village built over it, which was cleared by Mariette (*see p. 33*) in the 1860s. The mosque of Abu L'Haggag, however, that had been built in the northeastern corner of Ramesses' open courtyard was permitted to remain where it was and now stands on top of a wall far above the visitors' heads on the left as they walk through the temple entrance.

Royal additions

The front pylons, built by Ramesses II, are carved with accounts of his battles in the north against the Hittites. Two seated and two standing colossal statues are also his. Of an original pair of obelisks only the eastern one remains; the western obelisk was removed in 1831 and now stands in the centre of the Place de la Concorde, Paris.

The open court of Ramesses II is out of line with the rest of the temple, probably done deliberately so as to incorporate a small temple of Tuthmosis III, which used to stand outside the temple. Granite statues between the columns of this court depict Amenhotep III, although Ramesses II usurped them.

The tall colonnade was built by Amenhotep III. On the inside face of the walls here, a lightly carved relief shows the celebrations of the Opet festival, the reason for the existence of the temple of Luxor. Once a year the statues of Amun and Mut would be taken from their temples in the Karnak complex, shuttered inside the cabin of the ceremonial boat carried shoulder-high by priests. In the midst of great rejoicing, with the streets packed with people dancing, eating and drinking, the divine procession would make its way to the temple of Luxor. Here the statues of Amun and Mut would be placed together in the sanctuary for 24 days to celebrate a 'divine honeymoon', during which their son Khons was to be conceived. At the end of the period, the statues were returned, again with great festivity, to Karnak. The reliefs were carved on the order of Tutankhamun to celebrate the revival of Amun's cult after the traumatic Amarna period (*see p. 106–09*). Aside from his tomb, these reliefs are his sole surviving monument.

The large open courtyard was built by Amenhotep III, and with a graceful surround of papyrus-bud columns is thought to be one of the finest courts to have survived from ancient Egypt. Beyond this, the hypostyle hall is sadly dilapidated, and contains a modest 32 columns.

The zodiac of Dendera. *This disc of carved stone, some 2m (6½ft) in diameter, adorned the ceiling of the western upper chapel above the main temple. Carved with Egyptian figures, it depicts the constellations of the zodiac according to Greek, rather than Egyptian, understanding of them. Every modern star sign can be found on its inner circle. The original, shown here, was removed and can now be seen in the Louvre; a plaster cast is in its place in the temple of Dendera.*

Where once the front of the ancient sanctuary stood, a wall was added with two granite Corinthian columns flanking a Christian apse over an altar. Some traces of the original painting of Christ and the apostles still remain.

The sanctuary was rebuilt by Alexander the Great, and on its west outer wall, a depiction of him can be seen dressed as a pharaoh making an offering to Min, the ithyphallic aspect of Amun.

Ptolemaic temples

Although the older temples dedicated to the major gods have vanished, their sites were built over during Greek and Roman times. The cult temples outside Luxor all date to this period. Since they are of more recent date than Karnak, they are better preserved.

The temple of Dendera

Few ancient temples are as charming as that of the goddess Hathor (*see p. 134–35*) at Dendera. The temple stands on the west bank opposite the town of Qena, about 64km (40mi) north of Luxor. Although it is known to have been a site of major importance from at least the Old Kingdom, none of the buildings on the site dates earlier than 350 BC.

The outer enclosure wall and its gateway were built in the time of the Emperor Domitian, in the first century AD. On the right stands the birth-house, or mammisi, where an annual festival like the Opet of Luxor celebrated the birth of Ihy to Horus and Hathor. On the outer walls, carved with superb reliefs, the traditionally attired Pharaoh Nectanebo makes offerings to Hathor who suckles her son. Inside the sanctuary, reliefs depict the god and goddess seated on a bed, holding hands.

Past the mammisi stands a Coptic church, built during the sixth and seventh centuries, and beyond that, mud-brick walls mark the site of an ancient sanatorium, or hospital. The discovery of dream papyri on this site suggests that those who were ill could have come here to have their dreams interpreted by priests.

The main temple of Hathor is approached through a hypostyle hall, containing 24 columns topped with capitals carved as heads of Hathor, many of which retain much of the original paintwork. To the left, the ceiling is painted with a series of stellar constellations and symbols of the zodiac.

Walking through the next, smaller, columned hall, a door to the right leads to a gently rising, twisting staircase to the roof of the temple. The

walls of the staircase are carved in fine relief showing priests ascending to the roof; a staircase opposite shows them descending in an eternal petrified procession.

From the very large roof, in complete safety, fine views can be gained of the whole temple complex, including the now overgrown sacred lake. In one corner of the roof, a tiny, open-topped shrine was used by priests once a year to allow the statue of Hathor to feel the rays of the sun-god, Re. In the northeast corner, a low chamber was dedicated to the rebirth of Osiris. On the ceiling of this chamber, to the left of the entrance, is a plaster-cast of the 'Zodiac of Dendera' – the original is in the Louvre. Descending into the temple again by means of a straight staircase in the southeast and walking beyond the sanctuary, in a side chamber is found the entrance to one of the temple crypts. Here, it is believed, many of the temple treasures were stored, and although they have long since disappeared, the walls of the tiny crypt are carved with superb reliefs of some of the objects, including a fine jewelled collar. An inscription here records that the first temple on the site was built during the predynastic period, records of which were said to have been found written on leather when the present temple was built.

On the back outer wall of the temple, reliefs show offerings being made to the goddess by Cleopatra VII. This is one of the few depictions showing this most famous of the Cleopatras, while in front of her, in traditional Pharaonic dress, is her son by Julius Caesar, Caesarion.

The temple of Edfu

The temple of Horus stands within the modern town of Edfu on the west bank of the Nile, 103km (64mi) south of Luxor. It was built between 237 and 57 BC. Like Dendera, though, it was a most ancient site; blocks recently retrieved from under the forecourt have been found to belong to an earlier New Kingdom building on the same site.

Edfu is the most complete extant temple in Egypt, and its reliefs among the best preserved. The entrance pylon, 35.9m (118ft) tall, shows Ptolemy XII conquering his enemies shortly before the Roman conquest in 30 BC.

The open court is surrounded on three sides by columns, while the wall reliefs show the festival of 'Happy Reunion', when the statue of Horus left the temple to meet that of Hathor of Dendera on the Nile and bring her back in a

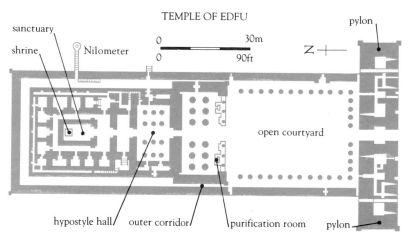

TEMPLE OF EDFU

sanctuary
shrine
Nilometer
pylon
0   30m
0   90ft
open courtyard
hypostyle hall   outer corridor   purification room   pylon

boat to Edfu to celebrate their marriage. To the front of the front pylon and within the court-yard stand superb statues of the falcon Horus.

The doorway at the rear of the court leads into a closed 12-columned hall. The reliefs on the walls show the foundation of the temple, from its design, based on the ancient Perwer shrine of Hieraconpolis (see p. 52), to the 'stretching of the cord' ceremony to measure the boundaries, the cutting of the first hole in the ground by the king, and the purification of the site. On either side of the entrance door, small chambers are built against the courtyard wall. The one on the left contained ritual jars used for the temple ceremonies, while the one on the right was the temple library, its walls carved with the titles of the rolls it once contained.

At the rear of the temple, the sanctuary still contains a magnificent, mirror-polished granite shrine inside which the cult statue of Horus once stood. In the side chamber behind the sanctuary can be seen a modern reconstruction of the ceremonial boat shrine in which the cult statue would have been placed at the time of the reunion festival.

The most informative area of the temple is the outer corridor, approached through door-ways from the open court. The walls here contain fine reliefs showing the story of the ancient struggle between Horus and Seth for the throne of Egypt. Horus, on the papyrus skiff accompanied by his mother Isis, is shown hunting Seth, who appears as both a hippo-potamus and a crocodile, with a spear. From the inscriptions here, the whole story of the battles between these gods can be read, one of the few theological accounts to survive from ancient Egypt.

The temple of Kom Ombo
This temple lies about 165km (102mi) south of Luxor, and is uniquely dedicated to two gods, Horus the Elder, avenger of his father (see p. 134), and Sobek, the crocodile god. As a result it has two parallel processional routes leading to twin sanctuaries. Both are now destroyed. The temple was built originally around 150 BC on an ancient site, but was added to and completed by Roman emperors, from Augustus and Tiberius Caesar through to Macrinus (AD 217).

The most interesting reliefs are preserved on the outer wall at the rear of the temple. Here, on the left at eye level, can be seen the figures of two goddesses seated on birth stools. Behind

them appears to be a table laid out with a panoply of surgical instruments including forceps, shears, scalpels and a set of balances.

On the opposite wall, along the centre line of the temple a small inset stone is flanked by curious carvings of a pair of eyes and a pair of ears. This is the place to which the local people could come to consult the god by getting as close as they were permitted to the sanctuary. Behind this stone, in a chamber hidden in the thickness of the wall, a priest would sit and respond to the questions he was asked. The eyes and ears thus refer to the watching and listening god whom, no doubt, the people believed they were addressing. Inside the temple, behind the wall, the secret entrance to this chamber can still be seen in an open shaft in the floor between the places where the sanctuaries once stood.

The plan of the temple of Edfu (top). Fine granite statues of Horus, the falcon god who presided over Edfu, can be seen in front of the main pylons and in the inner courtyard. The polished granite shrine is one of the finest to survive in Egypt. The front pylons of the temple (above) are covered with huge reliefs. At the top, Ptolemy III who began the temple, makes offerings to the god; while below, Ptolemy XII, who completed it, is shown defeating Egypt's enemies in the presence of Horus and his consort, Hathor.

141

HOUSES FOR IMMORTALITY

**Edouard Naville
(1844–1926)**

Naville was born in Geneva and trained in both Egyptology and theology, attending the universities of Geneva, London, Bonn, Paris and Berlin. He studied under Lepsius, and was the first excavator appointed by the Egypt Exploration Fund, in 1883. Naville's early digs were all in the delta, but in 1893, he moved south to Deir el Bahri, where he helped to clear the temple of Mentuhotep Nebhepetre. His last excavation, at Abydos in 1910, saw the clearing of the Osireion at the rear of the mortuary temple of Seti I. His formidable brainpower and wide knowledge won Naville many admirers, though he and Petrie often disagreed. Among many publications and articles, his translation and commentary on the Book of the Dead was perhaps the most important.

The mortuary temple *of Hatshepsut at Deir el Bahri (above, right) stands secluded in a great cliff-encircled plain on the west bank of Luxor. When Naville first saw the site in 1892, it was little more than a mass of rubble. The reconstruction of the temple was begun in 1893 and continues to this day. The third, topmost terrace is being rebuilt by the Polish Archaeological Institute and it is hoped that it will be opened to the public within the next few years.*

The earliest mortuary temple was built by the first king of the Twelfth Dynasty, Mentuhotep Nebhepetre, in a curving bay of the cliffs on the west bank of Luxor, now known as Deir el Bahri. This was not a true mortuary temple, though. It took the form of a series of colonnades one above the other and approached by a sloping ramp. On the top of this was a small pyramid. A shaft from the pyramid descended through the buildings and into the bedrock.

When the kings of the New Kingdom had their tombs cut in the Valley of the Kings, they needed to make provision for the mortuary cult. By building their mortuary temples on a large scale and quite separate from their tombs, no doubt they hoped robbers would not be directed to the tombs by large stone superstructures. As a result, there grew up on the plains of the west bank of Luxor a great swathe of mortuary temples. Few of them stand today, however, because the local people have been removing and re-using the stone for centuries.

Deir el Bahri
Alongside the Middle Kingdom funerary complex of Mentuhotep Nebheptre, Queen Hatshepsut chose to build her mortuary temple to an identical, though larger, design. Towards the

end of her 20-year reign, blocks from her Red Chapel show she allowed her stepson to rule as co-regent. When she finally died (or was removed), this co-regent became Tuthmosis III, one of the greatest kings ever to rule Egypt, and he defaced Hatshepsut's great monument. When H. E. Winlock of New York's Metropolitan Museum of Art, came to the site in the 1920s, little could be seen save rubble and sand. However, he systematically retrieved smashed blocks from the temple from two quarries where they had been thrown, and rebuilding commenced, a work still under way today.

On the walls of the lowest colonnade, badly damaged blocks on the left side show the removal of two obelisks from Aswan and their transport by ship to Karnak. Little remains on the right, save a chiselled image of Hatshepsut as a sphinx.

A ramp leads to the second colonnade, where the walls contain two remarkable and unique scenes. On the far left of this colonnade is a small temple dedicated to Hathor, with coloured reliefs showing Hatshepsut being suckled by the goddess in the form of a cow.

The colonnade to the left shows an expedition to the land of Punt, sent by the queen to bring back incense and incense trees for this temple. The officials of Egypt are shown arriving in Punt where they are welcomed by the queen of that land who appears to have suffered from elephantiasis. The land of Punt (still to be found, but believed to lie north of the Horn of Africa, perhaps in Eritrea or Tigre) is lush, with thick trees, domed houses built on stilts between them, while fat cattle graze beneath them. Everyone greets the Egyptian delegation, from the mayor to the local dogs, and then goods are laid out for barter.

The right-hand colonnade shows Hatshepsut's conception and birth. On the night she was conceived, the god Amun took over the body of her father Tuthmosis I. Queen Ahmose is shown being led by the gods and goddesses to the birth chamber where Hatshepsut, true child of the god, is born. Even her upbringing is depicted, with ranks of gods protecting the growing child.

On the far right of the colonnade is another small chapel, dedicated to Anubis. Its paintings here are superbly preserved.

The colossi of Memnon

Two giant colossal statues are all that remains of what was once the mortuary temple of Amenhotep III, the biggest ever built on the west bank. A monolithic stela about .4km (¼mi) behind them marks what was once the back of the temple. An inscription on it records that the temple was 'inlaid with gold throughout, its floors paved with silver and all its doors panelled with electrum'. Some foundations still stood in Wilkinson's time (see p. 36–37), but today no trace of the great temple remains.

The Ramesseum

This huge, though badly damaged, temple stands in the village of Sheikh Abd el Qurna on the west bank of Luxor. It measures 277.4 by 167.6m (910 by 550ft) and was built for the cult of Ramesses II. Entry today is through the side of the temple where a wall once stood. The front pylons are badly damaged and blocked by rubble and vegetation. Reliefs here show the army assembling ready to march north; on the southern pylon is depicted an account of the battle of Kadesh, a common temple scene.

This same scene is shown in finer detail on the wall behind the Osiriform statues on the left as the visitor enters the complex. One division of the Egyptian army, led by the king, camped at the foot of the town mound, assured by a spy that the Hittite army was miles to the

north. In fact, they were massing on the other side of Kadesh, out of Ramesses' line of sight. As a second Egyptian division crossed the river to join the king's troops, the Hittites attacked. Some of the soldiers were drowned, while others panicked and fled into the Egyptian camp. Ramesses despatched a messenger to alert more divisions marching at the rear and then, with the might of Amun strengthening his arm, faced and vanquished the Hittite foe virtually single-handed. In an amusing incident on this wall, the Prince of the Hittites is fished out of the Orontes and held upside down by his ankles to drain him of river water. Ancient artificial respiration seems to have been crude but effective!

Similar scenes can be seen on the badly damaged ruins of the courtyards and hypostyle hall of the temple.

Most noticeable and quite magnificent, however, are the remains of a huge seated granite colossal statue of Ramesses II, now smashed and lying on the ground. When it was still standing it must have been one of the largest ever cut. Its removal from Aswan to this site must have been a gargantuan task, since it weighed an estimated 1000 tons. Today, even the fragments of feet and toes dwarf the visitor.

Shelley was so inspired by the sheer might embodied in this statue that he penned a poem using the still remembered coronation name of Ramesses II – Usermaatre, or as it was popularly recalled 'Ozymandias'.

In the Ramesseum, *the second courtyard with its row of statues, showing Ramesses II in the guise of Osiris, is dominated by a massive broken statue that lies where once the entrance to the front courtyard was. This granite statue originally depicted Ramesses sitting and would have been more than 16.7m (55ft) high, weighing in excess of 1000 tons. Cut from a single piece of stone in the quarries of Aswan, nearly 240km (150mi) to the south, its shaping, polishing and moving to the site was a triumph of ancient technology. In the 19th century, it inspired Shelley to write his famous poem 'Ozymandias'. In the foreground, the carved cartouche bears part of Ramesses II's coronation name.*

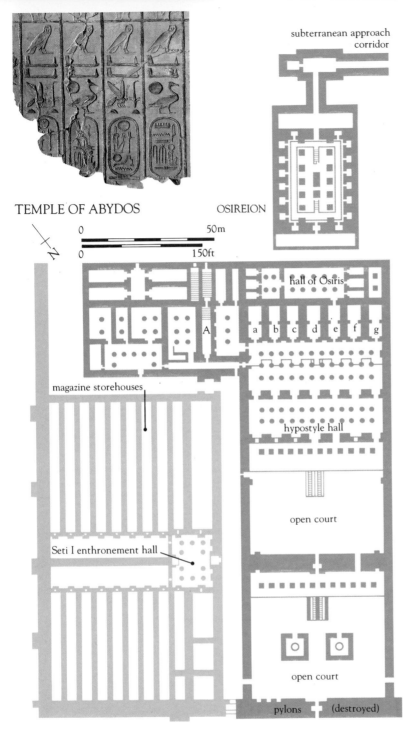

TEMPLE OF ABYDOS

OSIREION

subterranean approach corridor

hall of Osiris

A a b c d e f g

magazine storehouses

hypostyle hall

Seti I enthronement hall

open court

open court

pylons (destroyed)

0   50m
0   150ft

N

The plan of *the temple of Seti I at Abydos (above) shows its curious L-shape, probably built to avoid the subterranean Osireion (top, right) to the west. The sanctuaries are dedicated to: Seti I (a), Ptah (b), Re-Horakhte (c), Amun (d), Osiris (e), Isis (f), and Horus (g). The famous King List is found carved in relief on the* northern wall of a corridor (A) just beyond the sanctuaries. A similar list, a portion of which is shown above left, is from a small temple built by Ramesses II, to the north of the great temple of Seti I at Abydos. This fragment bears the birth and coronation names of Ramesses II, appearing in alternate cartouches.

Abydos: Temple of Seti

The finest and best preserved of all mortuary temples is at Abydos, near Balliana some 145km (90mi) north of Luxor. The site was venerated from ancient times as one of the most sacred places in Egypt. Here on a wide desert plain the first kings of Egypt were buried (*see p. 56–57*). One of their tombs, later declared to be the burial place of Osiris, the Great God, became the focal point for pilgrims. Once a year, a festival of revival and resurrection was held on the site. So popular was it that it was attended by people from all over Egypt, and so vital were its links with resurrection that even the souls of the dead were encouraged to join in. In most Middle and New Kingdom tombs, models and paintings depict boats carrying a sarcophagus sailing to Abydos and then returning to the tomb.

On this ancient site Seti I, second king of the Nineteenth Dynasty, around 1300 BC, decided to build his great temple – not strictly a mortuary temple. He dared not forget the god to whom the place had always belonged, while the lure of Abydos, bringing visitors together from every town of Egypt, encouraged him to remember the other great gods also. The temple of Abydos is unique, for besides serving the mortuary cult of its builder, six other deities are venerated here. Seti built over the foundations of many earlier temples.

Seti I did not live long enough to see his new temple completed. The fine reliefs carved by his craftsmen are often dominated by the cruder, hastily cut, sunk reliefs added by his son, Ramesses II. As well as having a mortuary temple in Luxor, Ramesses built another here, north of his father's. Although little of it remains, the walls contain brightly coloured reliefs, making it well worth a visit.

The temple of Seti I

The temple is built of the finest limestone, built in a curious L-shape, with the storerooms that usually stand behind the sanctuary actually built to the side and south of it. This appears to have been done firstly to avoid the subterranean chapel of Osiris, the Osireion, at the rear of the temple, and secondly, to permit the false doors at the rear of the sanctuaries to lead directly to the Osireion.

The front pylon and court have been largely destroyed. The base of the second pylon and the open court beyond lead to a pillared façade where Ramesses II is shown with the gods.

The first hypostyle hall with 24 papyriform columns, leads into a second hall, at the west of which are the entrances to the seven sanctuaries. These rooms are dedicated to Horus, Isis and Osiris (the only sanctuary with a door into the sacred chamber beyond); Amun; Re-Horakhte and Ptah; and finally, Seti himself.

To the left of the sanctuaries, a corridor contains the famous King List. Seti I, with his young son Prince Ramesses, is shown burning incense before the cartouches of every king of Egypt from Menes to himself, with the omission of Hatshepsut and the Amarna pharaohs.

On the right-hand side of this passage, another corridor leads to shallow steps to the back of the temple. Scenes on these walls show the young Ramesses watched by his father, roping a bull; and a fine depiction of the ceremonial boat of Abydos, with its unusual high prow and many oars, dedicated to the funerary god, Sokar.

At the top of the staircase, outside the temple, the Osireion can be seen below ground level. Although the eastern wall depicts and names Seti I, the massive granite blocks and monolithic columns are reminiscent of the valley temple of Chephren at Giza and it is possible that this temple dates to the Old Kingdom.

Medinet Habu

This great mortuary temple was built for Ramesses III during the Twentieth Dynasty, around 1150 BC. It stands on the west bank of Luxor south of the Ramesseum and the Colossi of Memnon, from which temples the royal builder removed many blocks to re-use in his own. The entrance to the temple is under a unique tower, the Migdol gateway.

On the right, inside the first open courtyard, stands an earlier temple of Hatshepsut, and beyond that rise the great front pylons of Ramesses III's temple – an exact copy of the Ramesseum, though better preserved.

The first pylons show scenes carved in relief of Ramesses III's victory against the Libyans, while the second pylons are carved with inscriptions commemorating his famous victory over the Sea Peoples. These same battles are also shown on the outer faces of the temple walls. The battle with the Sea Peoples, the first recorded naval battle in history, was fought in the eighth year of the king's reign, when the northern coast of Egypt was attacked by an allied force of ships from the north and eastern Mediterranean.

The statues that stand before the columns on the north wall of the second court are squat and stunted in comparison with the graceful Osiride statues in the earlier Ramesseum, showing how low the tradition of art and craftsmanship had already slumped. Behind these columns, reliefs, with their colour remarkably intact, depict the Festival of Min that was held here annually. On these occasions, the ithyphallic god's statue was processed along the west bank, and offerings were presented to it of long-leafed lettuce. These were considered the most potent aphrodisiacs by the Egyptians, and thus a suitable gift for Min!

The hypostyle hall and the sanctuary beyond are badly damaged, and the roof has long since disappeared. This once secret area is now open to the sky, as if it were an open courtyard.

Along the southern face of the outer wall, are the stone foundations of a palace that the king used when he was in Luxor. Among the rooms preserved here is the only extant example of a royal throne room, with steps leading up to a dais on which the throne once stood.

To the rear and north of the temple stand the remains of mud-brick buildings that cluster around the outer temenos wall. After the workmen's village of Deir el Medina fell into disuse, many of the inhabitants of the west bank came to live here. In Christian times this village, then called Djeme, was one of the largest settlements in the area of Luxor, with its own church and monastery. Many documents from the village archives, together with older material from the mortuary temple archives, were found here intact, an invaluable source of information on the full history of the building.

Medinet Habu, the mortuary temple of Ramesses III on the Twelfth Dynasty, stands on the plain of the west bank at Luxor. In the foreground, low walls are all that remain of a royal palace the king used when he visited the area from his palace in the delta. Behind the temple, mud-brick houses mark the Coptic settlement of Djeme that flourished until the 9th century AD.

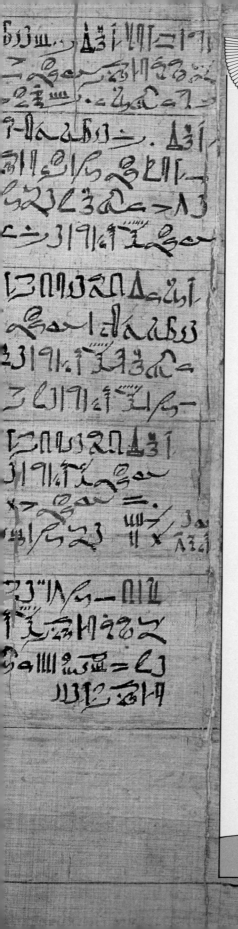

EGYPT'S LEGACY

VI

'The Egyptians, in their manners and customs, seem to have reversed the ordinary practices of Mankind. For example, women attend market and are employed in trade while men stay at home and do the weaving . . . In writing and mathematics, they go from right to left and, obstinately, maintain that theirs is the best method, ours being left-handed and clumsy.'
Herodotus, Book II, 36

All knowledge of Egyptian hieroglyphs was lost during the fifth century AD and not rediscovered until the early 19th century. Over the intervening decades, scholars tried to guess what the pictures meant – and the meaning of the strange artefacts – but with little success. Even Egyptian art was found baffling, with its total absence of perspective and any resemblance to the traditionally accepted standards of Classical beauty.

The decipherment of hieroglyphs was one of the greatest leaps forward made in the field of Egyptology. But modern scientific technology, when applied to archaeological evidence, can also produce interesting, often startling, results, revealing methods of technology or manufacture, allowing a more complete picture of their civilization to be drawn.

Surviving papyri provide a variety of texts concerning ordinary people's lives, from their love letters to their tax bills, from medical diagnoses and prescriptions to the method of calculating the slope of a pyramid or the capacity of a grain bin. From the mummies of the Egyptians we can not only discover information about their diet and their diseases, but we can also tell what their blood group was, and how hard – or how little – they worked.

The Rhind Mathematical Papyrus *was written during the reign of the Hyksos king, Apophis, of the Seventeenth Dynasty. It deals with the calculation of areas and slopes.*

PAINTINGS FOR ETERNITY

Upon a regular *squared grid, the shapes of the figures and hieroglyphs would be sketched by the ancient artist to a predetermined design. The standing figure of the woman on the left shows quite clearly that her face and body are shown in profile; only her shoulders and her eye are shown full face, resulting in the typically Egyptian posture that appears so rigid. The grid for the seated figure on the right displays the same rigidity of form. No allowance was made for the alteration of proportions of muscles of seated figures. Note that the left foot is invariably shown slightly forward of the right. It is curious to note that most pictures of human figures show them facing towards the right, the usual direction also for hieroglyphic inscriptions. This implies that the Egyptians saw little distinction between art and writing, but that larger pictures such as this could also be part of an inscription.*

To a Western eye attuned to the grace of Classical art and sculpture, ancient Egyptian art appears clumsy and ill conceived, though well executed. Early travellers, trying to record what they saw, frequently re-interpreted wall paintings to make them more understandable.

Structure of Egyptian art

There was very little attempt on the part of the Egyptian artist to achieve perspective, as we know it, in their art. However, at a very early date, tumultuous and disorganized scenes were resolved into registers – parallel horizontal bands of pictures forming one entire scene. Each band provided a ground line, for figures.

On the whole, the ancient artist attempted to portray objects as they were in reality. So pools of water must be square or rectangular, tables must have a square surface and round loaves of bread must be depicted as circular and not elliptical. In order to show the contents of buildings, for instance, often a cutaway view is used in addition to the exterior aspect, but with the same rigid maintenance of shape.

Form and layout were strictly controlled, leaving little leeway for individual expression. As a result, except by archaeological accident, the identities of the artists can seldom be elicited. On the whole, the Egyptian paintings that have survived were done for practical and not aesthetic reasons, in order to provide, magically, for a person's afterlife.

The Canons of Proportion

Everything that was to be drawn or written on any wall, from human and animal figures to hieroglyphs, was drawn first by the artist on a small board within a standard set of squares.

The width of each square was established as the width of a hand of any of the human figures in the scene. Until the Amarna period, human figures would occupy 18 vertical squares, from the sole of the feet to the hairline. Within the grid, the face from the hairline to the base of the neck filled two entire squares; the chest, from the shoulder to the waist, five squares; and the legs from the knees to the sole of the foot, six squares. Only posture and facial features are capable of showing different interpretation.

In the width of each grid, the arm would occupy one full square, while a central vertical line, running past the front of the ear, divided the body into two halves. While the shoulders are depicted as facing fully forwards, the face and trunk are always in profile, so that female figures, for instance, appear to have only one breast. Emphasis on eye delineation, making them three-quarters of a square wide, puts the eye too far forward in the face for reality, while the depiction of the eye in full face rather than side view, gives the human figure the typical, if strange, ancient Egyptian appearance.

During the Amarna period, in the early years of the reign of Akhenaten in the Eighteenth Dynasty, a disturbing artistic distortion of the human form occurred, but this has been proven to be no more than an artistic convention. Dr Gay Robins, of Cambridge University, has shown recently that in fact a standard grid of 20 squares high was used for all Amarna figure scenes. The rejection of the 'old' strict conformity in favour of 'outrageous' new ideas by Akhenaten is indicative of the feel of the whole period.

The end of the Amarna period, marked by the accession of Tutankhamun, signified a return to the old grid, but the result appeared stumped and graceless. As a result, in the Nineteenth Dynasty, a 21-square grid was introduced, with human figures being 'stretched' to appear exceptionally tall and slender.

Working method

Whenever the local stone was hard enough, it is clear the Egyptians favoured relief carving rather than flat painting. On the west bank of Luxor, where the limestone is particularly friable, few artists even attempted reliefs in tombs, but instead stonemasons made the walls and ceilings as smooth as possible using copper or bronze adzes and chisels. On top of this, a thin layer of lime, or gesso plaster was applied and allowed to dry, making a fine surface for

paint. A large-scale grid would then be marked on the wall using strings dipped in red paint. Both ends would be held in position against the plaster surface and lightly 'snapped' to leave a strong and accurate line. Onto this grid the smaller pictures designed by fully trained artists were carefully copied by scribes using black paint. Behind them came the master artist, who would make minor adjustments, in red ink.

The painting of the figures was achieved using flat colour pigments with little if any attempt to represent shading or highlights. The paint was prepared from pigments provided by the royal workshops through the office of the vizier. Ochres were ground to produce reds, yellows and browns; soot or some other form of carbon for black; limestone for white; malachite (copper ore) for green; the single-fired coloured glass (frit) for blue.

Sequence of painting

The paints were water-based and applied onto plaster, with whole areas being filled in sequence. The artist started with flesh tones. The background would be painted in next. In early periods this was plain white. At the end of the Eighteenth and the start of the Nineteenth Dynasties, royal tombs used a strong blue background, while from the reign of Ramesses II onwards, yellow was favoured for royal and nobles' tombs alike.

In order to show the fine quality of Egyptian linen, an overlay of white on to the skin tones resulted in a pleasing attempt at transparency, while delicate pleated fabrics were indicated by fine black or yellow lines on to a white background. Details, such as facial features, jewellery, wig curls and dress patterning were added on top of the base paint at the end.

The walls *in the tomb of the Nineteenth Dynasty pharaoh Horemheb in the Valley of the Kings were abandoned by their craftsmen before completion. Their unfinished work shows clearly the sequence that was followed to achieve the finely carved and painted scenes that fill Egyptian tombs. The dark outline figures were the initial drawings on the grid made and then corrected from a 'pattern book' that showed the things in miniature. The first artists would later be followed by sculptors or stonemasons who would carefully chisel away the background. The whole thing would be painted last of all. The scene above shows one of the stages of the Egyptians' vision of the passage through to the afterlife that King Horemheb's ka would have to pass and triumph over in order to achieve eternal rest.*

RELIEF AND SCULPTURE

From earliest times the Egyptians mastered the art of working the hardest stone with an ease and accomplishment that belies their lack of what we would believe to be even the most basic tools. Their monuments and statues were designed to withstand the ravages of time almost unscathed, unlike many of their more recent Classical counterparts.

Tools for the job

The few iron objects that survive were either imported or of meteoric metal. Although copper was extracted from Sinai and used from the Archaic period onwards, there was no native tin to form the harder and more useful bronze. From the start of the New Kingdom, with imported tin from the Aegean, bronze was used in greater quantities, but only for votive statues and special tools.

Egyptians had to use other means, then, to extract and work stone. For the softer limestone used in building, blocks would either be hewn to shape from roughly cut pieces, or would be sawn using copper-bladed saws. Perhaps these might have flint-tipped edges or sand would be used as an abrasive. Such saws were very short; one example, found in a First Dynasty tomb at Saqqara, had a blade only 35cm (14in) long. However, circular saw marks that can still been seen on the faces of many stones are an indication that these must have been effective, at least to a certain extent.

For harder stone, cutting marks in the granite quarries of Aswan show that a series of wedge holes was gouged along a line on the face of the stone, probably using pounders of dolerite, an exceedingly hard stone found in natural 'balls' in the Eastern desert. Into the wedge holes blocks of wood would have been hammered, and then water poured over them. The slow expansion of the wood thus caused immense sideways pressure to be exerted on the stone, making the stone split, hopefully in a straight crack. It has been suggested that fires would have been lit along the line of the crack to heat the stone. Water thrown on this hot stone would have caused the surface of the granite to crumble allowing the stone cutters to gouge a trough along the crack line using their pounders. Although progress on any one block would thus be very slow, quarrying would be carried out simultaneously at many places. In this way, blocks of the fine granite were extracted, varying from small pieces for T-shaped offering tables or stone vases, to blocks

weighing between 6 and 30 tons for use in pyramid chambers or temples, and up to 1152 tons for obelisks.

The obelisks were always cut in one piece. Such work was obviously very highly skilled, from the choosing of an unflawed area of stone, to its accurate cutting along lengths of up to 41.7m (137ft). As a result, the cutting of obelisks was always specifically recorded, their removal from the quarry and erection at the site being a time of great national rejoicing. In one of the quarries of Aswan – the northern – one such obelisk lies still partly attached to the bedrock, abandoned by an unknown architect when it unexpectedly ruptured along a flaw.

Another stone that was highly prized was calcite, a translucent white to yellow stone incorrectly termed alabaster. This was cut from the quarries of Hatnub between Tell el Amarna and Assiut. It is a soft stone that is also brittle to work, but the Egyptian craftsmen mastered its use during the Archaic period if not before. During the New Kingdom, the intricate and slender curves of elaborate calcite jars that were found in the tomb of Tutankhamun show a craftsmanship that can barely be matched today. One exceptionally fine example, a goblet, has a bowl made of two shell-fine layers of calcite that fit one inside the other. Although the goblet appears unadorned in natural light, with a small candle inside to illuminate it, a charming scene of the young king and queen is revealed, painted on the outer face of the inner shell. This must surely rank as one of the masterpieces of ancient Egyptian craftsmanship.

Relief work

On the fine stone walls of temples and many tombs, the Egyptians carved, rather than painted, scenes of both religious and secular nature. In general, relief on outside walls would be carved deeply into the face of the stone. The figures and hieroglyphic inscription would first be drawn on the wall in ink on a grid in accordance with a sketch plan (see p. 148–49). The sculptor would then trace the outline using a chisel and mallet, bevelling the edges of the shape of the figure and adding in whatever detail he deemed necessary. The sharp edges of these sunk reliefs would be enhanced by shadows cast in the brilliant sunshine.

For indoor walls, where lighting was more subdued or cast only by lamps on low stands or torches in the hands of priests, raised relief was used. After the initial grid sketch was complete,

This magnificent pair of painted statues belonged to Prince Rahotep, a son of King Snofru, and Princess Nofret, his wife. Found in a mastaba tomb at Meidum, their wonderful state of preservation makes it hard to believe that these statues are over 5600 years old. In common with all Egyptian statues, the finished stone was overlaid with a fine layer of plaster and painted. The skin tones for men and women were completely different, women being depicted as paler through less exposure to the sun. Nofret, unusually for a woman, wears a long cloak over her dress; her jewels are detailed in brightly coloured paint. The inlaid eyes of both statues – rock crystal with amethyst irises – give them an astonishing liveliness, especially when illuminated in a beam of light. It is interesting to note that the majority of such inlaid eyes show blue-grey and not brown colouring.

Sculpture

Statuary of life size or colossal scale was achieved from the Old Kingdom onwards. These pieces, made of the hardest stone and polished to a high sheen with painstaking labour, were commissioned from workshops by the king to stand in public places. The monumental nature of their purpose often resulted in rigid poses that many people find lacking in character and individuality.

A block of stone would be taken to the sculptor's workshop to be shaped. A grid would be marked on all the stone's surfaces, with a sketched outline of the different faces of the finished piece. Initial shaping, as can be seen in several relief scenes, was done with dolerite pounders (*see above*). The finer shaping was achieved either with chisels or small adzes, or by rubbing down with pieces of sandstone. To reach the larger standing figures, scaffolding constructed of wood lashed together with ropes would have been used.

Whether the Egyptians were intentionally mindful of protecting weaker sections of statues, or whether it was an aesthetic preference, all sections of human figures carved in stone would be left attached to a stronger section. Thus, arms would either be kept straight by the sides of the figure, carved in relief on the body, or depicted lying along the thighs; the neck, naturally one of the weakest parts of the statue, would either be supported by a headdress or else left attached to a back pillar; while the legs remained joined by stone either to the chair of a seated figure or to the back pillar of a standing one. Since standing figures invariably have the left foot slightly forward of the right, this has the strange result of making the figure look as if it is casually reclining when viewed from the left side!

The eyes of such statues were frequently inlaid with rock-crystal orbs set with irises of amethyst and pupils of obsidian that look startlingly lifelike when illuminated. They were pegged into the empty eye sockets using vertical dowels inserted through the forehead.

When completed, and polished, the statues would usually be overlaid with a fine skin of gesso plaster and painted to resemble closely the living person. Without doubt two of the finest extant examples are the statues of Rahotep and Nofret, dating from the Third Dynasty. So realistic are they that when first seen by the light of a candle, the workmen fled in terror.

the sculptor would painstakingly cut away the background, leaving the hieroglyphs and figures standing proud of the wall. These could then be shaped, often with great skill and a fineness that was exaggerated in the oblique light.

In both cases, the finished figures and inscriptions, inside buildings and out, would be painted in brilliant colours. In some temples, in places sheltered from the wind and abrasive sand, enough paint survives to show that they would originally not have been the mellow, gold-hued stone that we see today, but boldly coloured, with applications of deep bright blues, reds and greens standing out vividly against a whitewashed background.

TO LIVE FOREVER

The earliest preservation of human remains in Egypt appears to have been accidental. Predynastic burial sites consist of shallow pit graves in which the body, in curled foetal position, lay in direct contact with the sand. The combination of intense heat and dryness desiccated the bodies naturally. Since all of these burials were accompanied by grave goods, and since the face of the dead person invariably faced the west (the later traditional place of entry to the land of the dead), it is clear that the belief in the same form of afterlife existed from most ancient times. Whether this afterlife was intrinsically linked with the preservation of the body at this time is unclear.

The elements of life
The Egyptians believed that human life comprised several different elements, the survival of all of which ensured immortality.

The ka (represented by a pair of upraised arms over a human figure) was a spirit double, created at the time of birth by Khnum, the creator god, on a potter's wheel. It resembled the owner physically. During a person's lifetime it could be freed from the body during sleep and could, indeed, cause damage to its owner. At death, the ka left the body and travelled through the underworld to meet and be judged by Osiris, the god of the dead. Each morning, it returned to the land of the living with the rising sun, and was drawn back to the tomb by pictures, statues and the mummy. Several times each day a mortuary priest (i.e. ka priest) would visit the tomb to leave offerings of food and drink to refresh the ka.

The ba (represented by a human-headed bird sometimes with arms as well as wings), was the impersonal life force of the person and thus only left the body at the time of death. It was seen then to be free to leave and enter the tomb at will, using the body as a perch.

The body was needed for the ka to identify, and for the ba bird to perch on, and thus the eternal survival of both depended in the first instance on the preservation of the corpse.

Other aspects of the human being were the Akh, the 'shining form' a spirit took after death and satisfactory burial in the tomb; the Shadow, without which in a land of brilliant sunshine no living human could exist, and thus was deemed to have an existence of its own; and the Name, remembrance and repetition of which ensured that the memory of the deceased would be perpetuated.

The mummy
The term appears to derive from the Persian-Arabic word 'moumiya', meaning 'bitumen' or 'pitch', and refers to the hard, black resinous coating encrusting Egyptian mummies. The black material is the result of chemical interaction between the oils, perfumes, unguents and resins with which the body was anointed.

From the medieval period onwards, bitumen was regarded by the Arab physicians as a powerful curative. An apothecary in a 10th century treatise wrote, 'Where any difficulties arise from procuring bitumen, corpses may be substituted in its stead.' Whether as a result of this advice or not, Egyptian mummies were exported, the tissue reduced to powder and sold as a form of medicine.

The history of mummification
Early attempts to preserve the dead appear to have been very basic. As the desire to provide a comfortable grave or tomb grew, and more elaborate coverings and coffins were provided, the separation of the body from the desiccating sand resulted in decay. It is clear, however, that the bodies in those times were well wrapped in linen bandages, and covered with wet plaster, which was pressed and smoothed to take the form of the body beneath. When the plaster dried, the outer shell was painted – sometimes green from head to foot, resembling, presumably, the colour of regrowth – and the face decorated to resemble the person during life.

During the Middle Kingdom, mummification techniques were far more accomplished, though few mummies of this date have survived. One remarkable cache was discovered in a cave at Luxor by H. E. Winlock, who was excavating for New York's Metropolitan Museum of Art. What at first sight appeared to be a late, perhaps Coptic, intrusive burial was discovered much later to be a group of 60 soldiers who had served in the army of Mentuhotep Nebhepetre during the battles to re-establish centralized control during the early years of the Eleventh Dynasty. The bodies, all of men killed in battle, had lain exposed on the sand for some time after death, having suffered from the ravages of animals preying on them, before being gathered together, cursorily bandaged and thrust into the cache tomb.

Mummification was perfected during the New Kingdom. The royal mummies that have survived (see pp. 96–9) are among the finest examples of the embalmer's art. During the late

These are two of a set of four canopic jars that were designed to hold the viscera of a deceased person after mummification. On the left, Duamutef, the dog-headed jar, would have held the stomach, and on the right, Qebekh-sennuef, the falcon, the intestines. The other two jars would have depicted a human, Imsety (for the liver) and Hapi (a baboon, for the lungs). The four make up the four sons of Horus. Canopic jars are frequently made of calcite, and would have been stored in the tomb in a specially made chest. The term canopic jars was given to them by Classical scholars. Canopus, the pilot of the ships of Menelaeus, was supposedly revered in the form of a jar with a human head.

New Kingdom and the Third Intermediate Period, in a vain attempt to restore more natural features to the body, paddings of linen and other materials reintroduced the decay the embalmers sought to eliminate, with the result that many mummies of the period appear to have collapsed.

The process was still being used in Greek and Roman times. Although the bodies were less well preserved, great care was taken over the elaborate bandaging, with many hundreds of yards of folded and dyed linen being wrapped around the body to produce an intricate diamond pattern on the exterior. The image of the deceased was faithfully reproduced on a portrait board painted in a wax-based medium. Herodotus records that many of these mummies were kept in the houses of the living to remind them of their mortality. Many excavated sites in Egypt reveal that, from time to time, an earlier tomb would be uncovered and frequently set alight to destroy the previous owner's goods before placing whole families or local groups of mummies within, in caches.

As Christianity spread through Egypt, mummification was gradually abandoned. However, pockets of 'pagan' worshippers existed throughout Egypt until at least the fourth century and the cult acolytes, though only crudely mummified, were buried in painted linen shrouds bearing still the elements of the old religion.

The process of mummification

No contemporary account, either in pictures or in inscriptions, has survived to give a clear understanding of the New Kingdom mummification process. Herodotus' description, however, written in the fourth century BC, appears from modern analysis to be quite accurate.

According to him, three separate categories of mummification existed, priced at different levels. Treatment only varied during the initial stages. For the simplest and cheapest method, the body was merely washed and cleansed; for the second method, a corrosive fluid (hardly the 'palm-oil' to which many translators of Herodotus refer) was poured into the body orifices, which were then plugged. After some days, the plugs would be removed, and the inside thoroughly cleansed.

For the third, the most expensive and finest method, an abdominal incision would be made through which the intestines, stomach, liver and lungs would be carefully removed. The kidneys, often referred to as the seat of emotions, and the heart, required by the deceased for the Judgment, would be replaced within the shell of the body. The brain would also be removed, either through an incision at the back of the skull, or via the nostrils, a metal scoop being inserted, cracking through the fine foramen magnum at the rear and thus entering the cranial cavity. The viscera would be embalmed alongside the body, and wrapped in separate parcels. In the earliest periods they would be placed in a chest, internally divided into four compartments and covered with lids in the shape of human heads. Later, canopic jars were used with the same four heads, though from the Ramesside period onwards stoppers were in the form of the heads of the 'four sons of Horus'. From the Late Period, the viscera were replaced inside the body at the end of the process.

The body would then be packed in mounds of dry natron. This is a natural salt that occurs plentifully in a dried lake bed in the western delta, today called the Wadi Natrun. Primarily sodium chloride (common salt), it contains a high proportion (about 17%) of sodium bicarbonate. Modern experimentation at Manchester University, in the 1970s, has shown that the high level of bicarbonate is vital for the success of the process. The natron absorbed the body fluids, resulting, after around 40 days, in a stable shell no longer affected by decay.

The mummy of *King Seti II, of the Nineteenth Dynasty, a son of Merenptah and grandson of Ramesses II, shows how badly preserved many mummies are. Interaction of the oils and unguents poured over the bodies caused great carbonization, while the eviscerated trunks have frequently collapsed, the result of inadequate packing. In common with many mummies, royal and non-royal, the abrupt unwrapping Seti's mummy suffered at the hands of robbers caused further damage to his arms and head. It is a great privilege to be able to look at all, however, upon one of the faces of our distant ancestors. From careful and respectful examination of such remains we can deduce much information about the way the ancient Egyptians lived and the physical problems they had to endure.*

The mummy was then cleansed, and priests would supervise the bandaging. Linen bandages, often strips of household linen – except for the finest burials for which new, specially woven bands were used – would be wrapped first around each individual joint and limb, and then around the whole body, binding arms to the body and legs tightly together. As the layers of linen were applied, amulets would be placed at specially appointed spots, each to be accompanied by a spoken recitation by the priest to ensure its efficacy.

Often, when the bandaging was complete, a mask would be placed over the head of the body. While in royal burials this might be of gold or silver, for the less wealthy, the masks would be of cartonnage, a type of papier mâché made of papyrus or linen secured in gesso plaster and painted or gilded when dry.

The mummy would then be placed within one, or a whole series of, anthropoid coffins. These, painted to bear some idealized resemblance to the deceased in life, were frequently made of wood, comprising small pieces jointed and dowelled together and the whole plastered and painted. For the upper ranks of society and royal burials, at the time of burial these coffins would be lowered within a stone, rectangular sarcophagus.

At every stage of the bandaging, encoffinment and entombing, liberal quantities of precious oils and perfumes were brushed or ladled over the finished burial, forming the hard, characteristic pitch-like substance.

The burial

The mummy, in its coffins, would be dragged on a flat sledge to the tomb, with a canopy over it resembling the sky and stars. Behind, a funeral procession would bear food and drink, furniture and personal possessions, for the equipping of the tomb chambers, while mourning women (often professionals, paid to attend) wept and shrieked like the kites that circle over Egyptian hills today. At the tomb entrance, the mummy would be stood upright briefly while priests from the local temple performed the last ritual ceremonies. While the correct words were read out loud by a lector-priest, another priest would touch gently the eyes, nose, lips, ears, hands and feet of the coffin with a model carpenter's adze, as though lifting the wood of the coffin at these places to permit the senses to function. This is referred to as the 'Opening of the Mouth' ceremony.

The coffins would then be lowered into the tomb, and surrounded by the burial objects, then the entrance would be sealed, usually with loose stones faced with mud plaster. In the western hills of Luxor, the oval stamp over the necropolis guard – a recumbent Anubis over nine bound and tied captives – would be impressed into the plaster. Often a series of baked clay cones bearing the owner's names and titles would be pushed into the mud plaster while it was still soft.

Although some tombs were sealed, many were clearly left open, as Classical and even hieroglyphic graffiti inside attest. Within the tombs of the noble or courtier, the burial chamber was underground. The superstructure, often a T-shaped chamber cut into the rock, served as a mortuary chapel to which the relatives or the ka-priest would bring offerings of food and drink.

Analysis of mummies

Relatively few mummies survive today; it has been estimated at barely 1000 worldwide. As a result, this irreplaceable source of archaeological evidence must be treasured by the expert, and examined with the least damage possible caused. Modern scientific techniques permit this to be done very effectively, often without need to unwrap the mummies. Such was the interest, however, in 'unrolling' mummies during the last century that many museum collections around the world hold numbers of exposed mummies, and in recent decades, scientists have availed themselves of the opportunity to recover vital information.

X-rays, available for many years, have revealed a number of abnormalities, such as arthritis and gout, as well as fractures both ante- and post-mortem. Electron microscopy of tissue samples has brought to light a whole host of medical problems. Most mummies have been discovered to have particles of sand and carbon in their lungs – both unavoidable to those who live in the windy desert areas – that would have resulted in breathlessness and severe coughs brought about by pneumoconiosis.

Evidence of disease

High numbers of mummies also bear traces of parasitic infestations, including bilharzia, still prevalent today. This minute worm, entering the body via the skin of the foot of those who stand in infected irrigation ditches, attacks many organs of the body including the lungs,

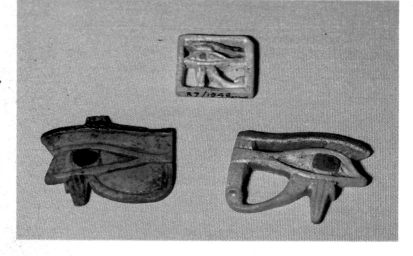

and, from time to time, severs the optical nerve, resulting in instant and irreversible blindness. In the workmen's village of Deir el Medina a man, Neferabu, lamented bitterly on a series of stelae the blasphemy he had perpetrated which had, he was assured, caused him to see 'darkness by day'. Even more pernicious was guinea-worm infestation, the female of which often grows to several metres in length, winding itself around the body just below the skin before erupting through an ulcer. These, together with intestinal worms, must have left the average sufferer feeling very tired, often severely anaemic, and in great pain.

Virtually every mummy examined reveals severe dental attrition – not the modern cavities, resulting from our sweet, soft diet, but the abrasion of surface enamel to the very dentine of the tooth, caused by the high quantities of sand in the bread that formed the basic Egyptian diet. Infections entering through these severely painful nerves resulted in abscesses that caused holes to form in the jawbone; many mummies have whole series of such holes.

More sophisticated techniques, using rehydration, have allowed very accurate blood- and tissue-typing of the remains to be established, frequently assisting in the identification of family relationships. The mummy of Tutankhamun (see p. 113) and that of the mysterious body in Tomb 55 (see p. 102) have both been shown to be of blood type A_2MN. Most surprising of all modern experiments, however, must be the recent discovery that within the cells of mummified tissue, the genetic molecular structure, the DNA, is still intact, and cells have been successfully cloned. Truly it can be said, therefore, that in at least this respect the Egyptians achieved their aim of 'living forever'.

Among the bandages of mummies large numbers of amulets were carefully placed where priests deemed they would offer the greatest magical protection. Most potent of all amulets were these wadjet eyes. The name 'wadjet' means 'healed' and refers to an incident in the story of the battle between Horus and Seth. On one occasion, while Horus slept, Seth removed one of his eyes. When Horus awoke, he sought out his mother, Isis, who fashioned a replacement: the healed or wadjet eye. So great was its magical power, it could be sent out on the god's behest, to do his command. The shape of the eye bears close similarity, viewed sideways, to the king's double crown which, like the eye, was revered for its magical powers.

HIEROGLYPHS: THE STORY OF DECIPHERMENT

Thomas Young
(1773–1829)

Young was the eldest of 10 children born to a Quaker family in southwest England, and was incontrovertibly a genius. He read by the age of two and by 14 knew competently at least 12 languages, including Syriac, Chaldee, Samaritan and Persian. Even though he later became both a doctor and physicist, his ability for languages never left him; he reviewed 400 different languages for the Encyclopaedia Britannica. Young's research into ophthalmology resulted in his identifying astigmatism for the first time. His interest in Egypt having been stimulated by an article he read, he started work on the decipherment of hieroglyphs. His analysis of the signs used on the Rosetta stone proved almost completely correct several years before Champollion's complete grammar was published. Young, unfortunately, was forced to abandon his researches into Egyptology through lack of funding.

This Egyptian *stamp, issued in 1972 to commemorate the one-hundred and fiftieth anniversary of the decipherment of hieroglyphs, bears the portrait of Jean-François Champollion – the author of the first Egyptian grammar – and the Rosetta stone, now in the British Museum, which gave him the clues he needed to decipher hieroglyphs successfully for the first time.*

Virtually all understanding of Egyptian hieroglyphs was lost during the fourth century AD, and even the Egyptian language was gradually forgotten with the exception of some words and structures that survived into Coptic. After AD 452 when the last vestiges of the language vanished along with Demotic at Philae, ancient Egyptian was truly lost. For centuries afterwards people attempted to understand the strange hieroglyphic characters in the light of Arabic insistence that they were idiomatic, each sign encapsulating a whole word or magical meaning.

Even interest in Coptic was beginning to decline in the 17th century and, but for the work of a Jesuit priest, Athanasius Kircher, it too might have died. Kircher not only produced a Coptic dictionary, but boldly attempted to translate hieroglyphs. His explanations, though scholarly, were works of imagination and such monstrous error as to set back the study of hieroglyphs by many years.

The Rosetta stone

But in 1799 a French soldier, while digging a fort at Raschid on the Rosetta branch of the Nile, found the black basalt stone that was to change the course of Egyptology. Although damaged, it contained three sections of writing: the upper part in hieroglyphs; the centre section in demotic, the last and cursive form of writing the Egyptian language; and on the lower part, upper case Greek letters. The importance of the stone was recognized at once by an engineer, Lieutenant Bouchard, who alerted the French commander Menou. Menou gave orders for the Greek section to be translated immediately, and for inked impressions and plaster casts to be made of the stone and copies sent to all interested scholars.

One cast fell into the hands of a Swedish diplomat, Akerblad, a man who had studied several Oriental languages in his youth. By comparing the three texts, he was able to prove that wherever royal names occurred in the Greek section, they appeared in virtually the same positions in the demotic text. In 1802, he wrote a letter to his friend, the Orientalist Silvestre de Sacy, showing not only that the three sections were indeed translations of one and the same text, a temple endowment decree of Ptolemy V dated to 27 March 196 BC, but also the existence of several recognizable words in demotic – 'temple', 'Greek' and 'his'.

The first breakthrough in decipherment was made by an Englishman, Thomas Young. Young was a genius by any understanding of the term. He could read his native language at the age of two and understand 12 different languages by the age of 14, including many Middle Eastern dialects; later he wrote an authoritative study on 400 languages for the Encyclopaedia Britannica. He trained as a mathematician and physicist, and was the discoverer of the wave-form nature of light.

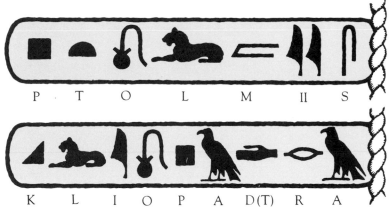

Young became interested in Egyptology by chance, studying first a papyrus bought in Egypt, and only later, a copy of the Rosetta stone text. Not only was he able correctly to decipher most of the demotic signs, but he was the first to recognize that the 'rope-loops', now called cartouches, in the hieroglyphic text contained the names of the kings. Within a short time, he was able to read the name of Ptolemy. By comparing the name on the Rosetta stone with those on an obelisk that was brought back by Belzoni from Philae, Young was able to read, correctly, six different signs, with another three partly correct, and was the first to realize that the signs were not idiomatic, but partly alphabetic and with a strict grammatical form. He also read and understood the mathematical hieroglyphic symbols. The results of his work he sent to Champollion in France. It is instructive to note that it would take Champollion two years after this to abandon the notion that hieroglyphs were simply symbolic, although he never fully admitted the debt he owed to Young's work.

However, the final and conclusive decipherment of hieroglyphs, and the rediscovery of the Egyptian language in which they were written, belongs to Champollion alone.

Champollion

Jean François Champollion's interest in Egypt was triggered as a boy, when first he read about the Rosetta stone. It is reputed that he swore one day to be the first to read hieroglyphs. Certainly, like his counterpart Young, he was a genius with a gift for languages, including Coptic which he mastered early, believing, correctly, that it would be the key he would need one day to understand Egyptian. His education was not gained from schools, however, but at the hand of his elder brother Jacques-Joseph. His brother was 12 years older and was studying classics, including Egyptian culture, when the French Revolution interrupted. He was forced to find a job and, while working for the government, begged to be allowed to go with Napoleon's savants to Egypt. To his lifelong regret, he was rejected. There can be little doubt that much of Jean-François' interest in Egyptology sprang from his elder brother's frustration.

The young Champollion was only 16 when he presented a paper to the Grenoble academy, stating unequivocally that Coptic was the ancient Egyptian language. He so impressed his peers that he was appointed a lecturer at the university at only 19, and was made professor at the age of 28. His first book on Egypt, *Egypt under the Pharaohs*, was published in 1811, when he was 21.

His progress in deciphering hieroglyphs was at first slow. But once he was finally convinced of the phonetic value of the symbols, he was able very rapidly not only to identify the hieroglyphic signs but also to discern enough of the lost language to be able to make a reasonable translation of the hieroglyphic section of the Rosetta stone in its entirety. The final proof of his theories he received in the early months of 1822, when he was sent copies of the texts from the rock-cut temple of Abu Simbel. Using his theories, he found he could read the inscriptions, including the name of the pharaoh, Ramesses II. Immediately he wrote a letter to the Secretary of the French Academie Royale des Inscriptions, Baron Joseph Dacier, outlining his discovery. This 'Lettre à M. Dacier' is regarded as the definitive document by which hieroglyphs could be translated and the start of the modern field of Egyptology. Champollion wrote, 'I have now reached the point where I can put together almost a complete survey of the general structure of these two forms of writing, the origin, nature, form and number of signs, and the rules of their combination . . . thus laying the first foundations for the grammar and dictionary of these scripts which are found on the majority of monuments.'

The publication of his grammar, however, was to elude him, for in 1832, at the age of 42, he died unexpectedly, after suffering a stroke. It was ironically to be his elder brother Jacques-Joseph who collected together the many notes left by Champollion, edited them and supervised their final publication. After almost 1500 years of silence, at last the ancient Egyptian texts could be read and a whole new vista of information opened to scholars.

The two cartouches *above provided the early 19th century scholars with all the information needed to decipher two royal names and thus prove that some of the symbols stood for sounds and were not symbolic. These two names, enclosed in cartouches, were inscribed on the Rosetta stone and also on an obelisk from Philae, brought to England by Belzoni. Young guessed that the enclosed areas contained names and from the Greek section of the Rosetta stone, he determined that these names were Ptolemy and Cleopatra – Ptolemy spelled the Greek way, Ptolemais. The first letter of the first cartouche was the same as the fifth in the second – and the letter 'p' matches identically. Thus the rectangle was the sound 'p'. Similarly, the third letter of the first name was identical with the fourth letter in the second – and the letter 't'. So a semicircle was the sound 't'. Slowly, Young was able to read, in the first cartouche (top): P – T – O – L – M – II – S; and in the second K – L – I – O – P – A – T – R – A. If you look at the hieroglyphic alphabet, you will see that in the name Cleopatra, the Egyptians used 'd' as the seventh letter instead of 't'. This tells us how 'd' was pronounced in Graeco-Roman times.*

HOW TO READ HIEROGLYPHS

Two fine *examples of hieroglyphs. The wooden panel (top), carved in raised relief, belonged to the Chief of Dentists and Physicians, Hesire, who served Djoser-Netcherikhe during the Third Dynasty. His name can be read at the bottom of the left-hand vertical column. The second example (below) shows part of a stela bearing the name in the cartouche on the right of King Menkaure-Mycerinus, of the late Fourth Dynasty. It was found by George Reisner near the king's pyramid at Giza and is now in the Boston Museum of Fine Arts, in the United States. In the centre, the four large signs read: 'May he be given life, stability and prosperity'. On the left is Mycerinus' Horus name, calling him a 'mighty bull'.*

Hieroglyphs are pictures used to write the language of the ancient Egyptians. The ancient Egyptian language is still not fully understood, although it can be read sufficiently to understand exactly what the ancient Egyptian scribe was trying to communicate.

It depends on the pronunciation of the word and not its spelling. If hieroglyphs were used to write English, 'there' and 'their', or 'threw' and 'through' could be written using the same signs.

The hieroglyphic signs were first used soon after unification simply to record the king's possessions throughout Egypt when they became too numerous and complex to use tally sticks. By drawing a picture of an ox or a boat followed by a number (*see p. 165*), scribes could record the facts without needing to use grammar. However as the need for written records extended, so more and more signs had to be used to represent the way the language sounded. It is not easy to write 'The King of Upper and Lower Egypt triumphed over the Delta-Dwellers in a mighty victory, holding them captive' simply by using pictures.

The language is a mixture of North African and Semitic elements, suggesting that it had developed from many strains long before it was written down. As time went on it also absorbed other foreign words. During the Greek administration, so many words were adopted that the language became very complex, being written with more and more signs. This Ptolemaic form of the language was then written in Greek characters and called Coptic. In Coptic, the essential structure of the Egyptian language was preserved, enabling us to understand how a sentence may have been formed in ancient Egyptian.

Written language

Hieroglyphs can be written in three ways. *Hieroglyphs*, written with pen and ink or carved on stone with a chisel, are carefully drawn, with attention paid to making the signs as accurate as possible. *Hieratic* was a cursive form of writing, as handwriting is to printed letters. It allowed the scribe to adapt the various signs, reducing them to a pattern of lines that still bore some resemblance to the hieroglyph. *Demotic* was a shorthand version of the writing which was adopted during the Late Period in Egyptian history. Since many people could read this form of script (the signs are not joined up but written separately and simply), it took the name 'demotic' – the people's writing.

The picture signs can be written from left to right; from right to left; or vertically downwards. Look for the figures of men, birds and animals. They all face the *start* of the line. If a 'man' sign faces left, the inscription is read from left to right. Hieroglyphs are not just a way of writing, but were still essentially pictures, and as such, a hieroglyphic inscription aimed to please the eye aesthetically. The Egyptians loved symmetry and balance. Thus over a doorway or around the walls of a chamber, the hieroglyphs always face the centre. Often the texts over a lintel and the doorjambs of a door are duplicated on each side, with the figures of the people looking inwards, leading the eye through the doorway.

Imagine trying to write the English language, using pictures instead of letters. A picture of an 'eye' could stand for a single letter 'i'; a wavy line could stand for the letter 'c' (sea). Put them together and the word 'icy' is formed. This, in principle, is the basis of the Egyptian language as it is written.

However, to write every word using these single signs would be both time-consuming, clumsy and often simply impossible. So instead, whole groups of sounds could be used. Imagine, in English, that in any word in which the sound 'car' or 'ka' appears, a picture of an automobile is used. By adding a picture of a flag after it, standing for the syllable '-nation', the word would read 'car-nation'. In the same way, by using pictures that were recognizable to them, the Egyptians could use 'group signs' to make up other words.

Yet the composite words 'icy' and 'carnation' have a meaning all of their own, with no relevance to the pictures they use. By adding another picture at the end of the word, the sense of the word can be understood. So, after 'icy' a picture of a 'shivering man' or an 'icicle' could be used; and after 'carnation' the picture of a 'flower'. The same method was used in hieroglyphs. After all of the group signs, a final picture was added to give the sense of the whole word. These we call *determinatives*. So for a verb of action, e.g. 'to go', a picture of 'walking legs' would be added! For the verb 'to cry' or the noun 'tears' a picture of an eye with tears dripping from it was added.

As a result of the use of determinatives, with relative ease and only little guidance the meaning of some words whe written in hierolyphs can be readily understood without ever knowing exactly how the word was meant to be pronounced.

THE HIEROGLYPHIC ALPHABET

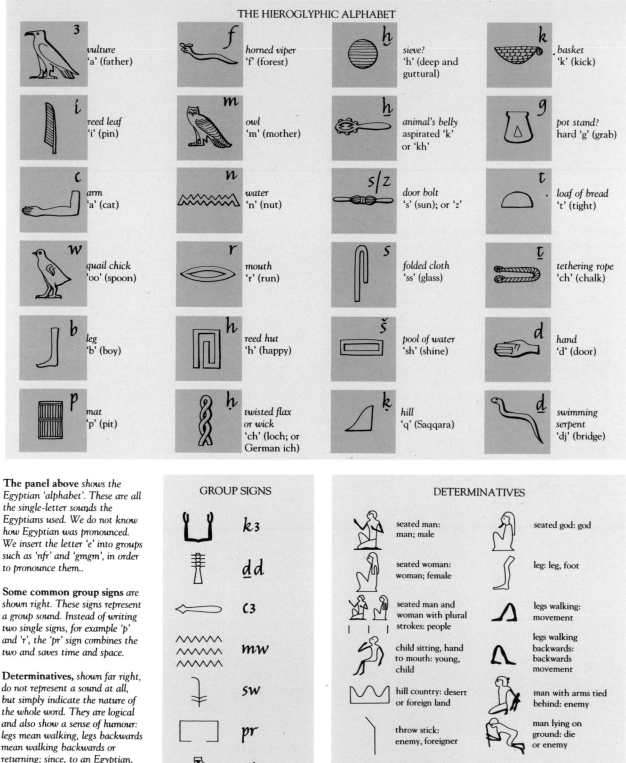

ꜣ vulture 'a' (father)	**f** horned viper 'f' (forest)	**ḥ** sieve? 'h' (deep and guttural)	**k** basket 'k' (kick)
i reed leaf 'i' (pin)	**m** owl 'm' (mother)	**ḫ** animal's belly aspirated 'k' or 'kh'	**g** pot stand? hard 'g' (grab)
ꜥ arm 'a' (cat)	**n** water 'n' (nut)	**s/z** door bolt 's' (sun); or 'z'	**t** loaf of bread 't' (tight)
w quail chick 'oo' (spoon)	**r** mouth 'r' (run)	**s** folded cloth 'ss' (glass)	**ṯ** tethering rope 'ch' (chalk)
b leg 'b' (boy)	**h** reed hut 'h' (happy)	**š** pool of water 'sh' (shine)	**d** hand 'd' (door)
p mat 'p' (pit)	**ḥ** twisted flax or wick 'ch' (loch; or German ich)	**ḳ** hill 'q' (Saqqara)	**ḏ** swimming serpent 'dj' (bridge)

The panel above *shows the Egyptian 'alphabet'. These are all the single-letter sounds the Egyptians used. We do not know how Egyptian was pronounced. We insert the letter 'e' into groups such as 'nfr' and 'gmgm', in order to pronounce them..*

Some common group signs *are shown right. These signs represent a group sound. Instead of writing two single signs, for example 'p' and 'r', the 'pr' sign combines the two and saves time and space.*

Determinatives, *shown far right, do not represent a sound at all, but simply indicate the nature of the whole word. They are logical and also show a sense of humour: legs mean walking, legs backwards mean walking backwards or returning; since, to an Egyptian, an enemy should be either tied hand and foot or dead, the determinative for an enemy makes this point clearly.*

GROUP SIGNS

Sign	Value
	kꜣ
	ḏd
	ꜥꜣ
	mw
	sw
	pr
	sḏm

DETERMINATIVES

seated man: man; male	seated god: god
seated woman: woman; female	leg: leg, foot
seated man and woman with plural strokes: people	legs walking: movement
child sitting, hand to mouth: young, child	legs walking backwards: backwards movement
hill country: desert or foreign land	man with arms tied behind: enemy
throw stick: enemy, foreigner	man lying on ground: die or enemy
village with crossroads: village; town	three vertical strokes: plural

Most of the sites open to visitors, both temples and tombs, were made on a grand and formal scale by and for the kings of Egypt. Since many of them are worked in stone, the hieroglyphs are easy to pick out; and also are so standard that the same phrases are repeated time after time, not just within one building, but over the full span of Egyptian history. With the knowledge of a few phrases then, it is often possible to read whole panels of texts. To read the words of long-dead civilizations for oneself is deeply satisfying, for it is as though the stones speak to you and you alone.

Although each king had up to five different names read out at the time of his coronation, only two were commonly used. The 'Son of Re' name was given to the infant prince at birth, and is the one by which we invariably know the kings – Ramesses or Tutankhamun, for example. The 'King of Upper and Lower Egypt' name was given to them only when they received the double crown, and it was by this name that the Egyptians and peoples of other nations knew the kings. Each of these names is unique, but they are often very complicated. Egyptologists use the simple 'Son of Re' name – usually the only exception of this rule is the early kings, for whom there was no Son of Re name. Finally, although we refer to kings by sequence number – Seti I or Ramesses II, for example – the Egyptians did not use numbers as part of the king's name. The inscriptions in the panel to the right are the common titles accompanying the names of kings, queens, princes and princesses throughout the history of Egypt, and will help anyone to read most of the inscriptions on the monuments.

King of Upper and Lower Egypt (coronation name)	May she be given life!
nsw-bity	di·ti ʿnh
Lord of the Two Lands	Living forever
nb t3wy	ʿnh dt
Lord of the Throne of the Two Lands	Forever and ever
nb nswt t3wy	dt nhh
Son of Re (birth name)	Given life, like Re, forever
S3 Rʿ	di ʿnh mi Rʿ dt
The good god	Life, prosperity, health!
ntr nfr	ʿnh wd3 snb
beloved of . . .	True of voice (i.e. vindicated by Osiris – dead)
mry	m3ʿ hrw
Lady of the Two Lands	Son of the King, Prince . . .
nbt t3wy	S3-nsw
Great Royal Wife (above queen's cartouche)	Daughter of the King, Princess . .
hmt-nsw wrt	s3t-nsw
Given life! (after or below cartouches)	of his own body
di ʿnh	n ht·f

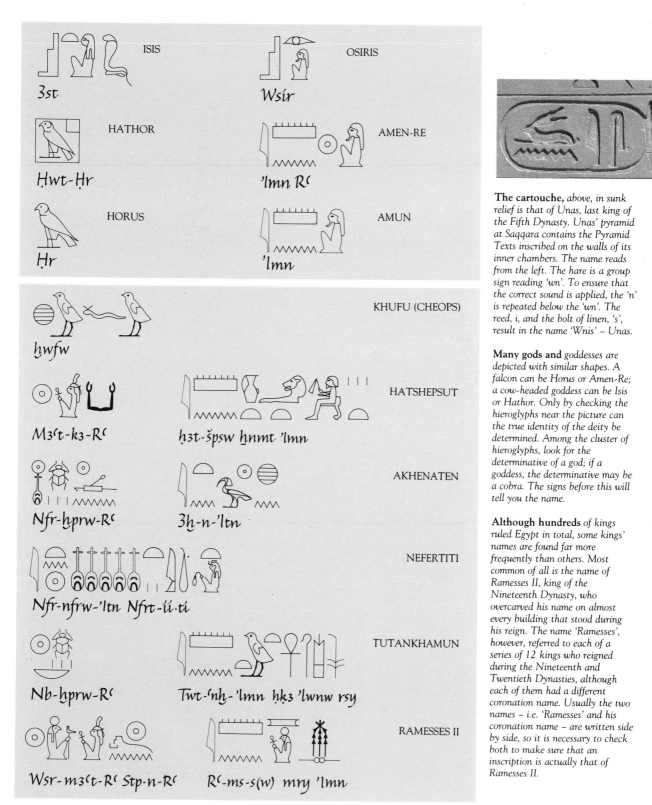

ISIS
3st

OSIRIS
Wsir

HATHOR
Hwt-Hr

AMEN-RE
'Imn Rʿ

HORUS
Hr

AMUN
'Imn

KHUFU (CHEOPS)
hwfw

HATSHEPSUT
h3t-špsw hnmt 'Imn

M3ʿt-k3-Rʿ

AKHENATEN
3h-n-'Itn

Nfr-hprw-Rʿ

NEFERTITI
Nfrt-íí·tí

Nfr-nfrw-'Itn

TUTANKHAMUN
Twt-ʿnh-'Imn hk3 'Iwnw rsy

Nb-hprw-Rʿ

RAMESSES II
Rʿ-ms-s(w) mry 'Imn

Wsr-m3ʿt-Rʿ Stp-n-Rʿ

The cartouche, *above, in sunk relief is that of Unas, last king of the Fifth Dynasty. Unas' pyramid at Saqqara contains the Pyramid Texts inscribed on the walls of its inner chambers. The name reads from the left. The hare is a group sign reading 'wn'. To ensure that the correct sound is applied, the 'n' is repeated below the 'wn'. The reed, i, and the bolt of linen, 's', result in the name 'Wnis' – Unas.*

Many gods and goddesses are depicted with similar shapes. A falcon can be Horus or Amen-Re; a cow-headed goddess can be Isis or Hathor. Only by checking the hieroglyphs near the picture can the true identity of the deity be determined. Among the cluster of hieroglyphs, look for the determinative of a god; if a goddess, the determinative may be a cobra. The signs before this will tell you the name.

Although hundreds of kings ruled Egypt in total, some kings' names are found far more frequently than others. Most common of all is the name of Ramesses II, king of the Nineteenth Dynasty, who overcarved his name on almost every building that stood during his reign. The name 'Ramesses', however, referred to each of a series of 12 kings who reigned during the Nineteenth and Twentieth Dynasties, although each of them had a different coronation name. Usually the two names – i.e. 'Ramesses' and his coronation name – are written side by side, so it is necessary to check both to make sure that an inscription is actually that of Ramesses II.

ROLE OF THE SCRIBE

This hieroglyphic sign shows the equipment used by a scribe; the palette with two wells, for black and red ink; the shoulder strap, reed pens and water pot. In Egyptian, this sign represents the sound 'sesh'. With the figure of a man after it, it means 'scribe'; but with a papyrus roll after it – the Egyptian symbol for anything abstract – it meant 'to write' or 'to paint'. Both writing and art, to the Egyptian way of thinking, were aspects of the same craft.

When a young scribe learned to read and write in ancient Egypt he would first be taught hieratic (*see p. 158*) and would have to copy out wise sayings and old stories many times until he eventually became familiar with the words. This copying would be done on ostraca – small broken fragments of pot or limestone flakes. When proficient, he would graduate to papyrus.

Material and methods

Papyrus was made from papyrus reed, which grew commonly on the riverbanks during the Old Kingdom, but which became more scarce as time went on. The name 'papyrus' appears to come from the Egyptian phrase 'pa per-aa' meaning 'that which belonged to the king,' implying that it was made and issued under a royal monopoly. Cutting the reed stem, which grew to the thickness of a forearm, the outer green sheath would be peeled away to reveal the white inner pith. This would be cut vertically into thin slivers, and these slices would be laid on a slab side by side, just touching; first a vertically arranged row and then on top, a horizontal row. This 'mat' would be beaten with a mallet, and then left under a heavy weight for several days. When it was dry, the natural sap of the pith bonded it into a firm sheet. These sheets measured, at their largest, about 50 by 40cm (20 by 16in). These sheets could be stuck together side by side to form a long roll, ensuring that the side with the horizontally-laid fibres was on top. This ensured that the papyrus, when rolled up, would not crack on the written side.

Before writing, the scribe would rub the surface of the papyrus with a polished stone to smooth it. With the papyrus roll in his left hand, the scribe either stood, sat cross-legged or occasionally squatted at a low desk to write. The Egyptian scribe is invariably shown writing with the right hand, though this may be artistic convention rather than evidence that no one was left-handed. Over his shoulder he would have a strap; at the front would be suspended an ink-palette, and at the back, a pen holder and a small water pot. Two indentations in the ink-palette contained small discs of ink – black, made from carbon, and red, from ochre – mixed with gum and allowed to harden. Using a brush-pen made from a softened maritime reed the scribe would moisten his brush in the water pot, dab it into the ink, and paint, rather than write, with his hand suspended over the surface of the papyrus.

Usually texts would be written horizontally from right to left. If the scribe used horizontal lines, he would be able to use only a small section of the papyrus at a time. When he had completed a section, he would wait for it to dry, roll it with his left hand and unroll a new section to his right. This was a time consuming procedure. If he wrote in vertical lines, however, he could write constantly without pause. Some papyri vary in the direction of the lines within the one roll.

Learning to write hieroglyphs, rather than hieratic, was the province of the selected few. Those scribes who were finally apprenticed to stonemasons, carpenters and painters, would have to learn exactly how to draw hieroglyphs within a marked grid so that painters could transfer them onto walls.

Reading and writing was confined to a very small group of men; there is no positive evidence that women ever learned to read and write. The vast majority of Egyptians, some 98 per cent, were quite illiterate. Documents show that every town and village would have a scribe, and those who wanted or needed to write – letters, legal documents or bills – would pay him in kind to write for them, sometimes attaching their 'mark' at the foot. Those who mastered the art, however, together with the ability to reckon, were assured of a prosperous and relatively easy life.

Young scribes were constantly advised by their teachers on the ultimate advantages of being able to read. 'See, there is no job without a master except for the scribe: he is the master. If you know how to write, it will serve you better than any other job,' one teacher wrote. Yet the boys were not always convinced, and many played truant. A teacher writes to his pupil: 'I know that you frequently abandon your studies and whirl around in pleasure, that you wander from street to street and every house stinks of beer when you leave it . . . if only you would realize that alcohol is a curse, you would put wine aside, and leave beer alone.' When the pupil did attend school, his teacher would often punish him as an impetus to learning – 'A boy's ear is on his back and he only listens when he is given a good hiding;' or would simply insult him – 'You, boy! You do not listen when I speak! you are thicker than a tall obelisk 100 cubits high and 10 cubits wide.'

The texts the schoolboys copied have frequently survived, together with teachers' corrections of their mistakes, while the originals

A portion of *a papyrus written during the reign of Merenptah, who reigned in the middle of the Nineteenth Dynasty. Written in hieratic in horizontal lines from right to left, it records a calendar of days deemed to be lucky and unlucky. The good days were marked in red. Such papyri would be copied innumerable times in various temples by scribes and consulted whenever priests were faced with people's questions. Through the use of such papyri, the influence of the educated man within the temple grew considerably in communities from the New Kingdom onwards.*

have been lost. Compilations of schoolboys' exercises frequently allow whole stories to be put together. During the Middle Kingdom, copyists' workshops set up by the king worked hard to write down many stories that had been simply passed from mouth to mouth for generations. This Middle Egyptian form of the language became the Classical form. Many of the stories, though frequently having an underlying message of morality or propaganda, are delightfully amusing and are the forerunners of modern fairy tales.

In Harris Papyrus 500 in the British Museum, the story is told of a king who lived to the north of Egypt. 'He had no children except for one daughter. For her, a tower had been built whose window was 70 cubits from the ground. He sent for all the princes of Syria and told them, he who reaches the window, of my daughter shall have her as his wife.' Unlike Rapunzel, the princess did not let down her hair, but a passing athletic Egyptian prince caught her eye. 'He jumped, and he reached the window of the princess, and she kissed him and hugged his body. Her father was informed: a man has reached your daughter's window.' Despite the king's natural reluctance to bestow her hand on a casual passer-by, the prince naturally got his wife!

In another story that survives in a New Kingdom copy in the Berlin Museum, King Cheops, the Old Kingdom ruler who built the Great Pyramid, was bored and instructed his children to amuse him. One son told him of a day when the King's own father, Snofru, was similarly bored. Finally Snofru sent for a magician: 'I have wandered through the palace in search of amusement, but I can find nothing,' His Majesty said. Djadjaemankh (the magician) replied, 'Let His Majesty go down to the palace lake; fill a boat with all the beautiful girls of the palace and your Majesty's heart will be amused watching them rowing up and down.' 'Indeed – I shall go boating!' His Majesty replied . . . 'Let there be brought to me 20 women with the shapeliest bodies, breasts and hair, who are virgins. Let there also be brought 20 nets, and give them to them instead of clothes.' Naturally, the king was indeed entertained, until a girl dropped a pendant into the lake and stopped rowing. When she insisted on it being retrieved, the magician intervened and, using a magic spell, folded the water of the lake in half. He collected the pendant from the bottom, and then replaced the water.

Besides stories, other material that survived includes poetry – based on rhythm and repetition rather than rhyme – and love letters, as well as other kinds of letters, tax demands, trial accounts and bills of sale. In total, although it has been estimated that only a tiny proportion of actual written material may have survived, what remains does allow us to look into the minds and lives of ordinary people.

CALENDARS AND CALCULATIONS

Numbers would be written as many times as were necessary to make up the total figure. Emphasis would always be placed on laying out the signs as neatly as possible. Example 1 shows how the Egyptians would have written 645.

In arithmetic, the Egyptians used only addition and subtraction, and they had no knowledge of theorems. Instead, to find out an area or capacity of a shape, they would follow a laid-out pattern of action, such as 'Take a half of the height of it, add it to itself 10 times, add to it a quarter of its total' and so on. The answer would not be in abstract measurements, such as 'square' or 'cube' measures, but in practical quantities. Thus, a ramp would be calculated in the number of mud bricks required, and the capacity of a jar in the number of sacks of grain needed to fill it.

Although the Egyptians had no concept of zero, and thus no decimal system for numbers less than one, they did use fractions, using the letter 'r' (*see p. 159*) with a number underneath. This represented $1/\ldots$. As a result, fractions with a numerator of more than one had to be expressed by a whole series of fractions that had to be added together; so $2/7$ is $\frac{1}{4} + \frac{1}{28}$. Quite a daunting system!

Measurements

These were standardized at a very early date, with lengths, weights and capacities being set and invariable. Whole series of marked rods, jars and weights have been found to show exactly what these measurements were.

Volume

The principal use for volume measurements was in the assessment of grain, and reckoned in jar-sizes, the basic size called a 'hekat', which held 4.54 litres (just over a gallon). Sixteen of these 'hekats' made a sackful, or a 'khar'. The average wage for a fieldworker and his family would be $1\frac{1}{2}$ khars per month of emmer wheat, with perhaps a small allowance of barley. From the ground grain, loaves of bread would be made; the barley bread, soaked in water, would ferment to form a creamy, lumpy alcohol to be drunk as beer. This would either be poured through a strainer or drunk through a fine clay tube.

Length

A cubit, theoretically the length from the elbow to the tip of the thumb, was approximately 52.5cm (20.6in). This subdivided into 'hands', which equalled $\frac{1}{7}$ of a cubit.

Weight

A standard metal ring called a 'deben' weighed 91g (about 3oz). The value of a deben depended on whether it was copper, silver or gold. The value of most objects on bills of sale are listed in debens, and it is unclear whether the rings were actually used as mediums for exchange, i.e. as coinage; or whether the value was purely theoretical, with inflation and devaluation in the theoretical rate changing what could be bartered for what.

One-tenth of a deben was a 'kite' (pronounce 'kitay'), a standard measure for very precious materials.

Liquids

The Egyptians measured liquids in a series of graded jar sizes. The standard liquid measurement was called 'hin', and contained approximately .5 litres (18fl oz).

Dates

There was no starting date for Egyptian history, but every day was calculated according to how many years the king had been on the throne. The year was divided into 12 months, four months making up a season. Three weeks of 10 days formed a month; thus the basic Egyptian year amounted to 360 days.

A date was expressed by year . . . of king . . .; month (1, 2, 3 or 4) of (season); day (number).

At the end of the year, five extra or 'epagomenal' days were added. These were holy days, the days on which, according to legend, Osiris, Isis, Seth and Nephthys were born. They were a time free from work, a time for festivities and general merriment.

The civil calendar always stuck rigidly to this structure. However, the ignorance of the one-quarter day each year (which we allow for every Leap Year), meant that every four years the civil calendar moved one day out of step with the land. Thus the first day of inundation of the civil calendar gradually moved further and further away from the day on which the farmers expected the river to start to rise. The two calendars only moved back into step once every 1460 years (i.e. 365×4).

Sothic cycle dating

With the dark velvet skies of Egypt, the stars were observed particularly well from earliest times by both priest-astronomers and the ordinary people. Among the brightest visible stars was Sothis, or Sirius, the Dog Star. For 70 days every year, Sothis would vanish, eclipsed by the sun. It would reappear at the very time that the inundation was expected to begin. The expectation of the inundation was naturally one of the high points of the Egyptian year; and thus on several occasions the priests or scribes would record the exact date in the civil calendar when Sothis reappeared. The Classical writer Censorinus recorded that the two calendars, civil and agricultural, coincided in AD 139; and from this it is but a short step, making minor adjustments from astronomical tables, to trace the cycles of 1460 years back through Egyptian history.

The first recorded date in Egyptian history for a reappearance of Sothis was in year 7 of the reign of Sesostris III of the Twelfth Dynasty, the fourth month of winter, day 16. From this can be obtained a date of 1870 BC, with a deviation of + or − 1 to 5 years, depending on where in Egypt the observation was made, allowing for the curvature of the earth between Alexandria and Aswan. In fact, other observations marked during Sesostris III's reign allow the date to be fixed exactly at 1872 BC. Because there is plenty of information available about how long the kings of the Eleventh and Twelfth Dynasties reigned, it is possible to set the start of the Middle Kingdom at 2134 BC.

Dates before the Middle Kingdom, however, are much less easy to establish, since the lengths of the various reigns and even the names of the kings and their sequence on the throne, are far from established. The Turin Papyrus gives a total of 955 years of the duration of the first eight dynasties. Allowing this to be approximately correct, and adding sufficient time for the Ninth and Tenth Dynasties, the start of the First Dynasty, and the unification of Egypt, can thus be dated to around 3100 BC.

Another significant date is that of year 9 of King Amenhotep I, of the Eighteenth Dynasty, third month of summer, day 9. Again, calculations show a date of between 1544 and 1534 BC; bringing the start of the New Kingdom to around 1550 BC.

These dates have been checked against the far less accurate C-14 dates (dates established from the radioactive decay rate of the Carbon-14 element in organic material) and in every case have been found to be correct. As a result, the Egyptian dating system is generally regarded as so firmly fixed as to allow other fields of archaeology to use it for cross-chronology.

NUMBERS

| 1 10 100
1000 10,000
100,000 1,000,000
645
143023

SEASONS

year month day
Akhet (Inundation)
Peret (Winter)
Shemu (Summer)

DATING

Year 2
Month 2
Winter
Day 27
Under the Majesty
of
King
Pepi

EVERYDAY LIFE

The quantities of inscribed material surviving from Egypt under the rule of the pharaohs is often patchy both in distribution and content. Until late in the 19th century, vast quantities of papyri were lost when the local people who discovered it either dug it back into the ground as fertilizer, or burned it as fuel for cooking. However, with the increase in foreign travellers and museums willing to pay high prices for genuine papyri, from around 1880 onwards, there was a growing awareness of the vital information about life in ancient Egypt that these pieces might contain.

The Oxyrhynchus Papyri

Bernard Grenfell, working in Oxford between 1893 and 1895, published two volumes of assorted Greek papyri, recently acquired in Egypt and thus brought to public attention the vast quantity of information these pieces might contain. As a result, in 1895, he was appointed by the Egypt Exploration Fund to explore Graeco-Roman sites for papyri before they disappeared under cultivation. He was so successful that, after barely eight weeks in the field, he requested his colleague, Arthur Hunt, to join him, thus forming a partnership that was to last for many years. Their second season saw them excavating at Bahnasa (a town in Middle Egypt on the west bank), ancient Oxyrhynchus, and after much painstaking labour they brought out of the ancient town midden (i.e. refuse pile) 150 complete rolls, and almost 300 cases of fragments of inscribed papyrus.

Each season for the following 15 years, Grenfell and Hunt excavated together from dawn to dusk, often with the assistance of as many as 200 local workmen at a time cutting trenches. The hardwork yielded great fruit, however, and the inscribed papyri, Grenfell reported, 'are found continuously down to a depth of 5 or even 8 metres. As a rule, the well-preserved documents are within 3 metres

Grenfell supervising native workers as they systematically dig through the dusty layers of the town rubbish dump where the remarkable papyri were found. Tens of thousands of texts, some considerably old, some fairly new were found and are still being restored and studied. Grenfell employed around 160 men daily, supervised by 30 trusted foremen, all from local towns and villages. He was quick to praise their skills and honesty and wrote that little, if anything, was lost. Nevertheless, extreme vigilance was required by day and night on the large site as antiquities dealers did all they could to get hold of examples of the remarkable finds.

of the surface; in the lower strata, papyri tend to be more fragmentary, though our trenches in a few mounds have reached 9 metres at the highest parts before coming to a damp level.'

Once the pieces had been collected, Grenfell and Hunt laid the better sections flat between sheets of newspaper. The fragments required virtually no conservation. So vast was the quantity of material retrieved that no attempt was made to draw, label or photograph any of it on site. Publication was to be carried out studiously and gradually back in England. The two Egyptologists, with numerous collaborators, advisors and editors worked assiduously over the summer months every year translating and analyzing the mounting number of finds resulting from the excavations of all the previous seasons' work. The process was laborious, even though they worked fast.

Grenfell fell ill in 1908, and never returned to Oxyrhynchus. Hunt also resigned from the excavations, with the result that after a few seasons' tentative explorations at Antinoe by their successor J. Johnson, all excavations for Graeco-Roman papyri by the Egypt Exploration Fund ceased.

The work continues

Publication of the papyri is continuing to this day under various editors, while more papyri of the same period are coming to light in excavations at Saqqara and Qasr Ibrim. In 1985, *Volume 52* was published, and still vast quantities remain untouched.

The papyri date between the third century BC and the fifth century AD, and they cover every aspect of written records that one might expect of any society – letters, bills and accounts, legal documents as well as literary pieces and fragments of gospels and other religious texts.

Among the discoveries have been many lost Classical works of Pindar and Euripides, commentaries on Thucydides and Sophocles and poetry of Sappho, Alcaeus, Aeschylus, Hesiod and others, mixed with personal letters and notes: a veritable cross-section of a lost Graeco-Egyptian society. As Grenfell himself wrote in the first volume of the published memoirs, 'Sometimes the mass was so great that these most probably represent the whole of the local archives thrown away ... We sometimes found not only the contents of a basket altogether, but often whole baskets full of papyri.'

Extracts from Texts
Marriage Contract between a Bridegroom and his Mother-in-Law (AD 260)

Aurelia Thaesis has given her daughter Aurelia Tausiris in marriage to the husband Aurelius Arsinoos ... to whom the giver contributes as dowry for her said daughter, the bride:

In common gold of the Oxyrhynchite standard, 1 necklace, having a stone and weighing (apart from the stone) 13.25

A brooch, with 5 stones, set in gold

A pair of earrings with 10 pearls

A small ring

Clothing, a silver striped dalmation veil – 260 drachmae

White, single-tasselled, striped dress – 160

Another white dalmation veil, with purple edge – 100 drachmae

'Let husband and wife therefore live blamelessly together, observing all the duties of marriage. But if (which heaven forbid) in consequence of an estrangement, a separation takes place, the husband shall restore to the giver of the bride (if she be living) or to the bride (if she is not) the aforesaid dowry in full within 60 days from the date at which a demand for restoration is made.

If at the time of separation the bride should be pregnant, the bridegroom is to give her, on account of the expenses of the birth, 40 drachmae. In connection with the demand of the aforesaid dowry, the bride's representatives shall have the right of executors upon the husband and all his property.'

Letter from a Boy to his Father (second century BC): Theon, to his father Theon, greeting.

It was a fine thing of you not to take me to the city! If you won't take me to Alexandria I won't write you a letter, or speak to you, or say goodbye to you, and if you go to Alexandria I won't hold your hand or ever greet you again. This is what will happen if you won't take me ... but send me a lyre, I beg you. If you don't, I won't eat and I won't drink. So there!

Chastisement of a Secret Egg-Seller

'From Aurelius Nilus son of Didymus ... I hereby agree on the august divine oath by our Lords the Emperors and the Caesars (AD 327) to offer my eggs in the market place publicly for sale ... and I acknowledge that it shall be unlawful for me in future to sell them secretly or in my own house.'

SPELLS FOR THE AFTERLIFE

Part of the spells, *known as the Pyramid Texts, that cover the walls of the burial chambers in the pyramid of King Unas. Unas, whose name is written here inside the cartouches, ruled Egypt at the very end of the Fifth Dynasty, around 2490 BC. His was the first pyramid in which texts were carved.*

The notion that the dead must be cared for and protected in their afterlife began in very ancient times. Even at the beginning of the predynastic era (*see p. 50–1*), the provision of mats, food and drink in even the humblest graves shows that there was a strong belief in a life after death. There are no inscriptions to show what form this was believed to take, but the inclusion of baked clay figurines of women, wide-hipped and heavy-breasted and with upraised arms, have been identified as Mother Goddess figures. Clearly, even the early settlers on the Nile believed in some god.

The first inscriptions that tell of conceptual beliefs in an afterlife appear in the burial chambers of pyramids at the end of the Fifth Dynasty and during the Sixth Dynasty. The chambers of the Middle Kingdom pyramids, however, are bare of these texts. Thus the first intimations we have of what form the Egyptians expected an existence after death to take do not appear until around 2400 BC; this was 700 years after the time of unification – and probably about 2000 years after the cult of the dead actually began.

The Pyramid Texts

It is clear from the language and writing of the first texts that appear in the pyramid of Unas that hundreds of years of spoken traditions had been encapsulated in what is often wrongly considered a single body of texts. They comprise a total of 759 different spells or utterances, and no pyramid has them all inscribed on its walls. Many of the spells are very ancient indeed, while others were probably contemporary with the building of the pyramid. They appear to have originated as recitations spoken while the king's body was being prepared for burial, while the mummy was being placed in the sarcophagus and while grave goods were being carried into the tomb: '*O Osiris, King, I give to you the Eye of Horus. May your face be provided with it. The Eye of Horus is spread over you (in) incense and fire*' (Spell 25)

Many of the spells date back to a time when the king's body was simply placed in a shallow sandy pit grave: '*O King, collect your bones together, assemble your limbs, cleanse your teeth and throw off the sand which is over your face!*' (Spell 666) At this time, the king in his form of Mighty Bull was expected to join the company of gods who lived among the stars: '*You are the son of the Great White Cow! She conceived you, gave birth to you, she places you in her protection.*

She will cross the lake with you, for you belong with those who surround the sun, who encircle the Morning Star!' (Spell 554)

The king's soul went to the gods not as a supplicant but as a victorious conqueror: '*How pleasant to see you! They* (i.e. the gods) *say when this god rises in the sky, when you ascend to heaven with your might about you, your fearfulness about you, your magic on your feet . . . There come to you, the gods of Pe, the gods of Nekhen* (*see p. 52*), *the gods who are in the sky.*' (Spell 306)

In their company, the king was expected to become a star himself: '*The sky is clear and Sothis flourishes because I am alive, the son of Sothis, and the gods have cleansed themselves for me in the Great Bear* (constellation), *the imperishable stars.*' (Spell 302) ·

It is clear that he was not allowed into that exalted company by right, but had to vanquish the gods who may oppose him. In one famous spell, the king must kill his opponents and eat them to acquire their power. This has led some scholars to infer that in ancient times, cannibalism was practised along the Nile: '*The king eats their magic and swallows their power. The old ones are for his morning meal; the middle ones for his evening meal and the young ones are for his night-time meal. The oldest men and women are fuel for him.*' (Spell 273)

Yet as time went by, the spells become less vicious and the king is believed to sail to heaven on a raft, to be welcomed by the gods: '*O you western, eastern, southern and northern gods! The four purified reed-rafts which you laid down for Osiris when he came to the sky so that he could sail across the sky with his son Horus beside him, so that he could lift him up and make him appear as a great god in the sky – lay them down for me too!*' (Spell 303)

The last group of spells, dating from the time of the late Old Kingdom, show that the concept of the afterlife had completely changed. No longer was the king associated with Osiris as a god of the stars but with Re, Lord of the Sun. The elevation of Re as a national god during the Fifth Dynasty (*see p. 81*) probably was the origin of this belief. From this time onwards, one of the king's destinies was to sail every day with the sun god in a solar boat across the sky: '*I am pure! I take my oar and sit in my seat. I sit in the prow of the barque of the Two Enneads. I row with Re to the West and he makes my place firm over the Lord of Kas, he writes (my name) over the living!*' (Spell 469)

In all these varied texts, there is no mention of any living person but the king enjoying this afterlife – not even his wives and family. Even he, at first, had to fight for the right of coexistence with the gods.

The Coffin Texts

The downfall of the living god that was Pharoah at the end of the Old Kingdom caused the people of Egypt to reconsider their own position. During the Eleventh and Twelfth Dynasties those people who could afford it were buried in brightly painted rectangular wooden coffins. Although the walls of their burial chambers were left bare, spells were written on the inner walls of the coffins. These Coffin Texts offer protection against eternal hunger, thirst and the fierce heat of the sun, and for the first time, speak of the perilous journey the soul of the deceased individual must undertake to reach the land where it can live eternally. The soul had to face many terrors and, in addition to the spells, on the inside of the coffin, a map of the underworld ensured that the deceased would find his way.

The Coffin Texts are more difficult to understand than the Pyramid Texts and have an atmosphere of fear about them – fear of death and fear of the traumas to be faced by the soul: *'I shall not be afraid in my body, for words and magic shall overcome this evil for me. I shall see the Lord of Light, I shall live there. Make way for me! Let me see Nun and Amun! They dare not speak for fear of the One whose Name is Hidden in my body. I know him! I am equipped to pass through his door!'*

Ushabtis

The land of eternal life after death was seen as an everlasting, spiritual Egypt. For this reason alone, the deceased had to fear that the gods might call upon him to work for them just as the king had demanded work from him for three months every year during life. To counteract this eternal servitude, in the Middle Kingdom, for the first time tiny worker figures were provided to 'answer' when the god summoned the soul. Since the Egyptian for 'answer' is 'usheb', the figures are called 'ushabtis'. In later times, in a perfectly equipped tomb there would be 401 ushabtis: 365, one for every day of the year, and 36 overseers, one for every 10 workers! The front of the ushabti was either inscribed simply with the deceased's name or, often, with a spell to make it work: *'O Ushabti, if I am summoned or assessed to do any work which is to be done in the land of the dead – if problems are piled up for me by (any) man concerning his (own) work in sowing fields, irrigating the arable land or in shipping stone from east bank to west bank, say – I shall do it! I am here! You shall answer to it!'*

These hundreds of *ushabti figures, together with the coffins from five ancient Egyptian burials were found in 1949, during excavations at Saqqara. When studied by Etienne Drioton, then Director General of the Egyptian Department of Antiquities, hieroglyphic inscriptions on some of the figures revealed the name of one of the deceased as Kanefer, a scribe in the temple of Ptah in Memphis.*

THE BOOK OF THE DEAD

At the beginning of the New Kingdom, the journey of the deceased's soul through to the afterlife was firmly based on the story of Osiris, with its notions of a judgment and then rebirth into a land of eternal contentment. After the terrors faced by the dead of the Middle Kingdom included in the Coffin Texts, these fears could not be removed altogether. As a result, the dead person in the New Kingdom was provided in his tomb with all the magic he would need to pass safely through all the troubles. These spells, quite different from the Pyramid and Coffin Texts, were usually written on a papyrus roll. At first, these were wrapped inside the bandages of the mummy, often between the legs. During the middle of the Eighteenth Dynasty, however, tall wooden statues in mummiform shape, mounted on a plinth, were included in most tombs. These statues were hollow and the papyrus roll would be hidden inside. The Egyptians called the roll *The Book of Coming out into the Day*; but generations of Egyptologists have known it better as *The Book of the Dead*.

The Book of the Dead
The earliest examples date from the start of the New Kingdom, but they were used right through to the Graeco-Roman period and the end of the ancient religious beliefs. The papyri are generally written in hieroglyphs and the finest examples include beautifully painted pictures. They vary in length from 23.7m (78ft) to tiny scraps only centimetres square. In total they contain approximately 200 spells, but no collection includes them all.

It appears from many surviving examples that most of the rolls were copied at leisure from older master copies, and were stored until someone bought them. Blank spaces were left for the name of the deceased to be added. Many of the Books of the Dead that have survived are carelessly written. Sometimes the scribe appears to have misjudged the amount of space he had available for a spell, so he either crammed many signs into a small space, spilled the text into the margin or omitted sections altogether.

The finest examples were written and painted with great care at the specific request of a wealthy nobleman. These show the correct forms and order of the spells, while the illustrations are a delight to the eye. During the 19th century, these illustrated Books of the Dead were such collectors' items that many dealers split rolls and sold sections separately.

The spells in the Book of the Dead start with recitations spoken by priests over the mummy of the dead person as they provided amulets to be placed in specific points among the bandages for protection:
To be said over a knot-amulet of red carnelian and placed on the neck of the mummy: '*You have power, O Isis! You have magic, O Isis! This amulet is a protection for this Great one. It will drive away those who would perpetrate evil against him!*' (Spell 156)

When the mummy was complete, it was taken to the front of the tomb and stood upright while the Lector Priest recited the Opening of the Mouth ritual, touching its eyes, nose, lips, ears, hands and feet with a model carpenter's adze as he spoke: '*My mouth is open! My mouth is split open by Shu* (god of the air) *with that metal "spear" of his that he used to split open the mouth of the gods. I am the Powerful One. I shall sit beside her who is in the great breath of the sky!*' (Spell 23)

Once in the tomb, the soul must leave the body and pass by demons and demiurges. These often take the form of reptiles or crocodiles armed with sharp knives: '*Get back! Get away from me! Stay away, you evil one! Do not come against me, do not live upon my magic! Do not make me tell your name to the great god who sent you here . . . O you who would speak against this magic of mine, no crocodile who lives on magic will take it away from me!*' (Spell 31)

Finally the deceased, in accordance with the legend of Osiris, must be judged for his deeds while alive. Horus comes to meet him and leads him forward to the throne where Osiris himself sits, supported by Isis and Nephthys. He now had to confess any misdemeanours he committed on earth in the form of 400 statements of the things he did not do. He speaks in the name of the demigods who will judge him:
'*O Bone-Breaker who comes from Heracleopolis, I have not told lies.*

O Green Flame who comes from Memphis, I have not stolen food.

O Nefertem who comes from Memphis, I have not done any wrong, I have witnessed no crime' (Spell 125)

Having spoken, the soul of the deceased was led into the Hall of Judgment. Using a spell inscribed on the back of a large stone scarab beetle and wrapped among the bandages of the mummy, the soul produced its heart from its body and presented it to the gods: '*O my heart, do not stand as a witness against me! Do not*

In this beautifully *illustrated section from a Book of the Dead, the deceased – Nakht – makes his way to the fields of the Rushes (i.e. of Iaru) where he hopes to spend a blessed eternity. In the top register, he paddles his papyriform boat into the hereafter. Below, he reveres the magical Bennu bird, the phoenix responsible for abundance of crops; while at a later date he cuts grain with a sickle and pulls up flax by the root for linen making. In the bottom register, oxen plough and then tread grain near the river that will supply everlasting fresh water. Nakht expects to spend the rest of eternity doing everything he did during life, without fear of problems, unhappiness or hunger.*

oppose me in the judgment. Do not be hostile to me in the presence of the Keeper of the Balance.' (Spell 30b)

The Keeper of the Balance, Anubis, carefully placed the heart in a weighing-pan and measured it against the feather of Ma'at (*see Glossary*). The heart was allowed a little leeway as Anubis moved a weight across the top bar of the balance. Thoth waited, pen in hand, for the heart to be judged truthful so he could record the verdict. Behind him, Amenti sat, a gobbling monster with crocodile's jaws, the forepart of a leopard and the hindquarters of a hippo. Should the heart be found wanting in the scales, he would devour the soul and the deceased would die a second time. But with the protection of the Book of the Dead, this would not happen, and Osiris would declare the soul 'True of Voice'. It then rejoins its ancestors in the Land of Reeds.

The Book of the Gates

In the tombs of the Valley of the Kings, the walls are painted with potent spells to enable their royal inhabitants to overcome the most fearsome tribulations.

There is not just one series of these spells, but several. The *Book of what is in the Underworld*, or the *Imy-Duat* in Egyptian, shows the king the route he must take while accompanying Re, the sun god, in his solar boat. After the sunset, this boat entered the realm of the dead beyond the western horizon, and the king must help with its navigation through untold perils. Beyond this point, the soul also needed the *Book of the Gates* and then the *Book of the Caverns* to find his way past the monsters that guarded the gates of the 12 hours of the night. Another book deals with the route through the land of the dead and gives instructions as to how the king can pass successfully through it until, with the aid of Nut the sky-goddess, the *Book of the Sun* enables him to re-emerge with Re in the solar boat every morning.

Not every tomb is inscribed with all these texts. Often only chapters of spells from each book are included along the long passages of the deceased's tomb.

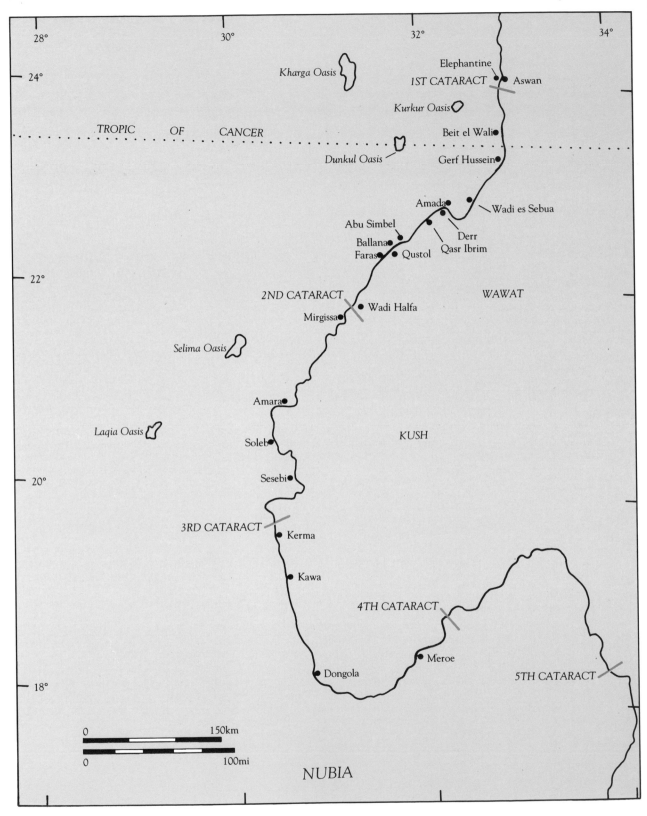

NUBIAN RESCUE

It is important *to realize that Egypt's links with Nubia, immediately to the south, go back to predynastic times and that by the beginning of the Old Kingdom, the pharaohs regarded Nubia as Egyptian territory. The struggle to dominate Nubia was a continuing fact of life throughout Egyptian history. In addition, it was the sole source of Egypt's gold until the Eighteenth Dynasty. Nubia was also the place from which the Egyptians obtained hard stone, the pink and black granite, diorite and porphyry so heavily favoured by them in building and sculpture. All historical evidence of any links would have been destroyed by the High Dam, which eventually opened in 1971, for this was to create a lake that was to obliterate Nubia entirely. As a result, surveys on an unprecedented scale were undertaken and sites were photographed and excavated at lightning speed before time ran out. These surveys, together with the moving of entire temples, weighing thousands of tons, to higher ground demanded all the knowledge and skill that archaeology had acquired. The land of Nubia is now lost forever, but the objects that were moved are continuing to reveal new stories.*

Egyptian links with the land of Nubia to the south go back to the beginning of their history. The word 'Nubia' comes from the Egyptian word 'nub' which means 'gold' – and this was what the Egyptians sought and found there. In addition, they prized Nubia's hard pink and black granite for their finest buildings and statues. From carvings found on rocks in the First Cataract we know that even the earliest pharaohs sent expeditions to Nubia; and the Palermo stone, which lists the main events of each year of the reigns of the first five dynasties, tells how an army sent by Snofru, father of Cheops the builder of the Great Pyramid of Giza, brought back to Egypt 7000 captives and 200,000 head of cattle.

During the Middle Kingdom, between 2040 and 1640 BC, a string of huge mud-brick garrison towns were built on the banks of the Nile in Nubia to control gold extraction while repelling the Nubians. Even when the gold-mines began to run out some time during the late Eighteenth Dynasty, the Egyptians did not relinquish their hold, but appointed a viceroy, the 'King's Son of Kush' to maintain the Egyptian presence.

Yet in some way the Nubians were proud of their powerful Egyptian neighbours, and maintained many Egyptian customs alongside their own. When, during the Late period, one of these Nubian princes, Piankhy (or Piye), conquered Egypt, the Nubians were able to restore to Egypt some of the traditions that had been in danger of dying out. When, in their turn, the Nubian conquerors were expelled by the Assyrians, the Nubian princes took back with them their Egyptian heritage and maintained ancient Egyptian ways long after the rest of the world had begun to forget.

The First Nubian Survey

Before the beginning of the 20th century, almost no archaeological work had been done in Nubia; Egyptian references to it were the sole sources of information. The final opening of the British dam at Aswan, in 1902, though it only closed off part of the Nile, raised the level of the Nile behind it and several sites were flooded. The flooding of the beautiful temple of Philae, called by a Napoleonic soldier 'the pearl of Egypt', caused great distress and protest. The archaeological community became aware of the risk of losing valuable information, especially since the new dam brought such benefit to Egypt that plans were immediately put into

action to raise its height. The new threat alerted the attention of Sir Gaston Maspero, who appointed Arthur Weigall to inspect all the Nubian antiquities between the Egyptian border and Abu Simbel. As a result, in 1907, the First Nubian Archaeological Survey was organized, with Dr Reisner at its head. Reisner's meticulous recording of the subsequent excavations was regarded as a masterpiece of scholarly research, and he was described, as a result, as 'the greatest archaeologist that the United States has ever produced in any field'. His team was appointed to survey Lower Nubia, while a second, comprising Gauthier, Günther Roeder and A.M. Blackman and funded by the Antiquities Organization was sent to copy inscriptions in Nubian temples.

The University of Pennsylvania put together its own independent team, the Eckley B. Coxe expedition under Dr Randall McIver, assisted by Leonard Woolley; and between 1907 and 1911, they explored many sites in Lower Nubia, between the First and Second Cataracts.

From 1910 to 1912, an Oxford University team under Professor Griffith excavated at Faras, close to the modern border with Sudan, and uncovered a cemetery that had been used continuously from early dynastic times right through to the Christian era.

By 1910, the official survey team was running into administrative difficulties. Reisner had moved away to Palestine, and his replacement, Firth, had to manage almost single-handed. He excavated both sides of the Nile between Dakkeh and Wadi es Sebua.

By 1911, the First Survey was closed, yet the limited excavations that had been done had alerted the world, and especially the black market, that a new source of relatively unguarded material had been located. Illicit plundering of Nubian sites destroyed much information that could have been valuable.

The Second Nubian Survey

In 1929, the Egyptian government decided once more to raise the level of the Aswan dam, and yet more sites were under threat. Moreover the spectre of a bigger dam, one that would seal off the Nile altogether, had begun to raise its head and, once again, the world of archaeology was alarmed. The Antiquities Organization approached W.B. Emery to head a Second Nubian Survey, a post he accepted willingly, for, as he said, 'Nubia, an ancient land, is now under sentence of death'.

**Professor A.M. Blackman
(1883–1956)**

Aylward Manley Blackman obtained a degree in Oriental Studies in Oxford in 1906. In the First Archaeological Survey, he worked for three years recording and publishing inscriptions from the temples. Blackman continued to work in the field, but most of his time was spent lecturing, first at Oxford, then as Professor at Liverpool University.

**Professor H.W. Fairman
(1907–1982)**

Herbert W. Fairman worked in Luxor and then in Tell el Amarna before moving on to Nubia. Here he dug first at Sesebi and then in Amara West. During World War II, he continued his work on Ptolemaic inscriptions. He succeeded Blackman in the Chair of Egyptology at Liverpool, a post he held until retirement in 1974.

The Second Survey began its work at Wadi es Sebua, where Firth had finished in 1911. In 1930, the massive Middle Kingdom fortress of Quban, previously unharmed by the waters of the Nile, was thoroughly excavated before it was lost forever. The walls of this great fortress, built around 1800 BC, stood up to 8m (26½ft) high. Emery recorded, 'To walk up stairways and to stand on the upper flooring of buildings constructed more than 3800 years ago was an unforgettable experience. In some ways it was like entering an empty house only recently vacated, particularly when one stood before a small fireplace still containing the remains of charcoal and burnt wood.'

Discoveries begin

In November 1931, Emery arrived with his team for what they thought would be the last season of work at Abu Simbel. On the west bank here, locally known as Ballana, he came across a 'confused jumble' of dunes of circular and regular form, and wondered whether they might be man-made. As they were about to dig, guards warned them that another site directly over the river, at Qustol, was being plundered by robbers. A quick inspection proved, from one of the holes dug at Qustol, that tomb entrances had been discovered. Within hours, a 15.2m (50ft) deep passage was opened, leading to an underground vaulted chamber. Although plundered, containing nothing but fragmentary remains of wood, it was decided to investigate further. The team began to dig the outside of one of the tumuli. After several weeks, a ramp was found, and along it, a whole pile of skeletal material that was found to be horses, donkeys and camels. At the foot of the ramp, the owner's horse had been slaughtered to accompany him to his eternity, furnished with silver-mounted saddles and full silver trappings.

It was thought that more evidence was needed, so the team was moved to another large mound, Tomb 3, and here another ramp to a tomb was uncovered, with a similar group of slaughtered animals along it. At the foot, the bricked-up doors of a chamber were revealed. When broken down, an intact burial chamber was seen. Behind the skeleton of a man lay the remains of six fine horses, their jewelled and gilded bridles and trappings exceeding anything previously found. Even the reins were made of silver chains, almost a metre (yard) in length, the workmanship so fine that it could scarcely be matched today.

The mounds of Ballana proved even more exciting and informative than those on the opposite bank. In 1934, the opening of a large mound, called by the team Tomb 80, revealed the first intact burial, and a royal one at that. As the sand of the mound was removed, the roof of a chamber was discovered, and the archaeologists found they had emerged into the burial chamber itself. As Emery reported, 'One of the first objects that the knives of our workmen laid bare was a massive silver crown on the head of a King.' The discovery of crowns, necklaces, and sword and scabbard followed, each of them made in accordance with traditional Egyptian design. The reconstructions of the crowns, the only ones ever uncovered anywhere in Egypt, suggest what some of those worn by the later kings of Egypt were probably like.

Results of the Second Survey

The Second Nubian Survey, however, proved to have a more practical outcome than purely archaeological. While at Ballana, the courses of several ancient irrigation canals were marked, and it was discovered that 30cm (1 ft) below the surface of the sand was a thick layer of old black alluvial silt. Though by 1934 the area was a desert, the Egyptian Ministry of Agriculture was able to install new pumping systems and valuable land was reclaimed, which served for many years to feed some of the Nubians who had been displaced by the encroaching waters of the Nile.

Although the Second Survey came to an end in 1934, the artefacts that had been found needed restoring and the information collected had to be published. This was to occupy the team, in Cairo, for a further four years.

While they had worked at Ballana, other expeditions had also been busy in Nubia. Teams from Oxford University had examined the sites of Kawa and Firka. Kawa proved to be especially interesting, with the remains of temples from the New Kingdom being traced. A temple built by Amenhotep III, and added to by Akhenaten and Tutankhamun, was shown to have served the town of Gematen, expanded by Akhenaten to promote his religion in Nubia. In recognition of the work done by the team, Oxford University was given a finely decorated shrine from the temple showing King Taharka of the Twenty-fifth Dynasty making offering to Egyptian gods. It is now in the Ashmolean Museum, Oxford.

The High Dam is planned

Between 1934 and 1960, the population of Egypt doubled to approximately 28 million and the restricted fertile belt each side of the river proved too limited to feed them. In the 1950s, the decision was taken at last to build the Great Dam, a dam that would stop up the full width of the Nile. The area of the First Cataract was chosen, and here, in January 1960, work finally began on its construction, a project that was to take 11 years. The thickness at the dam's base is 980m (3215ft); its width across the top from river bank to river bank is 3.6km (2¼mi), and it soars 109.7m (360ft) above the original level of the Nile. It has been calculated that the dam contains more than 17 times the material used to build the Great Pyramid. Behind it a lake was to be created 500km (310mi) long, 9.6km (6mi) wide and 182.8m (600ft) deep.

Lower Nubia would vanish completely. The entire civilization, whose study had barely begun, would disappear forever. The mud-brick fortresses that had so impressed Professor Emery would dissolve as the Nile water covered them, and all the fine temples so recently examined would lie below great depths of water. As for the Nubian people, several times forced to move as the water rose behind the old dam, they would lose their land altogether. A hundred thousand people had to be found new homes. The Egyptian Government allocated them new sites, and many Nubian villagers moved northwards into Egypt, taking their culture with them and forming small, tight Nubian communities in Upper Egypt. Others chose to move southwards into Sudan. But the question of the monuments remained.

The temples on *the island of Philae were removed and rebuilt on the nearby island of Agilkia to save them from the rising waters of Lake Nasser. The plan to the right reflects how the temples are in exactly the same position and orientation as on Philae. The visitor arriving at the island (above, right) is welcomed by the graceful columns of Diocletian's gateway (right) and Trajan's kiosk (left), here mirrored in the glassy waters of the lake. The great entrance pylons to the temple of Philae (above, left) show the figure of Ptolemy XII conquering his enemies and offering them to Isis, Horus and Hathor. The granite lions by the doorway are of Byzantine date; the temple still flourished long after every other temple in Egypt ceased to function. The gateway to the right leads via a processional way, to Trajan's kiosk.*

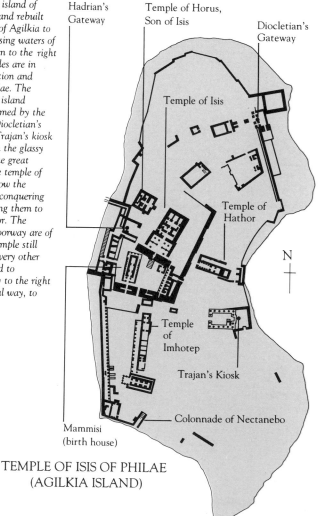

TEMPLE OF ISIS OF PHILAE
(AGILKIA ISLAND)

International rescue

In 1955, Egypt and Sudan approached UNESCO and asked that a massive archaeological rescue mission be mounted to save what could be saved. The cost was too high for them to take action alone, and within a matter of weeks work began on a map of the threatened lands with a view to discovering what could be done. By 1959, a committee was formed from eight countries to decide whether the monuments should be left where they were, whether barrage dams should be built to keep the water back from them, or whether they could be moved entirely out of the reach of the new lake. An appeal was mounted. Any government willing to assist would receive half of the objects found, while archaeologists from those countries would be allowed concessions to dig within Egypt.

The raising of Abu Simbel

The bid to rescue the Nubian temples was a success. It was decided that whole structures needed to be moved, and engineers and heavy lifting and cutting equipment poured into Nubia. The most ambitious project was to be the lifting of the temples of Abu Simbel. The two rock-cut temples, built by Ramesses II for himself and his Great Royal Wife, Nefertari, were unique in scale and design.

The front of the main temple is 31.m (102ft) high, with four colossal seated statues of the king 20.1m (66ft) high in front of them. The inner passage, cutting through two columned halls, reaches 54.8m (180ft) back into solid rock. At the rear, in the sanctuary, four sandstone statues are cut as though seated on a bench facing the entrance of the temple; these

This cutaway view shows the internal structure of the large temple of Ramesses II at Abu Simbel, within its man-made concrete dome. The temple was removed and rebuilt in exactly the same orientation, so that twice a year, rays from the rising sun strike the statues seated in the sanctuary at the rear. This modern technological achievement must one day rank with the building of the pyramids themselves.

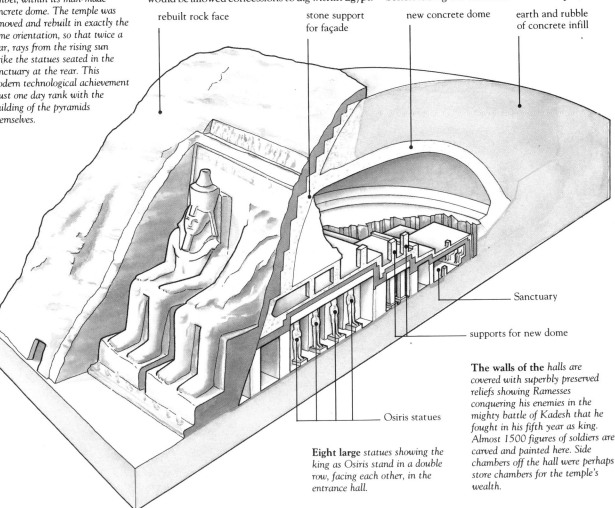

rebuilt rock face

stone support for façade

new concrete dome

earth and rubble of concrete infill

Sanctuary

supports for new dome

Osiris statues

Eight large *statues showing the king as Osiris stand in a double row, facing each other, in the entrance hall.*

The walls of the *halls are covered with superbly preserved reliefs showing Ramesses conquering his enemies in the mighty battle of Kadesh that he fought in his fifth year as king. Almost 1500 figures of soldiers are carved and painted here. Side chambers off the hall were perhaps store chambers for the temple's wealth.*

represent Ramesses II in the company of the great gods Amen-Re, Re-Horakhte and Ptah. Twice a year, at the summer and winter solstices, the rays of the sun as it rose over the eastern horizon shone straight through the temple and illuminated the faces of the king and the gods for 3000 years.

To rescue these temples alone was an almost superhuman feat. Various methods were discussed, including encasing them in concrete and lifting them 60.9m (200ft) on huge hydraulic jacks. When the cost of this proved prohibitive, it was decided to cut the temples up, block by block, and move them to a plateau above the cliff in which they had been cut. The site on which they were to be rebuilt was planned as carefully as the original site had been, with the correct orientation of the passage of the main temple such that the sun's rays would continue to illuminate the sanctuary. It was without doubt the most ambitious civil engineering project of modern times, and attracted the world's media to such an extent that money flooded in from around the world to help finance the removal of the temple.

The other temples

In all, 23 temples and sanctuaries were saved, being moved to new sites and re-erected. Below the High Dam, on a promontory of rock, the temple of Kalabsha, dedicated to the Nubian Horus, Mandulis, was moved several miles northwards by the German government. The largest temple to be moved after Abu Simbel, it forms the nucleus of a small group of monuments, along with the Kiosk of Qertassi and the tiny rock-cut chapel of Beit el Wali. Further to the south, the temple of Amada was moved in one operation on railway lines by the French government to a higher site, in company with another rock-cut chapel, that of El Derr. A little to the north of Amada now stand the temples of Wadi es Sebua (built by Ramesses II), Dakka and Maharraka. Other temples left Egypt entirely. The temple of Dendur, given to the United States in gratitude for its support during the rescue operation, has been reconstructed in its own building in the Metropolitan Museum of Art, New York; Debod temple now stands in Madrid, and El Lessiya in Turin.

The rescue of Philae, the remarkable and beautiful island temple dedicated to Isis, was at the heart of the rescue operation, but so expensive was it to prove that a separate appeal had to be mounted. The money raised by the

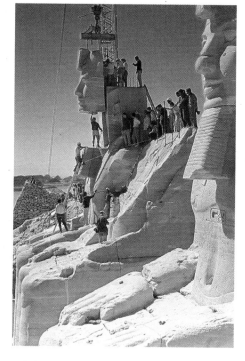

Workmen stand 20m (65 ½ft) above the ground on the shoulders of the colossal statues of Ramesses II and supervise the exact repositioning of each stone. No gap wider than 0.5cm (3/16in) remained to be filled once building work ceased. The lifting and repositioning of the blocks within the new concrete dome began in 1960; the project was completed with UNESCO's financial backing, received from all over the world, in December 1968.

exhibition of Tutankhamun's treasures, which began in London in 1972, provided a significant part of the sum needed. Already flooded after the opening of the earlier dam it was vital that it too should be moved. A neighbouring island, that of Agilkia, was chosen, and a barrage dam was built around the old site to keep back the water while work progressed. Like Abu Simbel, the temple of Isis was dismantled stone by stone and moved to its new home. Since it was re-opened several years ago it has been one of the highlights of any trip to Egypt.

Continuing work

The High Dam, Sadd el Ali, was officially opened by President Sadat on 15 January 1971. But excavation in Nubia has by no means finished. A few sites were high enough to escape the waters of Lake Nasser. Among them, the fortress of Qasr Ibrim, built on a high rock by the Roman Prefect Gaius Petronius in the reign of the Emperor Augustus over an older site, has been the location of a British excavation since 1974. In the past few years, the unexpected low level of the waters of Lake Nasser because of the drought in Africa has enabled the team to investigate sites low down on the hill that have been flooded for years. Among other things a series of rectangular cuttings in the rock appear to have been tombs previously unrecorded, although nothing remains in them. Among the major finds from Qasr Ibrim have been thousands of textual fragments, invaluable for research.

SUGGESTED FURTHER READING

The following list contains books for the general reader and the specialist alike. The serious student, however, must expect to have to consult international journals to find more detailed information that is often not incorporated into books; among these:

Annales du service des Antiquités de L'Égypte; Bulletin de L'Institut Français d'Archeologie Orientale (IFAO); Bulletin of the Metropolitan Museum of Art, New York; Chronique d'Égypte; Göttinger Miszellen; Journal of the American Research Center in Egypt (JARCE); Journal of Egyptian Archaeology (JEA), London; Mitteilungen des Deutschen Archaeologischen Instituts, Abteilung, Kairo (MDAIK); Révue d'Égyptologie; Zeitschrift für Ägyptische Sprache und Altertumskunde

General Reading

Aldred, C. *The Egyptians*, Thames and Hudson, London and New York, 1984

Baines, J. and Malek, J. *Atlas of Ancient Egypt*, Phaidon, London; Facts on File, New York, 1980

Gardiner, A.H. *Egypt of the Pharaohs* Oxford University Press, Oxford and New York, 1961

Hayes, W.C. *The Scepter of Egypt*, 2 vols., Metropolitan Museum of Art, New York, 1953, 1959

James, T.G.H. *Introduction to Ancient Egypt*, British Museum Publications, London, 1979

Ruffle, J. *Heritage of the Pharaohs*, Phaidon, Oxford, 1977; E.P. Dutton, New York, 1977

Sandars, N. *The Sea Peoples*, revised, Thames and Hudson, London and New York, 1985

Discovering the Past

Ceram, C.W. *Gods, Graves and Scholars*, Alfred A. Knopf, New York; Victor Gollancz, London, 1967

Clayton, P. *The Rediscovery of Ancient Egypt*, Thames and Hudson, London and New York, 1982

Drower, M. *Flinders Petrie – A Life in Archaeology*, Gollancz, London, 1985

Edwards, A. *A Thousand Miles Up the Nile*, Century, 1982

Fagan, B.M. *The Rape of the Nile*, Macdonald, London, 1975; Scribner's, New York

Herodotus *The Histories*, Penguin, London and New York 1980

James, T.G.H. (Ed.) *Excavating in Egypt – The Egypt Exploration Society, 1882–1982*, The British Museum, London, 1982

Kinglake, J. *Eothen*, Oxford University Press, Oxford and New York, 1984

Moorehead, A. *The Blue Nile* and *The White Nile* (both revised), Penguin, London and New York, 1984

Wilkinson, C.K. *Egyptian Wall Paintings – The Metropolitan Museum of Art's Collection of Facsimiles*, New York, 1983

Egyptian Origins

Adams, B. *Ancient Hierakonpolis*, Aris and Phillips, Warminster, 1974

Ancient Hierakonpolis: Supplement, Aris and Phillips, Warminster, 1974

Brunton, G. and Caton-Thompson, G. *The Badarian Civilisation and Prehistoric Remains near Badari*, London, 1928

Butzer, K. *Early Hydraulic Civilization of Egypt – A Study in Cultural Ecology*, University of Chicago Press, 1976

Carr, C. *The Kharga Oasis in Prehistory*, London, 1952

Childe, V.G. *New Light on the Most Ancient East*, New York, 1953

Clarke, J.D. *Atlas of African Prehistory*, University of Chicago Press, 1967

Emergy, W.B. *Archaic Egypt*, Penguin, London and New York, 1972, 1985

Great Tombs of the First Dynasty Kings, 3 vols., London, 1949–58

Hayes, W.C. *Most Ancient Egypt*, University of Chicago, 1965

Hoffman, M. *Egypt Before the Pharaohs*, Alfred A. Knopf, 1979; Routledge & Kegan Paul, London, 1980

Petrie, W.M.F. *Abydos*, London, 1902

Diospolis Parva, London, 1901

Nagada and Ballas, London, 1896

Quibell, J.E. *Archaic Mastabas*, Cairo, 1923

Hierakonpolis, 2 vols., London, 1900

Randall-McIver, D. and Mace, A. *El 'Amrah and Abydos*, London, 1902

Wendorf, F. and Marks. A. *Problems in Prehistory – North Africa and the Levant*, Southern Methodist University Press, Dallas, 1975

Pyramids: Houses for Eternity

Aldred, C. *Jewels of the Pharaohs*, Thames and Hudson, London, 1971

Edwards, I.E.S. *The Pyramids of Egypt*, revised, Penguin, London and New York, 1985

Fakhry, A. *The Pyramids*, University of Chicago, 1961

Goneim, M.Z. *The Buried Pyramid*, London, 1956

Jenkins, N. *The Boat Beneath the Pyramid*, Thames & Hudson, London, 1980; Holt, Rinehart and Winston, New York, 1980

Landström, B. *Ships of the Pharaohs*, Doubleday, New York, 1970

Lauer, J.P. *Saqqara – the Royal Cemetery of Memphis*, Thames and Hudson, London, 1976; Scribners, New York, 1976

Malek, J. and Forman, W. *In the Shadow of the Pyramids*, Orbis, London, 1986; University of Oklahoma Press, 1986

Mendelssohn, K. *The Riddle of the Pyramids*, Thames & Hudson, London; Holt, Rinehart & Winston, New York, 1974

Reisner, G.H. and Smith, W.S. *History of the Giza Necropolis, Volume 2 – the Tomb of Hetepheres, Mother of Cheops*, Harvard University Press, Massachusetts, 1955

Spencer, A.J. *Death in Ancient Egypt*, Penguin, London and New York, 1982

Winlock, H.E. *The Treasure of El-Lahun*, New York, 1934

The Shifting Sands

Aldred, C. *Akhenaten and Nefertiti*, The Brooklyn Museum, Viking, New York, 1973

Akhenaten Thames and Hudson, London and New York, 1988

Bierbrier, M. *The Tomb Builders of the Pharaohs*, British Museum Publications, London, 1982

du Bourguet, P. *Coptic Art*, Methuen, London, 1971

Carter, H. and Mace, A. *Tomb of Tutankhamen*, 2 vols., London 1923

   Tomb of Tutankhamen, condensed, Century, 1983

Cerny, J. *A Community of Workmen at Thebes in the Ramesside Era*, IFAO, Cairo, 1973

   The Valley of the Kings, IFAO, Cairo, 1973

Desroches-Noblecourt, C. *Life and Death of a Pharaoh: Tutankhamen*, Penguin, London, 1972; New York Graphic Society, 1972

Edwards, I.E.S. *Tutankhamun – His Tomb and its Treasures*, Metropolitan Museum of Art and Alfred A. Knopf, New York, 1976; Gollancz, London, 1976

Fakhry, A. *The Oases of Egypt*, 2 vols., Cairo, 1982

Harris, J. and Wente, E.F. *An X-Ray Atlas of the Royal Mummies*, University of Chicago Press, 1980

Kitchen, K.A. *Pharaoh Triumphant*, Aris & Phillips, Warminster, 1982

Manniche, L. *City of the Dead*, British Museum Publications, London, 1987

Peet, T., Pendlebury, J.D.S. et al *The City of Akhenaten*, 3 vols, London 1922–35·

Redford, D. *Akhenaten – the "Heretic King"*, Princeton University Press, 1987

Romer, J. *Valley of the Kings*, Michael Joseph, London, 1981

Samson, J. *Amarna* – City of Akhenaten and Nefertiti, second edition, Aris & Phillips, Warminster, 1979

Smith, G. Elliot *The Royal Mummies*, Cairo, 1912

Thomas, E. *The Royal Necropolis of Thebes*, Princeton University Press, 1966

Temples: Mansions of Gods

Cerny, J. *Ancient Egyptian Religion*, Hutchinson, London, 1952

David, A.R. *A Guide to Religious Ritual at Abydos*, Aris & Phillips, Warminster, 1981

Erman, A. *A Handbook of Egyptian Religion*, London, 1952

Frankfort, H. *Ancient Egyptian Religion*, New York, 1948

Frankfort, H. (Ed.) *Before Philosophy*, University of Chicago, 1946

Griffith, J. Gwyn *The Conflict of Horus and Seth*, University of Liverpool, 1960

Hart, G. *A Dictionary of Egyptian Gods and Goddesses*, Routledge & Kegan Paul, London, 1986

Lurker, M. *The Gods and Symbols of Ancient Egypt*, Thames & Hudson, London and New York, 1982

Murnane, M. *The Penguin Guide to Ancient Egypt*, Penguin, London and New York, 1983

Rundle-Clark, R.T. *Myth and Symbol in Ancient Egypt*, Thames & Hudson, London, 1959; reprinted London and New York 1978

Sauneron, S. *The Priests of Ancient Egypt*, New York, 1980

Shorter, A. *The Egyptian Gods*, Routledge & Kegan Paul, London, 1937; reprinted 1981

Spencer, P. *The Egyptian Temple – A Lexicographical Study*, Kegan Paul International, London, 1984

Thomas, A. *Egyptian Gods and Myths*, Shire, Aylesbury, 1986

Egypt's Legacy

Aldred, C. *Egyptian Art in the Days of the Pharaohs*, Thames and Hudson, London, 1980, and New York, 1985

Andrews, C. *The Rosetta Stone*, British Museum Publications, London, 1985

Cockburn, A. and E. *Mummies, Disease and Ancient Cultures*, Cambridge University Press, Cambridge and New York 1984

David, A.R. and Tapp, E. *Evidence Embalmed*, Manchester University Press, 1984

Faulkner, R.O. *Ancient Egyptian Coffin Texts*, 3 vols., Aris & Phillips, Warminster, 1978

   Ancient Egyptian Pyramid Texts, Aris & Phillips, Warminster, 1969

   The Egyptian Book of the Dead, British Museum Publications, London, 1985

Gardiner, Sir Alan *Egyptian Grammar*, third edition, Griffith Institute, Oxford, 1978

Glanville, S. (Ed.) *The Legacy of Egypt*, first edition, Oxford University Press,1942 (**Note:** this is substantially different in content from the Harris edition, below.)

Habachi, L. *The Obelisks of Egypt – Skyscrapers of the Past*, Cairo, 1984

Harris, J.R. (Ed.) *The Legacy of Egypt*, second edition, Oxford University Press, 1971 (**Note:** this is substantially different in content from the Glanville edition, above.)

Iversen, E. *Canon and Proportion in Egyptian Art*, second edition, revised, Aris & Phillips, Warminster, 1976

Lange, K. and Hirmer, H. *Egypt – Architecture, Sculpture and Painting*, Phaidon, London and New York, 1956

Lichtheim, M. *Ancient Egyptian Literature*, 3 vols., University of California Press, Berkeley, 1975–80

Michalowski, K. *Art of Ancient Egypt*, Abrams, New York, 1985; Thames and Hudson, London, 1985

Schaefer, H. *Principles of Egyptian Art*, Clarendon Press (Oxford University Press), Oxford, 1974

Smith, W. Stevenson *Art and Architecture of Ancient Egypt*, revised by W.K. Simpson, Penguin, London and New York, 1981

Nubian Rescue

Africa in Antiquity, 2 vols, Brooklyn Museum

Dunham, D. and Janssen, J.M. *The Second Cataract Forts*, 5 vols., Boston, 1967

Emery, W.B. *Egypt in Nubia*, Hutchinson, London, 1965; also published as *Lost Land Emerging*, Scribner's, New York, 1967

Emery, W.B. and Kirwen, L. *Excavations and Survey Between Wadi es Sebua and Adindan*, Cairo, 1935

Lumley, J.M. *Nubian Studies*, Aris & Phillips, Warminster, 1982

Save-Soderbergh, T. (gen. ed.) *Temples and Tombs of Ancient Nubia*, Thames and Hudson, London and New York, 1987

Trigger, B. *Nubia under the Pharaohs*, Thames and Hudson, London, 1976

GAZETTEER

Any visit to Egypt should be organized through a recognized travel group. In this way the itinerary can be worked out by experienced travellers aware of the problems that may occur. The tour companies are able to negotiate group rates, so to travel independently may be more costly. It could also prove to be difficult because during the popular season the tour companies invariably book up the best hotels.

For more details, the following firms can help individual travellers worldwide:

Bales Ltd, Bales House, Barrington Rd, Dorking, Surrey RH4 3EJ, England.
Telephone: 0306-885991.

Swan Hellenic, 77 New Oxford St, London WC1A 1PP, England.
Telephone: 01-831 1515.

Swan Hellenic Inc, 500 Fifth Avenue, New York, N.Y. 10010, USA.
Telephone: 212-719-2000.

The International Travel Guild, 330 Sutter St, San Francisco, California 94108, USA.
Telephone: 415-397-7160.

Misr Travel, 40 Great Marlborough St, London W1V 1DA, England.
Telephone: 01-734 0238.

Misr Travel, 630 Fifth Avenue, Suite 555, New York, NY 10111, USA.
Telephone: 212-582-9210.

Hotels
Accommodation in the better hotels of Alexandria, Cairo, Luxor and Aswan will be well up to international standards. However, outside the main centres there may not be a choice of hotel at all, so the visitor must be prepared for somewhat basic conditions.

Travelling within Egypt
The cost of transport between the major towns in Egypt is very cheap by air, rail or road. For information on flights contact Egyptair: London 01-734 2864 or New York 212-581-5600. Information on rail times can be obtained from any Thomas Cook Agency. Transport by coach can easily be booked in Egypt. The most reliable company with constant services both throughout the country and locally is Misr Travel, PO Box 1000, 1 Talaat Harb St, Cairo. Telephone 750010.

Once in the major towns, travelling to and around some of the sites may be more complicated. Provided you are willing to take a donkey or camel ride from time to time there will be little problem. Luxor and Aswan have a system of *barouches* (horse-drawn carriages). It is customary to agree a price before setting off. Bicycles can be hired by the day at little cost in all of the major towns.

When to go
The ideal time for a visit to Egypt is during the period from early October to the end of February. The summer months up to early October are extremely hot and therefore not really suitable for visiting the monuments and sunbathing. It is recommended when travelling – especially during the summer period – to take adequate precautions against the sun – a wide-brimmed hat and salt tablets or pills are essential in peak temperatures. During December and January the nights can be cold, so carry a warm outer garment.

Before you go
A visa is required and can be obtained from the Consulate of the Arab Republic of Egypt. Vaccinations are not required for visitors travelling directly from western countries, but protection is recommended against hepatitis, malaria, polio, cholera, typhoid and tetanus. Check the current regulations with your travel agent well before your scheduled date of departure.

Opening times
Shops are open most of the day. They may close on Friday. The opening times of monuments and sites vary according to the season. Check with the Egyptian Tourist Information Offices for details.

Photography
Generally photography is not permitted inside the tombs or pyramids. However, a permit may be granted for a fee if an application is made to the Egyptian Consulate well in advance. All video equipment must be registered with Customs and Excise on arrival.

Things to remember
– Always have a good torch, or flashlight. Power failures are not infrequent, and light in some monuments is poor.
– Always carry notes of small value (10 and 25 piastres) to use as *baksheesh* (tipping).
– Do not wander too far from the desert sites because often many of the surrounding areas are in restricted zones.
– Always bargain hard for anything you want to buy.
– Be careful what you eat and drink. Avoid salads or fruit unless you can peel it or wash it yourself with bottled water. Drink only mineral water from sealed bottles – they are inexpensive and widely available – and never have ice in drinks.

SITES
Abbreviations
OK – Old Kingdom
MK – Middle Kingdom
GR – Graeco-Roman
NK – New Kingdom
LP – Late Period

CAIRO
In walking distance of the major hotels is the viewing gallery of the **Cairo Tower** on Gezira Island. It offers panoramic views of the city and can be reached by crossing the Tahrir Bridge. The **Egyptian Museum** should not be missed, to see **Tutankhamun's treasure** along with the **jewels of the princesses of the MK** and **Queen Hetepheres' furniture**. Allow a full day to explore the museum.

Venture further by taxi or local coach tour to see the **Citadel** in Old Cairo. This building was begun in 1176. The **alabaster mosque** within it was built between 1827 and 1857 by Mohammed Ali, the Father of Modern Egypt, and it contains his tomb.

The **Coptic Museum** should also be seen. Greek, Roman, Byzantine and Early Christian pieces can be viewed. Old Cairo contains typical examples of Coptic churches such as **Apa Sergius**, which dates possibly from the 6th century and is said to have been built over the crypt where the Holy Family rested after their flight from Nazareth. The **Ben Ezra Synagogue**, originally a Coptic church, once stored thousands of Hebrew manuscripts, now in the university.

Try to pay a visit to the **Khan el Khalili**, a large Souk, or open bazaar, on the Nile Corniche. It is one of the largest souks in the Middle East, and is famous for its coppersmiths, perfume oils, jewellery and spices.

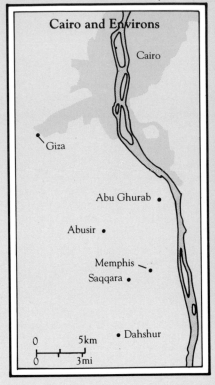

Cairo and Environs

Giza
Leave the city to the west over the southern tip of Roda Island to reach the three massive **Pyramids** of the kings of the 4th Dynasty, to the west of the city. All three pyramids are open to the public. The **Boat Museum** should be visited as well as the **Sphinx**.

A **Son et Lumière** performance takes place each evening. Most hotels arrange trips, but the languages the performance takes place in vary, so do check when you make your arrangements.

Memphis
The capital of Egypt for almost 400 years. What little remains now lies near the village of Mit Rahina, 25km (15mi) south of Cairo. The open-air museum here contains objects from the main temple of Ptah; embalming tables of the Apis bulls; and an undated, but striking, alabaster sphinx. The impressive **colossus of Ramesses II** also lies here covered by a specially constructed building for its protection.

Saqqara
This desert necropolis lies about 3km (2mi) west of Memphis and is dominated by the **Step Pyramid** complex of King Djoser. On entering the complex turn right into the **Sed Court**. Emerging at the north end notice the doorway into the southern building. To the rear of the pyramid lies the **Mortuary Chapel** with the attached **Serdab**.

The visit may continue on to the **Pyramid of Unas**. It was here that the earliest *Pyramid Texts* were discovered. To the east of the pyramid runs the causeway, with enough fine reliefs on the remaining blocks to show how splendid it originally was.

From the coach park a roadway passes the Step Pyramid to its east. On the right lies the **Pyramid of Teti**, its burial chamber decorated with texts. Opposite the entrance lies the 'street' of nobles' tombs, including the **mastabas of Mereruka and Kagemni** with their elaborately carved reliefs. Walking westwards the visitor passes the **Pyramid of Userkaf** and the mastaba **tombs of Ptahhotep** and **Ti**, the internal walls of which are carved with reliefs of wild animals – hippopotami and crocodiles. The **Serapeum** lies at the end of this route, beyond the **Dromos**, a semicircle of Greek statues.

Meidum

A quiet site with few tourists, dominated by what appears to be a tower. This is in fact the core of an early OK pyramid. Take a look at the **mastaba of Rahotep and Nofret**.

Southwards to Beni Suef, and then west, lie the pyramids of Illahun and Hawara. (Illahun is too dangerous to enter.)

Medinet el Faiyum

A big market centre for local produce. The road through the town to the lake passes through some of Egypt's richest agricultural land, a part of the country where little has changed since ancient times.

MIDDLE EGYPT

The journey up the Nile Valley is usually taken with at least one stop at El Minya.

El Minya

The first site to see is **Beni Hasan**. The tombs here belonged to MK nomarchs, and are built in a long terrace. Make sure to visit **tomb of Khnumhotep** with its caravan of Bedouin traders on the left wall and gardening scenes, with vineyard and a tree full of birds. If time permits, see **tomb of Khety**, with its scenes of spinning and weaving; dancing; wrestling; siege of a fortified town.

About 1.5km (1m) south lies a small unfinished rock-cut temple of Hatshepsut, **Speos Artemidos**, dedicated to the lioness Pakhet, with long inscription outside and coloured reliefs of the queen inside. Allow at least one and a half hours to see it. Returning to the west bank, follow the main road south 22km (14mi) to El Ashmunein.

El Ashmunein

Remains of ancient town of Hermopolis, dedicated to the god Thoth, depicted both as an ibis and as a baboon. As you approach the mud-brick walls two **granite baboon statues** with name of Amenhotep III (NK) inscribed on the base. Notice the granite columns of a Christian church built over foundations clearly visible. About 6.5km (4mi) south and west of Ashmunein lies the necropolis of Tuna el Gebel.

Tuna el Gebel

Set into the face of a cliff at this site is the western **boundary stela** of Tell el Amarna, together with statues of Akhenaten and Nefertiti. The climb up the cliff is relatively steep, but short. To the left of the statues note the addition of a third daughter; this was **Ankhesenpaaten**, future wife of Tutankhamun. The small temple-tomb of **Petosiris**, High Priest of Thoth at time of Greek conquest, has carvings inside of peculiar Greek/Egyptian style. To the south lie remains of the **Temple of Thoth**, with a deep well that supplied the area with water. On the way out of the necropolis on the left is an entrance via what seems an unprepossessing hut to the **Ibis and Baboon Catacombs**. Undergound staircase leads to well-lit chambers packed solid with mummified baboons and ibises. NK-GR date. From El Minya, allow a long half-day to visit Tell el Amarna.

Tell El Amarna

Follow road south from El Minya through Mallawi to Deir Mawas and turn left to the river bank. Cross by ferry. The plain where once the city of Akhenaten stood appears virtually bare. Go south along the road. Mud-brick walls mark the site of the royal palace and the temple of Aten.

In the north cliffs you will see the **northern tombs** cut for officials of the city. Notice particularly the tomb of **Huya**, steward of Akhenaten's mother; the tomb of **Meryre I**, high priest of Aten, with its scenes of boats moored by the palace walls and, finally, the tomb of **Panehesy**.

In the south cliffs, some 6km (4mi) away are situated the **southern tombs**. Special permission must be obtained from the Antiquities Service to visit these. Worth the effort, however, is the tomb of **Ay**, King of Egypt after Tutankhamun. On its walls is carved the hymn to the Aten.

On the east bank of Mallawi are the rock-cut tombs of the nobles of **El Bersheh**. They are at the top of a difficult climb and are badly damaged. They are little visited, but they do have great charm. Visit also the tomb of **Djehutihotep** with its unique depiction of the moving of a colossal statue on a sledge.

LUXOR

The town of Luxor – also commonly called Thebes, the name given to it by the Greeks – lies about 675km (420mi) south of Cairo. It is a major tourist centre, rapidly expanding, with many new hotels being built. It can be reached from Cairo by road or air (the flight takes about an hour), or take the overnight sleeper (**note**: this is a popular form of travelling and must be booked well in advance).

The first sights to visit from Luxor are **Abydos** and **Dendera** to the north.

Abydos

The ancient site lies to the west of El Balliana, 150km (95mi) south of Cairo. Here you will see the impressive **Mortuary Temple of Seti I**. This building is much restored. Pass through two badly damaged courtyards to the pillared façade to view the reliefs of Ramesses II making offerings. Inside walk through two columned (hypostyle) halls to a series of seven doorways; these are the sanctuaries. All have similar scenes showing the sequences of the daily offering ritual. Notice the superb carving and wonderful preservation of colour. Outside and to the left, enter the **Gallery of the King List** where Seti I and his son, Prince Ramesses, make offerings to names of all the kings of Egypt down to their own time. Turn right into the corridor that leads outside. On your left is a bird-trapping relief, on your right bull-roping. Shallow and uneven steps lead to the back of the temple; here the **Osireion**, an underground temple devoted to the mortuary cult of Osiris, with fine painted reliefs and figure of Merenptah, fourteenth son of Ramesses II.

Beyond the Osireion lies the wide plain of Umm el Qa'ab. To the west lies the site of the burials of the Archaic period kings, though nothing but depressions in the sand can be seen. South of the Osireion (.5 km (1 mi)) are the massive mud-brick walls of the **Shunet es Zebib**, standing approximately 12m (40ft) tall, though they are at least 500 years old.

North of the temple of Seti I are the remains of the **Temple of Ramesses II**. Though the walls stand only 2m (6ft) high, the coloured reliefs are beautifully preserved. Travel south 90km (55mi) from Abydos and on the west bank, opposite Qena, visit **Dendera**.

Dendera

The Graeco-Roman temple of Hathor here is one of the most charming in all Egypt. Park at the front of the temple and walk through a monumental gate into the front court. On the left, a brightly coloured relief on a block of Bes, the ugly dwarf demigod. On the right the **Mammisi**, the outside walls with superb reliefs of Hathor and her child, Ihy. Visit the sanctuary, decorated on the right with scenes of the divine conception and birth of Ihy. Adjacent to the mammisi is the **Christian Church**. Next to this lie the mud-brick foundations of the **Sanatorium**, the inside cubicles where patients were treated. South of this is what remains of the **Sacred Lake**, now filled with plants.

In the main temple, enter the columned hall to view on the left the **Astronomic Ceiling**. The next small hall, with six columns, is flanked with small side chambers showing reliefs of vessels once stored within them. On the right of the sanctuary lie a series of small chambers. In the corner room, a narrow staircase in the floor leads to one of the temple **Crypts**. Fine carved relief of jewellery once stored here and of the falcon Horus the Elder, husband of the goddess Hathor.

Returning to the front of the sanctuary, a staircase on the left leads to the roof. Here in the open temple of Osiris, once a year the cult statue would be placed to receive the first light of dawn. To the left, steps lead to the front of the temple roof.

Descend to the front of a side-chapel on the left. Inside the first chamber above the head, a carved relief of Nut, the sky goddess extending the width of the ceiling. To the left on the ceiling a huge black-painted plaster disc, a copy of the famous **Zodiac** (now in the Louvre), with Egyptian figures forming easily-recognized astrological signs. In the rear room, reliefs on the walls depict the dead and mummified Osiris being brought to life by the wings of the kite Isis and her impregnation by him of her son Horus.

Returning downstairs, leave the temple and walk to the rear wall. Here carved reliefs show **Cleopatra VII** and her son by Julius Caesar, **Caesarion**.

At dusk, the temple is dramatically illuminated with coloured lights; it is a sight that will be long remembered. Allow a full day to visit the sites of the east bank of Luxor. Travel between the temples of Karnak and Luxor by *barouche*.

Temple of Karnak

The front of the temple is approached down a short staircase from the main road to an avenue of ram-headed sphinxes in front of the main pylon. The front open courtyard contains two smaller temples; to the left, one of Seti II; to the right, one of Ramesses III. Both originally stood outside the temple, but were incorporated in the later building.

The processional way leads past a colossal statue of Ramesses II, overcarved with the name of the High Priest Pinedjem, into the **Great Hypostyle Hall**. The 134 columns of this hall are one of the most photographed sights in Egypt! Don't miss the **Clerestory Windows** on the first row of side columns, by which this once dark hall was lit, or the overcarving of names on the columns, where successions of kings tried to claim responsibility for their building. A door to the left leads to the outside wall, where fine reliefs show Seti I's battles in lands to the north. Returning to the hypostyle hall and leaving on the opposite side, reliefs on the outer walls show Ramesses II's battles with the Hittites at Kadesh. A stela text on the left contains a copy of the **Peace Treaty**.

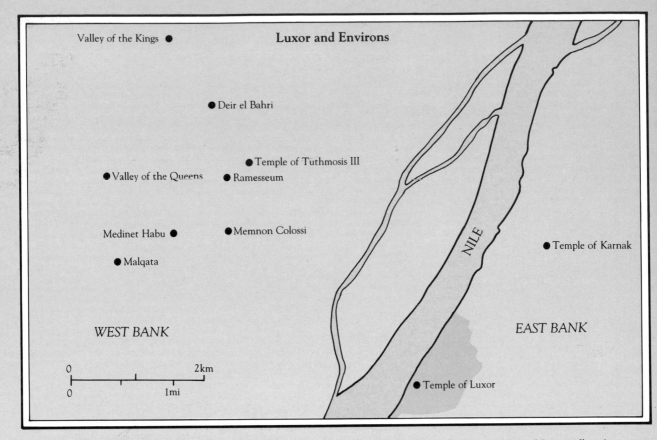

Luxor and Environs

Valley of the Kings ●

● Deir el Bahri

● Temple of Tuthmosis III

● Valley of the Queens

● Ramesseum

Medinet Habu ●

● Memnon Colossi

● Malqata

● Temple of Karnak

NILE

WEST BANK

EAST BANK

0   2km

0   1mi

● Temple of Luxor

Walking back to the hypostyle hall and continuing along the processional way can be seen two obelisks. The one on the right was cut for Tuthmosis I; the one on the left, for Hatshepsut.

At the end of the processional way is the **Sanctuary**. Inside, a stone base once held the god's ceremonial boat. The outer face of the sanctuary, carved with reliefs that are still brightly coloured, show Philip Arrhidaeus, brother of Alexander the Great, celebrating the Opet festival.

Behind the sanctuary, cross an open courtyard to the **Festival Hall of Tuthmosis III**, built to celebrate his victories over Syria and Palestine. The small side rooms were store chambers, although one contained the **King List** (now in the Louvre). At the back of the columns lie the foundations of several other rooms; climb up and down a short staircase, and then walk to the left to enter the **Botanical Hall**, the walls of which are lightly carved with pictures of plants and animals brought back by Tuthmosis III from abroad to found a small zoological collection.

Returning to the temple, walk to the obelisks and turn left to find the **Sacred Lake**, the fallen obelisk, carved with the coronation of Hatshepsut by Amen-Re and the scarab statue, built for Amenhotep III.

Walking back through the hypostyle hall into the open court, turn right and leave through a side door to find the **Open-Air Museum**, the **Kiosk of Sesostris I** at the rear left, one of the finest examples of relief carving to survive in Egypt. For those with time and energy, a visit can also be made to the Temple of Mut.

Temple of Mut

Leave the main temple, and on the main road turn immediately left and keeping the precinct wall on your left, walk about 1.5km (1mi), through a cluster of small houses, until a large stone gateway is reached. On the right, an **Avenue of Sphinxes** leads across open sand to a wooden gate. The remains of the temple of Mut lie beyond the gate, and are heavily overgrown with vegetation; in front of the temple was once an open courtyard flanked with a circle of black granite **Sekhmet Statues** of a woman with the head of a lioness. These are still there, peeping through long grass. The temple can best be surveyed from on top of one of the side walls where the outline of the columned halls and siderooms and the sanctuary can clearly be seen. Behind the temple is a large **Horseshoe Lake**, still filled with water.

To the front of the temple, turn right to see a small temple recently excavated. The remains of a pylon bear the names of Psammetichus I, though the inner walls show the first building was erected under Amenhotep III. On the left inner wall, is a remarkable painted relief of a circumcision operation. Returning to the front of the temple, 3km (2mi) to the south lies the temple of Luxor, once connected to Karnak by an avenue of sphinxes.

Temple of Luxor

Built by Amenhotep III and enlarged by Ramesses II during the NK for the Opet festival. Here once a year Amun and Mut of Karnak came for a divine 'honeymoon'.

Enter the temple from the main road at right angles to the front pylon. Here stand the colossal statues of Ramesses II and a single obelisk (its twin is in Paris).

In the courtyard, to the right, is the small temple of Tuthmosis III. Between the columns of the courtyard are statues of Amenhotep III, carved over with the name of Ramesses II. In the right-hand corner of this court, the reliefs on the inner face depict a procession of some of the sons of Ramesses II, and a unique depiction of the temple as it was when it was built.

Pass into the colonnade. Here fine reliefs on the right inner wall depict the Opet Festival, carved under Tutankhamun, with scenes of the temple store-houses of Karnak and the festivities along the river-front.

The open court, flanked by some of the most graceful columns standing in Egypt, leads to the small **Hypostyle Hall** and then to the **Sanctuary**. The apse, of Christian date with remains of some original paint, shows Christ and some of the saints. The rooms behind the sanctuary were probably storerooms and a copyists workshop.

Leaving the temple, walk along the outer wall on the western (river) side, watching out for reliefs of Ramesses II's battles in the north.

Luxor Museum

This museum lies about halfway between the temples of Karnak and Luxor on the Nile Corniche. Opened in 1975, it is one of the finest displays of Egyptian objects to be seen anywhere. The few choice pieces are freestanding, rarely behind glass, and beautifully lit. The museum opens only in the late afternoon. 4 p.m. until 9 p.m. in winter; 5 p.m. to 10 p.m. in summer.

The West Bank

There are a great many sites to visit here, and making several trips is advisable. A ferry from the front of the Winter Palace Hotel takes about 10 minutes to cross the Nile. If travelling independently, taxis can be hired on the west bank to take you to the sites, wait for you and bring you back. Donkeys can be hired more cheaply, though naturally they take longer and are less comfortable. *Tickets to the sites must be bought at the river bank.* The road from the river goes west past the **Colossi of Memnon**, statues that once stood at the front of the Mortuary temple of Amenhotep III, of which nothing remains.

At the major crossroads ahead, to the left lies **Medinet Habu** (the mortuary temple of Ramesses III); straight in front is the **Valley of the Queens** and the workmen's village of **Deir el Medina**; to the right, in the cliffs are the **tombs of the nobles**. The road curves past the mortuary temples of Hatshepsut at **Deir el Bahri** and of Ramesses II – the **Ramesseum** – and then winds behind the hills to the **Valley of the Kings**. All the sites lie at least 3km (2mi) from the river. The road to the Valley of the Kings is about 8km (5mi) long. Allow at least an hour at each site.

The Mortuary Temples
Medinet Habu
Enter under the unusual **Migdol Gateway** with its battlemented top. Inside the open courtyard, the temple of Hatshepsut lies to one side, north of which is a small sacred lake. In front, the pylons on the temple are carved with scenes of the king's victories. Entering through them into an open courtyard, the inner face of the northern pylon, shows a relief of the severed hands and genitals of enemies being offered to the god.

The walls of the courtyard show more battle scenes; the second pylons depict the **Sea Peoples**. The left wall formed the front of the **Royal Palace**. Inside this, at the rear, a stone dais is in what was once the throne room and to the right, a tiny side room that was the royal bathroom. Returning to the temple itself, enter a **second court**. On the right wall, behind the curiously squat statues are reliefs of the **Festival of Min**.

Of the hypostyle hall and the sanctuary only column bases and low walls mark the major features.

The Ramesseum
At the side of the temple, a short path leads directly into the second court. To the left, descend past the fallen **Colossus of Ozymandias**, once one of the largest granite statues ever erected in Egypt, to the overgrown first court, which contains the remains of the main pylon.

Back inside the second court, notice the reliefs on the wall immediately to the right of the statue, showing the **Battle of Kadesh**.

On the west side of court are the Osiris statues of the king. To the left of this the Processional Way enters what remains of the temple. Next to the door, the wall to the left contains scenes of the siege of the Hittite city of Dapur. On the opposite wall, the sacred persea tree where Amun and Seshat (personification of writing) inscribe the king's name on leaves of the tree. The rest of the temple is destroyed.

Deir el Bahri
The bay of cliffs is reached from the Ramesseum by turning right on the road (north) and then left after about 1km (0.5mi). Park in the front of the temples and follow a flat path about 90m (300 ft) to the temples. Behind the temples a steep ancient path leads over the hills to the Valley of the Kings. It is about an hour's walk and has spectacular views over the Nile, the temples and the Valley of the Kings.

To the south of the bay is the ruined mortuary temple of **Mentuhotep Nebhepetre** (11th Dynasty, MK) with remains of the pyramid on the top under which the king was buried. To the north of the bay is the great temple of **Hatshepsut** (18th Dynasty, NK); between them and level with the second terrace of Hatshepsut's temple is the recently revealed court-

yard of the temple of **Tuthmosis III**, built from, and over, stones from Hatshepsut's temple.

The Temple of Hatshepsut
In three terraces, but the second terrace contains the most interesting scenes.

On the first terrace to the right, though badly damaged, on the left wall, the queen as a sphinx (chiselled out so carefully it is easily recognized). To the left, reliefs of boats moving two great obelisks from Aswan to Karnak.

On the second terrace, turn right and walk to the far end. The temple of Hathor overlooks the other two temples. Notice the relief of the queen suckled by cow goddess, Hathor. Next, in the colonnade are the superb reliefs of the **Expedition to Punt**; on the side wall the Queen of Punt (copy of the original block); the Egyptian army delegation and under them the river, with squid, shark and huge turtles.

In the centre of the terrace, enter the inner rooms used for the mortuary offerings. In two small dark 'cupboards', use a torch on the side walls to see a small carved image of a man with his name, Senmut, in hieroglyphs; he was Hatshepsut's chief advisor and Treasurer and, some say, her lover.

In the northern side of the terrace, the reliefs depict Hatshepsut's conception and birth. Amun sits with Queen Ahmose on a bed and offers her the symbol of life (ankh). Khnum forms the baby and her ka on his wheel and the pregnant queen is led into the birth chamber. Finally the child is presented by the god to ranks of other gods who nurture Hatshepsut.

In the far northern corner is a chapel to **Anubis**. Here the wonderful intact colouring gives an impression of what the whole temple once looked like.

The Workmen's Village
The walled village of Deir el Medina gives a good idea of housing in ancient Egypt. To enter, a doorway in the west wall leads to the central street where most of the houses were built. Halfway through the village on the right is the larger house once occupied by the village foreman. At the north end of the village, at the single main entrance are the houses which belonged to the janitors who controlled entrance and exit of the villagers. Beyond this note the mud-brick foundations of a temple built in the time of the Ptolemies. Opposite, in the cliff face, lie remains of a tiny temple cut during the 19th Dynasty.

Returning to the car park at the south end, to the west lie the **Pyramidions** that cover the entrances of tombs of the workmen. The tomb of **Sennedjem**, small but wonderfully preserved; tombs of **Ipy, Inkherkhau** and **Pashed** are all beautiful, though not always open to the public.

The Valley of the Queens
From Deir el Medina, return to the main road and turn right. After 1km (½mi) the road terminates at the entrance to the Valley of the Queens.

Tombs were built here from the 19th dynasty onwards for the queens and princes of the Ramesside kings. Usually only two tombs are open. The famous tomb of **Nefertari** is closed because of continuing damage to its fine paintings.

The tomb of **Queen Tyti**, though one of the finest in the valley, has long been a mystery, as the tomb does not record who she was, nor the name of the king with whom she was associated. It has been suggested that she was a wife of Ramesses III and possibly the mother of Ramesses IV. The queen is shown in the company of

gods and goddesses. She shakes a sistrum before Horus.

The tomb of **Amenhirkhopshef** belonged to a crown prince, a son of Ramesses III, who died when he was only a young child. The fine wall paintings are well-preserved.

The Valley of the Kings
Allow a good half day, or, if energetic, a full day. There is a large, comfortable rest house that provides snacks, drinks – and shade. Your entrance ticket entitles you to enter as many tombs as you wish within the valley. All the tombs lie within a 1km (½ mi) radius.

The tomb of **Tutankhamun** is in the floor of the valley behind a wall just inside the entrance. The body of the king still lies there, so silence is respected. The tomb lies at the foot of a stone staircase, but is shallow and easy to enter. Inside only the burial chamber is painted: At the rear, King Ay, as crowned pharaoh, 'opens the mouth' of the mummified Tutankhamun; Tutankhamun and his ka meet Osiris. The sarcophagus contains the lid of the outer coffin of the king under glass; the king's body lies under this.

At the side of Tutankhamun's tomb is the entrance to the tomb of **Ramesses VI**, built for Ramesses IV and usurped. Again it is an easy tomb to reach. The corridors are brightly painted with scenes from the *Book of The Gates* and the *Book of What is in the Underworld*.

Outside the tomb, turn right, to a 'crossroad' and then right again. On the right, find the tomb of **Horemheb**. It is very deep and steep. The steps lead to one of the finest preserved tombs open in the valley. Since it was unfinished, it gives the unique opportunity of following exactly the sequences of decorating the tombs, from sketch to carving to painting, and even the sequence of painting. Notice that the sarcophagus is almost identical to Tutankhamun's. In a side chamber is a beautiful painting of Osiris.

Leave Horemheb's tomb and turn right to the head of the side-bay, and find the tomb of **Amenhotep II**. The stairs lead to two large chambers, whose bright preserved paintings are in hieratic, i.e. cursive writings and stick-figures on a background that resembles papyrus. This is where one of the caches of royal mummies was found.

Return to the 'crossroad' and turn right. Where the path splits, take the left fork and approach the head of the valley. A metal staircase leads up the side of the cliff to the entrance of the tomb of **Tuthmosis III**. The climb both up the cliff and down into the tomb is strenuous. At the foot of the stairs, enter a rectangular painted chamber with walls decorated in hieratic. A shaft in one corner, with a staircase leads down to a lower chamber that is unique in its oval shape, with brilliantly preserved hieratic paintings.

Tombs of the Nobles
The village of Sheikh Abd el Qurna, with its brightly painted houses and alabaster workshops, lies off the main road, opposite the Ramesseum. The tombs lie just west of this village; some on a lower level, others up a steep rise behind the village. Tickets cover entry to two or three tombs, usually clustered in groups. Check at the tourist office at the riverbank to see which tombs are open and request permission here if you wish to visit any others.

The large tomb of **Ramose** (No 55) dates from the reign of Amenhotep III/Akhenaten. The one large columned chamber contains remarkable scenes: On the left a fine raised relief carving of Ramose and his wife, his brother Amenhotep and his wife and guests at

183

a banquet. On the adjacent wall: above, a funeral with the sarcophagus on a sledge; below, mourners wailing for the deceased. Rear wall, left shows Ramose in traditional style before Amenhotep IV and goddess Ma'at. On the right an incomplete sketch shows Ramose in deformed Amarna style appearing before Akhenaten and Nefertiti, receiving foreign ambassadors on their behalf. This change of art style' is unique in these tombs and is the main evidence for the co-regency of Amenhotep III and Akhenaten.

Outside to the south lies Tomb 56, of **Userhet**, smaller but beautifully preserved with unusual scenes. Depictions of the Opening the Mouth ceremony, taxation, recruiting soldiers, hair cutting.

Next door, Tomb 57, of **Khaemhet**, depicts scenes in relief rather than paintings.

Return to the path and walk north uphill to Tomb 100 of **Rekhmire**, vizier of Tuthmosis III, with unique accounts of the life of a vizier during the time of the New Kingdom.

Outside the tomb, turn left up the hill to Tomb 96, of **Sennefer**. Narrow, steep and twisting steps lead to two chambers. Notice the remarkable painted ceiling hanging with bunches of grapes and the goddess emerging from a tree to give offerings to Sennefer.

Either walk downhill eastwards towards the lower group of houses, or return to the main road opposite the Ramesseum, turn left and left again.

The tombs of **Menna** (No. 69) and **Nakht** (No. 52) lie near each other. Though small, both contain superb paintings of lively humour. Menna was Overseer of the Granaries during the reign of Tuthmosis IV. Nakht, an astronomer, was a contemporary of Menna's.

ASWAN
The 232km (144mi) journey from Luxor to Aswan can be done by river, road, air or rail.

Many boats cruise the Nile between these two towns, from elegant and huge cruise ships to small feluccas, and can be booked locally. The journey by felucca, sleeping in the bottom of the boat and eating food prepared by the crew is both cheap and truly memorable.

The flight by Egyptair lasts about 40 minutes. Taxis will be needed to Luxor airport and from Aswan. The rail journey takes about four hours. The journey by coach also takes about four hours, but allows you to visit all the sites between the two towns en route: the GR temple of **Esna**. The temple of **Edfu** and the tombs of **El Kab** are equidistant from both places. **Kom Ombo** is easiest reached from Aswan.

Esna
To the south of Luxor 55km (34mi), the temple of **Khnum** is on the west bank. This small Ptolemaic temple lies under the level of the main street, and only the hypostyle hall remains. It was built from the 1st to the 3rd centuries AD, dedicated to Khnum, the ram-headed creator god. Reliefs are well preserved, and show Roman emperors dressed as pharaohs.

Note that Esna market is one of the best places to buy cotton clothing, including galibeyas, the native long robe, at cheap prices.

El Kab
This site is on the east bank of the Nile 85km (53mi) south of Luxor, 146km (91mi) north of Aswan. It was the site of the ancient city of **Nekheb**, which venerated Nekhbet, the vulture goddess, and stands straight across the Nile from Kom el Ahmar, the predynastic capital of Upper Egypt, ancient Hieraconpolis. The old town site of El Kab lies behind a huge NK mud-brick wall 11m (37ft) thick. To the east of it, cut into the hillside are several well-decorated tombs dating from the early NK. The area has been much restored and the tomb chambers are well lit and in a far better state of preservation than those of Beni Hasan further north.

The tomb of **Paheri** dates from the time of Tuthmosis III (18th Dynasty) and though the pictures are a little damaged, the colour is well preserved. Fine painted reliefs depict Paheri supervising harvesting and collection of taxes. He is also shown, uniquely, with the crown prince on his knees.

The tomb of **Ahmose** son of Ibana is historically important. Ahmose was a soldier, grandfather of Paheri who fought during the wars to evict the Hyksos rulers from the delta. His autobiography records how the final battle was won.

The tomb of **Setau** dates from the 20th Dynasty, during the reign of Ramesses III. In design it is very similar to the tomb of Paheri though Setau's more badly damaged.

Edfu
The large town of Edfu stands on the west bank of the river 103km (64mi) south of Luxor, 129km (80mi) north of Aswan. Though a very old town dedicated to Horus, nothing is left save the huge **Graeco-Roman temple** about 1.5km (1mi) from the river. The main road west from the river bank leads into the town of Edfu, and terminates by the outer temenos wall at the back of the temple. The building was begun on a much older site in 237 BC, but was not dedicated to the god until 142 BC. The front pylons and courtyard were not finished until 57 BC.

On the right stands the small Roman mammisi, or birth house to which the cult statue of Hathor was brought once a year; here she is shown giving birth not not to Ihy, as in Dendera, but to Horus the Child.

Passing to the front of the temple and looking back at the great pylons, the massive size and undamaged state of the temple can be appreciated. At the front of the gate stand a fine pair of black granite falcon statues some 2m (6ft) tall.

Inside the pylons is a large open court surrounded by elaborately carved columns. Another falcon statue stands by the colonnade entrance to the temple. Under this courtyard, in 1984, were found coloured blocks from the previous temple on the site, depicting kings of the 25th Dynasty (LP). On the walls each side of the doorway is carved an account of the annual festival meeting between the cult statues of Horus, and Hathor of Dendera.

The front columns of the temple are joined to a half-height curtain wall. Inside the first hypostyle hall, to the rear of the curtain wall a small chamber stands each side of the doorway; to the left, a room for the priest to be robed and purified before the daily ritual; to the right, the temple library. The inner faces of this hall are carved with scenes from the founding of the temple. The second, and smaller, hypostyle hall has small side-chambers where pictures of temple vessels are carved. Beyond this hall lies the sanctuary within which is the fine, polished **granite shrine** where the cult statue was kept.

Returning to the front open courtyard, a doorway each side of the curtain wall leads to the outer corridor, on the walls of which are carved details of the story of the legendary battles between the eternally warring gods, Horus abd Seth.

Kom Ombo
The **Temple of Kom Ombo** lies on a wide marshy plain on the east bank of the Nile, 164km (102mi) south of Luxor, 67km (42mi) north of Aswan. It stands atop a mound right on the riverfront.

A short flight of steps leads to the entrance which is on the south side of the façade. The temple is unique, in that it was dedicated to two gods: Horus the Elder or Haroeris; and Sobek, the crocodile god. It had two parallel processional ways and twin sanctuaries. The site is one of the oldest in Egypt, but the temple dates to the 2nd century BC, its inscriptions usurped by later Roman Emperors.

On the right as you enter, a small side chapel with padlocked gate contains many stacked crocodile mummies.

The temple is much damaged, though the façade still stands to its full height, and the twin processional routes can clearly be seen. At the rear a shaft in the floor leads to a secret chamber where priests answered questions of petitioners. Behind the rear wall, in the outer corridor, the square space can be seen flanked with ears and eyes to which the petitioner addressed himself. Approaching this, on the left a table laid out with medical instruments, before which two goddesses sit on birth stools.

Aswan
The town stands on the first cataract, where the desert comes right to the river's edge, and rocks and islands fill the Nile. It marked the ancient frontier between Nubia and Egypt, and its quarries provided kings with finest granite throughout the Pharaonic period. Today, the high dam, the **Sadd el Ali** has brought new prosperity to the area. It is without doubt the prettiest and least spoiled town for visitors to Egypt. Feluccas ply the swift-flowing river taking visitors to the various islands; a sail on one in the fabled scarlet Egyptian sunset is a must.

From the town of Aswan, several sites can be reached easily by taxi and by felucca.

The East Bank Sites
A mile south of the town is the north quarry where stands the **Unfinished Obelisk**, 42m (137ft) long. It was abandoned when it cracked during manufacture. It is not known for whom it was started.

About 8km (5mi) south of the town is the high dam, a marvel of modern technology. (**Note**: special permission to visit the dam must be obtained in Aswan.) From this can be seen Lake Nasser and beyond, the open-air museum site of **the Temple of Kalabsha**.

West Bank Sites
A felucca will take between half and a full hour, depending on the breeze, to sail to the foot of **Qubbet el Hawa**, where the tombs of the nobles are cut. These can be seen illuminated at night, and by day, the long **coffin slides** from the river to the tomb entrances are a distinctive landmark.

The climb to the tombs from the river-bank is hard but for the view alone, it is worthwhile. At the top is a long row of tombs dating from the late OK and early MK. The furthest tomb to the north belonged to **Sarenput** (No. 36). It has six pillars in an open courtyard as a façade, while the wall shows domestic scenes of Sarenput hunting, with his pets and his family.

Around the face of the hill to the south are the tombs of **Pepynakht**, then **Harkhuf**, the façade of which bears a long autobiographical text that includes a copy of a letter sent to him by the young **Pepi II** (OK), exhorting Harkhuf to take great care of a pygmy he had brought back from southern Nubia. The hieroglyphs showing the dancing pygmy can be made out towards the centre of the long text. Inside, only a false door is of any interest.

On the corner of the hill, the tomb of **Khunes** was turned into a Christian anchorite's cell; further on can be found the tomb of **Sarenput II**. Inside, beyond a columned hall is an unusual passage flanked with brightly painted life-size mummiform statues in niches with an offering scene at the rear. The last large tomb belonged to two local governors of the OK, **Sabni** and **Mekhu**, the inside showing offering scenes and hunting in the marshes.

Take a felucca from the east bank also to visit the **Mausoleum of the Aga Khan**. The huge white tomb dominates the southern west bank. Camels or donkeys can be hired from here to visit the deserted **Monastery of St Simeon** built in the 6th century and abandoned in the 13th. The mud-brick enclosure wall is 7m (23ft) high, and contains a church. Take a look at the paintings on the inside of the dome of Christ together with saints and angels. The monastery buildings – dormitories, refectories, kitchens and stables – are also of interest and allow insights into monastic life.

The Islands

Opposite the town of Aswan lies the island of **Elephantine**. Here are the ruins of the great **Temple of Khnum**, the god of floods. Take a felucca and land near the **Nilometer**, a long stone staircase which descends into the Nile, with markings on the walls where the height of the inundation could be marked every year. Behind the temple lies the tall mud-brick ruins of the ancient town of Elephantine.

Returning towards the landing stage, a small building houses the **Aswan Museum**. This very small and old-fashioned museum contains several interesting pieces including the mummy of a sacred ram. To the west and slightly north of Elephantine Island is **Kitchener Island** sometimes called Botanical Island. The entire island is one huge garden, containing many rare and exotic plants and trees. Its coolness and greenness is a delight in the hot dryness of Aswan.

About a mile to the south of Aswan, an hour's felucca sail will take you to the little-known and seldom visited island of **Seheil**. This island has a small hill at its centre which is covered with rocks bearing hundreds of hieroglyphic graffiti, dating from the earliest times through to the GR period and giving much interesting information.

Philae

Take a coach or taxi south of Aswan beyond the British Dam, and then a motorboat to the island of **Agilkia** where now stands one of the most beautiful temples in all Egypt, the reconstructed **Temple of Isis of Philae**. The temple and all the surrounding buildings were moved from their original position (still marked by the coffer dam that can be seen to the southeast of the temple) to rescue it from the water that had engulfed it ever since the opening of the British Dam in 1901.

The Temple of Isis was considered 'the pearl of Egypt', and functioned as an Egyptian temple for many years after all other temples were closed by Roman decree. Even after Christianity came to the area, Nubians continued to worship Isis.

The boats halt at the landing stage by the ancient quay at the south of the island. Up the steps is a

Portico built by Nectanebo, the oldest part of the island. The large forecourt of the main temple is flanked by two colonnades. Behind the east colonnade are, first, at right angles to it, the temple of Aresnuphis (a GR god associated with Isis); behind are the ruined Temple of Mandulis (the Nubian Horus); and by the front of the main temple, the Temple of Imhotep (builder of the Step Pyramid, who came to be venerated in GR times as a healer and wise man).

The main pylon shows Ptolemy XII offering to the gods; at right angles in front of the east pylon is a gateway built by Ptolemy II, and probably the original approach to the temple. In the pylon entrance on the right is a long inscription carved by Napoleon's army in 1799. Inside the inner courtyard on the right, the **Mammisi**, built by Ptolemy VI, where the birth of Horus was celebrated. The second pylon stands at an angle to the first and follows the main route of the temple. The inner halls and rooms of the temple are decorated with the usual scenes of temple ritual.

Returning to the second pylon, turn right to the side of the temple to find **Hadrian's Gateway**, a staircase that leads to a passage down to the river. On the walls are carved several interesting scenes: on the left near the river a crocodile carrying the mummy of Osiris to the rocky island of Biggeh; above, Osiris resurrected, with Horus under a star-studded sky canopy; on the right the Nile god, Hapy, hidden in a cave under Biggeh island, the entrance hidden by a magic serpent, its tail in its mouth. To the right of this, a crudely carved figure of a man has a badly written inscription adjacent to it; this is the last recorded text ever written in hieroglyphs, dating to AD 394.

On the other side of the island, lies the small **Temple of Hathor**. On the right musicians including the dwarf-god Bes dancing and playing a harp and a unique depiction of an ape figure playing a lute. To the south lies the beautiful **Trajan's Kiosk**, also known as Pharaoh's Bed. This was built as an entrance to the island, and with its 14 graceful columns, is regarded as one of the finest pieces of GR architecture.

A **Son et Lumierè** performance on the island began in 1985 and is by far the most moving sound and light show in Egypt. It is, at present, little known, but a special experience never to be forgotten.

Aswan is the starting point for visiting the rescued monuments of Nubia. The flight south to **Abu Simbel** takes barely half an hour. An alternative is to travel by coach. This is far cheaper, and though it takes about four hours, enables the visitor to experience Nubia and Lake Nasser more fully. En route by road it is worth paying a visit to the **Temple of Kalabsha**. (**Note**: special permission must be obtained to see Kalabsha and this should be done several months in advance and confirmed on arrival.) This was the second largest building, after Abu Simbel, moved before the opening of the dam. It was dedicated to **Mandulis**, the Nubian Horus. The temple is of Roman date, with many fine reliefs. Notice a fine carving of Horus emerging from reeds on the inner curtain wall; a long inscription carved by the Roman Governor Aurelius Besarion in AD 250, forbidding pigs in the temple, an inscription on the far right of the Nubian King Silko, carved during the 5th century and recording his victory over the Blemmyes and a picture of him dressed as a Roman soldier on horseback. From the sanctuary chambers a staircase leads up to the roof of the temple from where you get a marvellous view of the temple itself and lake.

Outside the temple, rocks by the south wall propped on other stones contain predynastic rock sketches of

animals (including an elephant and a giraffe), and a high-prowed boat. To the south, on a rocky promontory, stands the graceful **Kiosk of Qertassi**. This is unfinished and not inscribed with the name of the architect, but it is probably contemporary with Trajan's Kiosk at Philae.

To the rear of the temple, a pathway leads northwest around a curved face of rock where stands the charming rock-cut temple of **Beit el Wali**, built by Ramesses II. Though only very small, it is quite delightful. On the walls of the open court, on the right are scenes of battles with Syrians and Libyans, while Ramesses' son, Prince Amen-her-wenemef, presents captives to his victorious father. On the left, Ramesses and two of his sons fight the Nubians; unique scenes include: a village with palm trees where a woman crouches over a fire, cooking a meal; women and children fleeing in terror; the presentation of booty, including ostriches, giraffes, lion skins and elephant tusks; the delighted viceroy of Kush, Amenemope, presented to Ramesses. Inside the temple, Ramesses is shown in vividly preserved colour with statues of the gods of the cataract, Khnum, Anukis and Satis.

Abu Simbel

Coaches collect visitors from the airport and whisk them to the new location of the rock-cut temples of Abu Simbel. The site can be very busy. The two rock-cut temples built by Ramesses II, one for himself and the other for his Great Royal Wife Nefertari, were moved 64m (210ft) up the face of a cliff to save them from the new lake, an unprecedented feat of technology. At the back of them a concrete dome was built; this can be visited, and is almost fascinating as the temples themselves.

The main temple to the left has four colossal seated sandstone statues of the king each 20m (65ft) high. The top of the temple is 31m (102ft) high. You can see the tiny statues of the king's wife by his legs and on the side of the colossal statues, there is a text which records the marriage of Ramesses to a Hittite princess.

The temple reaches 55m (180ft) deep into the face of a cliff, with two columned halls leading to the sanctuary. The first hypostyle hall contains square-cut pillars cut from the rock with statues of the king as Osiris in front of them. The walls at each side are carved with raised relief on which the colour is finely preserved. To the left, Ramesses is shown charging a fortress in Syria while mounted on a chariot, and spearing an enemy. On the right, the camp of Ramesses surrounded by shields; Hittite spies are captured and beaten; the battle of Kadesh; piles of severed hands being inspected by the king.

Off the hall are eight small side-chambers which were once used to store the temple's treasures. Stone benches are cut against the walls.

In the second hall, reliefs show Ramesses with the gods; in the sanctuary four statues are seated on a bench: Ptah, Amun, Ramesses and Re-Horakhte. Twice a year, at the time of the solstices, the rays of the sun at dawn shone straight into the temple and illuminated the statues at the rear. The rebuilt temple was exactly aligned so that this still happens today.

The second, smaller, **Temple of Nefertari and Hathor** lies to the north of the great temple. The statues depict the queen, with tiny figures of her children by her feet. Inside, the columns of the hypostyle hall are decorated with carved Hathor heads. Reliefs on the walls show the king and queen in the company of the goddesses Isis, Hathor and Anukis.

GLOSSARY

Note: all terms which appear in **bold** within entries refer to other entries in the Glossary.

Akhetaten Egyptian: 'Horizon of the Aten'. City built by Akhenaten for his god, the Aten.

Amarna Modern name for city site founded by Akhenaten. Aspects of culture of that period.

Amen-Re King of the gods from the New Kingdom onwards; a fusion of Amun and the sun god Re.

amulets Good-luck charms, often in form of **hieroglyphs** or gods.

Amun God of Luxor. During New Kingdom, regarded as king of the gods.

ankh Hieroglyph meaning 'to live' and 'life'. Adapted by Coptic Christians as their cross.

Anthropoid Greek: 'man-shaped'. In Egyptology refers to inner wooden coffins of human shape.

Anubis Wild-dog–headed god who presided over mummification; controlled weighing of the heart.

Apis Bull sacred to Osiris. Revered from Archaic times; prominent during Graeco-Roman era.

Aten God promoted by Akhenaten, during the **Amarna** period, in the 18th Dynasty to the exclusion of all previous deities.

Atum Primeval cosmic god; appeared spontaneously from **Nun**. Progenitor of elements of universe.

ba Element of soul, in form of human-headed bird. Left body at death and inhabited tomb. *See also ka.*

barrel vault A roof of hemi-cylindrical shape. In Egypt, used for lids of Old Kingdom **sarcophagi.**

Benben stone Obelisk-shaped focal point of a 5th Dynasty **solar temple.**

Book of the Dead Modern name for magical texts protecting the dead on their way to the afterlife.

Calcite Crystalline form of limestone. Often incorrectly called alabaster.

canopic jars Four jars, often of **calcite**, used to store mummified viscera of a deceased.

carnelian Blood-red semiprecious stone.

cartonnage Papyrus or bandages soaked in gesso plaster, shaped around a body and painted.

cartouche Oval-shaped loop encircling a royal name.

cataracts Outcrops of rocks in the Nile from Aswan southwards.

causeway Path from pyramid to canal cut from river. It was enclosed and decorated inside.

cenotaph Tomb built for ceremonial purposes; never intended for a burial.

Coffin Text Magical spells on inner faces of Middle Kingdom wooden coffins.

Colossi of Memnon Name given by Classical visitors to pair of colossal statues in front of the mortuary temple of Amenhotep III.

Coptic Greek: 'aegyptios' (Egyptian). Refers to Egyptian Christians and language of their liturgy.

corvée Annual three-month work period required of all men as taxation.

cubit Ancient Egyptian measurement based on length of forearm from elbow to tip of thumb.

delta Fertile area between Cairo and the Mediterranean, usually called **Lower Egypt.**

demotic 'Shorthand' variety of hieroglyphs.

dolerite Hard black rocks found as small nodules; used for mining.

Dendera Temple site dedicated to Hathor.

Duat Land of the dead. Regarded as similar to Egypt in climate and nature.

encaustic Wax-based paint.

ennead Group of nine gods.

faience Glazed material; base of steatite or clay with crushed quartz, overlaid with coloured glass.

false door Focal point of tomb; painted or carved door through which the **ka** could enter and leave.

funerary offerings Bread, beer, wine, etc. provided by mourners and later magically.

Geb A god; son of Shu and Tefnut, brother of Nut. He represented the earth.

Hathor Goddess portrayed with cow's horns. Consort of Horus.

headrest Curved piece of wood or stone on a vertical post, used as a pillow.

hieratic Cursive writing derived from **hieroglyphs.**

hieroglyphs Picture signs used to write the ancient Egyptian language, based mainly on sounds.

Hittites People of a nation located in what is now central and southern Turkey.

Horus Ancient god; opponent of Seth of Naqada. Absorbed into Osiris legend as son of Osiris and Isis.

Horus name Earliest versions of king's names written inside a **serekh**, with a Horus falcon above.

Hyksos People of unknown origin who settled in the **delta** and ruled Egypt during the Second Intermediate Period.

hypostyle Greek: 'many columns'; refers to the large columned hall in most temples.

intermediate periods Brief times of confusion in Egyptian history, during which Egypt was split and ruled simultaneously by different kings.

inundation Annual flooding of Nile from August to November.

Isis Greatest of goddesses. Wife of Osiris and mother of Horus. Venerated as ideal mother.

ka Element of soul; physical, spiritual double of its owner. Created at time of birth by **Khnum**, was finally released at death. *See also ba, false door, funerary offerings, mortuary cult, mortuary priest.*

Khepri Scarab beetle aspect of the sun which pushed 'ball' of the sun over the horizon at dawn.

Khnum Straight-horned, ram-headed god of the First Cataract; often shown as a potter, creating human beings on his wheel. *See also ka.*

king list Listing of all the kings from the **unification** onwards; usually found in temples.

kiosk Small, elaborate temple-like structures, usually minor feature of a larger site. Could have been a quay or processional entrance to a site.

kohl A black powder, used as eyeliner.

lapis lazuli A dark-blue semiprecious stone.

Lower Egypt Land around **delta**, from modern Cairo to Mediterranean coast. So named because Nile runs from south to north.

Luxor City on east bank of Nile, 675km (420mi) south of Cairo; site of Temple of Karnak. On west bank, site of royal and noble burials. *See Thebes.*

Ma'at Goddess depicted with ostrich feather in her hair; or feather by itself. Both represented order, balance, correct attitudes, morality and justice.

malachite Green-coloured copper ore. When ground to powder, used as pigment for paint and colouring for glass and **faience.**

mammisi Coptic: 'place of birth'. Name for subsidiary temple or chamber attached to temple and to which residing goddess retired once a year to 'give birth' to child with whom she and her 'husband' god were associated.

mastaba Arabic: 'bench'. Mud-brick or rectangular superstructures built over tomb shafts for Archaic period kings, and Old Kingdom courtiers.

Menes Legendary first king of unified Egypt.

Middle Egypt Term loosely applied to area south of the Faiyum and north of Luxor, especially to sites around Beni Hasan and Tell el Amarna

Mitanni Area of northern Mesopotamia between Tigris and Euphrates rivers.

mortuary cult Provision of regular **funerary offerings** for the well-being of the deceased.

mortuary priest A person appointed to bring **funerary offerings** daily to a tomb.

mound of creation Land mass arising from **Nun** upon which gods and humans came into existence.

mummy Any preserved corpse. In Egypt, refers both to bodies naturally preserved by the desiccating effect of sand in graves, and to bodies preserved artificially by mummification. *See also natron.*

Naqada Village near Luxor adjacent to which was a huge cemetery of prehistoric and Archaic date.

naos Greek: 'dwelling of a god'. Refers in Egypt to stone cubicle, or shrine, at heart of temple and in which cult statue of the god resided.

Narmer palette Ceremonial shield-shaped **palette**. Relief on both sides shows Narmer, one of first kings of united Egypt. On one side he wears the crown of **Upper Egypt**, on the other that of **Lower Egypt**.

natron Natural salt used as a cleansing agent and as a preservative during mummification.

necropolis Greek: 'city of the dead'. This refers to Egyptian cemeteries dating from all periods.

nemes Striped headcloth. It had lappets either side of the face; the back gathered into a 'tail'.

Nephthys Sister of Isis, Osiris and Seth. With Isis, one of the 'Two Kites', screeching birds that sounded like mourners. A protectress of the dead.

nilometer Staircase down to a passage, usually in a temple, leading to Nile. During **inundation**, the maximum level could be marked on the staircase as a means of assessing the future yield of the land.

nome Administrative area, controlled by a governor or nomarch. There were 22 nomes in **Upper Egypt** and 20 in **Lower Egypt**.

Nubia Land south of Aswan; source of gold and hard stones, especially granite. Name most likely derived from Egyptian 'nub' ('gold').

Nun Watery void of chaos, present before the existence of the world. *See also Atum.*

Nut Goddess of the sky, portrayed as stretching in an arc over the earth with fingers and toes touching the ground. *See also Geb.*

obelisk Tall, thin, square-based stone capped with **pyramidion**. Often erected in front of temples; always made of one block of granite. During New Kingdom, may have been sheathed in gold.

Opening of the Mouth Rite performed on a mummy, whereby the priest, with an adze, frees the **ka** from the body and magically restores its senses.

Osiris God and king of the dead.

ostracon Potsherd or limestone flake used by scribes for practising to write, and as a cheap and easily available medium for letters, daily documents and quick sketches. Plural – ostraca.

palette Flat stone, often slate – sometimes shaped in form of a fish or animal – with a shallow depression for grinding of **malachite**.

papyrus A reed now virtually extinct. Used in prehistoric times for boats. When split into layers and dried, it formed a strong writing material.

pectoral Jewelled plaque worn as a pendant.

pharaoh Title used for King of Egypt from the **Amarna Period**. Comes from name for royal palace, the 'per-aa', or Great House.

Ptah Creator god of **Memphis**. Associated with wife, Sekhmet, and son, Nefertem.

Punt A country to which Egypt sent expeditions to obtain ivory, ebony, incense and animal skins. Possibly in region of modern Tigre or Eritrea.

pylon Greek: 'gate' or 'door'. In Egypt, refers to monumental gateways at the front of temples.

Pyramid Texts Spells on burial-chamber walls of late Old Kingdom pyramids to effect passage of **ka** into afterlife as a god.

pyramidion A small pyramid. Generally one small hard stone used to cap a pyramid or **obelisk**.

raised relief *See relief.*

Ramesseum Mortuary temple of Ramesses II on west bank of Luxor.

register Base, or ground, line used as a 'floor' for figures in Egyptian art.

relief Carving effected without undercutting any of the surface; either sunk, with figures cut out of the stone; or raised, with background cut away.

reserve head Stone portrait head placed in a **serdab** in burial shafts of Old Kingdom courtiers.

Rosetta stone Black basalt stone found in 1799 on Rosetta branch of Nile. It contains three identical texts in Greek, **hieroglyphs** and **demotic.**

sarcophagus Greek: 'flesh eater'. Name given to outer rectangular or oval stone container within which coffins and **mummy** were placed.

scarab Dung beetle that pushes balls of dung from which ancient Egyptians believed larvae emerged as if by spontaneous generation. Believed to be form of rising sun, as ball of sun was thrust over the eastern horizon by a cosmic beetle, **Khepri.**

Sed festival The 30–year jubilee festival celebrated by kings of Egypt.

serapeum Underground burial chambers for the sacred **Apis** bull at Saqqara.

serdab Arabic: 'cellar'. Small walled-up chamber in a mortuary chapel or burial shaft containing image of the deceased. *See also reserve head.*

serekh Rectangular panel enclosing a King's name.

Seth God associated with evil. Adopted in Osiris legend as brother and murderer of Osiris.

shawabti *See ushabti.*

sherd Variant, shard. A piece of broken pottery.

Shu God, son of Atum, husband and brother of **Tefnut.** Symbolizes emptiness or the void'; occupies space between heaven and earth.

sistrum Rattle or musical shaker. Forked metal stick with discs threaded onto a bar across the prongs.

solar boat Mythical high-prowed boat in which sun god was believed to navigate the heavens.

solar temple Open-air courtyard dominated by a **Benben stone.** Here offerings could be made to sun.

sphinx Statue of a reclining lion with the head of a human or animal.

steatite Soapstone, form of compacted talc; soft stone, very hard after firing; base for **faience.**

stela Inscribed stone slab, or similar inscription on wall or cliff. Memorial to the dead; commemoration of an event; or formal decree.

sunk relief *See relief.*

Tefnut Goddess referred to as daughter of Atum. Sister of Shu and mother of Geb and Nut.

Tell el Amarna *See Amarna.*

temenos Massive mud-brick walls surrounding a temple, pyramid or palace site.

Thebes Greek version of Egyptian name of what is modern Luxor – 'ta ipet'.

Two Lands Believed to refer to **Upper** and **Lower Egypt.** Some theorize that the two lands could also be the river valley and the desert.

unification The political joining of **Upper** and **Lower Egypt.** Its date is uncertain, but between 3100 and 3000 BC.

Upper Egypt Southern Egypt, between Luxor and Aswan; sometimes included **Middle Egypt.**

Uraeus Greek: 'a type of snake'. Refers to cobra motif worn on crown or royal headdress.

ushabti Mummiform statuette placed in tombs to perform work on behalf of deceased in the afterlife.

Valley of the Kings Wadis on west bank of Luxor containing tombs of New Kingdom kings, their families and close associates.

Valley of the Queens Wadi used for burials of queens and royal children of 19th and 20th Dynasties.

vizier Head of administration; chief ambassador; supreme civil and criminal judge; royal adviser.

wadi Dried-up riverbed in the desert.

INDEX

Page numbers in italic refer to
illustrations and captions

ACKNOWLEDGMENTS

The author wishes to thank Eric, Mark, and Antony for their unfailing support and assistance in the preparation of this book. Thanks also to Professors A.F. Shore and K.A. Kitchen, and Pat Winker in the Department of Archaeology and Oriental Studies at the University of Liverpool. And very special thanks to Elizabeth Longley, who as friend and editor has given her unstinting support to this project from its inception.

The publishers wish to acknowledge with gratitude the generous help and guidance of Dr Mohammed Saleh of the Cairo Museum, Dr G.T. Martin of University College, London, Dr Patricia Spencer of the Egypt Exploration Society and Dr Rosalind Hall of the Petrie Museum.

The publishers would like to acknowledge the following individuals and organizations to whom copyright in the photographs used in this book belongs:

Cairo Museum 17 (top), 32, 49, 57 (bottom), 72, 86, 87, 97 (left), 101, 103, 112, 113, 122, 123
Peter Clayton 28, 29, 30, 31, 38, 68, 96, 98, 116, 117, 119, 149, 156, 168
Colorific 177
Egypt Exploration Society 35, 39, 58, 142, 166
Egypt Exploration Society/Leiden Expedition 115
Griffith Institute, Ashmolean Museum, Oxford 14, 109
Eric Hobson 22, 71, 89, 120, 121
Michael Holford 52, 60–1, 63, 90–1, 93 (top), 105, 124, 126–27, 136, 137, 141, 143, 144, 146–47, 163, 171
National Portrait Gallery 25, 26, 27, 36
Courtesy of the Petrie Museum of Egyptian Archaeology, University College, London 40, 41, 42, 43, 46–7
John Ross frontispiece, 15, 16, 17 (bottom), 20–1, 23, 45, 50, 53, 54, 55, 57 (top), 59, 64, 65, 66, 73, 75, 79, 80, 81, 82, 85, 88, 94, 95, 97 (right), 100, 106, 110, 111, 118, 125, 130, 131, 133, 138, 139, 140, 142, 145, 151, 158, 161
Ronald Sheridan 18, 24, 84, 107, 132, 153, 154, 155, 175
Sunday Times of London 83
John Topham Picture Library 69, 169
University of Liverpool 92, 93 (bottom), 108, 174

In addition, the publishers wish to acknowledge with gratitude the contribution of the following illustrators:

Ian Bott, 56, 59, 62, 65, 67, 71, 74, 81, 89, 115, 129
Susanne Haines 159, 160–61 (*calligraphy*)
Aziz Khan 15, 76–7, 77, 102, 108, 148, 159 (*Alphabet*), 162, 176
Chris Moore 12, 100, 107, 173, 180, 182
Alan Suttie 157
Tracy Wellman 104, 111, 132–33, 134–35, 137, 141, 144, 159 (*Group Signs; Determinatives*), 160–61, 165, 175